# RHETORICS OF EVIDENCE

# Visual Rhetoric
Series Editor: David Blakesley

Visual culture studies and visual rhetoric have been increasing areas of emphasis in scholarly studies. Drawing on the work of a variety of theorists, from Kenneth Burke in rhetorical studies to Roland Barthes in semiotics, and addressing a wide range of subjects, from supermarkets to new media, scholars established visual cultural studies as a thriving and significant area of inquiry for the new century. The impetus for such study has been the awareness that primary information sources (television, streaming media, film and the internet) are strongly graphic (or visual) rather than print- or text-based in nature. This series encourages scholars working in rhetoric, cultural studies, and communication to create new scholarly works that analyze visual phenomena and theorize visual rhetoric itself.

The previously unquestioned hegemony of verbal text has beeng challenged by what W. J. T. Mitchell labels the "pictorial turn" (*Picture Theory*)—a recognition of the importance and ubiquity of images in the dissemination and reception of information, ideas, and opinions—processes that lie at the heart of all rhetorical practices, social movements, and cultural institutions. The Visual Rhetoric series brings together the work currently being accomplished by scholars in a wide variety of disciplines, including art theory, spatial rhetorics and architecture, rhetoric, cultural studies, media studies, neuropsychology, and cinema studies.

## Books in the Series

*Rhetorics of Evidence: Science–Media–Culture*, ed. Olaf Kramer and Michael Pelzer (2024)

*The Afterlife of Discarded Objects: Memory and Forgetting in a Culture of Waste* by Andrei Guruianu and Natalia Andrievskikh (2019)

*Type Matters: The Rhetoricity of Letterforms*, ed. by Christopher Scott Wyatt and Dànielle Nicole DeVoss (2018)

*Inventing Comics: A New Translation of Rodolphe Töpffer's Reflections on Graphic Storytelling, Media Rhetorics, and Aesthetic Practice*, ed. and trans. by Sergio C. Figueiredo (2017)

*Haptic Visions: Rhetorics of the Digital Image, Information, and Nanotechnology* by Valerie L. Hanson (2015)

*Locating Visual-Material Rhetorics: The Map, the Mill, and the GPS* by Amy D. Propen (2012)

*Visual Rhetoric and the Eloquence of Design*, ed. by Leslie Atzmon (2011)

*Writing the Visual: A Practical Guide for Teachers of Composition and Communication*, ed. by Carol David and Anne R. Richards (2008)

*Ways of Seeing, Ways of Speaking: The Integration of Rhetoric and Vision in Constructing the Real*, ed. by Kristie S. Fleckenstein, Sue Hum, and Linda T. Calendrillo (2007)

# RHETORICS OF EVIDENCE

## SCIENCE–MEDIA–CULTURE

Edited by
Olaf Kramer and Michael Pelzer

Parlor Press
*Anderson, South Carolina*
www.parlorpress.com

Parlor Press LLC, Anderson, South Carolina, USA

© 2024 by Parlor Press
All rights reserved.

Printed in the United States of America
S A N: 2 5 4 - 8 8 7 9

Library of Congress Cataloging-in-Publication Data

Names: Kramer, Olaf, editor. | Pelzer, Michael, editor.
Title: Rhetorics of evidence : science - media - culture / edited by Olaf Kramer, Michael Pelzer.
Description: Anderson, South Carolina : Parlor Press, [2024] | Series: Visual rhetoric | Includes bibliographical references and index. | Summary: "Sixteen essays examine the use of evidence in culture, media, and science communication, ranging from paleontology, meteorology, neurological science/computation to literature, film, photography, and civic rhetoric. In full color"-- Provided by publisher.
Identifiers: LCCN 2024060737 (print) | LCCN 2024060738 (ebook) | ISBN 9781643174440 (paperback) | ISBN 9781643174457 (hardcover) | ISBN 9781643174464 (pdf) | ISBN 9781643174471 (epub)
Subjects: LCSH: Evidence. | Logic. | Truth.
Classification: LCC BC171 .R45 2024  (print) | LCC BC171  (ebook) | DDC 121/.68014--dc23/eng/20250114
LC record available at https://lccn.loc.gov/2024060737
LC ebook record available at https://lccn.loc.gov/2024060738

978-1-64317-444-0 (paperback)
978-1-64317-445-7 (hardcover)
978-1-64317-446-4 (pdf)
978-1-64317-447-1 (epub)

2 3 4 5

Book design by David Blakesley.
Cover design by Michael Pelzer.

Printed on acid-free paper.

Parlor Press, LLC is an independent publisher of scholarly and trade titles in print and multimedia formats. This book is available in paperback, hardcover, and eBook formats from Parlor Press on the World Wide Web at http://www.parlorpress.com or through online and brick-and-mortar bookstores. For submission information or to find out about Parlor Press publications, write to Parlor Press, 3015 Brackenberry Drive, Anderson, South Carolina, 29621, or email editor@parlorpress.com.

# Contents

| | |
|---|---|
| Acknowledgments | ix |
| Introduction<br>    Olaf Kramer and Michael Pelzer | xi |
| **Theoretical Approaches** | *1* |
| 1 The Telescope. Evidence in Rhetoric<br>    Joachim Knape | 3 |
| 2 Evidence in Visual Rhetoric<br>    Thomas Susanka | 29 |
| 3 Evidence on the Micro Level: What Rhetoric Can Learn from Hans Fallada's *Every Man Dies Alone* and New Objectivity<br>    Olaf Kramer | 45 |
| **Rhetorics of Evidence in Science Communication** | *61* |
| 4 Visual Rhetoric and Evidence in Scientific Images: Imaging Brains and Imagining Minds in Cognitive Neuroscience<br>    Kirsten Brukamp | 63 |
| 5 Using Images, Films and Colors When Communicating Neuroscientific Results<br>    C. Giovanni Galizia | 79 |
| 6 Communicating the Uncertainty in Weather Forecasts<br>    David M. Schultz | 98 |
| 7 The Communicative Construction of Evidence: Presentational Knowledge in Computational Neuroscience<br>    Hubert Knoblauch, Eric Lettkemann, and René Wilke | 115 |
| 8 Narrative, Rhetoric, and Science: Opportunities and Risks<br>    Jenny Rock and Julia Siebert | 141 |

9 Humans after *Heidelbergensis*: The Spirited Rhetoric
of Paleoanthropology *160*
*Jeffery Gentry*

10 Civic Science: Applied Rhetoric as a Facilitator
of Scientific Knowledge *190*
*Colleen E. Kelley*

**Rhetorics of Evidence in Media and Culture** *205*

11 Beyond Literalism: Reality and Imagination in the Public Image *207*
*Robert Hariman and John Louis Lucaites*

12 "The Journalism of Tomorrow." Medium-Specific Evidence in
Nineteenth-Century Illustrated Magazines *233*
*Anne Ulrich*

13 "The Best Battlefield Scene of All Time": The Feeling
of History and the Problem of Realism in *Saving Private Ryan* *256*
*Philipp Löffler*

14 An Analysis and Criticism of Chaïm Perelman's Approach
to Evidence and Argument as Developed in *The New Rhetoric* *276*
*John W. Ray*

15 Carl Friedrich von Weizsäcker's Rhetorics
of Evidence Construction *287*
*Klaus Hentschel*

16 Timeless Demonstration: Abraham Lincoln's Cooper Union
Address and Cicero's *officia oratoris*: To Teach, to Delight,
and to Move *319*
*William M. Purcell*

Contributing Authors *335*
About the Editors *339*
Index *341*

# List of Illustrations

*Introduction*
The "Arts belonging to the Speech."                                              xv

*Chapter 1*
Galileo Galilei, holding a telescope.                                            10
Galileo showing the Doge of Venice how to use the telescope.                     15
Bertolt Brecht and Charles Laughton, 1947.                                       22

*Chapter 2*
Example of an electron microscopic picture.                                      39
Example of an image evoking evidence by clarity of form.                         41
The hockey-stick graph.                                                          42

*Chapter 3*
*Hetzkarte* to denounce Hitler as pictured in Hans Fallada's *Every Man Dies Alone*.   46
Gestapo file cover sheet case as pictured in Hans Fallada's *Every Man Dies Alone*.    47

*Chapter 4*
Classification of Science Images.                                                66

*Chapter 5*
Depiction of the human brain by Vesalius (1543).                                 81
Dryander (1537, fol. D2$^r$), shows the presumed role of brain
    ventricles in the human head.                                                83
Avicenna (1374, fol. 64$^v$) shows the connections between sensory organs
    and the brain ventricles.                                                    84
fMRI (functional magnetic resonance imaging) measurements of
    subjects in a moral judgment situation.                                      86
Spatial glomerular activity patterns for a series of odors in the
    honeybee antennal lobes.                                                     88
Example of an odor response in a honeybee antennal lobe.                         90
Spatial odor response patterns in the honeybee antennal lobe.                    92
Examples for color scale effects.                                                93
Using different background colors has a strong effect on the image.              93
Examples of how colors are seen by color blind people.                           95

*Chapter 6*
Postage stamp plots of sea-level pressure.                                      103
Spaghetti plot of two contours of the 500-hPa surface.                          104
Experimental forecast product during the 2012 Summer Olympic Games.             105
Box-and-whisker plots of cloud cover, precipitation, surface
    wind speed, and surface temperature in the ECMWF ensemble.                  106
Cone of uncertainty for Tropical Storm Dean.                                    107
The *Warn on Forecast* concept from the U.S. National Weather Service.          108

viii    *Illustrations*

| | |
|---|---|
| An example of weather icons from Google. | *109* |

*Chapter 7*

| | |
|---|---|
| Introductory PowerPoint slide with bullet points and virtual images. | *123* |
| Speaker changing a PowerPoint slide. | *126* |
| PowerPoint slide showing a schematic depiction and diagrams. | *130* |
| PowerPoint slide showing illustrations. | *132* |

*Chapter 8*

| | |
|---|---|
| Visualization of narrative techniques in Laurence Sterne's *Tristram Shandy*. | *149* |
| Spandrels (detail of Nidaros Cathedral's sanctuary, Trondheim). | *151* |
| Paradigm of primitive. | *153* |
| Biological Man. | |

*Chapter 9* *155*

| | |
|---|---|
| Example RAO Phylogenic Branching Model. | *166* |
| *The Temptation of Eve*, painting by Jean-Baptiste Marie Pierre. | *167* |
| Inter-racial American family from European, African, and Middle Eastern descent. | *168* |
| Example MRE Trellis Model. | *170* |
| Similarities Chart: Recent African Origin (RAO) and Multiregional Evolution (MRE). | *171* |
| Differences Chart: Recent African Origin (RAO) and Multiregional Evolution (MRE). | *171* |
| Neandertal/Cro-Magnon. | *173* |
| Rhetorical and Scientific Advancement. | *179* |
| Wolpoff's Seizure of Presumption. | *182* |
| Center and Edge Construct. | *184* |
| Neandertal and Cro-magnon Skulls. | *186* |

*Chapter 11*

| | |
|---|---|
| Example photograph, by Nassar Ishtayeh (AP; April 30, 2013). | *223* |
| Example photograph, by Josh Newton (AP; June 7, 2014). | *225* |

*Chapter 12*

| | |
|---|---|
| Photoengraving of Chevreul on "L'art de vivre cent ans." | *236* |
| Synchronization of words and images in "L'art de vivre cent ans." | *237* |
| The final quartet of photos in "L'art de vivre cent ans." | *244* |

*Chapter 13*

| | |
|---|---|
| *Saving Private Ryan*, D-Day scene. | *261* |
| *Saving Private Ryan*, D-Day scene. | *261* |
| *Saving Private Ryan,* D-Day scene. | *262* |
| *Saving Private Ryan*, D-Day scene. | *262* |
| *Saving Private Ryan*, Private Mellish. | *264* |
| *Saving Private Ryan*, Private Mellish. | *264* |
| *Saving Private Ryan*, cemetery scene. | *268* |

# Acknowledgments

The work of the *Presentation Research Center* at the Rhetoric Department of Tübingen University (Germany) focuses on the role of presentations in science communication—be it in scientific discourse, education, or communicating to a wider public. This wide and challenging field is highly dependent on—and, indeed, could not be tackled without—a close cooperation between specialists from diverse scientific and practical backgrounds, and it needs the support of various communicative and institutional stakeholders involved. Thus, we are very thankful and indebted to the inspiring, open, and fruitful exchange with all colleagues and supporters who contributed to this volume and, in fact, made it possible.

In particular, the publication of this book would not have been conceivable without the generous and reliable support of the Klaus Tschira Foundation (Heidelberg, Germany), which not only funds our research center, but also enables us to explore various ways and formats of researching and promoting science communication. We especially would like to thank the foundation's chief executive, Beate Spiegel, for her continued support and belief in the project.

The idea for this volume originated from the conference *Rhetoric of Evidence* in Heidelberg, where we started our endeavor to reconstruct the concept of evidence. In this context, we would like to thank Carmen Lipphardt, who organized that conference, as well as the entire team of our *Presentation Research Center* for their dedicated and valuable work. Moreover, we are grateful to David Blakesley from Parlor Press for his guidance, patience, and support in preparing the manuscript for print. During the final review of the book, Steven B. Katz provided valuable feedback.

Last but not least, we want to express our gratitude to all authors who contributed their thoughts and essays to this volume—working together in creating this book has been an inspiring and rewarding pleasure.

—Olaf Kramer and Michael Pelzer

# Introduction

*Olaf Kramer and Michael Pelzer*

How can knowledge be conveyed in a vivid way? What kinds of linguistic and visual techniques exist for the presentation and representation of evidence? What is the significance of evidence in the natural sciences, in scientific communication—and in schools, in art, and in culture?

Driven by these questions, the present volume examines the phenomenon of evidence in the nexus of culture, media, and science communication from a rhetorical perspective. It aims to foster interdisciplinary collaboration in studying the rhetoric of evidence, and presents a collection of diverse approaches pursuing a common goal: to deepen our understanding of "evidence" and build communicative bridges between science, culture, and society.

## Why Evidence Matters: Chances and Challenges

In antiquity, evidence was seen as a largely *linguistic* phenomenon investigated with special respect to the setting of forensic speech; today, however, evidence is also increasingly established *visually*, through the use of photographs, films, and presentation media. With contemporary communication getting more and more reliant on visual illustration and clarity of expression, the traditional category of "evidence" gained considerable relevance in various fields. For instance, striving for clarity and well-structured models forms a basis for the wide use of presentations in the natural sciences, and influences presentations in courtrooms, auditoriums, and conference halls as well. In all these cases, there is a high need to sustain proof by giving visual evidence. Consequently, evidence can be regarded as a culturally established and very effective presentation technique whose importance is recognized not only in the field of rhetoric, but in a wide range of disciplines and applications. At the same time, the study of evidence exhibits a long and rich tradition stretching from Aristotle's ancient demand to use vivid language, via the empiricism of scientists such as Galileo or Darwin, to contemporary approaches developing new strategies to achieve evidence, for example in the fields of neuroscience or meteorology (see chapters 4–7 in this volume). Contemporary research and scientific discussion are, however, still in need of catching up with the rapid development of modern (digital) media, as well as the communicative and sociocultural changes connected to it.

## Evidence and the Extension of Knowledge

In today's digitalized world, the fast development of new media causes a constant development and change of human media usage; this influences our perception and affects our cognition, as Marshall McLuhan prophesized in his seminal works *The Gutenberg Galaxy* (1962) and *Understanding Media* (1964). At the same time, the accelerated specialization of research and knowledge calls for new ways to illustrate (and vividly communicate) increasingly complex insights.

To organize and share our knowledge under these challenging circumstances, we need to communicate efficiently, and we need the means and techniques to vividly convey the gist of even the most complex findings and insights to a general audience. It is at this point that the significance of evidence becomes crucially apparent: in a globalized and digitalized society that is both highly *complex* and *connected*, evidence can assume the role of a mediating tool that allows for efficient sharing of knowledge. In this context, evidence has the potential to be to the communication of human knowledge what the new media are to the extension of the human mind; but in order to make successful and proficient use of it, we need to *thoroughly understand how it works*.

## Risky Evidence

Closely connected to the possibilities of evidence as a facilitator of fast and convincing mediation and communication are, however, also challenges and potential risks that must be considered: techniques of evidence (as rhetoric in general) are very powerful tools that call for scientifically sound, ethically responsible, and thoughtful usage to avoid potential misinterpretations and fight unethical practices. In particular, what is conceived as being 'evident' might not necessarily be 'true.' Hence, any examination of the power of (visual) evidence should always include a reflection on the processes and potential pitfalls underlying the creation and communication of knowledge. In this sense, investigating the rhetorics of evidence also entails important implications in regard to the ethical and epistemological ramifications of the rhetoric of science—and indeed the complex relations between evidence, (visual) rhetorics, and scientific soundness and credibility in general. This is particularly true, for instance, in the realm of the digital scientific image (e.g., Buehl 2014; Mitchell 1992), but it is also true in regard to visual rhetoric (cf. Allen 1996; Manning and Amare 2006) and the creation of "facts" in scientific contexts in general (cf. Latour and Woolgar 1979; Kuhn 1996).

Our contributors are aware of this—and critically explore, among other aspects, the connection between visual evidence and what counts as "truth" (chapters 11 and 12), the potentially misleading effects of false-color images (chapter 5), the challenges of communicating uncertainty in weather forecasts (chapter 6), or the fundamental rhetorical constructedness of scientific process (chapter 8), debates (chapter 9), and scientific discourse in general (chapter 10).

Communicative tools and techniques that are powerful in their effect—as the use of evidence certainly is—need to be *applied* (and *deliberated*) with skill and consideration. And while evidence might, in the worst case, even be misused to make "alternative facts" and "fake news" seem plausible, it is, at the same time, also the best tool to expose and contest those potential fallacies and deceptions: Studying the functions and effects of evidence allows us to strengthen our *critical analytical awareness* towards potentially misleading effects—and helps us in developing the *productive skill to vividly and reliably share* news, insights, ideas, and information that are, to the best of our knowledge, 'true'.

Indeed, as this volume seeks to illustrate, exploring the *Rhetorics of Evidence* is a pathway to actively addressing the call for responsibility that results from the growing necessity and influence of evidence within our digitalized knowledge society. In discussing the ideal of a perfect communicator, ancient rhetoric called for a person who is both of "good" character and skilled at speaking (*vir bonus dicendi peritus*). Similarly, we might call for a communicator who is both honest and skilled at using techniques of evidence (*vir bonus evidendi peritus*).

## A Survey of Evidence

Seeking answers to the questions presented at the very outset of this introduction, our volume presents a survey of techniques and strategies of evidence. In three overarching sections featuring a total of sixteen essays, an international and interdisciplinary set of contributors convenes and collaborates to discuss the topic of evidence from a varied number of perspectives.

In our first section, rhetoricians explore basic *Theoretical Approaches* and fundamental questions in respect to *evidence* as a core concept of rhetoric (chapters 1–3). Within the second section (chapters 4 to 10), specialists from diverse fields such as neuroscience and meteorology discuss the *Rhetorics of Evidence in Science Communication* and elaborate on the impact that concepts of evidence have on their work. Finally, in the third section of our book (chapters 11–16), academics investigating the *Rhetorics of Evidence in Media and Culture* look for the meaning of evidence regarding cultural, philosophical, linguistic, and media-related themes.

Combining these multilayered perspectives, we do not only explore abstract concepts and commonly used techniques to create evidence, but also scrutinize on concrete examples of rhetorical practices in various disciplines: our contributors analyze theoretical concepts of *evidence* (and its fundamental implications in regard to visual and narrative rhetoric)—but also look at ways in which scientists *gather* evidence; they explore how communicators *make use of* evidence in informing or persuading others, but also discuss which special techniques are applied in the cultural realms of literature, photography, and film. In this way, we hope to appreciate evidence not only as a phenomenon that can be observed in various applications and contexts but also as a general epistemic principle.

## Dimensions of Evidence

Having addressed the wide-ranging relevance and thematic breadth of the concept of evidence in today's society and communicative practice, we need to take a step back and deliberate on the systematic complexity of the subject: When we use the term *evidence* (as we did in our earlier remarks, but also in the very title of this book), we are unavoidably confronted with a question of definition: What, exactly, are we talking about—and what are we referring to?

Following the increasingly broad significance of evidence that we broached above, the usage of the term itself has grown manifold and complex—and thus, at least at first glance, elusive. The word evidence has multiple meanings and connotations: Readers from a background of *science* might have in mind the epistemic dimension of evidence, that is, ways of gathering proof of a hypothesis. Experts of *law* might have in mind gathering evidence at a crime scene or presenting evidence before the court. *Educators* and *communicators* might wonder about visual means to make complex topics and research results accessible to students, or ways of appealing to a general audience. Finally, *rhetoricians* and *literary scholars* might relate to techniques to create vivid language, descriptive passages in

*Introduction* xv

literary texts, perhaps also Aristotle or Cicero and their theories of *enérgeia* and *evidentia*. The following overview aims to shed some light on these different perspectives—and the *dimensions of evidence* they allow us to discover and distinguish.

A Basic Distinction: The Descriptive and Dynamic Dimensions of Evidence

To gain a more immediate access to our definitory discussion, let us start with a look at a children's book—and, as a matter of fact, a rather old one: the so-called *Orbis pictus* (which translates to "Visible World in Pictures"). It is an illustrated textbook that was first published by the Czech educator and theologian Johann Amos Comenius in 1658 and is widely considered to be the first picture book specifically intended for children. The book was very successful and spread rapidly all over Europe, with the first English translation being published in 1659. In this book, there is a page dedicated to the "Arts belonging to the Speech" (figure 1).

## Arts belonging to the Speech.     *Artes sermonis.*

Figure 1. The "Arts belonging to the Speech" as pictured in Comenius (1659), 202. Public domain work.

On this page, we see allegorical depictions of Grammar (1), Rhetoric (5), Poetics (12), and Music (13)—and the annotation tells us: "Rhetorica 5. pingit 6. quasi rudem formam 7. Sermonis Oratoriis pigmentis, 8. ut sunt Figurae . . ." ("Rhetoric paints unpolished forms of speech with oratory colors such as figures of speech").[1] If we look closely at the illustration, we notice that the woman who stands for rhetoric (5) is actually depicted as *painting a picture*. Comenius, we might infer, seems to have centered rhetoric on the stylistic concept of evidence, or—to use the Latin word—*evidentia*, that is, on techniques that convey (as Quintilian put it) a "mental picture of a scene" to the audience (Quintilian [1922, trans. Butler] *Inst.* 8.3.64).[2] This is the first dimension of evidence: evidence in the sense of *evidentia*, a stylistic device to appeal to the imagination. And while vivid language that "paints pictures" for the audience (so that they can clearly envision what the speaker is talking about) seems to be just one of many stylistic effects according to Comenius, it is a central feature of rhetoric.[3]

Evidence is a topic that most ancient books on rhetoric address, even if hardly one of them identifies it as *the* central principle. Yet, today, there is a tendency to underestimate the importance of evidence in modern introductions to rhetoric. They treat evidence predominantly as a stylistic quality of language that has little theoretical resonance. Therefore, a part of the present book will be specifically dedicated to investigating the fundamental rhetorical significance of evidence.

The word *evidentia* is a Latin translation introduced by Cicero in his dialogue *Lucullus* (section 17) for the Greek word *enárgeia*, which means "clarity" or "lucidness" and is derived from the Greek word *enárgos* (which means "to shine by itself"). Cicero tried to stick to this etymology when he created the noun *evidentia* from the Latin verb *evideri* ("to shine out" or "shine through"). According to Cicero, the orator should make his point clear by presenting it as if the audience was observing something with their own eyes. Thus, Cicero considered evidence to be a stylistic concept that regulates verbal expression and has a high persuasive potential: "For the *dwelling* on a single circumstance has often a considerable effect; as has a clear *illustration* and *exhibition* of matters to the eye of the audience, almost as if they were transacted before them" (Cicero [1970, trans. Watson] *De or.* 3.202). The core linguistic technique Cicero had in mind here is *description*—and, based on this, we can further define the systematic form of evidence in the sense of Cicero's concept of evidentia as *descriptive evidence*.

The ambiguity of the word evidence is not just a modern phenomenon, however: Cicero had to deal with it as well. As mentioned above, he specifically developed his concept of evidentia on the basis of the Greek word *enárgeia*, a word Aristotle actually did *not* use in his *Rhetoric*, at least as far as we can tell (the similarity between the words *enérgeia* and *enárgeia*—just one different character—might have led to various cases of misreading and misspelling over the ages). What is clear is that Aristotle focused on techniques of *energetic* writing, and therefore, when scrutinizing vivid language, reasonably referred to *enérgeia* (rather than the notion of detailed description inherent in *enárgeia*): to him, it was most important that speakers should use language in a way that presents a dynamic development. Following this position, we can identify a second systematic form of evidence: *dynamic evidence*.

Indeed, Rüdiger Campe (1990, 230) proposed that there are two separate traditions regarding the use of language that can be observed in the distinction between *enérgeia* and *enárgeia*: he differentiated between a static representational Roman use of language, and the dynamic language use of Aristotle—but that generalizing distinction appears a little far-fetched.

What we can say is that Cicero and Quintilian both concentrated—in contrast to Aristotle's earlier take on the subject—on descriptive evidence: they put special emphasis on the importance of details and the necessity of describing things carefully. In order to gain a better understanding of what exactly this means, it is helpful to consider some examples of descriptive evidence that Quintilian quotes:

> There is, then, to begin with, one form of vividness which consists in giving an actual word-picture of a scene, as in the passage beginning, "Forthwith each hero tiptoe stood erect." Other details follow which give us such a picture of the two boxers confronting each other for the fight, that it could not have been clearer had we been actual spectators. (Quintilian *Inst.* 8.3.63)

As this example shows, descriptive evidence can actually be achieved in a very economical way: The concept of emphasizing the *importance* of details in creating descriptive evidence does not necessarily imply that a speaker has to extensively elaborate on as many details as possible. Rather, the *quality* and *adequacy* of the details presented seems more important than their *quantity* and *level of elaboration*. As long as an author identifies the *right* details, which means, the details that are able to rouse the imagination of the audience, descriptive evidence can be created effectively.

Another example Quintilian quotes actually combines descriptive and dynamic evidence, that is, combines both attention to detail and dynamic movement:

> I seemed to see some entering, some leaving the room some reeling under the influence of the wine, others yawning with yesterday's po-

tations. The floor was foul with wine-smears, covered with wreaths halfwithered and littered with fishbones. (Quintilian *Inst.* 8.3.66)

Once again, we see that appeals to imagination do not necessarily require much elaboration. Descriptive and dynamic evidence can be achieved if the author has a strategy of how to appeal to an audience. Moreover, we learn that attention to detail and dynamic representation go together very well—as Quintilian himself pointed out:

> For the mere statement that the town was stormed, while no doubt it embraces all that such a calamity involves, has all the curtness of a dispatch, and fails to penetrate to the emotions of the hearer. But if we expand all that the one word "stormed" includes, we shall see the flames pouring from house and temple, and hear the crash of falling roofs and one confused clamour blent of many cries: we shall behold some in doubt whither to fly, others clinging to their nearest and dearest in one last embrace, while the wailing of women and children and the laments of old men that the cruelty of fate should have spared them to see that day will strike upon our ears. Then will come the pillage of treasure sacred and profane, the hurrying to and fro of the plunderers as they carry off their booty or return to seek for more, the prisoners driven each before his own inhuman captor, the mother struggling to keep her child, and the victors fighting over the richest of the spoil. (Quintilian Inst. 8.3.67–69)

It is this kind of dynamic that Aristotle had in mind when he put forward the concept of *dynamic evidence* and connected *enérgeia* with motion (*kinesis*, cf. *Rh.* 1412a). He encouraged speakers to show things "in activity" (1410b), and considered *enérgeia* as a verbal technique of "actualization" (as George A. Kennedy translated the term, cf. Aristotle [2007] *Rh.* 1410b).[4] Tellingly, Aristotle also believed that, in order to effectively persuade an audience, a speaker needs to present "things . . . as being done rather than as going to be done" (*Rh.* 1410b). Both dynamic and descriptive evidence deal with appeals to imagination, that is, with the importance of being able to rouse the imagination of addressees (who are not only guided by rational discourse and arguments, but also by this kind of aesthetic appeal).

## The Visual Dimension of Evidence

In all of ancient rhetoric, the discussion of evidence is primarily tied to effects that can be achieved through the use of *words*, that is, by verbal means. Yet, as we already noted in our considerations regarding Comenius' *Orbis pictus* from the seventeenth century, the evolution of media has progressively widened this perspective. With the development of printing techniques that made it possible to reproduce pictures in increasingly economic, efficient, qualitatively sophisticated, and accessible ways, communicators were enabled to feasibly and effectively reach (wider) audiences by *showing* pictures instead of *describing* them with words. Coherently, visual techniques to present evidence gained broader usage, appeal, effect, and attention. Today, a common method for presenting evidence is to show an image or moving images (film) instead of describing them. Going into detail and presenting dynamic developments is nowadays often (and predominantly) achieved through visual means. Thus, we should add *visual evidence* as another overarching technique and third dimension of evidence.

Even though the basic dimensions of *enérgeia* and *enárgeia* can be applied to grasp some core effects of visual evidence (as Thomas Susanka discusses in more detail in chapter 2 of this volume), there are aspects of visual evidence that transcend these basic categories. Indeed, Cicero himself believed in the special and unique impact of visual presentation, holding that

> the most complete pictures are formed in our minds of the things that have been conveyed to them and imprinted on them by the senses, but that the keenest of all our senses is the sense of sight, and that consequently perceptions received by the ears or by reflexion can be most easily retained in the mind if they are also conveyed to our minds by the mediation of the eyes, with the result that things not seen and not lying in the field of visual discernment are earmarked. (Cicero [1942, trans. Sutton and Harris] *De or.* 2.355)

The power of verbally producing dynamic and descriptive evidence (see chapter 3) eventually resides in the power of visual apprehension. As a result, it does not come as a surprise that modern communicators apply new techniques for the visual presentation of evidence. Acknowledging this special importance of visual evidence in today's communication, several of our contributors discuss examples of visualization, as well as principles, possibilities, and challenges of visual evidence in general (see chapters 2, 4, 5, 6, 11, and 12).

When we talk about visual evidence, however, we also have in mind presentation media such as PowerPoint or Keynote (see chapter 7). For visual evidence is not just the result of representative illustrations, photographs or films that allegedly depict something real. Visual evidence is—just as descriptive and dynamic evidence—the result of a communicative process initiated by the orator as a strategic communicator. In a similar vein, there also is a *deictic* dimension of evidence that is particularly noticeable when a speaker actively points towards concrete objects related to a presentation. It is important to note that this idea of evidential *deixis* is not restricted to performative gestures of pointing and showing within a face-to-face situation. As a matter of fact, *deixis* is a rather fundamental aspect of many evidential techniques: a communicator might deliberately point addressees towards connected references within a given communicative situation, frame, or wider (textual) context to create evidential immediacy and meaning—be it by means of performative gestures or other (visual, textual, vocal, etc.) cues.[6]

In considering all this, it is crucial to stress the systematic importance of always keeping the addressee in mind—just as Aristotle, Cicero, or Quintilian started all their considerations with thoughts about the recipients and the effects the orator wants to achieve. Thus, it seems possible to reconfigure the idea of descriptive and dynamic presentation from verbal expression to the way that images (or "moving images" in films) should be designed in order to maximize their effect *on* the addressee. Indeed, the reductionism involved in the examples given by Aristotle and Quintilian could be particularly instructive here: visualizations must build on a thorough reflection on the recipient in order to be regarded as "evident"—be it a PowerPoint slide, a photograph, or a movie.

Even abstract visualizations (as commonly used in PowerPoint or Keynote presentations) can involve evidence and can have the effect that we believe in something that we see because it appeals to us as being "clear." To give an everyday example: Picture a meteorologist presenting a model about the development of the weather over the next few days. The visualization used might show the streams of high and low pressure areas in a very simple animation, but this visualization can be sufficient to make us believe that the predictions are right—as long as the communicator presents the evidence in an adequate manner (see also chapter 6).

Whether a visualization is evident (or not) can be determined by considering the effects it has (or does not have) on the recipients. Similarly, we need to note, there are also *textual* qualities such as reductionism or details that stand *pars pro toto* for larger contexts, and that help to achieve evidence in verbal or visual texts.

## The Epistemological Dimension of Evidence

We have reached an important point now: Evidence is a communicative effect, the result of a communication process and the context it provides. The idea of self-evidence, of something that is clear in and by itself, has to be questioned from a rhetorical perspective. Historically, Descartes was probably the last thinker who tried to further the idea of self-evidence. He held that there is a form of insight driven by clear and distinctive perception. Yet, this form of evidence is more of an ideology than an epistemologically convincing approach. What appears to be evident is produced with rhetorical means, and this is the *epistemological dimension* of evidence.

Forensic experts who gather evidence at a crime scene will not find proof there: the items they gather and the constellation they find can be turned into evidence and can be used as evidence in different ways when arguing. To call these findings evidence is a strategic move that turns them into proof of a hypothesis. Fingerprints found, for example, might be used to prove that a suspect probably was the offender, but that suspect could also just have been a visitor. Evidence is *produced*, and this is true even in the natural sciences, since modern science tries to explain our world with the use of models. As Popper taught us, these models cannot be proven right, but only be proven wrong (falsification). Scientists need to build a strong model in accordance with the data they have gathered, and often use visual evidence to do so. Yet, it should be clear—to both the scientists applying this kind of evidence and the addressees grasping it—that what seems to be a perfectly simple model that appeals to the intuition of the recipients is, as a matter of fact, the result of a process of construction, information management, and effective communication (see also chapter 5). Moreover, there is the closely related challenge of adequately communicating such models to a general public. All these considerations outline the importance of evidence in science, and our book deliberately devotes a strong focus to the complex and topical role of evidence in science and science communication (chapters 4–10).

## Constructing Evidence: Strategies of Imagination and the Role of the Creative Process

As we have stressed above, it is—from a rhetorical perspective—crucially important to understand that evidence is *relative* and highly dependent on *context*: a general audience might find a specific model or illustration of data complex and obscure, while experts might find the same model simple, clear, and perfectly evident: "Question and evidence are therefore," as Chandler, Davidson, and Harootunian (1994, 1) argue, "'correlative' in the strong sense that facts can only become evidence in response to some particular question." And it is in finding adequate and effective strategies of successfully correlating questions with evidence, of *turning* facts and information *into* evidence, that the special role of rhetoric (and rhetorical studies specifically concerned with strategical and persuasive communication) comes to bear.

After all, Comenius might have been right in ascribing such a central role to vivid language and visual evidence when he discussed rhetoric: the epistemic, stylistic, and visual dimensions of evidence are, indeed, closely connected. The *production* of evidence where it is not readily available and where we are challenged to deal with the uncertain is central to the rhetorical perspective—and touches on persuasiveness as the heart of rhetoric. In this respect, it might appear somewhat irritating that Quintilian not only put forth the idea that evidence has to be produced by the orator (in the sense of emphasizing specific aspects and details, and attempting to construct and aesthetically polish texts in order to reach persuasive goals), but actually also recommended the use of fiction: "And we shall secure the vividness we seek, if only our descriptions give the impression of truth, nay, we may even add fictitious incidents of the type which commonly occur" (Quintilian *Inst.* 8.3.70).

The production of evidence dwells on the ability to find the available means of persuasion in each case.[5] In producing evidence, we regularly turn to fiction and to the possible—even in science. Aspects we do not know or understand often make it necessary for a scientist to design a model by using assumptions and postulations:

> It should not be supposed that the ad hoc appropriation of evidence occurs only when there is a single unquestioned paradigm of explanation. The loose relation between observation and theory in systems of complex causation can also allow opposite theories to consume the same evidentiary nutrition. (Lewontin 1994, 484)

The production of evidence is possible in either direction—as long as it takes the logic of media and textual conditions into account. Without this, an orator will not have any rhetorical impact.

With this, we arrive at a question that is central to discussing the concept of evidence from a specifically rhetorical perspective: Which *strategies* are available to optimize both knowledge transfer and persuasive effects through the interplay of image and text?

Evidence is closely connected to imagination. Imagination is needed to identify what could be evident to others; and evidence, in turn, appeals to the imagination of an audience.[7] Kant was perfectly clear on this point, as Ludwig Jäger (2006) discussed in his contribution to *Listen der Evidenz* ("Ruses of Evidence," Cuntz et al. 2006): as Kant put it, imagination makes concepts "understandable" and "communicable"—and without it, understanding and knowledge would be quite limited. For Jäger, the rhetoric of evidence implies the performance of evidence on a macroscopic level, while the attribution of sense on the micro level is a semiological issue.

When we are confronted with visual evidence, the creative process underlying it is often neglected—because we tend to believe what we see, frequently without actively realizing that what we see is actually the product of a process of several strategical choices that the creator of an image needed to make. Visual and verbal evidence alike are products of active construction, attribution, and enactment of sense. Scientists who believe that theirs data speaks for itself when they visualize it will find it hard to effectively and convincingly present those findings to the public, as well as to an expert audience. When it comes to addressing the problem of establishing evidence, science and communication are, just as education and communication, closely connected.

In addition, it is important to emphasize that the process of strategically constructing and creating evidence is closely related to historical and cultural developments, and, of course, the target audience addressed: In regard to verbal as well as visual evidence,

> [a]ttention needs to be . . . directed: toward the configuration of the fact-evidence distinction in different disciplines and historical moments, . . . toward the relative function of such notions as "self-evidence," "experience," "test," "testimony," and "textuality" in various academic courses; or toward the ways in which the invoked "rules of evidence" are themselves the products of historical developments, and themselves undergo redifferentiation and reformulation. (Chandler 1994, 2–3)

In this volume, we will move forward and clarify some of the core characteristics of evidence by deliberately viewing it as a continuously developing and inherently diverse phenomenon. In order to grasp its diversity, we aim to explore as many of the dimensions distinguished above as possible: be it descriptive and dynamic evidence, visual evidence, or evidence as an epistemic principle.

Combining the perspectives of a wide range of disciplinary fields along the common goal of grasping the influence of evidence in science and society, the present volume pursues a unique approach to covering the diversity and complexity of the topic. There are some important publications that deal with certain aspects we address (see, e.g., van Belle 2014; Plett 2012; Schneck 2011)—but none of those follows the broad, integrative, and interdisciplinary approach we aim to present. At the same time, the phenomenon of evidence has, up until now, only rarely been discussed in specific relation to its *rhetorical* dimension and *production*; and individual research scattered over diverse disciplines has lacked fruitful combination and integration. We attempt to address this gap by collecting various approaches to studying evidence under the common umbrella of a *rhetorical perspective*, focusing on communicative *strategies* and *persuasion*. Moreover, *Rhetorics of Evidence* is not intended as a "how-to-book" (cf., e.g., Bowater and Yeoman 2012): while practical handbooks are useful, we deliberately want to follow a more theoretical and analytical orientation.

## Chapter Overview

### Theoretical Approaches

In the first chapter, titled "The Telescope: Evidence in Rhetoric," Joachim Knape outlines some fundamental reflections on the concept of evidence in rhetoric. Starting with observations regarding the "Unspoken Speech" John F. Kennedy wanted to present at the Dallas Citizens Club, Knape addresses, for instance, aspects of plausibility and possibility in relation to a supposed opposition between *rhetoric* and *reality*. Based on these considerations, the second part of his essay develops a theoretical framework that discusses the communicative necessity of actively expressing the way in which we functionalize and contextualize evidence in rhetorical processes of orientation.

Following these fundamental observations, Thomas Susanka specifically explores the core aspect of "Evidence in Visual Rhetoric" (Chapter 2): he examines the importance of evidence as a central persuasive mode in visual rhetoric—and argues that all visual artifacts used in persuasive communication share a common capability of evoking a sense of certainty about the subject-matter in the addressees. Supplementing his theoretical reflections with examples of both deductive and inductive analysis, Susanka illustrates how the techniques of detailing and vivification function in visual communication; but he also explores ways of creating visual evidence that seem to elude those traditional categories.

When exploring various "Dimensions of Evidence" earlier in this introduction, we already established that a communicator, instead of using pictures, can also apply vivid language to portray visual images with words. Further elaborating on this aspect, Olaf Kramer's contribution regarding "Evidence on the Micro Level: What Rhetoric Can Learn from Hans Fallada's Every Man Dies Alone and New Objectivity" (chapter 3) puts its focus on the persuasive efficiency of rhetorical micro-narratives in contrast to larger storytelling arcs. Kramer also returns to the general techniques of elaborating on details (*enárgeia*) and presenting information in an enlivening manner (*enérgeia*), and he specifically examines how Hans Fallada's economic style of writing succeeds in being particularly appealing to the readers' imagination.

## Rhetorics of Evidence in Science Communication

After the first section's chapters on theoretical approaches, we turn towards more concrete applications and case studies, starting with the highly topical field of science communication.

Given the steadily growing specialization and complexity of scientific research, vivid, clear, and easily intelligible communication is of key importance to ensure successful cooperation between experts of different scientific fields—and enable a wider public to grasp the meaning of scientific findings. Nevertheless, the relation between rhetoric, evidence, and science communication has hardly been explored so far, and collecting various essays that shed light on this highly dynamic and significant correlation seems both promising and valuable. Coherently, the second section of our book centers on some of the diverse functions and challenges that the concept of evidence exhibits in regard to communicating *in* and *about* science.

In many ways, Kirsten Brukamp's section-opening essay on "Visual Rhetoric and Evidence in Scientific Images" (chapter 4) provides a bridge between the theoretical discussions of our earlier chapters and the more specialized analyses of the chapters following it. Examining the usage of illustrations and figures as visual evidence in the specific field of science communication, Brukamp corroborates the assumption that visual rhetorics can help in understanding aspects of evidence in scientific images. In doing so, she proposes a set of categories to differentiate, classify, and analyze scientific images from a perspective of visual rhetoric, and she addresses the often-cited oppositions of image vs. evidence and logic vs. argument. Placing a special focus on the field of neuroscience, her discussion of the complex and various types of images used in functional brain imaging ultimately serves as a springboard to further conclusions stretching to the philosophy of mind and the status of the human subject in general.

Having gained a general understanding of the complex and far-reaching implications of the use of images in science communication, our focus turns to a number of more specific examples and analyses, the first of which, presented by *C. Giovanni Galizia*, further expands on the usage of images in neuroscience. His essay "Using Images, Films and Colors when Communicating Neuroscientific Results" (chapter 5) specifically addresses the increasing use of colored images in this field. He provides a critical appraisal regarding how colors are used in neuroscientific reports and how color choice can influence the apparent scientific message of illustrative figures. Drawing on a number of diverse examples, Galizia elucidates the long tradition of using image elements to communicate information in depictions of the human brain—and discusses contemporary challenges when using false-color images to communicate neuroscientific results. Pointing out potential problems and misunderstandings as well as communicative advantages with respect to selected examples of false color-coded images, he argues that actively deliberating these potential consequences is important for both the scientists creating the material and the readers digesting it.

The next contribution stays within the wider realm of visual evidence in science communication, but changes the scientific field: In his essay "Communicating the Uncertainty in Weather Forecasts" (chapter 6), David M. Schultz discusses limitations in the effectiveness of weather forecast and the potential problems arising with respect to their communication. Drawing on the example of Hurricane Katrina, he shows that effective communication is part of the path to effective forecasts and argues for "a new effort by weather forecasters, social scientists and graphic designers to construct more effective means to communicate weather forecasts."

Having explored the specific usage of images in communicating scientific data and insights, we shift our focus to the communication of scientific results in a presentational setting. In "The Communicative Construction of Evidence: Presentational Knowledge in Computational Neuroscience" (chapter 7), Hubert Knoblauch, Eric Lettkemann, and René Wilke examine the form evidence takes in communicating presentational knowledge in computational neuroscience. Assuming that "an argumentative role of evidence is exemplified by, and rooted in, the dialogic situation," they apply rhetorical analysis to explore the communicative generation of evidence. In addition to their empirical findings, they also provide a discussion of the peculiarities of presentational knowledge and highlight the wider context of their results.

After these various discussions of evidence in examples of visual and presentational communication, we consider aspects of narrative evidence in science communication: In "Narrative, Rhetoric and Science: Opportunities and Risks" (chapter 8), Jenny Rock and Julia Siebert follow the thesis that being "a scientist is not simply about generating and disseminating results, but about presenting a story in order to make one's work and its implications evident for a broader public." They explore the effects of narrative structures in science—and show that rhetoric provides a conceptual framework for analyzing various ways of creating narrative evidence. Moreover, their essay not only discusses the opportunities inherent in the evidential techniques they identify, but also the risks of obscuring scientific knowledge, eventually calling for "a consciousness of scientific process as always influenced by persuasive efforts."

Jeffery Gentry further elaborates on this relation between persuasive efforts and science, placing special emphasis to the rhetorical factor underlying scientific controversies. In his contribution "Humans after Heidelbergensis: The Spirited Rhetoric of Paleoanthropology" (chapter 9), he provides a rhetorical analysis of a fundamental scientific debate regarding human evolution: the opposition between advocates of the recent African origin model and supporters of the multiregional evolution approach. Aiming to "discern which human-origin theory produces the greater rhetorical effect," Gentry discusses the scientific evidence supporting the two competing theories. Ultimately, he recommends the rhetoric of scientific controversies as a salient genre for studies in rhetorical criticism, thus providing a closer look at the meta-level of evidence in scientific discourse analysis.

Similar to this conclusion, the following contribution by Colleen E. Kelley—titled "Civic Science: Applied Rhetoric as a Facilitator of Scientific Knowledge" (chapter 10)—is also concerned with the discursive creation and discussion of evidence. Widening Gentry's argument to an even broader, sociocultural level, Kelley assumes a rhetorical perspective viewing American science as contextualized narratives and texts. Here, at the end of our second overarching section, we arrive at one of the most essential aspects of science communication: the relation between science and society. Considering the "mediated reality of American science as discourse situated in, experienced by and, ultimately, argued through an interface between expert and lay opinion," Kelley argues for a closer cooperation between rhetoric and science, and calls for "civic scientists" who should be experts not only in their fields of research, but also in communicating with broader audiences.

## Rhetorics of Evidence in Media and Culture

We start our third section, which centers on the rhetorics of evidence in media and culture, with an essay by Robert Hariman and John Louis Lucaites, who contribute their view on the question of "Reality and Imagination in the Public Image" (chapter 11). Investigating the public dependence on visual images, they argue that "the evidentiary value of photography eludes simple conceptions of information and objectivity, and resides instead in understanding how seeing is an active engagement with the world." In their analysis, they put particular emphasis on the field of photographic reportage and maintain that to become evidence, a photograph has to simultaneously record reality and engage the imagination of its addressee. Furthermore, Hariman and Lucaites advance the claim that the evidentiary value of photography resides in understanding how seeing is an active engagement with the world, and that a more rhetorical conception of the photographic image can better account for how photography can "communicate profound truths about the human condition while also calling people into democratic community."

In her essay "'The Journalism of Tomorrow': The Anticipation of Liveness in Nineteenth Century Illustrated Magazines (chapter 12), Anne Ulrich takes us back to a seminal piece of media history: she presents a close reading of the pioneering photo interview between French chemist Michel-Eugène Chevreul and photographer Gaspard-Félix Nadar, published in 1886 in the *Journal illustré*. In Ulrich's reading, the interview serves as a case study of an early attempt at strategically creating an impression of immediacy and authenticity of depiction that "anticipates audio-visual liveness." Analyzing the interview from the perspective of rhetorical evidence and discussing it against the backdrop of the history of media, journalism, and photography, Ulrich underlines the interview's significance as a "transitory form" that combines traditional language and themes of the nineteenth century with progressive technological methods. In effect, Ulrich argues, it transcends both its temporal and medial boundaries, resulting in "an extraordinary realization of rhetorical evidence."

We expand these considerations on the use photographs and the evocation of authenticity with a closer look at how evidence works in the realm of (historical) movies: Philipp Löffler examines the theoretical implications of the return of realism for the creation of historical evidence, illustrating his considerations by an analysis of "The Feeling of History and the Problem of Realism in *Saving Private Ryan*" (chapter 13). In doing so, he explores the question of how "the subjectivity of an individual historical agent [can] be turned into the precondition for generating the idea of a universal historical truth," and provides a general discussion of Spielberg's movie as a reflection of the political world in the aftermath of the Cold War.

Following these considerations regarding visual evidence, we take a step back and turn to an essay that illustrates the broad philosophical reach of our subject. In "An Analysis and Criticism of Chaïm Perelman's Approach to Evidence and Argument as Developed in The New Rhetoric" (chapter 14), John W. Ray draws on Perelman's theory of evidence and argument as rhetorical constructs. Starting from the definition that evidence "is data that can prove or disprove a statement," Ray examines the concept of the universal audience and critically discusses whether it provides a usable test of evidentiary adequacy. He argues that "the universal audience furnishes a distinct method for viewing what constitutes sound argumentation and convincing evidence"—and explores philosophical antecedents in the works of Rousseau, Diderot, Kant, and Hegel.

After this, Klaus Hentschel focuses on a "master constructor of rhetorical evidence" whose works have—so far—not been easily accessible to an international readership: the German physicist, philosopher, and rhetor Carl Friedrich von Weizsäcker. In "Carl Friedrich von Weizsäcker's Rhetorics of Evidence Construction" (chapter 15), Hentschel provides a rhetorical analysis of von Weizsäcker's work—and makes it accessible to an international readership by providing faithful English translations of selected quotations. By analyzing examples taken from von Weizsäcker's talks, scientific papers, and books, Hentschel explores the reasons behind the wide impact of von Weizsäcker's publications. He illustrates how von Weizsäcker managed to be a very successful author despite the "highly nontrivial" content of his writings, showing that von Weizsäcker succeeded in making his theses sound evident by means of "sophisticated style" and "clever rhetoric."

We conclude this third section—and our volume—with an essay that, in many ways, closes a circle to the first chapter: Having started with Joachim Knape's theoretical reconsiderations of traditional rhetorical concepts and positions as well as a reference to John F. Kennedy's "Unspoken Speech", we end with a neo-classical rhetorical analysis of a speech by another highly regarded former president of the United States: Abraham Lincoln. In his essay "Timeless Demonstration: Abraham Lincoln's Cooper Union Address and Cicero's officia oratoris" (chapter 16), William M. Purcell employs Cicero's framework of the duties of the orator as a means of analyzing and appreciating Abraham Lincoln's address at Cooper Union. He argues that a "rhetoric of evidence must consider the nuances of oral rhetoric to be complete" and that the classical canon of rhetorical theory can be used as an analytical tool to appreciate the "oral magic locked into a speech text." Eventually, Purcell shows that Lincoln's speech goes beyond the "marshalling of evidence to marshal the aural texture of language to reinforce and, indeed, carry his points."

We hope that our book can help to spark further research in the field of evidence and provide a basis for fruitful discussion. As our contributors show and exemplify, exploring the *Rhetorics of Evidence* is not only a highly relevant task for a wide range of fields, but also a very productive topic for interdisciplinary exchange. By exploring the importance of evidence in the natural sciences and scientific communication as well as in education, art, and culture, we hope to kindle an interdisciplinary and lively discussion regarding how knowledge can be conveyed in a vivid way—and what kinds of linguistic and visual techniques exist for the presentation and representation of evidence in science and society.

## NOTES

1. To improve readability, we used our own translation here. The original seventeenth century English translation (given side-by-side to the Latin text) in Comenius (1659) reads: "Rhetorick, 5. doth as it were paint 6. a rude form of Speech with Oratory Flourishes, 8. such as are, Figures . . . " (202–03).

2. The English translation by Butler indicated here (Quintilian 1922) is also used in the following quotes from Quint. *Inst.*

3. In this context, also cf. the close relation between evidentia and the concept of *perspicuitas* (see, e.g., Asmuth 1996, esp. 814–16).

4. The English translation by Kennedy indicated here (Aristotle 2007) is also used in the following quotes from Arist. *Rh.*

5. Cf. Aristitotle's general definition of rhetoric as the competence of finding the possible means of persuasion in reference to any given subject (Arist. *Rh.* 1.2.1; cf. also Joachim Knape's observations in this regard in chapter 1).

6. For more on the connection between evidence, *deixis*, and indexicality, also cf. the contributions in Wenzel and Jäger (2008).

7. In the wider context of these remarks, also cf. insights regarding empathy and perspective taking, especially in the field of cognitive sciences (e.g., De Vignemont and Singer 2006).

## WORKS CITED

Allen, Nancy. 1996. "Ethics and Visual Rhetorics: Seeing's not Believing Anymore." *Technical Communication Quarterly* 5:87–105.
Aristotle. 2007. *On Rhetoric. A Theory of Civic Discourse*. Translated by George A. Kennedy. New York and Oxford: Oxford University Press.
Asmuth, Bernhard. 1996. "Perspicuitas." In *Historisches Wörterbuch der Rhetorik*, vol. 6, edited by Gert Ueding, 814–74. Tübingen: Niemeyer 1996.
Belle, Hilde van. 2014. *Verbal and Visual Rhetoric in a Media World*. Leiden: Leiden University Press.
Buehl, Jonathan. 2014. Toward an Ethical Rhetoric of the Digital Scientific Image: Learning from the Era When Science Met Photoshop. *Technical Communication Quarterly* 23 (3): 184–206.
Bowater, Laura and Kay Yeoman. 2012. *Science Communication: A Practical Guide for Scientists*. Chichester: Wiley-Blackwell.

Campe, Rüdiger. 1990. *Affekt und Ausdruck: Zur Umwandlung der literarischen Rede im 17. und 18. Jahrhundert*. Tübingen: Niemeyer.
Cicero, Marcus Tullius. 1922. *Academicorum reliquiae cum Lucullo*. Edited by Otto Plasberg. Leipzig: Teubner.
—. 1970. *Cicero on Oratory and Orators*. Translated by J. S. Watson. Carbondale: Southern Illinois University Press.
—. 1942. *On the Orator*. Books 1 and 2. Translated by E. W. Sutton and Harris Rackham. Loeb Classical Library 348. Cambridge, MA: Harvard University Press.
Chandler, James, Arnold I. Davidson, and Harry D. Harootunian. 1994. "Introduction." In *Questions of Evidence: Proof, Practice, and Persuasion Across the Disciplines*, edited by James Chandler, Arnold I. Davidson, Harry D. Harootunian, 1–10. Chicago: University of Chicago Press.
Comenius, Johann Amos. 1659. *Orbis sensualium pictus, hoc est, Omnium fundamentalium in mundo rerum, et in vita actionum, pictura et nomenclatura / Visible world, or, A picture and nomenclature of all the chief things that are in the world, and of mens employments therein*. London: Printed for J. Kirton. Original version published 1658 (Nürnberg: Endter).
Cuntz, Michael, Barbara Nitsche, Isabell Otto, and Marc Spaniol. 2006. *Listen der Evidenz*. Cologne: DuMont.
De Vignemon, Frédérique and Tania Singer. 2006. "The Empathic Brain: How, When and Why?" *Trends in Cognitive Sciences* 10 (10): 435-41.
Jäger, Ludwig. 2006. "Schauplätze der Evidenz: Evidenzverfahren und kulturelle Semantik. Eine Skizze." In *Listen der Evidenz*, edited by Michael Cuntz, Barbara Nitsche, Isabell Otto, and Marc Spaniol, 37–52. Cologne: DuMont.
Kuhn, Thomas S. 1996. *The Structure of Scientific Revolutions*. 3rd ed. Chicago, IL: University of Chicago Press.
Latour, Bruno and Steve Woolgar. 1979. *Laboratory Life: The Construction of Scientific Facts*. Princeton, NJ: Princeton University Press.
Lewontin, Richard C. 1994. "Facts and the Factitious in Natural Sciences." In *Questions of Evidence: Proof, Practice, and Persuasion across the Disciplines*, edited by James Chandler, Arnold I. Davidson, and Harry D. Harootunian, 478–91. Chicago: University of Chicago Press.
Manning, Alan and Nicole Amare. 2006. "Visual-Rhetoric Ethics: Beyond Accuracy and Injury." *Technical Communication* 53, 195–211.
McLuhan, Marshall. 1962. *The Gutenberg Galaxy. The Making of Typographic Man*. Toronto: University of Toronto Press.
—. (1964) 2001. *Understanding Media*. London and New York: Routledge.
Mitchell, William J. 1992. *The Reconfigured Eye: Visual Truth in the Post-Photographic Era*. Cambridge, MA: MIT Press.
Plett, Heinrich F. 2012. *Enargeia in Classical Antiquity and the Early Modern Age: The Aesthetics of Evidence*. International Studies in the History of Rhetoric 4. Leiden, Boston: Brill.

Quintilian. 1922. *The Institutio oratoria of Quintilian*. Vol. 4. Translated by Harold E. Butler. Loeb Classical Library 127. Cambridge, MA: Harvard University Press.
Schneck, Peter. 2011. *Rhetoric and Evidence*. Berlin, New York: De Gruyter.
Wenzel, Horst, and Ludwig Jäger, eds. 2008. *Deixis und Evidenz*. Freiburg/Br.: Rombach.

# Theoretical Approaches

# 1 The Telescope. Evidence in Rhetoric

*Joachim Knape*

> *A poet turns solutions into puzzles*
> —Karl Kraus
>
> *An orator turns puzzles into solutions*
> —JK

## Introduction

On November 22, 1963, the American president John F. Kennedy brought a speech to Dallas that he wanted to present to the invited guests of the Dallas Citizens Club. As we all know, he never made it to the speech. Still, about half a year later, it was released to the public as "The Unspoken Speech" (Kennedy 1964). Kennedy's subject was the connection between America's leading role in the world and the educational efforts of the country (the "link between leadership and learning"). For the President, the connection was

> not only essential at the community level. It is even more indispensable in world affairs. . . . America's leadership must be guided by the lights of learning and reason—or else those who confuse rhetoric with reality and the plausible with the possible will gain the popular ascendancy with their seemingly swift and simple solutions to every world problem. (Kennedy 1964, 1–2)

In this quotation, President Kennedy touched on a few points that I will also be dealing with in my following observations: questions of power and influence in connection to knowledge, science, and education, as well as questions of plausibility and possibility in connection with a supposed antagonism between *rhetoric* and *reality*. I would like to use this as a starting point in my comments on evidence in rhetoric. In the first part of my paper, I will begin by defining two general theoretical positions. In doing so, I will in fact discuss two theoretical "reintegrations." In the second part of my paper, I will then address the theory of rhetorical evidence more specifically.

## Two Theoretical Reintegrations

Let me begin with the alleged contradiction between rhetoric and reality, because it is relevant for my following comments and for the theory of rhetoric in general. In Kennedy's "Unspoken Speech," *rhetoric* is something that clearly exists without reference to reality; indeed, it seems to be the exact opposite of reality. Here, Kennedy and his unknown speech writer place rhetoric on the theoretical level of pure language games and fiction, which deal with unreal possibilities in the virtual spaces of *possible worlds*. In other words: on the one hand we have the unreal *rhetoric*, and on the other we have non-rhetorical political communication; apparently, only the latter concerns itself with reality. With these comments, Kennedy expressed a widespread prejudice found in post-antiquity Western culture that has culminated in the understanding of rhetoric as nothing more than empty word play.

Here, I would like to undertake the first theoretical reintegration. In contrast to the positions mentioned above, I would like to reintegrate rhetoric into reality. Rhetoric should not be abstracted to a phenomenon of some meta- or game-level; it is rather a component of the level of serious, socially binding facts in the real world. This abstract differentiation was undertaken as early as Aristotle (see Barthes 1988, 20–21). He clearly defined a theoretical level of semiotic simulation, which he called *mimesis*, and he developed a theory to describe it: his *Poetics*. Today, we assign the field of poetics that he described in that work to the study of aesthetics. According to Aristotle (*Poet.* 6), this theory deals with the "simulation of actions" (*mimesis praxeos*).

Aristotle wrote a second work: *The Art of Rhetoric*. What is the object of this theory? His topic here is not virtuality in the simulation of communicative practices, but rather exactly the opposite: a specific type of communicative action in political reality, namely socially effective persuasion. Hence, rhetoric is not equivalent to communication in general; it is restricted to the type of communication that seeks to guide and steer people. As Plato (*Phdr.* 261a) put it well, rhetoric is *psychagogia*, the leading of the soul.

According to ancient theory, rhetoric always deals with "truth." We could ask the ironic question (placed in the mouth of the Roman politician Pontius Pilate): *Quid sit veritas?* What is truth? Within the theoretical framework of rhetoric, Aristotle, like Cicero after him, was not concerned with truth as a philosophical principle, but rather with the factual and concrete life world of the *polis* or the roman *forum*,[1] which grappled with issues such as what is concrete and useful (the *sympheron*) within the social context (see Aristotle *Rh.* 1.5–6). "That is why Rhetoric assumes the character of Politics," in the sense of political science, and why it, similar to dialectics, "may be reasonably called Politics" (Aristotle [1975, trans. Freese] *Rh.* 1.2.7).[2] According to Aristotle, rhetoric is "useful for the enforcement of the true and the just (that is, for ensuring that this element is not lost in public debates)."[3] In the "life world" (according to Husserl)[4] we need rhetoric to "help ensure the effective enforcement" of just matters of concern "in the public domain."[5]

For this reason, the German philosopher Martin Heidegger interpreted "rhetoric" not as a theory that dealt with aesthetic products, but rather as a "first systematic hermeneutic for the everydayness of being-with-one-another" ([1927] 1996, 130). Heidegger saw in rhetoric a reference point in his search for the "existential-ontological constitution" of man, a foundation that was largely reflected in the fundamental communicative capacities of hearing, speaking, and remaining silent as well as their practical correlates of interpreting, understanding, informing, etc. In his 1924 lecture on Aristotle, one thing was clear to Heidegger:

> *Rhetoric is nothing other than the interpretation of concrete being-there, the hermeneutic of being-there itself.* That is the intended sense of Aristotle's rhetoric. Speaking in the mode of speaking-in-discourse—in public meetings, before the court, at celebratory occasions—these possibilities of speaking are definitively expounded instances of customary speaking, of how being-there itself speaks. With the interpretation of the *Rhetoric*, one aims at how basic possibilities of the speaking of being-there are already explicated therein. (Heidegger 2009, 75–76, §13)

Orators are committed to reality of the life world, and thus to the standard status of communication, according to roman theory as well. In their performance, they are "the deliverers of truth itself" (*veritatis ipsius actors*), and are contrasted with actors, who act within licensed communicative frames and are "only the imitators of truth" (*imitatores autem veritatis, histriones*, Cic. *De or.* 3.214). Games and *mimesis* (simulation), which, according to Austin and Searle do not constitute real speech acts (cf. Knape 2008, 899–900), are not the object of the orator. At most, he can instrumentalize them for brief moments to help meet his real-world goals. Cicero's orator, as an *actor veritatis*, must be understood as someone who deals with "true" circumstances and actualities, and who acts with and within the real and factual world. Thus, the rhetorical situation is defined by a standard communicative status, and we can say that communicative actuality is the foundation of rhetoric; the non-actual phenomena of licensed communication are only occasionally employed in the service of other goals.[6]

If we differentiate between two separate abstract theoretical levels of human action including communication: the level of factual practice (reality) and the level of fabricated practice (simulation)—which seems sensible for further scientific analysis—then there are still many questions that remain open that cannot be dealt with here. Still, one of these questions is of particular importance for our topic of evidence: what exactly are we humans dealing with when we act and interact at the real-world level?

In his essay titled "An Anthropological Approach to the Contemporary Significance of Rhetoric" (first published 1971 in Italian), German philosopher Hans Blumenberg (1987) sought to provide some answers to this question as related to the concepts of rhetoric and evidence. According to Blumenberg, the biggest problem that humans have in dealing with the environment and its realities is that we no longer live in harmony with nature as animals do; although we have gained the ability for self-reflection, we have lost too many of our natural instincts. Therefore, man is "defined by what he lacks," and he is "a creature of deficiencies, left in the lurch by nature" (Blumenberg 1987, 429). As the only biological species with a conscience, we stand at a certain distance (but not completely separate) from the environment around us (cf. Klein 2009). To a certain extent, man "is the observer of the universe, in the center of the world, *or* he is [literally] 'eccentric,' exiled from Paradise on an insignificant dust speck called Earth" (Blumenberg 1987, 429). Because we, in our human lives, are in many ways no longer predetermined, are driven too little by our instincts, and are constantly forced to find our own way through the thicket of the world, we are extremely dependent on our own cognitive faculties. We compulsively seek that which is *true* so that we can live *good* lives in society, or at least survive. In the end, we continually come to the realization that our cognitive faculties are insufficient, because we are never able to collect natural or "original" evidence through the use of our conscious mind. According to Blumberg, this means that we need "a theory of man outside the realm of Ideas, forsaken by evidentness" (Blumenberg 1987, 432). Here, Blumenberg understands evidence as a sort of "life-form tuning" to nature that could help us orient ourselves and live our lives in the right way. The possibility of gathering *original evidence* (in the sense of an immediate relationship of being or even a sudden, wordless understanding of being) is unobtainable.

What is Blumenberg's (1987, 433) conclusion from the realization of this "deficiency of pre-given, prepared structures to fit into and of regulatory processes for a connected system," a "'cosmos,'" and the deficiency of evidence connected to it? For Blumenberg, the answer is clear: "everything that remains, this side of evidence, is rhetoric." And: "rhetoric creates [model forming] institutions where evident truths are lacking" (435). What is this supposed to mean?

As I said, the question here is how we humans can live properly and how we can recognize what good is. How can we answer questions about what is good in the world, and how are these answers related to human understanding and cognition? According to Blumenberg's (1987, 433) reading, Platonic philosophy assumed that man could count on a "'substantial' base of regulatory processes" in life. The "Platonic Socrates's principle . . . that virtue is knowledge makes what is evident, instead of what is an 'institution,' the norm of behavior." Such a "philosophy of absolute goals did not legitimate the theory of means; instead, it repressed and suffocated it," because this ethic "takes the evidentness of the good as its point of departure" (431–32). In this respect, the mainstream of pre-modern philosophy was based on the assumption that there is such a thing as inherent evidence or "pure evidence" as "absolute self-foundation" (434), and that we as humans are capable of arriving at socially relevant insights outside of social discourse through the use of some "pure sensation" in a "moment of evidence," as Manfred Sommer (1987) might call it.[7] This viewpoint "leaves no room for rhetoric as the theory and practice of influencing behavior on the assumption that we do not have access to evidence of the good [as we can see it]" (Blumenberg 1987, 432).

Perhaps with the exception of Heidegger, modern philosophical thought no longer believes that *innate* evidence is within our ability to understand or perceive. For this reason, Blumenberg sought to fit rhetoric into the gap. His desire was to rehabilitate rhetoric as a philosophical replacement for evidence, and to install it as a method for arriving at insight. "Lacking evidence and being compelled to act are the prerequisites of the rhetorical situation" (Blumenberg 1987, 441). In such situations, rhetoric allows man to "deal with his lack of truth" (430). It is the "effort to produce the accords that have to take the place of the "substantial" base of regulatory processes in order to make action possible" (433). Put another way, "because the possession of [unfiltered] truth is unattainable, the traditional dichotomy between truth and effect must be dissolved and replaced with the insight that truth is provisional and can only be reached through a consensus that has been "effected" by rhetoric. That means that the only way for us to have any understanding of—and active access to—reality is through the indirect route of rhetorical consensus" (Höfner 2009, 27). Blumenberg quotes Aristotle's *Nicomachean Ethics* approvingly when he states "'we say that that which everyone thinks really is so'" (Aristotle [1941, ed. McKeon], *Eth. Nic.* 1173a 1; Blumenberg 1987, 433). Against this backdrop, Blumenberg (1987, 435–36) asserts that on "this side of evidence"—that is, on the side of cognitive man (with his distance to the World)—only rhetoric remains: today, rhetoric represents the "alternative to an evidence that one *cannot* have, or cannot have yet, or at any rate cannot have here and now."

Just as President Kennedy constructed a terminological opposition between rhetoric and reality, so too did Blumenberg construct a conceptual contradiction between evidence and rhetoric. Here too, I would like to undertake a theoretical reintegration—by reintegrating evidence back into rhetoric. I spoke here of a *conceptual* or *terminological* opposition because the contradiction implied by Blumenberg hinges on his interpretation of the word *evidence*. In both English and in German, the word is ambiguous, and we can only make use of it as a clear term if we define it in relation to its theoretical surroundings and mark it attributively. This is one reason, for instance, why Blumenberg's American translator almost always translated the single German word "Evidenz" with the marked English expression *definitive evidence*. I would say, however, that Blumenberg actually meant something more like "original" or "inherent" evidence.

In the following, I would like to compare two separate marked expressions in order to negate the contradiction assumed by Blumenberg. I would like to move away from speaking about a concept of *innate, direct evidence* in a philosophical sense (understood as a direct, quasi-intuitive experiential or cognitive access to being) and shift focus to the concept of a *socio-communicatively produced evidence*. This concept has been an essential part of rhetorical theory since antiquity, known as *enárgeia* or *evidentia* (see Knape 2012a, 19). This theoretical framework concerns itself with communicatively produced "evidence as a *result of a process*," that must "be based on intermedial or discursive procedures," according to the linguist Ludwig Jäger (2006, 43). These procedures "operate as *evidential processes*, as processes that take into account the fact that semantic evidence as apodictic self-evidence [in the sense of Husserl or Blumenberg, see Jäger 2008, 311] can no longer be had" (Jäger 2006, 42). The communicative "evidential processes, insofar as they are medial procedures, create the *settings for evidence*, stages for negotiation upon which cultural semantics executes its attribution of meaning and/or orchestrates the various anticipated formats of sense within the confines of rhetorics of evidence" (43).[8] Rhetoric has been familiar with such "stages for negotiation" since antiquity; among others, even the theater has been counted as a "moral institution" (Friedrich Schiller).

From a structural perspective, evidence here occurs as *deixis* (*showing*) that brings *vividness* and *distinctness* into play. *Subiectio sub oculos*, says Quintilian: something is placed before the very eyes. It is not reported as something that has already occurred (*non gesta indicatur*) but rather as something that is presented in the present moment (*ostenditur*) how it happened or could have happened (*Inst.* 9.2.40). To evaluate the plausibility of evidence-generating *deixis*, two components are particularly important: first, the reference-quality (fictitious or factual) of that which is shown, and second, its argumentative embeddedness (the quality of its connection to argumentative strategies to make it plausible). Within this framework, evidence becomes an element of a communicative operation in which (in a Hegelian sense) the addressee is expected to take the dialectic path from abstraction to intuition (sensory evidence) and then in reverse from intuition back to abstraction. The rhetorically active communicator (the orator) creates this motion with his communicative act in the hope that the addressee is able to follow him cognitively and perhaps emotionally as well.[9] The philosopher Catherine Z. Elgin (2007) believes this hope is justified.

## Bertolt Brecht's *Galileo* Drama and the Theory of Evidence

With that said, I would like to move on to the second part of my paper, in which I will discuss a famous case for evidentiary theory from the rhetorical perspective: Galileo Galilei (see figure 1), likely the most famous physicist of early modern times. Since 1600, his case has repeatedly agitated the Western world, most recently with the Roman Catholic Pope's 1992 apology, in which he recanted the behavior of the catholic inquisition in Galileo's times. Even at the height of the Second World War, the German dramatist Bertolt Brecht saw a reason to reflect on Galileo's case. In the political conditions of his time, Brecht saw in this case pointed questions about proper scientific knowledge, about freedom of thought, and about the relationship between power and knowledge as reflected in the political conditions of his surroundings. Is the scientist allowed to remain neutral, to retreat to his ivory tower, in light of the terrible conditions of the world? Is he allowed to bend to power? Brecht sought to take a clear position with respect to these questions, to rhetorically intervene with the means that he had available, and, in doing so, to create evidence for us.

Figure 1. Galileo Galilei, holding a telescope. Portrait by Justus Sustermans (1636). Public domain work.

Let us begin by taking a look at a brief passage from one scene of Brecht's Galileo drama.

*The Philosopher* begins:

*Galileo* by Bertolt Brecht. English version by Charles Laughton, 1947 (the following passage is cited after Brecht 1988, 134–38).

Act 4: Galileo's house in Florence in the year 1610

> Galileo Galilei, a physicist
> Philosopher, a Court Scholar of Florence
> Mathematician, a Court Scholar of Florence
> Federzoni, Galileo's lens polisher and collaborator
> Andrea, apprentice
> The Prince, Duke Cosmo de Medici, a boy of nine
> Lord Chamberlain, a courtier
> Two Ladies of the Court

PHILOSOPHER. . . . Before we use your celebrated instrument, Mr. Galilei, we beg the favour of a discussion-subject: can these moons [of Jupiter] exist?
MATHEMATICIAN. Of a formal discussion.
GALILEO. I strongly suggest you take a look first. You will find that a discussion would have wasted your time.
. . .
MATHEMATICIAN. Surely! You know your proposition that there is no support in the heavens is in contradiction to the wisdom of the ages?
GALILEO. Yes.
PHILOSOPHER. Apart from my mathematical friend's reservations, I as a philosopher ask you are these moons necessary? Quaedam miracula universi. Orbes mystice canorae . . .[10]
GALILEO. *interrupting.* Shall we speak in everyday language? My colleague Mr. Federzoni does not understand Latin.
PHILOSOPHER. Is it important that he should?
GALILEO. Yes.
PHILOSOPHER. Forgive me. I thought he was your mechanic.
ANDREA. Mr. Federzoni is a mechanic and a scholar.
PHILOSOPHER. Thank you, my boy. If Mr. Federzoni insists . . .
GALILEO, *interrupting.* I insist.
PHILOSOPHER. The quotation will lose its flavour, but it is your house. "Oh mystically musical spheres, oh crystal arches, oh enraptured architecture of the celestial globes." May I pose the question: why should we go out of our way to look for things

that can only strike a discord in the ineffable harmony of the divine classics?

GALILEO, *to the Prince.* Your Highness, one can see the unnecessary and impossible stars as large as life, you know.

MATHEMATICIAN. . . . it might occur to Your Highness that an eyeglass through which one sees improbabilities might not be a too reliable eyeglass?

GALILEO. How is that?

MATHEMATICIAN. With the utmost deference, Mr. Galilei, I suggest that what one sees in the eyeglass and what is in the heavens are two entirely different things.

. . .

FEDERZONI *to Galileo.* They think you painted the Medician stars on the lens.

GALILEO *to Professors.* You are suggesting fraud?

. . .

FEDERZONI. Are you going to look or not?

PHILOSOPHER. Surely, surely.

Mathematician. Surely.

A pause. Nobody goes near the telescope.

. . .

ANDREA. They are wicked. [*German version*: They are stupid.] *He exits* . . .

PHILOSOPHER. Poor child.

LORD CHAMBERLAIN. May I remind Your Highness, that the State Ball begins in three quarters of an hour.

MATHEMATICIAN. Why beat about the bush? Mr. Galilei has to face facts sooner or later. His moons of Jupiter would perforate the outer crystal walls. It is as simple as that.

FEDERZONI. There are no crystal walls; you'd be surprised.

PHILOSOPHER. Any school book will tell you that there are.

FEDERZONI. Let's have new school books.

PHILOSOPHER. My good man, my colleague and myself speak on the authority of Aristotle.

FEDERZONI. Aristotle had no telescope.

Mathematician. Quite.

GALILEO. "Truth is the daughter of Time, not of Authority."[11] Gentlemen, the sum of our knowledge is pitiful. It has been my singular good fortune to get hold of a new instrument which brings a small patch of the universe a little bit closer. It is at your disposal.

PHILOSOPHER, *he and Mathematician step in between the Prince and Galileo.* Your Highness, Ladies and Gentlemen, where is all this leading?

. . .

GALILEO. Your Highness! My work in the Great Arsenal of Venice brought me in daily contact with draughtsmen, mechanics and so on. Much less talented men than Mr. Federzoni here, have taught me many new ways of doing things. I have no difficulty with such men. They are unread, they go by the evidence of their senses regardless of where this evidence might lead them.

PHILOSOPHER. Oh! . . . I am sure Mr. Galilei has admirers down at the dockyard.

LORD CHAMBERLAIN, *bowing to Prince.* Your Highness, I find that this highly informative discussion has exceeded the time we had allowed for it.

In the "possible world"[12] or better: simulated world of this dramatic scene, the discussion hinges on the question of what "facts" are. For those present, it is clear that proof is necessary to be able to talk about fact(s) in a scientific sense. Among other things, this proof must be based on something that we could call *testimonial evidence*; this type of evidence is at the core of all scientific evidence. But what is scientific evidence in the scene above? Here, two irreconcilable opinions clash with one another: on the one hand, we have the valid concept of humanistic-philological *scriptural evidence*, on the other hand the concept of purely *observable evidence* (which is also referred to as *original evidence* in Blumenberg's reflections). For one side, testimonial evidence can only be based on written authority, for the other it can only be derived from empirical observations of the non-literary world.

At the very beginning, the philosopher asks to have a "discussion," while Galileo immediately and exclusively wants to "take a look first." The philosopher rhapsodizes about the harmony of a celestial architecture with "mystically musical spheres," while Galileo points out simply and clearly that the stars in question could be seen through the telescope. The philosopher questions the reliability of the instrument, the other side insists doggedly, "are you going to look or not?" The philosopher refers to the authority of Aristotle, which is the stuff of school books; the other side replies dryly that "Aristotle had no telescope." The philosopher expresses doubts that observation of the world leads to something that makes sense; Galileo says that craftsmen see things differently and rely on their senses and know "where this evidence might lead them," namely to a subversion of the current world order, something which Galileo admittedly does not mention here.

And exactly this is the critical point. It is necessary to express the function of one's method of gathering evidence, and it is always necessary to give evidence a meaningful framework to be able to rhetorically (communicatively) integrate it into an acceptable orientation process. Yes, the fact is that evidence only really becomes evidence and gains meaning within the framework of a strategy for generating plausibility. The fact that both sides in our scene are unable to reveal their argumentative strategies is a separate question; one side argues affirmatively, the other revolutionarily. Because this is never explicitly stated, we must infer it as observers of the scene.

About twenty years after Brecht's *Galileo*, Thomas S. Kuhn's famous *The Structure of Scientific Revolutions* (1962) made it clear that scientific methodology, and thus views about evidence, do not develop continually, but rather in fits and starts. For Kuhn, it was clear that new paradigms always meet resistance, because the existing research community first has to internalize the new cognitive structures. In the process, the community splits into two (or more) camps, ultimately resulting in a sort of revolution that ousts the old, preexisting paradigm. In such disputes, science needs rhetoric, because rhetoric enables us to overcome resistance through communication.

Brecht's Galileo, however, believes naively that he can go without rhetoric. He does not argue with his opponents; instead, he simply puts forward a methodological claim ("Empiricism is enough!") that he monotonously and repeatedly ties to a specific way to act: look and see for yourself! This strategy is unsuccessful because, within the three-way constellation of power (the Prince), established science (the Philosopher and the Mathematician), and new science (Galileo), he does not make any effort to make his claims seem plausible. The Philosopher outlines his ideal harmonist-Pythagorean theory of the cosmos and calls for (in the German version, Brecht 1988, 220): "Reasons, Mr. Galilei, Reasons!" What is the reaction? What does Galileo offer in this situation? No new theory, rather merely the derivation of his observational methodology from the concepts of evidence accepted by craftsmen.

Figure 2. Galileo showing the Doge of Venice how to use the telescope. Fresco by Giuseppe Bertini (1858). Public domain work.

According to the systems theoretician Niklas Luhmann (1980, 49–50), we could here ask the question of whether "the experiential content" of simple craftsmen "signalizes" an acceptable "reference for the society as a whole," within the "social context" of this scenic constellation. Thus, we can perhaps understand the established scholar's position. Luhmann wrote:

> The way in which the internal social environment influences the selection criteria in the evolution of ideas should be described with the terms *plausibility* and *evidence*. Semantic definitions are plausible when they are apparent without further justification and one can expect that others will find them apparent as well. Evidence is

reinforced plausibility. It exists when the exclusion of alternative interpretations is also apparent. Insofar as the social context for plausibility and evidence is not more clearly specified (is not outdifferentiated), this experiential content signalizes a reference for the society as a whole. . . . To the extent that the evolution of ideas is dependent on plausibility and evidence, it is not sovereign in its selective function, but in return, its results are more strongly secured by social relevance. (Luhmann 1980, 49–50)

In the scene above, only the established Philosopher and Mathematician (as nameless social institutions) possess this social relevance, and Galileo does not.

In our scene, Galileo is in need of a rhetorical strategy of persuasion that would make his new understanding of evidence more plausible. What does this mean? In his essay on plausibility ("Versuch über Plausibilität"), Lutz Koch (2002, 193)[13] established a contrast between evidence and plausibility when he apodictically observed that "certainty and evidence are in general only found in the mathematic disciplines." This is why we need plausibility, particularly when dealing with questions that require consensus (discussions about social norms, future decisions, etc.), in order to "characterize the persuasive power, the argumentative value, or simply the 'truth value' of claims and opinions" (194). If we literally translate plausibility from its Latin roots, it means something like "worthiness of approval" (lat. *plausus* = approval). Plausibility depends on the acceptance of the public and demands rhetorical intervention (194). This fits well with the Aristotelian definition of rhetoric, according to which the analytical rhetorical competence (*dynamis*) consists of determining what is believable or persuasive (*pithanon*) in any given communicative situation: "rhetoric then may be defined as the faculty of discovering the possible means of persuasion in reference to any subject whatever" (Aristotle *Rh.* 1.2.1). In this context, something is plausible if it is probable, which is, according to Immanuel Kant, a form of truth that is admittedly justified by "insufficient grounds" (Kant 1855, 209). In the end, Koch finds his way to the following definition:

> Plausible is thus that which is neither inconsistent and absurd nor obvious, to say nothing of that which can be counted, weighed, or measured. If we want to define it in a more positive sense, then it is good to remember that we can only speak about plausibility in the context of actions that require counsel and contemplation, and more generally of the type of thing that could also behave different-

ly, as Aristotle said. What should one adhere to if not "that which generally happens" [Aristotle *Rh.* 1.2.15]? (Koch 2002, 199)

I think we can understand why the Mathematician and the Philosopher feel that they are in the right. In our scene, Galileo should have remembered that by refusing to discuss *scriptural evidence* and asking his audience to just "take a look," he was simply ignoring the *consensus omnium* of the largely unquestionably accepted methodological paradigm established by the history of science up until that point. Galileo needed to make arguments to make his new model of investigation seem reasonable, regardless of the outcome in our scene. What was it that Aristotle wrote? "We say that that which everyone thinks really is so" (Aristotle *Eth. Nic.* 1173a 1). And not everyone was convinced of Galileo's approach to creating evidence.

There are two moments in the conversation where Galileo could have and should have acted rhetorically. The first is when the Philosopher asks the question (which for him is not absurd in the least, and stems from his accepted theoretical system): "are these moons necessary," which "can only strike a discord in the ineffable harmony" of the theory "of the divine classics?" At its core, this is a question about a better theory, which is a topic that experts are correct to continually discuss (see Knape 2013a, 14–15). In his answer, Galileo should have embedded his demand for observational evidence in an argumentative explanatory framework (in a new plausible theory).[14] Instead, he merely prompts the Philosopher to take a look without giving him any reason to do so.

The second opportunity for Galileo to construct an argumentative framework is when the scholars make the indirect accusation that the moons of Jupiter might be simply painted on the lens of the telescope. How does Galileo react? Only with moral indignation, "You are suggesting fraud?" Luckily, there is an interruption after his comments. It would have been much better for him to calmly make an argument about the utility of the device. He could have mentioned (as happens later in the drama) that the telescope gave the seafaring cities of northern Italy the advantage in naval battles and on their trade routes. The instrument certainly worked in those cases! Such a practical argument would have instantly caught the attention and interest of the representative of power (the Prince), and it would have given Galileo the chance to construct a new context of plausibility (cf figure 2). Unfortunately, nothing of the sort happens in our scene.

## Rhetorical Evidence in the Life World

In Brecht's literary world, Galileo fails because he naively believes that his concept of scientific evidence is self-evident. The intrinsic (that is, drama-internal) analysis of the communication in this scene and its historical background make it clear that the character and quality of evidence must always be clarified when there is no consensus about how evidence can be produced or *must* be produced for it to be accepted as legitimate. Self-evidence always requires a theoretical framework.

Another point must be made here. It may seem surprising that the telescope itself became a decisive point of conflict both in the *Galileo* drama and in the actual historical event. But the dispute surrounding this instrument cuts to the core of the decisive problems with culturally produced evidence. It is a dispute concerned with the question of whether or not it is better to depend on our immediate physical, intuitive, and spontaneous evidence—with all its lacks—as opposed to something external to us. "Technically" produced evidence depends on consensus concerning the relevant processes of creation, because it creates space for possible manipulation; we see in this case the accusation of fraud, for instance (cf. Kuhn 2000). "Visualization"[15] of that which is not naturally observable inevitably brings with it the experience of alienation. Every "attitude of the *retour au réel*," that is derived from rhetorical theory, "has to concern itself with the explanation of the illusions, deceptions, and seductions that have to be disposed of in connection with it" (Blumenberg 1987, 455). In principle, from its very beginning rhetoric has assumed a clear theoretical position in reference to communicative instrumentalism. The theory of rhetorical means is an instrumental theory. *Sub specie artis rhetoricae*, rhetoricians observe every linguistic text, and every other method of communication, as a tool. Communication needs instruments, above all the instrument of language or, more clearly: text.

In our *Galileo* scene, for instance, we see annoyance with the fact that the Philosopher prefers the hermetic instrument of Latin, while Galileo prefers the instruments of the trades people (including their vernacular language). We can produce evidence using a wide variety of means, but some groups expressly prefer only a very specific kind of means. Technically speaking, in the realm of text and communication, evidence can be created narratively or dramatically, to name just two of the ways that texts can "show."[16] Still, Quintilian thought it was important not to take things too far in cases of illustrative evidence:

I would not for this reason go so far as to approve a practice of which I have read, and which indeed I have occasionally witnessed, of bringing into court a picture of the crime painted on wood or canvas, that the judge might be stirred to fury by the horror of the sight. For the pleader who prefers a voiceless picture to speak for him in place of his own eloquence must be singularly incompetent. (Quintilian [1966, trans. Butler] *Inst.* 6.1.32)[17]

Let us leave our analysis of the world inside the *Galileo* drama behind and shift our thoughts to another level, to an analysis based on an extrinsic perspective. Here we must concern ourselves with the interface between texts and their environments. In this case, we should view Bertolt Brecht as a rhetorically active orator outside of the drama; as someone who not only wanted to construct the fictional world inside his drama, but who also wanted to influence his audience outside of the drama.

In 1933, on the three hundredth anniversary of Galileo's judgment, Brecht began doing historical research on the case. In Emil Wohlwill's monumental 1909 monograph on Galileo Galilei, he found (among other things) information on the contemporary opponents of Galileo's sensational discovery of Jupiter's moons.[18] This inspired Brecht. It was an "opposition of school scholars," wrote Wohlwill,

> [an opposition of] the men who didn't need to see in order to understand, and who ceased to accept for Clavius and Magini as authorities when they too could no longer deny that which could no longer be explained by Aristotle's authority. For them [the school scholars] the observations of many—which had once been the observations of the few—remained the deception of the lenses. With this conviction, Giulio Libri, the Pisan philosopher, persisted until his death in his denial of having seen the Medicean Stars. "Perhaps," wrote Galileo upon receiving word of his death, "he will see them on his way to heaven."[19] With the same stubbornness, Cremonini in Padua had refused all demands to make use of the telescope in order to recognize in the moon and stars the truth that he had declared to be impossible. And he remained steadfast in his refusal in the years to follow. That didn't prevent him, despite contradictory testimony from others, from claiming that nobody other than Galileo had seen what he described. (Wohlwill [1909] 1983, 335; own translation)

In a 1610 letter to the famous German astronomer Johannes Kepler, Galileo lamented such colleagues, "people of this sort think that philosophy is a kind of book like the Aeneid or the Odyssey, and that the truth is to be sought, not in the universe, not in nature, but (I use their own words) by comparing texts!"[20]

As Brecht read this, he faced the challenge of transforming the abstract nature of this historical information, and the fundamental methodological problem of modern science addressed in Galileo's letter, for his own communicative purposes: creating theatrical evidence. How could this historical commentary about the scientific empiricism postulate versus the ancient philological-humanistic postulate of traditional evidence derived from authoritative sources be communicatively conveyed in such a way that we (the audience) would recognize the problem and—if everything went well—would also come to the messages and inferences that Brecht had in mind?

As a professional dramatist, Brecht decided to use his own communicative methods, which I would like to designate with the term *poetic evidence*. According to its communicative function, we could classify this type of evidence as a form of what I call *illustrative evidence*, because it uses visual or narrative reification to shed light on or illustrate a posed or implicit argument (see Holert 2002). In the same sense, I myself am using Brecht's drama in this paper in order to create a form of illustrative evidence.

According to Quintilian, if I want to make a case in front of a court it is highly effective to create an *effet du reel*, as Holert (2002, 205–13) calls it, to describe things as if they were right in front of our eyes (*in occulis*): "From such impressions arises that *enárgeia* that Cicero calls *illustratio* [to bring to light] and *evidentia* [to take from sight], which makes us seem not so much to narrate as to exhibit the actual scene, while our emotions will be no less actively stirred than if we were present at the actual occurrence" (Inst. or. 6,2,32, see also Zanker 1981).

> The theory of rhetoric normally uses the term *evidentia* to denote literary visualization, that is textual processes that are especially stimulating for the imagination. Concrete evidence goes even further. When discussing the form that the conclusion of a speech should take, Quintilian states in his *Institutio oratoria* (6.1.30), "we may excite tears, however, not only by words (*dicendo*), but by acts (*faciendo*)." The core of Quintilian's theory of evidence holds that at the mere sight of a meaningful object an entire event unfolds again in the consciousness, and again generates an image of the event in the imaginations of the observers. (Knape 2012a, 19; own translation)

Quintilian saw a compelling example in the case of Marc Antony's famous *Oratio funebris* after Ceasar's murder:

> Hence, too, we see blood-stained swords, fragments of bone taken from the wound, and garments spotted with blood, displayed by the accusers, wounds stripped of their dressings, and scourged bodies bared to view. The impression produced by such exhibitions is generally enormous, since they seem to bring the spectators face to face with the cruel facts. For example, the sign of the bloodstains on the purple-bordered toga of Gaius Caesar, which was carried at the head of his funeral procession, aroused the Roman people to fury. They knew that he had been killed; they had even seen his body stretched upon the bier: but his garment, still wet with his blood, brought such a vivid image of the crime before their minds, that Caesar seemed not to have been murdered, but to be being murdered before their very eyes. (*Inst.* 6.1.30–31)

Thus, *illustrative evidence* is not a form of proof, because the facts are already known. Instead, it consists of bringing into play something that amplifies our sense of a situation within the context of an argument, in order to, for instance, stir up our emotions (Knape 2010a, 43–44).

Even Plato distinguished between two elementary communicative practices that had to be unified in the creation of evidence. He called these elements *dihegesis* and *mimesis* (Knape 2006, 107). For our own context, we could speak of the internal and necessary connection between *argumentation* and *demonstration*. Others distinguish these elements as *telling* and *showing* (James 2011), *description* and *dramatism* (Burke 1967, 341), or *saying* and *displaying* (Peters 2007).

If we had an actual historical report that our Galileo scene really happened the way it is described above, then Brecht could have attempted to historically reconstruct *scenic evidence*. In the terminology of modern documentary filmmaking, we could speak of a *reenactment* (the acting of a historically accurate scene). Because we lack such precise evidence, however, Brecht had no choice but to employ pure fiction and simulate a historical scene (in the sense of Aristotelian *mimesis*). Between 1944 and 1947, Brecht worked together with the famous British actor and director Charles Laughton to develop a poetically memorable scene for a Broadway production (see figure 3).

Figure 3. Bertolt Brecht and Charles Laughton, 1947, New York, USA. Photograph by Ruth Berlau.

From the perspective of rhetorical theory, the following process took place: Brecht transformed the abstractions of his source material into the concrete simulation of a scene (*poetic evidence* as a method) that was designed to lead to further abstractions in the minds of his audience, for example, the abstraction of a message (for instance, concerning the question of what counts as scientific fact and what rules there should be for the actions of scientists). In this way, the poetic evidence (as aesthetical factor) generated by Brecht was embedded in a rhetorical framework for action. Brecht himself spoke of *epic theater*—we should better say: *rhetorical theater*—by which he meant that this form of art should transcend pure illusion and continually seek to activate a rhetorical factor to influence people ideologically in their life world. The evidence in our scene is embedded in the argumentative macro-frame of his Marxist inspired political agitation in order to establish a scientific, non-speculative Weltanschauung. In doing so, he systematically reinserted the conditions and expectations of licensed communication (as they apply to art) back into the standard communicative frame of the life world with rhetorical intentions.[21]

Since the beginning of the so-called Art Period in the eighteenth century and the emergence of the *l'art pour l'art* ideology, an idea of the autonomy of artistic work has developed. Brecht's aesthetic stands in contrast to the spontaneous concepts of performance that have been developed within this context, according to which the meaning of a piece of art first develops in the moment of its performance. Such concepts hold that artistic messages are thus a phenomenon of a situatively linked emergence (cf. Knape 2012b, 17). With reference to literature, this would mean that poets write only for themselves, and then leave us their texts as mere stimuli for our own individual games. According to this ideology, literature or theater that has been fully detached from its author, like every other form of art, leads to an original experience of being.

Brecht saw the situation totally differently, and this made him an orator. He believed in controlled evidence: the idea that he could utilize his poetic resources within a rhetorical framework, and that his audience had the capacity to derive an authorial message from his work by transforming theatrical evidence into intellectual abstraction (Knape 2010b, 24–27). If that was actually the case, then indeed we do have here (in Brecht's theater) also an example of rhetorical communication and not only of aesthetic communication.[22]

## NOTES

1. For more on rhetoric's connection with the polis, see the commentary provided by Christof Rapp in his edition of Aristotle's *Rhetoric* (Aristotle 2002, vol. 2, 127–29, 171–73).

2. The English translation by John Henry Freese indicated here (Aristotle 1975) is also used in following when citing from Aristotle *Rh*.

3. Aristotle 2002, commentary by Rapp in vol. 2, 82; cf. 89, 91 (own translation). Cf. also Bultmann (1933, 239): "The adjective alethes [true] characterizes a situation as really so, as it is seen or illustrated now, and, especially as alethinos [true, correct], can take the meaning of actually, real" (own translation).

4. See Husserl 1970, §§33–34; Schütz (1936) 1996; Schütz 1971, 257.

5. Aristotle 2002, commentary by Rapp in vol. 2, 91 (own translation). The Sophist quote used by Aristotle (*Rh*. 2.24), "to make the weaker speech [*logos*] the stronger one" (Protagoras 1960, fragment 80 B 6), was also used by Cicero ([1962, trans. Hendrickson] *Brut.* 30) when he reported that the Sophists had promised "to teach how by the force of eloquence the worse (as they called it) could be made the better cause."

6. For more on the differences between standard communication and specialized or licensed communication, see Knape 2008, 898–906; Bauer et al. 2010, 9; Knape 2013b, 14–15.

7. Cf. the idea of "Punctum-Evidenz" from Barthes and Lucida 1981, 24–27, 49–59; see also Jäger 2008, 305–07.

8. In his reasoning, Jäger refers to Tom Holert (2002, 208).

9. For pathos and evidence, see Knape 2010a, 43.

10. English translation: "A kind of wonder of the universe. Mysterious melodic heavenly spheres . . . ."

11. According to Francis Bacon (1620, I, 84): "Veritas Temporis filia dicitur, non Authoritatis."

12. For more on possible worlds, see Kripke 1980; Surkamp 2002.

13. The following quotes from Koch (2002) are my own translations from the original German text.

14. With regard to this new theory, Galileo also would have had to take into consideration the religious taboo concerning curiosity and scientific research (*experientia*).

15. See Knape 2023; cf. also Flusser's theory of technocodes (see Knape 2000, 1–18).

16. A list of such technical possibilities can be found in Lanham 1991, 64 (under the keyword *Enargia*).

17. The English translation by H. E. Butler indicated here (Quintilian 1966) is also used in the following (with minor variations).

18. Cf. the commentary in Brecht 1988, 339; see also: 332–34; cf. Knape 2023.

19. Letter from Gualdo to Galileo, July 29, 1611. Printed in *Works of Galilei* (1901, 165).

20. Letter from Galileo to Kepler, August 19, 1610. Printed in Works of Galilei (1900, 423); own English translation based on the German version by Wohlwill ([1909] 1983, 335); also cf. Brecht 1988, 391.

21. For standard communication and specialized or licensed communication see again Heidegger 2009, 75–76, § 13.

22. This chapter was translated from German by Alan L. Fortuna.

## Works Cited

Aristotle. 1941. "Nicomachean Ethics." Translated by W. D. Ross. In *The Basic Works of Aristotle*, edited by Richard McKeon, 927–1112. New York: Random House.

——. (1926) 1975. *The "Art" of Rhetoric*. Translated by John Henry Freese. Vol. 22 of *Aristotle in Twenty-Three Volumes*. Cambridge, MA, London: Harvard University Press.

——. 2002. *Rhetorik*. Translated by Christof Rapp. 2 vols. Vol. 4.1–2 of *Aristoteles: Werke in deutscher Übersetzung*. Berlin: Akademie Verlag.

Bacon, Francis. 1620. *Novum organum*. London.

Barthes, Roland. 1981. *Camera Lucida: Reflections on Photography*. Translated by Richard Howard. New York: Hill & Wang. Original French version *La chambre claire. Note sur la photographie*. Paris: Gallimard, 1980.

Barthes, Roland. 1988. "The Old Rhetoric: an aide-mémoire." In Roland Barthes. *The Semiotic Challenge*. Translated by Richard Howard, 11–93. New York: Hill & Wang. Original French version "L'ancienne rhétorique. Aide-mémoire." *Communications* 16 (1970): 172–223.

Bauer, Matthias, Joachim Knape, Peter Koch and Susanne Winkler. 2010. "Dimensionen der Ambiguität." *Zeitschrift für Literaturwissenschaft und Linguistik* 158: 7–75.

Blumenberg, Hans. 1987. "An Anthropological Approach to the Contemporary Significance of Rhetoric." In *After Philosophy: End or Transition?* Edited by Kenneth Baynes, James Bohman, and Thomas McCarthy, 429–58. Cambridge, MA/London: MIT Press. German version "Anthropologische Annäherung an die Aktualität der Rhetorik." In *Wirklichkeiten in denen wir leben. Aufsätze und eine Rede*, 104–136. Stuttgart: Reclam, 1981. Original Italian version published in *Il Verri* 35.6 (1971): 49–72.

Brecht, Bertolt. 1988. *Stücke 5*. Edited by Bärbel Schrader and Günther Klotz. Vol. 5 of *Bertolt Brecht: Werke*. Berlin, Weimar, Frankfurt a. M.: Aufbau-Verlag.

Bultmann, Rudolf. 1933. "Der griechische und hellenistische Sprachgebrauch von alêtheia." *Theologisches Wörterbuch zum Neuen Testament* 1: 239–51.

Burke, Kenneth. 1967. "Dramatism." In *Communication: Concepts and Perspectives*, edited by Lee Thayer, 327–60. Washington, D.C.: Spartan Books.

Cicero, Marcus Tullius. 1962. "Brutus." In *Brutus*, with an English translation by G. L. Hendrickson. *Orator*, with an English translation by H. M. Hubbell. Vol. 5 of *Cicero in Twenty-Eight Volumes*, 1–293. London, Cambridge, MA: William Heinemann Ltd., Harvard University Press.

Elgin, Catherine Z. 2007. "Die kognitiven Funktionen der Fiktion." In *Kunst denken*, edited by Alex Burri and Wolfgang Huemer, 77–90. Paderborn: mentis.

Heidegger, Martin. 2009. *Basic Concepts of Aristotelian Philosophy*. Translated by Robert D. Metcalf and Mark B. Tanzer. Bloomington, IN: Indiana University Press. Original German version *Grundbegriffe der aristotelischen Philosophie*. Edited by Mark Michalski. Frankfurt a. M.: Klostermann, 2002.

Heidegger, Martin. (1927) 1996. *Being and Time: A Translation of Sein und Zeit*. Translated by Joan Stambaugh. Albany, NY: State University of New York Press. German version *Sein und Zeit*. 15th edition. Tübingen: Niemeyer, 1979 [originally published in 1927]. Citations refer to the English edition.

Höfner, Markus. 2009. "Leben als Reden. Rhetorik, Ethik und die Frage nach dem Menschen bei Hans Blumenberg und Martin Heidegger." In *Auf Distanz zur Natur: Philosophische und theologische Perspektiven in Hans Blumenbergs Anthropologie*, edited by Rebekka A. Klein, 23–41. Würzburg: Königshausen & Neumann.

Holert, Tom. 2002. "Evidenz-Effekte. Überzeugungsarbeit in der visuellen Kultur der Gegenwart." In *Korrespondenzen. Visuelle Kulturen zwischen Früher Neuzeit und Gegenwart*, edited by Matthias Bickenbach and Axel Fliethmann, 198–225. Cologne: DuMont.

Husserl, Edmund. 1970. *The Crisis of European Sciences and Transcendental Phenomenology. An Introduction to Phenomenological Philosophy*. Translated by David Carr. Evanston: Northwestern University Press. Original German version: *Die Krisis der europäischen Wissenschaften und die transzendentale Phänomenologie: eine Einleitung in die phänomenologische Philosophie*. Edited by Walter Biemel. Vol. 6 of *Husserliana*. Dordrecht: Springer, 1962.

Jäger, Ludwig. 2006. "Schauplätze der Evidenz: Evidenzverfahren und kulturelle Semantik. Eine Skizze." In *Die Listen der Evidenz*, edited by Michael Cuntz, Barbara Nitsche, Isabell Otto, and Marc Spaniol, 37–52. Cologne: DuMont.

Jäger, Ludwig. 2008. "Indexikalität und Evidenz. Skizze zum Verhältnis von referentieller und inferentieller Bezugnahme." In *Deixis und Evidenz*, edited by Horst Wenzel and Ludwig Jäger, together with Robin Curtis and Christina Lechtermann, 289–315. Freiburg i. Br., Wien, Berlin: Rombach.

James, Henry. (1934) 2011. *The Art of the Novel: Critical Prefaces*. With an Introduction by R. P. Blackmur and a New Foreword by Colm Tóibín. Chicago, London: University of Chicago Press.

Kant, Immanuel. 1855. *Critique of Pure Reason*. Translated by John Miller Dow Meiklejohn. London: Bohn. Original German version: Immanuel Kant, *Kritik der reinen Vernunft*. Edited by Wilhelm Weischedel. Vol. 3 of *Immanuel Kant: Werke*. Frankfurt a. M.: Suhrkamp, 1968.

Kennedy, John F. 1964. The Unspoken Speech of John F. Kennedy at Dallas November 22, 1963. El Paso, TX: Carl Hertzog.

Klein, Rebekka A. 2009. "'Auf Distanz zur Natur.'. Eine Beschreibung des Menschen." In *Auf Distanz zur Natur. Philosophische und theologische Perspektiven in Hans Blumenbergs Anthropologie*, edited by Rebekka A. Klein, 9–19. Würzburg: Königshausen & Neumann.

Knape, Joachim. 2000. "Die kodierte Welt. Bild, Schrift und Technobild bei Vilém Flusser." In *Perspektiven der Buch- und Kommunikationskultur*, edited by Joachim Knape and Hermann-Arndt Riethmüller, 1–18. Tübingen: Osiander.

—. 2006. *Poetik und Rhetorik in Deutschland 1300–1700*. Vol. 44 of Gratia. Wiesbaden: Harrassowitz.

—. 2008. "Rhetorik der Künste." In *Rhetorik und Stilistik / Rhetoric and Stylistics. Ein internationales Handbuch historischer und systematischer Forschung / An International Handbook of Historical and Systematic Research*, edited by Ulla Fix, Andreas Gardt, and Joachim Knape. Vol. 1. Vol. 31.1 of *HSK. Handbücher zur Sprach- und Kommunikationswissenschaft / Handbooks of Linguistics and Communication Science*, 894–927. Berlin, New York: de Gruyter.

—. 2010a. "Rhetorischer Pathosbegriff und literarische Pathosnarrative." In *Pathos: Zur Geschichte einer problematischen Kategorie*, edited by Cornelia Zumbusch, 25–44. Berlin: Akademie Verlag.

—. 2010b. "Zur Theorie der Spielfilmrhetorik mit Blick auf Fritz Lang's *M*." In *Fritz Lang: "M–Eine Stadt sucht einen Mörder": Texte und Kontexte*, edited by Christoph Bareither and Urs Büttner, 15–32. Würzburg: Königshausen & Neumann.

—. 2012a. *Was ist Rhetorik?* Stuttgart: Reclam.

—. 2012b. "Das Kunstgespräch." In *Kunstgespräche. Zur diskursiven Konstitution von Kunst*, edited by Joachim Knape, 11–62. Baden-Baden: Koerner.

—. 2013a. "Schönes im Wahren?" *Attempto. Forum der Universität Tübingen* June: 14–5.
—. 2013b. *Modern Rhetoric in Culture, Arts, and Media: 13 Essays*. Berlin, Boston: de Gruyter.
—. 2023. "Zur Theorie der Visualisierung, rhetorisch." In *Bildmedien*, edited by Frauke Berndt and Jan-Noël Thon, 9–25. Berlin, Boston: de Gruyter.Koch, Lutz. 2002. "Versuch über Plausibilität." In *Rhetorik, Argumentation, Geltung*, edited by Andreas Dörpinghaus and Karl Helmer, 193–204. Würzburg: Königshausen und Neumann.
Kripke, Saul A. 1980. *Naming and Necessity*. Revised and enlarged edition. Oxford: Blackwell.
Kuhn, Thomas S. 1962. *The Structure of Scientific Revolutions*. Vol. 2.2 of *International Encyclopedia of Unified Science*. Chicago: University of Chicago Press.
Kuhn, Thomas. 2000. *The Road Since Structure: Philosophical Essays, 1970–1993, with an Autobiographical Interview*. Edited by James Conant and John Haugeland. Chicago, London: University of Chicago Press.
Lanham, Richard A. 1991. *A Handlist of Rhetorical Terms*. Berkeley, Los Angeles, Oxford: University of California Press.
Luhmann, Niklas. 1980. *Gesellschaftsstruktur und Semantik. Studien zur Wissenssoziologie der modernen Gesellschaft*. Vol. 1. Frankfurt a. M.: Suhrkamp.
Peters, Sibylle. 2007. "Über Ablenkung in der Präsentation von Wissen. Freier Vortrag, Lichtbild-Vortrag und Powerpoint-Präsentation ein Vergleich." In *Powerpoint-Präsentationen. Neue Formen der gesellschaftlichen Kommunikation von Wissen*, edited by Bernt Schnettler and Hubert Knoblauch, 37–52. Konstanz: UVK-Verl.-Ges.
Quintilian. 1966. *The Institutio Oratoria*. Translated by H. E. Butler. Vol. 2. London, Cambridge, MA: William Heinemann Ltd., Harvard University Press.
Schütz, Alfred. (1936) 1996. "Das Problem der Personalität in der Sozialwelt." Quoted in Chung-Chi Yu. *Transzendenz und Lebenswelt im Spätwerk von Alfred Schütz*, S. 84–88. Bochum: Diss. Ruhr-Univ.
—. 1971. "Über die Mannigfaltigen Wirklichkeiten." In Alfred Schütz. *Gesammelte Aufsätze. Bd. 1: Das Problem der sozialen Wirklichkeit*. With an introduction by Aron Gurwitsch and a preface by H. L. van Breda. Translated by Benita Luckmann and Richard Grathoff. Den Haag: Nijhoff Original English version: "On Multiple Realities." *Philosophy and Phenomenological Research* 5 [1945]: 533–576.
Sommer, Manfred. 1987. *Evidenz im Augenblick. Eine Phänomenologie der reinen Empfindung*. Frankfurt a. M.: Suhrkamp.
Surkamp, Carola. 2002. "Narratologie und *possible-worlds theory*: Narrative Texte als alternative Welten." In *Neue Ansätze in der Erzähltheorie*, edited by Ansgar Nünning and Vera Nünning, 153–83. Trier: WVT, Wiss. Verl. Trier.
Wohlwill, Emil. (1909) 1983. *Galilei und sein Kampf für die copernicanische Lehre*. Vol. 1. of *Bis zur Verurteilung der copernicanischen Lehre durch die römischen Kongregationen*. Vaduz: Sändig.

Works of Galilei. 1900. *Le Opere di Galileo Galilei*. Edited by Sua Maestà il Re d'Italia. Vol. X. Firenze: Barbèra.

—. 1901. *Le Opere di Galileo Galilei*. Vol. 11. Edited by Sua Maestà il Re d'Italia. Firenze: Barbèra.

Zanker, Graham. 1981. "Enargeia in the Ancient Criticism of Poetry." *Rheinisches Museum für Philologie* N. F. 124, 3/4: 297–311.

# 2 Evidence in Visual Rhetoric

*Thomas Susanka*

## Introduction

The field of visual rhetoric is vast and almost unfathomable. It features messages created by a plurality of semiotic systems (and some also claim even non-semiotic visual artifacts) that are bound to copious different media. Consequently, pursuing the idea of a general theory of visual rhetoric in a way also means to find the lowest common denominator of communicative artifacts as diverse as memorials, photographs, theater, dance performances, paintings, graphs, protest techniques or film, to name only a few. A theory of visual rhetoric of such a scope must necessarily disregard those phenomena of communication that stem from the specific workings of the artifacts, first and foremost the involved semiotic systems. A statue presumably creates its meaning and becomes persuasive in a very different way than, for example, how typographic choices influence the rhetoricity of a written message. Hence, if we want to make claims about visual rhetoric in general, our answers must remain very general. At the same time, there seems to be a sound reason why very different communicative phenomena are conflated in the concept of *visual rhetoric*, there seems to be a certain form of rhetoricity that they share.

The theory of visual rhetoric has received great attention in the last two decades, and major critical contributions have been made (for example, to name only a few: Batra and Scott 2003; Hill and Helmers 2004; Prelli 2006; Hariman and Lucaites 2007, 2016; and Olson, Finnegan, and Hope 2008). We still lack a unified theory of visual rhetoric, but by now, we have an immense resource of case-studies. In this regard, Olson's study on the "Intellectual and Conceptual Resources for Visual Rhetoric" (2007) is still one of the most valuable contributions so far. In their entirety, these studies more and more paint a picture of how a general theory of visual rhetoric could look and what its major elements could be.

In this chapter, I argue that one defining persuasive mode of visual rhetoric is evidence, that is, it seems to me that all persuasively used visual artifacts share their evidentiary character and are capable of evoking a *sense of certainty about the subject-matter* of communication in the addressee. Clearly, there is some amount of ambiguity in the term evidence. In my argument, I refer to two distinct understandings of "evidence": (1) evidence in the sense of proof as in atechnical proofs (the *pisteis atechnoi*, with Aristotle) and (2) evidence in the sense of self-evidence, also known in the rhetorical tradition by the name of *evidentia* with Cicero or Quintilian.

## Visual Proof

Visual artifacts are used on a regular basis to prove a certain state of affairs in various contexts. The predominance of this usage is, for example, also well documented in Howells's and Matson's *Using Visual Evidence* (2009). Visualizations attest claims in political communication, in science and research, but also in private life. These visual artifacts are employed on grounds of their authority that seemingly excels the mere verbal claims of a speaker. Visual evidence apparently offers an unmediated, unfiltered access to reality that seems to be capable of circumnavigating the perils of the potentially deceptive speaker. "Picture or it didn't happen," is a vernacular internet-phrase to demand visual evidence for a claim, but by the same token, scientists use visuals to substantiate their findings or interpretations.

At the heart of any inquiry into a visual rhetoric of evidence lies the question of the role of factual proofs and truths in rhetoric in the first place. However, already the first texts loosely associated with rhetoric, such as the *Dissoi Logoi,* reveal a fundamental situational or relativist perspective on questions of truth and falsehood. While Plato, in the *Phaedrus,* tried to assign rhetoric the role of a truth-dispenser as an aid for the less intelligent, it was, of course, Aristotle who put forward the most influencing conception of rhetoric. Aristotle maintained that rhetoric is the *antistrophos* (the "counterpart") to dialectics, which deals not with truths but necessarily with those topics where no truth is to be had. Hence, rhetoric is never essentially concerned about facts or truths in the first place, but about credibility and probability. In this sense, Temilo van Zantwijk maintains that

> [i]t is of fundamental importance that truth appears in rhetoric only as a truth that has been made probable by rhetorical means. Truth, in a way, requires rhetoric's probabilities as midwife. With this, rhetoric has a problematic relationship with truth. This is because the other way around, the false can also be made to appear as being probable by means of rhetoric and consequently meets approval. (Zantwijk 2009, 1286; own translation)

Hence, rhetoric is actually not so much interested in facts, yet not because of an overall relativist worldview, but simply because the currency of rhetoric is probabilities not truths, *doxa* not facts or mere data. This, quite naturally, has influence on how rhetoricians have approached the question of proof. Especially in judicial rhetoric, practical rhetoricians always had to deal with evidences as they played an important role in the *argumentatio*. Aristotle made the influencing distinction between *pisteis atechnoi* and *entechnoi*, that is, atechnical and technical proofs. In this sense, the technical proofs are all forms of arguing that are based on rhetorical theory, first and foremost the *enthymeme*. The atechnical proofs, on the other hand, are those sources that the rhetorician finds connected to the case, such as documents, laws, reports, and the like. They can be brought to court but are not manufactured by the rhetorician himself and are located outside of rhetorical theory.

Another external resource in the *argumentatio* are the signs or *signa*, not in the sense of semiotic theory but as indicators, symptoms or evidence for certain circumstances, for example, blood or fingerprints, which seem to be closest to what is often quite colloquially referred to as facts. Quintilian (*Inst.* 5.9) is most enlightening here when he distinguishes between necessary, nondisputable signs (*signa necessaria*) and those which can be contested, the *signa non necessaria*. Blood, for example, may stem from violence but also from a mere nosebleed. Hence, given that the evidence is not compelling, rhetoric may step forward to dispute the probability of different truths resulting from facts, questioning the grounds of a case.

However, given that their prime characteristic is that they are outside of rhetorical theory, we only find very little hints for rhetoricians about how to use atechnical proofs and especially the nondisputable signs. Quintilian (*Inst.* 5.1.2) simply maintains that rhetorical artistry is required for the proper use of these proofs.

When we now look at how visual proof is employed in rhetorical contexts, we often find that rhetoricians employ them in the form of atechnical evidence. In his famous *An Inconvenient Truth*, Al Gore uses various kinds of visualizations in this very sense (for example, photographs of glaciers are shown) to support his rhetorical argument. This is pretty much how photographs are used in most rhetorical contexts: as objective evidence, devoid of human intentionality. Of course, this also applies to other machine-made images, for example, when we think of magnetic resonance imaging (MRI), thermography or seismography but also statistical diagrams that visualize sets of data as in the case of the infamous hockey-stick graph (cf., e.g., Schneider 2009). The cultural logic behind such usages maintains that these visualizations attain their evidentiary status, that is, their status as atechnical proofs, due to their apparatus-based genesis: the seemingly impartial production where a machine unwillingly detects some sort of signal and translates it into visual information—be it a pixel or a dot. This usage of visualizations as atechnical proofs critically hinges on the cultural myth of the *acheiropoieton*, a myth well reflected in the critical discourse on photography.

## The Case of Photography: The Cultural Myth of the *Acheiropoieton*

The invention of photography marked a sea change in the cultural production of images. For the first time, it was possible to create images without actually drawing them; instead, nature seemed to paint itself. One of the inventors of photography, William Henry Fox Talbot, quite tellingly entitled his first books of photographs *The Pencil of Nature* ([1844–46] 2011) and made it a point that the images were created solely by using optical and chemical means but explicitly without the aid of a painter. Photographs were essentially seen as *acheiropoieta*, that is, pictures made without the help of human hands (for detailed discussions, see Wortmann 2003; Andree 2005; and Geimer 2009). For the discourse on photography, two distinct consequences ensued: (1) photographs could not pass as art, as the camera was merely conceived of as a recording-device and (2) photographs were understood as an objective access to the world, due to their optical, chemical, and mechanical genesis and the seeming absence of subjective intent. In fact, the epistemological potential of photography was seen as so fundamental that photographically created images were imagined to even be capable of replacing reality itself, as, for example, argued by Oliver Wendell Holmes in his 1859 essay on stereography:

> Form is henceforth divorced from matter. In fact, matter as a visible object is of no great use any longer, except as the mould on which form is shaped. Give us a few negatives of a thing worth seeing, taken from different points of view, and that is all we want of it. Pull it down or burn it up, if you please. (Holmes 1859, 112)

In this conception, the photographer was seen as the mere operator of a machine that automatically renders pristine renditions of reality. The relation of image and reality was seen as pure and causative and was consequently later discussed in the semiotic terminology of the index (Krauss 1977).

Of course, this idea of pure and objective representation was soon contested. Amongst many, the pictorialists made efforts to highlight the role and influence of the photographer whom they saw not as the mere operator of a machine but as a creative image-maker. From these initial moments of debate, photographic criticism has ever since oscillated between affirmation and skepticism of the reliability or authenticity of photographic evidence. In a way, André Bazin (1960) later made a point when he even spoke of an *irrational power* of photography due to its dispassionate mechanical genesis (8), a power that stems just as much from the lack of human authorship (Geimer 2009, 65). In the words of rhetoric: from the beginning on, photographs were first-and-foremost described as *atechnical evidence*.

But clearly, the argument truly is irrational and photography never was an infallible and pristine access to reality. The history of image manipulation is well-documented and essentially coincides with the invention of the technique itself (see, e.g., Fineman 2012), as photographs were soon tampered with in the darkroom. But manipulation of various degrees also took place during the actual taking of photographs, as in the early and well-known example of Roger Fentons setting-up of the "Valley of the Shadow of Death" (1855). Even more, critics like Allan Sekula (1982), for example, vehemently attacked the alleged neutrality of photography by arguing that "[e]very photographic message is characterized by a tendentious rhetoric" (87).

But even despite all critical objections, the myth of objective photographic evidence has entered the digital age almost unblemished—yet only to witness another severe onslaught. In *The Reconfigured Eye*, William J. Mitchell famously argued that, due to the fact that digital processes enable the manipulation of every single constitutive pixel of a photographic image, photography was essentially stripped of its capacity for authentic representation: "From the moment of its sesquicentennial in 1989 photography was dead—or, more precisely, radically and permanently displaced—as was painting 150 years before" (Mitchell 1992, 20).

Indeed, the fact that photographs are just as much *made* as they are *taken* is today a subject of public awareness—and no longer only a matter of academic debate: It is widely known that photographers have a wide range of influence during production, even more, images undergo processes of selection before publication and, of course, they can almost at any stage be subject to image-manipulative action. In a way, the cultural logic that the photographic image has a privileged evidentiary status as atechnical proof has been shattered by the digital image. Yet, as is almost paradoxically documented by everyday culture, photography did not die at all. On the contrary, photography has never been more alive with billions and billions of photographs accessible online and more and more uploaded every day: The cultural myth of the acheiropoietic image, too, is still untouched and photographs are used as atechnical evidence for the recline of glaciers just as much as proof of one's social status on the internet.

In the end, the evidentiary usage of photography is based on convention and social practice. The technophile narrative of acheiropoietic image production (be it chemical, mechanical, or photo-electric) is essentially a cultural myth that does not reflect actual processes of photographic production but can be seen as a result of cultural discourse about the medial properties of photography (cf. Wortmann 2003; Susanka 2015a).

Photography is a fairly well researched form of visual communication, where we can quite finely (indeed, much finer than I did in my sketch of the debate) trace the discursive developments that established its paradoxical status right in the middle between atechnical and technical proof: In rhetorical communication, photographs are often used as atechnical proof, while, from the perspective of image-production, the photographic image is at will to the image-maker. It seems to me that this paradoxical evidentiary status applies to a large segment of visual rhetoric, and that most of photographic discourse about evidence is readily extrapolated to the entire realm of technical image production. The aforementioned techniques of MRI or thermography similarly derive their evidentiary status from the same cultural narrative of the acheiropoietic production—and consequently lend themselves easily for the usage as seemingly objective forms of evidence. From a rhetorical perspective, all forms of visual proof seem to linger between made and taken, between technical and atechnical proof. This, of course, puts forth the need for profound ethical considerations when we rely on visual proof in communications.

## Self-Evidence

Rhetoricians employ visual proofs by *presenting* them to their audience, just as the bloody cloth was presented to the audience in Shakespeare's *Julius Ceasar*. It seems that this is the very mode of all forms of visual artifacts entering rhetorical communication: they are given presence and hence become perceivable physical manifestations over a certain period of time. But even more, their primary communicative mode is that of giving presence to something potentially absent: they can show what is not there. Consequently, the philosopher Lambert Wiesing (2005) describes the creation of an *artificial presence* as the *irreplaceable capacity* of images. Their prime faculty is that they offer a glance at a reality devoid of physics (7). From the perspective of visual rhetoric, we can say that the creation of artificial presence is the proprium of the entire field of visual communication: be it a graph, a monument, or a picture—they all create an artificial presence of something. It is in this sense that Jens Kjeldsen (2013) describes *presence* as one key potential in his argument on pictorial rhetoric. Looking for corresponding conceptions in rhetorical theory, he links the presence of images to the concept of *evidentia*, as described by Cicero and Quintilian. Kjeldsen maintains that

> [t]he power to make events come alive before the eyes of the audience and create mediated evidentia and resonance is probably the most important rhetorical characteristic in representational images. (2)

Indeed, it seems to me that evidentia may be of central relevance even to the entire field of visual rhetoric, and not only to the limited field of pictures. The concept of evidentia can be approached from two perspectives: First, it can be regarded as a rhetorical effect in communication, and secondly, it can be referred to as a rhetorical technique. With regard to the first, Ansgar Kemman describes evidentia as "the immediate sense of certainty about the vividly apprehended or about what necessarily has to be thought" (Kemman 1996, 33, own translation), which is why evidentia also translates into *self-evidence*. In that, evidentia differs from the form of certainty and insight we get from, for example, retracing a logical argument or examining factual evidence. Even more, the certainty of insight, referred to in evidentia, is not linked to an actual and profound understanding as it is not an epistemological category (cf. Sandkühler 2011). Hence, an audience's experience of a sense of certainty about a given subject matter is not necessarily grounded in actual knowledge or understanding. This, of course, has profound ethical implications since evidentia presents itself as a potentially deceptive technique that we can see at work, for example, in conspiracy theories. The term was introduced by Cicero and the terminology is quite revealing here, stemming from the latin *evideri*, it refers to giving insight by shedding light on something (Kemman 1996, 33). When something becomes self-evident, it seems to need no further reasoning or explanation, it is immediately clear and understandable, which is why the term is also sometimes used synonymously with perspicuity. The concept of self-evidence documents, amongst others, that the early rhetoricians were already well aware of the persuasive power of the visual (cf. Kjeldsen 2003)—but the challenge that ancient rhetoricians faced was, of course, that visual communication was almost not available to them.

How then can we create self-evidence? Kemman retraces the winding conceptual history and maintains that self-evidence can be effected by the creation of visual presence by means of words:

> In oratory, such presence is attained when the orator lays out a matter clearly and precisely, vividly and graphically with the effect that the hearer is taken to believe to see it with his own eyes. (Kemman 1996, 33; own translation)

Hence, evidentia means making something self-evident by using verbal techniques to create vividness of imagination in the addressee. The concept essentially advises the orator to try to give the audience a visual understanding of the subject matter, and the more vivid the rendition is, the more persuasive the speech will be. That makes evidentia, as described by Cicero and Quintilian, essentially a *compensatory technique*: the ancient rhetoricians realized that visuality is capable of instilling an unhindered readiness to belief. But, given that orators almost exclusively had to stick to language, they had to look for verbal techniques that were able to instill a visual conception of a state of affairs in the audience. Two techniques were found to be very helpful in this respect: Aristotle already described techniques of *vivification*, which is referred to as *enérgeia*. Vivification includes the use of vivid metaphors, the *subiectio sub oculos*, the *phantasia* or the *visio*. The other technique of evoking self-evidence refers to all forms of detailing and goes back to stoic philosophy with the term of *enárgeia*. Detailing can be achieved by a minute and colorful description, but also by *hypotyposis*, *diatyposis*, *illustratio*, or the *demonstratio* (Kemman 1996, 40).

The techniques of vivification (enérgeia) and detailing (enárgeia) are systematically located in the field of *elocutio* and describe exclusively verbal techniques of creating self-evidence. They are ways to simulate a visual experience and instill the impression in the audience that they have seen themselves what the orator talks about. Clearly, these techniques vehemently rest on the semiotic restrictions of verbal language, especially sequentiality and its proneness to abstraction and generalization, while visual communication, on the opposite, favors simultaneity and concreteness. This means that the verbal techniques of detailing and vivification are in their very nature compensatory to the limitations of verbal languages.

## Challenges in Visual Rhetoric: Scope, Terminology and Method

What does that mean for visual rhetoric? In how far can we then even apply the concept of self-evidence and its associated techniques of detailing and vivification to visual rhetoric? Especially in light of their compensatory nature, the question about the applicability of techniques of enérgeia and enárgeia to visual communication touches the more fundamental question, how we can develop a theory of visual rhetoric.

In her seminal essay "Framing the Study of Visual Rhetoric: Toward a Transformation of Rhetorical Theory," Sonja K. Foss points out that most of rhetorical theory was written based on how verbal language works and generates meanings. She argues that, since the realm of the visual works quite differently in many ways, not all of rhetorical theory may be easily transferred to visual rhetoric (Foss 2004). This seems to be especially the case for those aspects of rhetorical theory that inform us about specific verbal techniques, such as, for example, the figures. Indeed, it might be of dubitable benefit to look for alliterations or anaphora in visual communication. Clearly, this deductive approach, as Foss calls it, is the central route as it is based on an already highly developed theory of rhetoric. Its validity, however, is never granted and certainly limited. Even more, working deductively in the field of visual rhetoric necessarily means working with a blind spot as those phenomena that are unique to visual communication must necessarily evade our attention. Hence, Foss argues, we must also work inductively, and potentially add new concepts and techniques to rhetorical theory to update it to the visual realm—evoking and applying concepts of rhetorical theory to visual communication might simply not suffice to account for how visual rhetoric works.

## Working Deductively: Details and Vividness in Visual Communication

As maintained above, self-evidence, as a general concept, refers to a communicative effect that pertains to the vividness of apprehension of a given subject-matter on the side of the addressee. With this, a conception of self-evidence as rhetorical effect seems to be productive and likewise applicable to the entire field of visual rhetoric. In this regard, self-evidence can be understood as *the immediate sense of certainty upon visual apprehension* (to paraphrase Kemman).

Since the techniques of detailing and vivification are compensatory in nature, we should also be able to trace them in visual communication. With regard to the techniques of detailing, I think it is almost self-understood that the realm of the visual works very differently than verbal language, and that the way a visual is able to provide details is very different than a vivid and minute description of something. Yet, I think Kjeldsen (2013) makes a point when he refers to detailing as a key potential for self-evidence in the case of photography. Ever since people indulged in the inspection of daguerreotypes with magnifying glasses, its potential for detail was seen as a defining characteristic of the technique. Additionally, pictures (understood as representational pictures) are defined by their similarity or iconicity (cf. Stöckl 2004), and hence their currency is concreteness and—if we will—details. However, there are other visual representations that carry the same potential for detailing: for example, visualizations can take us deep into cell-structures and reveal minute particulars. In this way, the electron microscope with a magnification of up to ten million times is the technological epitome of making details visible. Quite self-evidently, visual artifacts offer an immense potential for detailing that cannot be attained even through the minutest form of description (cf. Susanka 2015a).

The deductive transferal of techniques of vivification to visual communication can be deduced from a plethora of examples. First and foremost, all forms of so-called "moving-images" (film, video, animations) offer a potential for vivification, just consider computer animations that sequence complex processes. Just like in language, visual metaphors and other tropes may also be seen to vivify even a static visual artifact (Bonsiepe 1965).

In many forms of visual rhetoric, evidentia is produced by both techniques of detailing and vivification. In this sense, Markus Gottschling (2016) discusses the presentation software *Prezi*, where the actions of panning and zooming enable the presenter likewise to go into details and to vivify an otherwise static visual experience.

Indeed, as we should have expected, the compensatory verbal techniques to create self-evidence can be effortlessly detected in the realm of visual communication. Yet, there may be two caveats that should be expressed: Firstly, while we may argue that visual artifacts bear, as Kjeldsen puts it, a critical *potential* for self-evidence, we must maintain at the same time that not all visual artifacts necessarily create feelings of immediate insight. Hence, despite its excess of details, a picture created by an electron microscope is not necessarily rhetorically charged with self-evidence and not all animations will lead to instantaneous feelings of certainty:

*Evidence in Visual Rhetoric* 39

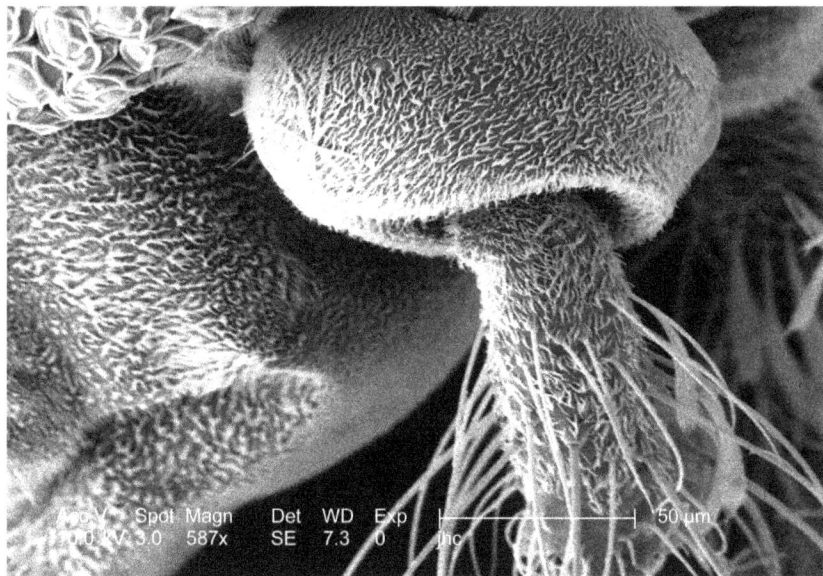

Figure 1. Electron microscopic pictures offer a great amount of details but do not necessarily create immediate feelings of insight. Public domain image by Paul Howel, https://pixnio.com/science/microscopy-images/insects/anopheles-dirus-mosquito/at-a-moderately-high-magnification-of-587x-this-scanning-electron-micrograph-sem-revealed-some-of-the-morphologic-features.

With Birgit Schneider (2009), we must maintain that self-evidence in visual communication is not just a given but has to be systematically created, amongst others, by the verbal framing of a visual. Otherwise, visualizations may remain ambiguous, unclear or underspecified and hence do not create feelings of insight but give rise for questions, for example, what is it that the picture shows me? (Susanka 2015b)

## Working Inductively: Purely Visual Self-Evidence

A second caveat pertains to Foss's argument: The deductive use of the techniques of enéreiga and enárgeia in a heuristic for visual rhetoric may tell us only half the story of how self-evidence can be effected through visual communication. Hence, as compensatory techniques, detailing and vivification may simply be too much tied to how language works, and leave unexplored how visual artifacts inspire immediacy of insight by purely visual means. A second, inductive step may be required.

Exploratively, we may look at some examples. The first example stems from Daniel Kahneman's bestselling *Thinking, Fast and Slow* (2011) in which he describes his award-winning studies with Amos Tversky. He asks, "How to write a persuasive message?"—and reports a study how typographic choices can affect how true or false a statement is rated (62). The idea behind the experiment was that relieving cognitive strain by means of clear and perceptible type is capable of instilling truth illusions. Kahneman gives the following example (63):

**Adolf Hitler was born in 1892.**
Adolf Hitler was born in 1887.

While both answers are false, experiments reported by Kahneman have shown that the bold version is more likely to be believed. In this minimalist example, the visual properties of the printed text somehow seem to exert an immediate influence on the reader about which statement is more likely to be true—and even if we know that the correct answer is 1889, it is hard to divest oneself of this form of visual self-evidence. Yet it seems to me that neither detailing nor vivification can be seen at work here. For Kahneman, it is a matter of contrast, as he concludes:

> If your message is to be printed, use high-quality paper to maximize the contrast between characters and their background. If you use color, you are more likely to be believed if your text is printed in bright blue or red than in middling shades of green, yellow, or pale blue. (63)

Visuals that are made to stick out seem to be likely to inspire a sense of immediate certainty, a critical component of self-evidence.

A second example that I would like to consider exploratively stems from the field of information visualization and could look something like this:

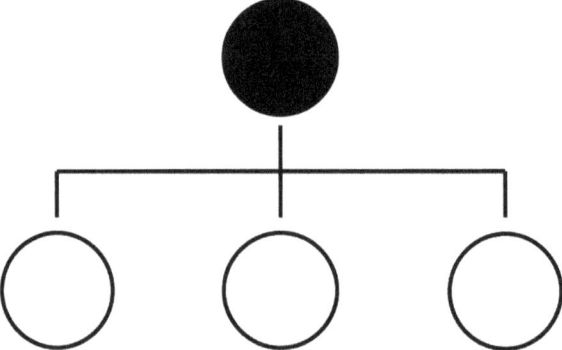

Figure 2. Example of an image evoking evidence by clarity of form. Created by Thomas Susanka.

While we may know nothing about what the white dots represent and what the black dot stands for, their relation to each other becomes self-evident. Hence, while we may not even be able to specify this relation, for example, by giving it a name, we gain immediate insight by means of a visual conception about their (potentially metaphorical) spatial relation to each other. Again, it seems to me, neither detailing nor vivification seem to be at work here. Rather, we can speak of clarity of form that sheds immediate insight about its own properties. This form of self-evidence seems to be often exploited by infographics, where the overall visual form is meant to give insight about the represented subject matter.

Lastly, a similar effect may be seen at work in other forms of data visualizations. The communicative value of diagrams, for example, does not lie in their potential of detailing—on the contrary, as diagrams often even restrict the access to specific data. Nor are diagrams known for the momentum of vivification, but they give their beholders an immediate insight into a potentially very ample and complex set of data, as in the infamous hockey stick graph, where the late rise of the curve immediately signalizes a drastic development of whatever kind.

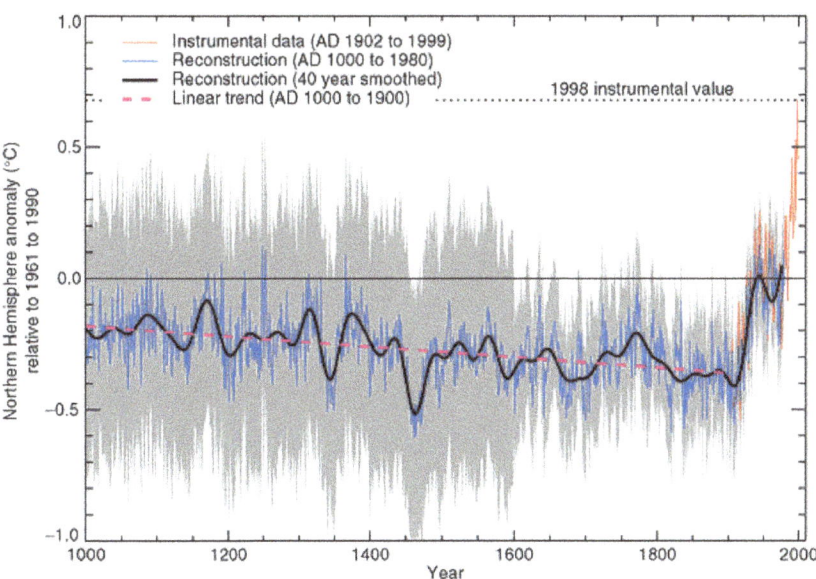

Figure 3. The hockey-stick graph as published on www.ipcc.ch.

These few briefly considered examples seem to point to the fact that there might be at least a third way of creating self-evidence that is different from the techniques of detailing and vivification. This third route of self-evidence would rely exclusively on visual techniques and may be a critical force in visual rhetoric that requires further exploration.

## Conclusion

In this chapter, I have argued that evidence may be seen as a central persuasive mode in visual rhetoric. I have approached evidence from two angles: (1) evidence understood as proof, and (2) evidence understood as self-evidence, known as evidentia in the ancient rhetorical tradition. In a deductive analysis, I have tried to show how the techniques of detailing (enárgeia) and vivification (enérgeia) can be seen at work in visual communication. In a final inductive and explorative step, I argued that in visual rhetoric, ways of creating self-evidence (i.e., feelings of immediate insight) may be at work that are not sufficiently explained by the categories of detailing and vivification; rather, clarity of visual form may be at work here. As in the case of the Kahneman study, the evidentiary force of visuality can be subtle but immense at the same time—and may be put to ethically questionable use. The rise of fake news and more recently deep fakes document these implicit dangers well. From the perspective of the rhetorical tradition, certain ethical limitations (e.g. the vir bonus ideal, see the introduction of this volume) regarding the use of visual evidence necessarily do apply. At the same time, rhetorical theory also offers tools and terminology to detect and describe deceptive uses of visual evidence. Lastly, self-evidence—or evidentia as communicative effect—can only be sufficiently accounted for in a complete analysis of a rhetorical act that especially includes acts of verbal framing. Visual rhetoric may be crucially tied to evidence, yet visual artifacts do not involuntarily exert an evidentiary force on their beholder.

## Works Cited

Andree, Martin. 2005. *Archäologie der Medienwirkung: Faszinationstypen von der Antike bis heute*. München: Fink.

Bazin, André. 1960. "The Ontology of the Photographic Image." *Film Quarterly* 13 (4): 4–9.

Bonsiepe, Gui. 1965. "Visuell-verbale Rhetorik / Visual-Verbal Rhetoric." *Journal of the Ulm School for Design* 14/15/16:23–40.

Fineman, Mia. 2012. *Faking it: Manipulated Photography Before Photoshop*. New York: Metropolitan Museum of Art.

Foss, Sonja K. 2004. "Framing the Study of Visual Rhetoric: Toward a Transformation of Rhetorical Theory." In *Defining Visual Rhetorics*, edited by Charles A. Hill and Marguerite Helmers, 303–313. Mahwah, NJ: Erlbaum.

Geimer, Peter. 2011. *Theorien der Fotografie zur Einführung*. Hamburg: Junius.
Gottschling, Markus. 2016. "Lend Me Your Eyes." In *Rhetoric, Knowledge and the Public Sphere*, edited by Agnieszka Kampka and Katarzyna Molek-Kozakowska, 57–72. Frankfurt am Main.
Hariman, Robert, and John L. Lucaites. 2007. *No Caption Needed: Iconic Photographs, Public Culture, and Liberal Democracy*. Chicago: University of Chicago Press.
Hariman, Robert, and John L. Lucaites. 2016. *The Public Image: Photography and Civic Spectatorship*. Chicago: University of Chicago Press.
Hill, Chales A., and Marguerite Helmers, eds. 2004. *Defining Visual Rhetorics*: Mahwah, NJ: Erlbaum.
Holmes, Oliver Wendell. 1859. "The Stereoscope and the Stereograph." *The Atlantic* 6:738–48.
Howells, Richard, and Robert W. Matson. 2009. *Using Visual Evidence*. Maidenhead: Open University Press/McGraw-Hill.
Kahneman, Daniel. 2011. *Thinking, Fast and Slow*. New York: Farrar, Straus, and Giroux.
Kemmann, Ansgar. 1996. "Evidentia, Evidenz." In *Historisches Wörterbuch der Rhetorik*, vol. 3, edited by Gert Ueding, 37–38. Tübingen: Niemeyer.
Kjeldsen, Jens. 2003. "Talking to the Eye: Visuality in Ancient Rhetoric." *Word & Image* 19 (3): 133–37.
Kjeldsen, Jens. 2013 "Four Rhetorical Potentials of Pictures." Paper presented at the conference Rhetoric in Society in Copenhagen, January 15–18.
Mitchell, William J. T. 1992. *The Reconfigured Eye*. Cambridge: MIT Press.
Olson, Lester C. 2007. "Intellectual and Conceptual Resources for Visual Rhetoric: A Re-examination of Scholarship Since 1950. "*The Review of Communication* 7 (1): 1–20.
Olson, Lester C., Cara A. Finnegan, and Diane S. Hope, eds. 2008. *Visual Rhetoric: A Reader in Communication and American Culture*. Los Angeles: Sage.
Prelli, Lawrence J., ed. 2006. *Rhetorics of Display*. Mahwah, Columbia: University of South Carolina Press.
Sandkühler, Hans Jörg. 2011. "Kritik der Evidenz." In *Wissen was wirkt*, edited by Johannes Bellmann and Thomas Müller, 33–55. Wiesbaden: VS Verlag.
Schneider, Birgit. 2009. "Die Kurve als Evidenzerzeuger des klimatischen Wandels am Beispiel des 'Hockey-Stick-Graphen.'" In *Sehnsucht nach Evidenz*, edited by Karin Harrasser, Helmut Lethen and Elisabeth Timm, 41–55. Bielefeld: Transcript.
Scott, Linda M., and Rajeev Batra, eds. 2003. *Persuasive Imagery: A Consumer Response Perspective*. Mahwah, NJ: Erlbaum.
Sekula, Allan. 1982. "On the Invention of Photographic Meaning." In *Thinking Photography*, edited by Victor Burgin, 84–109. London: Macmillan.
Stöckl, Hartmut. 2004. *Die Sprache im Bild—das Bild in der Sprache zur Verknüpfung von Sprache und Bild im massenmedialen Text ; Konzepte, Theorien, Analysemethoden*. Berlin: de Gruyter.

Susanka, Thomas. 2015a. *Foto/grafie: Zur Rhetorik von Medium und Bild*. Mit einer Fallstudie zu James Nachtwey. Berlin: Weidler.

—. 2015b. "Die Schuhe von van Gogh. Ambiguität vs. Unspezifität im Bild." In *Ambiguität: Sprache und Kommunikation / Ambiguity: Language and Communication*, edited by Susanne Winkler, 339–356. Berlin, New York: Mouton de Gruyter.

Talbot, William Henry Fox. (1844–46). 2011. *The Pencil of Nature*. Chicago: KWS.

Wiesing, Lambert. 2005. *Artifizielle Präsenz: Studien zur Philosophie des Bildes*. Frankfurt am Main: Suhrkamp.

Wortmann, Volker. 2003. *Authentisches Bild und authentisierende Form*. Cologne: von Halem.

Zantwijk, Temilo van. 2009. "Wahrheit, Wahrscheinlichkeit." In *Historisches Wörterbuch der Rhetorik*, vol. 9, edited by Gert Ueding, 1285–1340. Tübingen: Niemeyer.

Quintilian. 1966. *The Institutio oratoria*. Vol. 2, translated by H. E. Butler. London, Cambridge, MA: William Heinemann Ltd., Harvard University Press.

# 3 Evidence on the Micro Level: What Rhetoric Can Learn from Hans Fallada's *Every Man Dies Alone* and New Objectivity

*Olaf Kramer*

### A Surprising Success and the Exploitation of Evidence: Hans Fallada's *Every Man Dies Alone*

The re-edition of *Every Man Dies Alone*, a novel by Hans Fallada which was first published in 1947 and translated into English by Michael Hofmann in 2009, was an instant and surprising success in the US and the UK book market (where it was published under the title "Alone in Berlin"). The novel is based on the historic Hampel family (named Quangel in the novel), a Berlin working class couple which committed itself to the resistance movement against the Nazi regime after their son had died as a soldier in France. But how could it happen that a more than 60-year-old book became that popular all of a sudden? Certainly, there was an enthusiastic review in the New York Times book section (Schillinger 2009) that drew attention to the English edition of Fallada's novel and the book was promoted heavily by the publishing house. Yet, an aspect that made this re-edition of the 1947 novel in the US as well as in the UK special was the inclusion of historic documents as evidence: these documents further enhanced the strong emotional appeal of the text, which resonated with the readers. The 2009 English translation contains a chapter disclosing "The True story Behind *Every Man Dies Alone*," excerpts from the Gestapo (Secret State Police) File on the Hampels, and reproductions of historical postcards written by the Hampel family. As an act of protest against the Nazis, the Hampels had written and distributed these so called *Hetzkarten* ("hate cards") to denounce Hitler (figure 1).

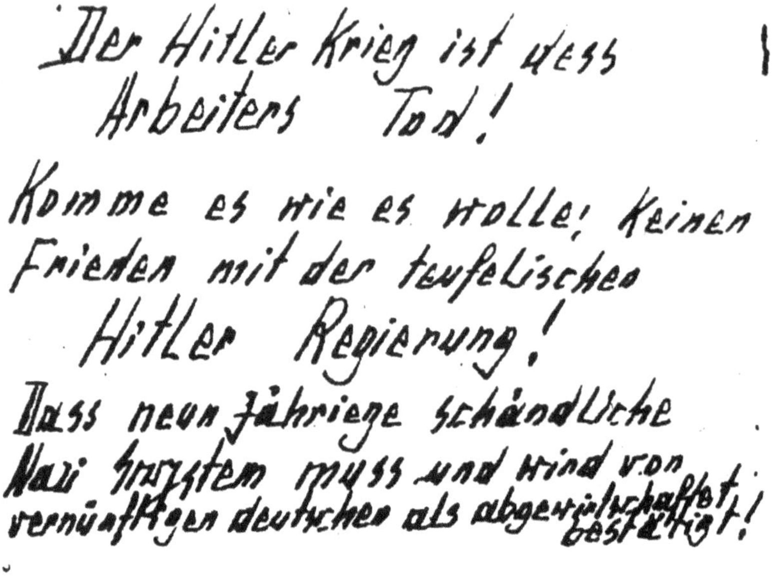

*Der Hitler Krieg ist des Arbeiters Tod! Komme es wie es wolle; keinen Frieden mit der teuflischen Hitler Regierung! Dass neun jähriege schändliche Nazi System muss und wird von vernünftigen deutschen als abgewirtschaftet gestellt!*

Figure 1. *Hetzkarte* to denounce Hitler as pictured in Fallada (2009), 534. The text translates to: "Hitler's war is the worker's death. Come what may: No peace with the diabolical Hitler government! The nine-year disgraceful Nazi system must be and is confirmed by reasonable Germans as run down!" (own translation)

These cards, hand-written in clumsy letters, as well as the reproduction of official Secret Police Files on the Hampels, are a form of *visual evidence*: they add an historic and realistic dimension to the literary text which, as a consequence, is no longer just a piece of fiction but interwoven with historic reality. What is particularly appealing about these cards and documents is not so much the verbal text printed on them; rather, it is their status as a reproduction of historic documents. The concrete visualization of historic documents establishes a bridge between fiction and reality, and therefore the distance between the actual world in which the readers live and the possible world that is constructed by the author is diminished (cf. Doležel 1998).

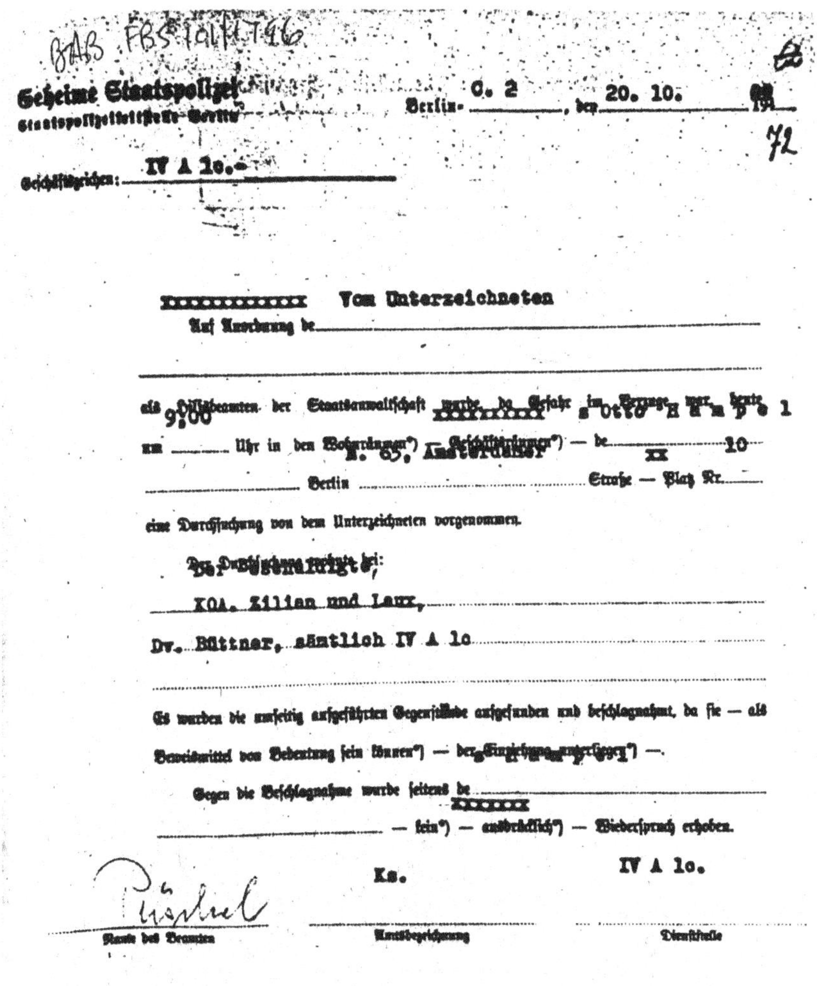
BAB FBS 191/14796

Geheime Staatspolizei
Staatspolizeileitstelle Berlin

Berlin C. 2, den 20. 10. 19

72

Geschäftszeichen: IV A 1o.-

xxxxxxxxxxxxx Vom Unterzeichneten
Auf Anordnung de

als Hilfsbeamten der Staatsanwaltschaft wurde, da Gefahr im Verzuge war, heute 9.00 Uhr in den Wohnräumen — Geschäftsräumen — de Otto H a m p e l N. 65, Amsterdamer xx 10 Berlin Straße — Platz Nr.

eine Durchsuchung von dem Unterzeichneten vorgenommen.

Der Durchsuchung wohnte bei:

KOA. Zillian und Laux,

Dr. Büttner, sämtlich IV A 1o

Es wurden die umseitig aufgeführten Gegenstände aufgefunden und beschlagnahmt, da sie — als Beweismittel von Bedeutung sein können — der Einziehung unterliegen —.

Gegen die Beschlagnahme wurde seitens de xxxxxxx — kein — ausdrücklich — Widerspruch erhoben.

Ks. IV A 1o.

Name des Beamten | Amtsbezeichnung | Dienststelle

Figure 2. Gestapo file cover sheet case as pictured in Fallada (2009), 529.

There are, of course, translations of the verbal text that are accompanying these documents, but they are not even complete; obviously, the paratexts marking these documents as authentic reproductions are more important than the translations. These paratexts turn the reproduction into visual evidence that is used to strengthen the immersive effect of the text, because they shape solid accessibility relations to the possible world (cf. Ryan 1991). The underlying aesthetic strategy that is employed here is to intermingle the fictional possible world defined by the novel with the actual world. Thus, the re-edition uses visual evidence as a kind of backing, and that fascinating interplay between fiction and the actual world is appealing to the readers. The importance of the visual representation of the cards and files (see also figure 2) becomes particularly obvious when envisaging an alternative way of including the information they contain: if the editors had just presented the same information as a written text, the effect would not have been as strong as it is with the visual representation included.

Rhetorically speaking, the postcards and Gestapo files are *signa* or, following Quintilian, "necessary signs" (cf. Quintilian *Inst.* 5.9.5, 5.9.15) that legitimate the conclusion that the novel is a close depiction of the situation in Nazi Germany. The visual representation of these documents has a strong argumentative force as we tend to accept as true what we see. The rhetorical use of evidence is not limited to visual evidence, of course: according to Cicero, speakers should make their points by presenting them as if the audience were observing something with their own eyes to influence and persuade them. Thus, Cicero considered *evidentia* as a style of writing that aims at conveying a visual impression towards the audience with the use of language, as a powerful rhetorical figure:

> For dwelling on a single circumstance often has a considerable effect; and a clear illustration and exhibition of matters to the eye of the audience, almost as if they were transacted before them. This has wonderful influence in giving a representation of any affair, both to illustrate what is represented, and to emphasise it, so that the point which we emphasise may appear to the audience to be really as great as the powers of our language can represent it. (Cicero [1860, trans. Watson] *De orat.* 3, 202)

The central linguistic technique that Cicero has in mind here is the verbal description of objects. This descriptive form of evidence is focused on observable details. However, the rhetorical concept of *evidentia* encompasses yet another approach: the dynamic representation of events. This dynamic evidence can be traced back to Aristotle and his idea of energetic writing. Aristotle encouraged speakers to show objects "in activity" (2007 [trans. Kennedy], *Rh.* 1410b36) and focus on events; he regarded *enérgeia* as a verbal technique of envisioning and actualization: for one must present "things as being done rather than as going to be done" (Rh. 1410b34f). Both dynamic and descriptive evidence appeal to the imagination of the audience.

Unsurprisingly, the use of evidence in Fallada's *Every Man Dies Alone* is not limited to the exploitation of visual evidence. If we analyze Fallada's style, we realize that descriptive and dynamic evidence are as central in this book as the visual evidence added in the re-edition. What is especially notable when analyzing the use of descriptive and dynamic evidence in Fallada's novel is his economic style of writing. Fallada is highly economic in his use of figurative language, and his work is a perfect model to underline the observation that not much ornamental effort is needed to achieve descriptive and dynamic evidence: evidence can be realized on the micro-level of the text and can focus on isolated details and minimalist representations of events. Let us have a closer look at the beginning of the novel to illustrate this point:

> The postwoman Eva Kluge slowly climbs the steps of 55 Jablonski Strasse. She's tired from her round, but she also has one of those letters in her bag that she hates to deliver, and is about to have to deliver, to the Quangels, on the second floor. (Fallada 2009, 9)

This letter that the postwoman is about to deliver to the Quangels is the letter announcing that their son died as a soldier. Fallada is a master of economic word use and comparable to Hemingway in this ability. The scene can be immediately imagined and is a splendid example for dynamic evidence. Only few words are sufficient to convey a mental image to the reader, and we get all the details we need: a tired woman moving slowly up the stairs. Fallada is great at this kind of reductionism that nevertheless allows him to write in a way that maximizes the appeal to imagination. This style has sometimes been referred to as *Kinostil* or *cinema style* and is typical for New Objectivism in the 1920s. Writer Alfred Döblin had already envisioned this style of writing in his so called "Berlin Program" that was first published in 1913:

> Given the enormous quantity of forms, the representation requires a cinematic style. The fullness of the faces has to pass by in the highest crowdedness and precision. To wrest from language the utmost of plasticity and vividness. (Döblin [1913] 2013, 121; own translation)

In his cinematic style of writing, Döblin goes even further than Fallada in building up aesthetic hyper-structures, opening up a perspective to the consciousness of his protagonists. In comparison, Fallada tends to stick more to external clues, he is more interested in what can be observed rather than in what is happening inside of a person. Yet, both authors show a special focus on sketching surfaces and outlining small events, a focus on perceivable objects and events typical for the *cinema style*. Obviously, the use of dynamic evidence allows the author to confront his readers with observable micro scenes from the life of his protagonists, thus creating a special sense of immersion.

This highly economic form of writing that is directed to (and heavily relying on) the imagination can also be observed if we focus on the use of descriptive evidence in Fallada's novel:

> In the meantime shop foreman Otto Quangel has taken the field post letter into the parlor and propped it against the sewing machine. "There!" he says, nothing more. He always leaves the letters for his wife to open, knowing how devoted she is to their only son Otto. Now he stands facing her, biting his thin under lip, waiting for her smile to light up. In his quiet, undemonstrative way, he loves this woman very much.
>
> She has torn open the envelope, for a brief moment there really was a smile lighting up her face, and then it vanished when she saw the typed letter. Her face grew apprehensive, she read more and more slowly, as though afraid of what each next word might be. The man has leaned forward and taken his hands out of his pockets. He is biting his underlip quite hard now, he senses something terrible has happened. It's perfectly silent in their parlor. Only now does the woman's breathing come with a gasp. (Fallada 2009, 9)

It just takes theses very few, but well selected details (the field post letter propped against the sewing machine, the open envelope, Otto biting his thin lips, a brief smile, a hard bite)—and we can see the scene developing in front of us. The few sketches are enough to convey the atmosphere to the reader. Fallada's reductionist style leaves a lot of gaps to be filled in: instead of describing the sewing machine in detail, it is up to the readers to put their prototypic sewing machine into the scene. These gaps, which allow the readers to fill in their own experiences and expectations, strengthen the effect of involvement and immersion.

Descriptive and dynamic evidence are characteristic for all narrative texts, but the intensity of description and dynamic evidence used in literary texts does vary heavily. On the micro level, evidence can be realized in a rich way (i.e., by precise descriptions of every detail and event, leaving very little space for the imagination of the readers) or in a reduced and economic way (i.e., with a lot of gaps to be filled in). It is the reductionist approach which is characteristic of Fallada and the New Objectivism.

Horaz already mentioned that a fictional work can be short, and in ancient rhetorical theory, the principle of brevity is repeatedly referred to with regard to narration, too. However, this principle of economy is opposed to more ornamental styles of writing. Accordingly, texts can be measured on a scale of saturation. The scale that measures the degree of saturation of a text and a possible world ranges from zero saturation to complete saturation. However, both extreme poles are only theoretically given. World-building with the help of a text cannot succeed entirely without saturation, otherwise it would contain little more than conjunctions; and similarly, complete saturation is just as inconceivable, even in a stream of consciousness or in a realism, however sprawling. Saturation is a powerful adjusting screw through which an author can control his or her addressees. Indeed, the process of simulatively creating a possible world can be described, as Wolfgang Iser has recognized, through the deliberate opening and closing of voids:

> Blank spaces, however, do not so much denote a lack in the determination of the intentional object or the schematized views, but rather the occupability of a certain system position in the text by the reader's imagination. (Iser 1984, 348; own translation)

In the sense of the principle of minimal departure, the addressee fills the gaps in a way that seems conclusive to him or her—and it is this process that Fallada induces in his readers with the help of a reductionist form of *evidentia*. With the stylistic figure *evidentia*, simulation processes can be studied on the micro level: evidence builds on the sensually concrete representation, and it results from the depiction of individual details—even (and, as we have seen, sometimes especially) without the complex context of these details necessarily becoming clear. With Wayne C. Booth (1983, ch. 1), we can argue that a style of writing related to showing is needed to create *evidentia*. Yet, showing is only successful if it is carried by deliberate procedures of simulation which consider the perception of the addressee, provides access relations, and purposefully sets empty spaces or indeterminacy places.

Focusing on a micro level form of vivid writing that avoids overdetermination and subjectivity, the cinematic style of the *Neue Sachlichkeit* or New Objectivity is obviously still able to resonate with modern readers today. As a matter of fact, it might even be especially appropriate for our age of visual media, in which objects are often expected to speak for themselves and visual impressions and surfaces capture the attention of the audience particularly well. Objects or surfaces are not self-evident, however: they gain evidence because an author produces this evidence with an aesthetical and rhetorical strategy.

## Narrative Evidence: The Use of Evidence in Rhetorical Storytelling

Since the late 1970s, Walter Fisher has promoted the idea that rhetorical communication should not be focused on rational persuasion alone. According to Fisher (1978), "Humans as rhetorical beings are as much valuing as they are reasoning animals" (376). From a rhetorical perspective this might not be surprising, as *logos*, *ethos*, and *pathos* are commonly accepted as the means of persuasion in the Aristotelian tradition and the mostly neo-Aristotelian revival of rhetoric in the twentieth century. Yet, in his narrative paradigm, Fisher goes even further by linking communicative influence via rational persuasion and a more aesthetic impact:

> The narrative paradigm, then, can be considered a dialectical synthesis of two traditional strands in the history of rhetoric: the argumentative, persuasive theme and the literary, aesthetic theme. . . . The narrative paradigm challenges the notions that human communication—if it is to be considered rhetorical—must be an argumentative form, that reason is to be attributed only to discourse marked by clearly identifiable modes of inference and/or implication, and that the norms for evaluation of rhetorical communication must be rational standards taken essentially from informal or formal logic. (Fisher 1984, 2)

Fisher's theory, therefore, not only identifies narration and storytelling as central rhetorical techniques, he even sees the narrative part of communication as an overarching paradigm that includes both rational argumentation and aesthetic design. While this is a very wide approach that might even go a step too far, we can definitely conceptualize narrative and argumentative communication as parts of a rhetorical paradigm. In fact, the use of *evidentia* in ancient rhetoric already illustrated the potential of narrative communication for rhetorical persuasion and its effort to inform and influence others. Yet, while *evidentia* in classical rhetoric is a strategy to be used within an argumentative approach, in the view of Fisher narration is a technique to influence others beyond argument—and in this sense reaching further than rhetoric. In a broader sense, Fisher's narrative approach can even be applied to conceptualize complex and argumentative structures of public discourse, as demonstrated by Jeff Gentry in chapter 9 of this volume regarding the example of the scientific debate surrounding the story of human evolution.

To a certain extent, Fisher's theoretical discussion of the narrative paradigm foreshadowed the rise of storytelling in public communication. As narration is a very powerful way to appeal to an audience, it is hardly surprising that it has been discovered (or perhaps rather re-discovered and promoted) to communicate in pragmatic situations in recent years: storytelling has become a communicative technique that is widely used for information and persuasion in the "real" world, not just as an aesthetic mode of communication as in Fallada's novels. However, the promises associated with storytelling sometimes might go too far. For instance, Aleida Gersie argues:

> Storytelling is currently experiencing a considerable revival of interest. This has led many educators to think about ways in which storytelling can be used to explore important shared themes and visions. The current concern about environmental issues is connected with this revival, since folktales about the relationship between the Earth and its human inhabitants have been at the heart of storytelling since earliest times. Not only do such stories offer a source of inspiration, they also contain a potential for understanding the many ways in which we value and devalue our beautiful green and blue planet. Stories provide us with practical insight into approaches to our most persistent environmental difficulties. (Gersie 1992, 1)

This quote from *Earthtales: Storytelling in Times of Change* illustrates how fascinated communicators became with storytelling in the 1990s. Gersie is among the first authors to rediscover narrative strategies for education and pragmatic communication contexts (see also Gersie and King 1991), together with Andrew Wright's breakthrough handbook for educators, *Storytelling with Children* (1995). To cut the story short: in the new millennium, storytelling somehow seemed to even outrun rhetoric as the main technique for public address and communication in general. To quote Maxine Alterio, another influential author on storytelling:

> [In education,] [s]torytelling is a powerful and enduring means of communication that has widespread appeal. It crosses cultures and communities; in fact, many of our earliest learning experiences most likely involved stories, some told to us directly, others read and, still more, played out around us. Even before we had the ability to articulate what we knew, felt and thought, we learned to make sense of our world through stories. (Alterio 2003)

In the end, many natural scientists as well as business and PR professionals seemingly discovered the method of storytelling as if we had never been telling stories before, and as if narrative elements and strategies did not play a role in public speeches ever since ancient rhetoric.

In the twenty-first century, storytelling has, moreover, often been considered as a master strategy for communicators when confronting audiences that hold different views, and the persuasive potential of narratives in conflicts has regularly been discussed (cf., e.g., Dal Cin, Zanna, and Fong 2004). Stories can create common ground if it is no longer given in a society that values diversity over mainstreaming: they appear as a way to reduce resistance because they are more open and inclusive than rational arguments, which rely on the choice between limited and clearly marked alternatives. Therefore, stories are told by business managers, in political speeches and scientific presentations. Indeed, stories can raise emotions and enhance involvement, as they allow immersion in a possible world. They transport information and may have influence on cognitive patterns without rising reactance in the same way as argumentative persuasive communication does. A story does not only convey knowledge and share information, it also is a way to manage conflicts in organizational contexts. Conflicting parties may buy into the same story, a common way to understand the past and shape the future of organizations, as stories stimulate the reasoning process by establishing information with an audience in a more indirect way.

Yet, an important aspect that we must recognize when considering the current storytelling hype is that most modern theories focus on long and complex stories, not so much on micro narratives. While the use of *evidentia* in rhetoric is mainly about small narrative elements, storytelling is primarily focused on more elaborate stories and larger storytelling arcs. However, Hans Fallada's *Every Man Dies Alone* and his reduced minimalist style tellingly remind us of the efficiency that micro narratives can have. If we consult handbooks about storytelling, we mostly learn that we should tell stories! And to tell a story, according to these handbooks, basically means to present events in a timeline as they develop or with flashbacks or flash-forwards. We are told to be neither too long nor too complicated, that a story needs a narrator and characters. Surprisingly enough, not much can be found about the use of *evidentia* as a more minimalist approach to *narratio*, or about the invention of a story with persuasive impact and emotional appeal that might be able to co-ordinate social behavior (cf. for instance Biesenbach 2018).

However, stories can be quite boring if they are told by someone who is not good at narrating, and they might turn out to be a risky strategy in presentations, talks, and speeches if a unified understanding is needed. For instance, there definitely is a need for a clear and coherent flow of information in science and medicine, as it would lead to disaster if an aircraft engineer or doctor acted according to narratively conveyed information that may be understood in very divergent ways by different addresses. In scientific presentations, the listeners themselves tend to be looking for clear argumentations, for good reasons—and even in a political speech, one might want to hear a clear agenda rather than a story that allows multiple interpretations. One might want to hear a story from time to time, but not all the time.

To reliably induce co-operation, the maxims of Paul Grice (1975) cannot be overruled by storytelling and narrative openness. From the maxim of quality (which includes not saying that for which we lack adequate evidence) and the maxim of quantity (which mandates to make contribution as informative as is required) to the maxim of relevance and the maxim of manner (which includes to be clear and structured): these communicative principles limit the application of storytelling in everyday communication.

## Evidentia and Storytelling as Rhetorical Techniques

In conclusion, it might be more beneficial and helpful for communicators to learn about techniques to imply descriptive and dynamic evidence on the micro level of a text—be it a speech or a presentation—than to focus on turning every speech or presentation in a story. An orator as a strategic communicator (see Knape 2013) should be able to design single episodes that appeal to the imagination of the audience to interest and motivate others to acquire new information, to promote understanding or persuade them to co-ordinate social interaction. It might be very important to appeal to the imagination to establish your arguments with the help of narrative elements as possible and probable. Yet, to successfully reach this goal, the old rhetorical concept of appropriateness is important and helpful: a technique of perspective taking (see Batson 2009) is necessary to anticipate the thoughts and attitudes of the audience, as their demands and needs must direct the choices of the orator if she or he wants to be successful.

Just as an author has to write with her or his reader in mind, the orator has to communicate with her or his audience in mind. With Daniel C. Batson, it is possible to differentiate three forms of perspective taking. Batson (2009) sees the "objective perspective," which he describes as, "simply attending carefully to the other's behavior" (268), as fundamental. This perspective seems to hold little promise for real empathy, because it remains focused on superficial signals. Nevertheless, such observations certainly provide the speaker with indications for the general character of the narrative elements that should be employed. The "imagine-self perspective" (267) involves simulating one's own thoughts and feelings from the perspective of an addressee; rhetorically, it is an important corrective to adopt arguments and performance in a way that it is apt to the audience. The "imagine-other perspective" (267) even goes beyond this point: it is defined as the process of placing oneself in the position of the addressees and looking at the situation through their perspective. Batson claims that this "imagine-other perspective" provides a higher degree of empathetic accuracy than the others, but also emphasizes that such a perspective is significantly more difficult to take. While it can be extremely valuable for speakers to simulate the mental states of their audience to better predict their reaction to their speech, it can be difficult to gain enough distance from one's own perspective.

As Nicholas Epely and Eugene M. Caruso have pointed out, the estimation of the addressees' mental states should be as accurate as possible (see Epely and Caruso 2009), and the technique of stereotyping carries with it a significant danger of inaccurate assessments. It is therefore important that speakers are aware that they are often using prejudices to understand their audiences, and they must have enough empathy to understand and realize when their prejudices have carried them into a wrong direction. Jones, Dovidio, and Vietze (2014) have made a good point in this context when they advocated a process of decategorizing and recategorizing of the other, in which we at least try to see everyone as individuals and think of "me and you" rather than "us and them" (134). However, this interplay between categorization and decategorization is needed for storytelling approaches as well as for argumentative communication. Stories may be more open to interpretation than arguments and may allow multiple perspectives (as storytelling theories claim), but stories can also promote a specific limited world view, legitimize certain options, and delegitimize others. Thus, it would be naïve to underestimate the hegemonial tendency of stories. Narratives are regularly developed with certain interests in mind and often start with the entitlement of the author that he or she is promoting the one and only "right" story.

Narrative communication and *evidentia* are hard to handle, and some skills are necessary to use them as efficiently and purposefully as Fallada did as a writer. Regarding the challenge that the invention and textual realization of a good story entail for an author, it might be more appropriate for a communicator in many cases to turn to *evidentia* as a technique to communicate with the help of narrative elements than to focus solely on storytelling. This means an author must use and cope with the production of narrative texts on the micro level. This way, he or she is no longer in need to tell the one big, fascinating and exciting story that might just turn out as a real challenge for most communicators. Whether a communicator aims at the one big story or uses *evidentia* to add narrative elements to his or her text, he or she should turn to literary examples and narratology to understand narration as a communicative practice and to identify effective ways to use narration as a means to communicate with others and create possible worlds that influence others in purposeful ways.

Nelson Goodman, in his influential monograph *Ways of World-Making* (1978), described how one can create a possible world, such as any narrative creates, from a reference world: one erases elements, adds new ones, or deforms them, for the "Worldmaking as we know it always starts from worlds already on hand; the making is a remaking" (Goodman 1978, 6). Direction is given by the perceived reality of the addressees, which includes other fictions. Thus, worldmaking as a form of remodulation of experienced reality—and David Herman (2009, 77f.) subsequently distinguished five forms of worldmaking according to Goodman:

1. *compostion / decomposition*, that is, world-building relies on the reassembling of elements from the actual world in new contexts and combination
2. *weighting*, that is, world-building implies that certain aspects come to the fore, others are put in the background, which entails a perspectivization.
3. *orderings*, that is, world-building happens through the adoption of systems of order.
4. *deletion / supplementation*, that is, world building means the erasure of certain aspects of the actual world, but also additions
5. *deformation*, that is, an alternative world is always associated with a deformation of the reference world.

Storytelling builds on a reduction of complexity that has consistently been implemented in the rhetorical figure of *evidentia* ever since ancient rhetorical theory, and that was masterfully employed by Hans Fallada in *Every Man Dies Alone*. Storytellers should, therefore, not try to have an effect through complexity, but should provide an economical arrangement of a narrative event. This keeps narrative elements manageable and easy to integrate into pragmatic communication contexts, as the appeal to imagination should never be underestimated in its complexity. As Francis Bacon (1974 [1605], 139) pointed out in his famous reflections on rhetoric: "[T]he duty and office of rhetoric is to apply reason to imagination for the better moving of the will." For Bacon, rhetoric takes a detour, so to speak, via the imagination, that is, it is supposed to help to arrive at rational insights by finding sensually evidenced forms of representation. "The end of rhetoric is to fill the imagination to second reason" (140).

In this sense, however, Bacon provides a theory that convincingly assigns narration and imagination a position in the context of pragmatic communication and limits them at the same time. In contrast to the storytelling hype that we have seen in public communication in recent years, *evidentia* as a rhetorical approach to narration might be more appropriate to public speeches than highly complex and ambitious forms of storytelling. Rather, the more economic and efficient approach to narration that we witnessed in analyzing the narrative techniques employed by Fallada seems particularly promising and appropriate from the perspective of rhetoric.

In a rhetorical context, good storytelling is about perspective, coherence, reduction, and amplification. With the addressee in mind, the orator has to create a coherent story that goes into detail at certain points, but also uses a reductionist, minimalist approach. Under this condition, the simulation of dynamic developments with verbal means (dynamic evidence) as well as the dwelling on isolated objects (descriptive evidence) remain very promising techniques to communicate to an audience, to inform and influence it by an appeal to imagination. There is no need to turn to visual evidence in every case just because we could in the age of presentations and visual media, nor is the use of storytelling a quality in and by itself for a strategic communicator. We should not give up on speech just because some people tell us to do so, and we should not try to blindly replace rhetorical micro narratives with bigger storytelling arcs. Emphasizing the importance of amplification in creating dynamic and descriptive evidence does not necessarily imply that a speaker must cover as many details as possible and tell a long and complex story. Rather, the quality and appropriateness of the details presented seem to be more important than their quantity or the degree to which they are elaborated. As long as an author identifies the right details, that is, the details that are capable of stimulating the audience's imagination in an appropriate way, descriptive and dynamic evidence can be achieved comparatively efficiently by a skilled communicator and are more promising and efficient than storytelling in many cases.

## Works Cited

Alterio, Maxine. 2003. *Using Storytelling to Enhance Student Learning.* Available online, https://www.researchgate.net/publication/241678570_Using_Storytelling_to_Enhance_Student_Learning, accessed July 2, 2021.

Aristotle. 2007. *On Rhetoric. A Theory of Civic Discourse.* Translated by George A. Kennedy. New York and Oxford: Oxford University Press.

Bacon, Francis. (1605) 1974. *The Advancement of Learning.* Edited by Arthur Johnston. Oxford: Oxford University Press.

Batson, C. Daniel. 2009. "Two Forms of Perspective Taking. Imagining How Another Feels and Imagining How You Would Feel." In *Handbook of Imagination and Mental Simulation*, edited by Keith D. Markman, William Martin Klein, and Julie A. Suhr, 267–79. New York: Taylor & Francis.
Biesenbach, Rob. 2018. *Unleash the Power of Storytelling: Win Hearts, Change Minds, Get Results*. Evanston, IL: Eastlawn Media.
Booth, Wayne C. 1983. *The Rhetoric of Fiction*. Chicago: University of Chicago Press.
Cicero, Marcus Tullius. 1860. *On Oratory and Orators*. Translated by J. S. Watson. New York: Harper & Bros.
Dal Cin, Sonya, Mark P. Zanna, and Geoffrey T. Fong. 2004. "Narrative Persuasion and Overcoming Resistance." In *Resistance and Persuasion*, edited by Eric S. Knowles and Jay A. Linn, 175–191. Mahwah, NJ and London: Lawrence Erlbaum.
Döblin, Alfred. 2013 [1913]. "An Romanautoren und ihre Kritiker. Berliner Programm." In *Alfred Döblin: Schriften zu Ästhetik, Poetik und Literatur*, edited by Erich Kleinschmidt, 118–21. Frankfurt a. M.: Fischer.
Doležel, Lubomír. 1998. *Heterocosmica: Fiction and Possible Worlds*. Baltimore and London: Johns Hopkins University Press.
Epley, Nicholas and Eugene M. Caruso. 2009. "Perspective Taking. Misstepping Into Others' Shoes." In *Handbook of Imagination and Mental Simulation*, edited by Keith D. Markman, William Martin Klein, and Julie A. Suhr, 295–309. New York: Taylor & Francis.
Fallada, Hans. 2009. *Every Man Dies Alone*. Translated by Michael Hofmann. New York: Melville House.
Fisher, Walter. 1978. "Toward a logic of good reasons." *Quarterly Journal of Speech* 64:376–84.
—. 1984. "Narration as a Human Communication Paradigm: The Case of Public Moral Argument." In *Communication Monographs* 51:1–22.
Gersie, Aleida. 1992. *Earthtales: Storytelling in Times of Change*. London: Green Print.
Gersie, Aleida, and Nancy King. 1991. *Storytelling in Education and Therapy*. London: Jessica Kingsley Publishers.
Goodman, Nelson. 1978. *Ways of World-Making*. Indianapolis: Hackett Publishing.
Grice, Paul. 1975. "Logic and Conversation." In *Syntax and Semantics*. Vol. 3: *Speech Acts*, edited by Peter Cole and Jerry L. Morgan, 41–58. New York and London: Academic Press.
Herman, David. 2009. "Narrative Ways of Worldmaking." In *Narratology in the Age of Cross-Disciplinary Narrative Research*, edited by Sandra Heinen and Roy Sommer, 71–87. Berlin and New Yorik: De Gruyter.
Iser, Wolfgang. 1984. *Der Akt des Lesens. Theorie ästhetischer Wirkung*. Revised edition. Munich: W. Fink.
Jones, James M., John F. Dovidio, and Deborah L. Vietze. 2014. *The Psychology of Diversity: Beyond Prejudice and Racism*. Chichester: Wiley-Blackwell.

Knape, Joachim. 2013. *Modern Rhetoric in Culture, Arts, and Media*. Berlin and Boston: De Gruyter.
Quintilian. 1966. *The Institutio oratoria*. Vol. 2. Translated by H. E. Butler. London, Cambridge, MA: William Heinemann Ltd., Harvard University Press.
Ryan, Marie-Laure. 1991. "Possible Worlds and Accessibility Relations. A Semantic Typology of Fiction." *Poetics Today* 12 (3), 553–76.
Schillinger, Liesl. 2009. "Postcards from the Edge." *New York Times*, February 27, 2009. Available online, https://www.nytimes.com/2009/03/01/books/review/Schillinger-t.html, accessed July 2, 2021.
Wright, Andrew. 1995. *Storytelling with Children*. Oxford: Oxford University.

# Rhetorics of Evidence in Science Communication

# 4 Visual Rhetoric and Evidence in Scientific Images: Imaging Brains and Imagining Minds in Cognitive Neuroscience

*Kirsten Brukamp*

### Introduction

The insights of visual rhetoric possess the potential to deepen reflection on the traditions of image use in scientific research. Natural sciences, life sciences, medicine, psychology, and neuroscience in particular rely on visual evidence, namely images that are integrated into, or even replace, verbalized arguments. Pointing to the so-called evidence in an image is supposed to convince at first sight and to silence the critics. Here, the focus will be on neuroscience because of the complexity of different image types in contemporary functional brain imaging. These images, appearing confusingly similar to non-expert audiences, are utilized to draw far-reaching conclusions in philosophy, particularly in the philosophy of mind, about the status of the human subject.

By and large, figures in scientific and research publications serve the intention to either provide testimony and show evidence or to arrange data in a meaningful way (Mersch 2008). This dichotomy corresponds to the image *versus* logic traditions in science (Galison 1997), according to which researchers are convinced either by obvious facts in visual representations or by reasoning on the basis of non-visual measuring devices and statistics. Consequently, categories of scientific images can be devised along the lines of the image *versus* logic tradition (Galison 1997) and the testimony *versus* arrangement function (Mersch 2008) of scientific images, which are undeniably related to each other (compare the section "Scientific Images between Evidence and Argument").

Since this opposition is eventually too simplistic, a spectrum of image types in the natural and life sciences reflects the gradual influx of extra-pictorial information into the image: from photography *via* representation of signal detection and through enhancement of information to overlay of additional information. This classification helps to identify specific points where the scientific results are dubious or in need of improvement. This way, the flawed analysis steps are connected with the appropriate features in the image representation (compare the section "Image Categories in the Life Sciences, Medicine, and Cognitive Neuroscience").

The insights can be applied to the prominent example of modern cognitive neuroscience, which relies heavily on images in functional brain imaging, frequently in the format of functional magnetic resonance imaging (fMRI). Neuroscience thereby illustrates the complexity of a wide range of different image types that appear deceptively similar to non-expert audiences. The focus on neuroscience allows conclusions about the status of the human subject, who is depicted by scientific endeavors. Therefore, this overview points out the foundations for appropriate interpretations regarding higher cognitive abilities in humans, including implications for consciousness, in the philosophy of mind.

Modern neuroscience intends to show "true" pictures of the human, that is, evidence for real facts. Many neuroscientists aim at revealing the experiment participant as a true subject and thereby at strengthening a subject-oriented stance in psychology, sociology, anthropology, and the philosophy of mind. Thus, a science addressing questions of consciousness is within reach (compare the section "Implications for the Philosophy of Mind").

In summary, visual rhetoric aids in understanding the degree of evidence in scientific images in the communication between scientists. Thereby, they contribute to the neuroscientific and philosophical insights into the functions of the human brain and mind (compare the section "Beginnings of a Visual Rhetoric Analysis for Neuroscience").

## Scientific Images Between Evidence and Argument

Visual rhetoric[1] may be regarded as the art of intentionally communicating by visual means. It relies on the onlookers' visual literacy, that is, the ability to understand an image. As an academic discipline, visual rhetoric is concerned with the analysis of communication and meaning related to visualization, not primarily with the art and the aesthetic composition proper. In general, it may consist of the examination of design, typography, fonts, colors, arrangements on a page, and image manipulation. In the following, these aspects will not all be addressed because, in the natural and life sciences in particular, the focus is on images, photographs, graphs, charts, diagrams, and illustrations. The latter confer meaning and are intended to convince, and thereby, they assume a rhetoric role.

"Science images" is an emergent topic for the theory and philosophy of science. Images have been called visual arguments (Mersch 2008), particularly in science, where visualization is a strategy for convincing the target audience, typically peer researchers, of theories by simply showing artifacts of evidence and pointing to the so-called facts. This process of trying to establish facts is usually not as straightforward as it sounds at first, especially in the field of brain imaging.

Images possess extraordinary power at persuading people. Everyday life teaches humans to trust images because visual information helps them to navigate their environment, to discriminate information, and to ultimately survive. Therefore, the result is a widespread acceptance of image contents when they are presented. The default stance is that images are "true," that is, correspondent to reality.[2] However, this need not be the case. Before the twentieth century, visual information either originated from reality, or it was clearly constructed. This changed with the advent of photography: Images conformed to the original scene or could be altered during the picture-processing stage. During the last decades, graphic software tools have become efficient enough to create or manipulate any image.

Artifactual visual information needs to be assessed in both supportive and critical ways. So far, academic education trains people primarily for a careful analysis of written texts and spoken words.[3] Analysis of images should eventually reach a similar level of scholarly attention and awareness in society at large.[4] An examination of scientific images helps to detect pitfalls in science that need correction. A criticism of this type does not dismiss some results of science as simple errors and as meaningless. Rather, it makes image analysis fruitful for understanding the process of science, for improving scientific results, and for reforming science overall.

A comprehensive "image science" (Mitchell 2008, 55) should address all of the following in a scientific manner: the modeling of images, their mathematical fabric, their interpretation, effect, constructedness, as well as their social and cultural determinants. The basis for such an "image science" is the fact that visual perception proper is a topic of science.[5] So, increasing knowledge about the fundamental characteristics of vision in humans will also result in a better understanding of how humans respond to different types of images.

Brain images have been regarded as highly processed technological products (see Brukamp 2012). A multitude of analysis steps separates the initial signal detection of an fMRI apparatus from the final image in a research publication.[6] The processing steps can falter, often unintentionally. It is not sufficient to merely examine the final image as an end result, which is typically a figure in a published scientific article. The process of obtaining the image is equally important—it may happen that the instruments of image acquisition and processing ascribe their features into the image (see Heßler, Hennig, and Mersch 2004, 3–4). In particular, faulty statistics may interfere with the intention to depict reality.[7] These problematic issues in functional neuroimaging require an image type classification that makes it easy to point to processing steps in the background, which become hidden from sight when only the final images are presented.

Science images may be categorized according to the content that they display, their origin, the intended function, and the target audience (see Hüppauf and Weingart 2008, 6). The following overview presents a list with examples for these types (Hüppauf and Weingart 2008, 6):

1. Images that are produced in the sciences as visual elements of scientific research and that are directed at the scientific community. Examples include photographs in peer-reviewed scientific journals and academic textbooks.
2. Images that are produced in the sciences as visual elements of scientific research and that are directed at the public. Examples are illustrations in popular science magazines.
3. Images that are produced by scientists about scientific objects and processes. Examples include photo series to document laboratory procedures and protocols.
4. Images that are produced by public media about scientific objects and processes. Examples are videos about scientists and their working environments.

Table 1. Classification of Science Images (based on Hüppauf and Weingart 2008, 6).

| Class | Origin: produced by | Content | Function and target audience: directed at |
|---|---|---|---|
| 1 | scientists | as visual elements of scientific research | scientific community |
| 2 | scientists | as visual elements of scientific research | public |
| 3 | scientists | about scientific objects and processes | scientific community |
| 4 | public media | about scientific objects and processes | public |

In physics, two approaches for generating data may be juxtaposed: the image and the logic tradition (Galison 1997). They use a "homomorphic" and a "homologous" representation, respectively, and are associated with "picturing" or "counting" machines. For the first one, the ideal is the mimetic preservation of form in an image;[8] the second deduces statistical arguments in science from, occasionally large-scale, data. They both exhibit their own pedagogical, technical, and demonstrative-epistemic continuity. Neither one of these traditions can claim superiority.[9] In other words, their distinction can be rephrased as one between aesthetics and iconoclasm, between vision and intellect. Electronically produced images are then an image-logic hybrid.[10]

Visualizations have been regarded as visual arguments (Mersch 2008). In science, images are either utilized in a testimony function or an arrangement function (Mersch 2008):

1. *Testimony*: For testimony, the visual artifact is presented as proof. The image typically is a photograph, or it is at least similar to a photograph. It highlights the existence of an entity of scientific interest and produces evidence for scientists' claims.
2. *Arrangement*: For the purposes of arrangement, a transformation of knowledge into figures takes place. The images clearly possess a constructive status for this function. Usually, graphs aid in depicting the results of calculations and scientists' dealing with numbers. These images constitute a hybrid between notationality and iconicity.

## Image Categories in the Life Sciences, Medicine, and Cognitive Neuroscience

The two related dichotomous classifications of science images, which have been presented above (see Mersch 2008 and Galison 1997, 181–98), do not yet seem far-reaching enough to tackle the complexities and intricacies of visual products in everyday life, medicine, and cognitive neuroscience. Therefore, a set of new categories for the testimonial[11] role of images will be presented and examined for usefulness. The following four categories of images can be found in everyday life, natural sciences, life sciences, medicine, psychology, and neuroscience:

1. *Photography*: Photography consists of the reproduction of typical visual perceptions that humans are commonly exposed to at every moment. It represents electromagnetic waves of the visible spec-

trum. Its depictions may be called "natural" images. These images have obvious spatial implications, while the temporal factor in observation is comparable to the usual human visual perception.[12]

2. *Representation of signal detection*: Images with representations of signal detection utilize either natural signals or responses to artificial signals. They depend on advanced technology because of their reliance on specialized detection devices. Two examples for the detection of natural and artificial signals in medicine are heat maps of body parts and X-ray images, respectively. So, these types of images include ones based on electromagnetic waves outside of the visible spectrum. There is evidence of spatial implications in the images, whereas the time period of detection is variable and ranges from milliseconds to minutes. Sometimes, there is a need for processing and computation, depending on the type of detection machinery.

3. *Enhancement of information*: Images may contain an enhancement of information that is already largely inherent in images of the types one and two. Based on a processing step, an interpretation and an alteration are introduced to direct attention and establish a focus. The groundwork for this information already resides inside the images or their computational constituents, but the uninitiated person is still assumed to require help in identifying their meaning. Examples in medicine include the use of arrows and circles to highlight regions of interest and the introduction of false colors for making spatial structures obvious.

4. *Overlay of additional information*: In an overlay of additional information, information is added that is not inherent in the images. This procedure requires outside knowledge or a sophisticated processing step. In medicine, examples are the inclusion of names for structures and associated legends as well as the depiction of statistics by color-coding[13] for numerical statistical measures.

To illustrate the classification into four image categories better, the following summary provides three examples for each category, namely from or concerning everyday life, medicine, and neuroscience. These examples demonstrate the possibility to classify images from a variety of sources according to the categories.

1. *Photography* examples include photo portraits from everyday life, photo documentations of skin changes in medicine, and photos during a procedure in neurosurgery.

2. *Representations of signal detection* would be heat radiation images from a building, heat maps of inflammation and surrounding areas, and X-rays of the skull, respectively.
3. *Enhancement of information* can be present in satellite maps with roads that are highlighted in color, in computer tomography with an arrow that indicates an anatomical entity, and in brain computer tomography with colors that highlight different structures.
4. *Overlay of additional information* may be found in a satellite map with overlaid city names, in a picture body atlas with anatomical names, and in an fMRI image with a color code to indicate statistical results.

This classification resonates with the distinctions presented above—image *versus* logic (Galison 1997) and testimony *versus* arrangement (Mersch 2008). Moreover, it reflects continuity between these two approaches: A photograph, already, is not an immediate recording from visual reality, but always mediated by camera technology. Statistics, conversely, is applied to real events, with optional visual representations as numbers, as graphs, or as colors that code for overlaid numbers in images. On both sides of the spectrum, the aim is to document and analyze the real world, but the different levels in the continuum exhibit various degrees of obvious constructedness.[14] Therefore, the classification hints at a spectrum with a gradual increase of extra-pictorial information that enters the image, or which needs to be available outside in a legend or description, in order to interpret it correctly.

How does the classification help to better characterize the problematic issues due to multi-step processing (see Brukamp 2012) and complex statistics (see Brukamp 2012) in contemporary fMRI? fMRI images with overlaid statistical information can now be understood and categorized as highly processed and constructed. They inhabit the realm of category 4, where information intrudes from the outside world, information that was not part of the individual image in stages two and three. Consequently, this novel level of information can be discussed and criticized separately. Awareness about the clearly hybrid character of an overlay image makes it easier to independently dissect the influx of additional knowledge.

This approach puts image theory and statistics criticism together. The problem with flawed studies is neither the black-and-white fMRI images nor the combination with statistical numbers in color-coded visualizations, but the inflow of faulty material. It is indeed appropriate to present a typical image with overlaid statistics, but the statistics better be correct. The image typically remains true to its testimonial function only with regard to the anatomy represented. The color code for statistical numbers is construed, and maybe wrongly. One image serves its many functions in differential ways, and a hybrid image can exhibit both adequate and inadequate features. Numerous processing steps lead to the final image as the end result, but these steps are hidden and not represented in the image. Looking at the image by itself may not arouse any suspicion; only an intricate knowledge of the processing steps enables the peer scientist to raise well-founded criticism. The scientists who produce or analyze scientific images utilize varying degrees of competence in visual rhetoric, insofar as it is understood as a discipline that regards images as communicative, intentional, or strategic artifacts.

## Implications for the Philosophy of Mind

Visual rhetoric in neuroscience benefits the field of philosophy of mind. A perspective on functional brain imaging from visual rhetoric not only advances cognitive neuroscience, but also the philosophy of mind. Regarding neuroscience, the scientific value improves due to increased expression and precision. Concerning philosophy, such analysis informs about the status of humans in the world because it helps to uncover individuals, their intentions and desires, their psychological and social basis, by means of scientific images. Ultimately, visual rhetoric may strengthen the connection between neuroscience and philosophy because it aids in drawing conclusions from scientific data for intellectual reflection. Moreover, rhetoric in general is needed to adequately describe the relationship between the body or the brain, which can be represented by images, and the mind, which is a theoretical concept.

What are the conclusions of cognitive functional neuroimaging for the philosophy of mind? How do the results deduced from brain images help to understand the mind-brain relationship? What is the status of the subject in a world that is filled with technology?

The following theses, discussed below, are compatible with current cognitive neuroscience research by way of functional brain images:

1. A science of subjectivity seems to be within reach.
2. The subject is not merely the object of scientific study, but also becomes visible and palpable as an individual in the research process through scientific images.
3. Cognitivism and embodied embedded cognition are compatible with each other.

4. An appropriate terminology for relating brain images and the understanding of the mind is still in the stage of development.

1. SCIENCE OF SUBJECTIVITY

Humans are subjects. Is a science about them possible? Philosophical anthropology laid the groundwork for such an endeavor over several thousand years, and psychology has aimed at experimental results for more than a hundred years. Studying a subject in science involves attention to all aspects, be they bodily, emotional, intellectual, and moral ones. But is science not supposed to be objective? In reply to this objection, the distinctions of subjectivity *versus* objectivity and ontology *versus* epistemology need to be related to each other:[15] A science needs to be epistemically objective to qualify as such, namely as a scientific discipline. The scientist is not supposed to experiment with a subjective prejudice, but to establish widely accepted facts. This requirement does not imply that subjects cannot be in the spotlight of investigation. Thus, ontological subjectivity is accepted and respected. In conclusion, a science of subjectivity is indeed possible.

A few examples of recent scientific studies will illustrate how cognitive research does undeniably inch forward to address questions about consciousness, the unconscious, subjectivity, and decision-making, issues that have formerly been discussed in the tradition and language of philosophy and the humanities. After Hans Helmut Kornhuber and Lüder Deecke (1965) discovered the readiness potential, Benjamin Libet (2004) began studies at the intersection of decision-making and consciousness. His studies demonstrated that, under certain conditions, humans attain consciousness about their willingness to perform an action only after this decision is already made, according to brain signals.

In an extension of these experiments, John-Dylan Haynes's group investigated the unconscious determinants of decision-making. One study (Soon et al. 2008) examined the possibility to predict the laterality of hand use from fMRI data. Indeed, the image sequence allowed conclusions about voluntary motor movements that occurred several seconds later. Although the participants in the experiment did not consciously think about the decision to either move the right or the left side, the experimenters were able to predict, to a certain degree, which side the participants were going to use in the future.

Some devastating neurological conditions result in dissociation between consciousness and sensorimotor communication with the outside world, most notably locked-in syndromes and some variants of vegetative and minimally conscious states. Patients may be incapable of communicating with their caregivers by usual means, such as verbal sounds, limb movements, and eye signals.

The coma science group, led by Stephen Laurys, demonstrated in a study of patients in vegetative and minimally conscious states (Monti et al. 2010) that five out of fifty-four patients showed cognitive capacities in the sense of activation in typical brain regions after they were told to follow mental imagery tasks. One patient was even able to communicate by this means: When visual and spatial imagery signified a "yes" or "no" answer, respectively, he answered several questions about his former life circumstances correctly.

The authors conclude that many patients who carry a label of vegetative and minimally conscious states are overdiagnosed in the sense that they still possess hidden cognitive abilities, although these cannot be tested at the bedside. Only sophisticated methods such as fMRI reveal remaining brain function and assess consciousness. Thereby, they potentially ease the patients' confinement somewhat, especially when advanced communication and treatment options will become available and prevalent in the future.

## 2. Experimental Subjects as Subjects Indeed

For a technology critic, it may seem as if the human being gets lost under a pile of technology in neuroscience. Although psychology started out with the intention to study the human subject with all characteristics, this results in an amassing of fragmented instruments that measure signals from the body. The intellectual, emotional, aesthetic, and moral dimensions appear to vanish in a nightmare scenario. According to some philosophical or social standpoints, the human quality is annihilated: the human is transformed into a virtual being, captured in images and subsisting in computers and machines.

However, a very different interpretation is also available, and it emerged from a sociological perspective. Its main thesis holds that the subject becomes visible and palpable through neuroimaging. One investigation[16] claims that the procedure of taking fMRI images during a cognitive task has the aim of "making visible" the research subject. It asks how the subject is present during the image acquisition and interpretation.

The participant in an experiment—or experimental subject, like he or she is indeed called—is not seen as an objectified origin of measurable signals that is barely alive. The person is taken care of during the procedure, and the experimenters make arrangements for his or her physical and psychological well-being. They, as humans themselves, are continuously capable of identifying with the participant and feel empathy, likening the participant to the patient in a doctor-patient relationship. The results are intersubjective and multimodal experiences, with a focus on the bodily presence of the participant, but obviously also recognizing the cognitive abilities that are the purpose of the study. Thereby, embodied feeling and enactment ensue effortlessly.[17]

## 3. Embodied Embedded Cognitivism

Cognitivism succeeded behaviorism as the main metatheory in psychology. Its victory was due to the abandonment of the treatment of humans as black boxes in favor of a focus on their mental processes and inner experiences. Cognitivism recognized the brain as the carrier of cognitive capabilities. So, this one organ became the focus of cognitive psychology and cognitive science at large, which also occupied itself with topics in neuroinformatics, robotics, and computer linguistics. To get meaningful results, cognitivism allied with neurobiology for practical reasons. Novel data on the brain, for example, by brain imaging, then gave rise to the public impression of the brain as a stand-alone entity, independent of the world.

Embodied embedded cognition[18] proposes that the brain needs to be connected back to the body and the outside world: The concept of *embodiment* emphasizes the place of the brain as an organ within the body, as it communicates with and depends on the organism. The model of embeddedness views the brain as part of the world, influenced by incessant streams of sensory perceptions, taking from and giving to the world by motor actions and the sheer presence as a body.

A fundamental opposition between cognitivism and embodied embedded cognition does not exist. They are only contrasted as mutually exclusive in a false dichotomy fallacy. Cognitivism has the potential to embrace the concepts of embodiment and embeddedness, after it temporarily neglected the connectivity of the brain as a whole to its surroundings. These aspects are now beginning to be investigated again under headings like emotionality and social neuroscience.

## 4. In Search of an Appropriate Mind-Brain Terminology

The use of language informs about the implications of thoughts. The term *brain* has spatial implications, like images derived from nature, whereas *mind* invokes associations of higher cognitive capabilities in the interaction with the world. This way, *brain* and *mind* are simply not identical. The brain is the material organ that can, in principle, be perceived; the mind is the logical center of cognition, of mental processes and thoughts. The brain can be imaged; the mind must always remain imagined.[19]

Nevertheless, this distinction in language is no argument for classic dualism. The brain is the central place that can be pointed to as an answer to the question about the biological basis of behavior. The brain as the organic basis for the mind "causes" or "leads to" cognitive abilities, and mental processes "take place" in the brain. This terminology is a seed for the appropriate language of relating brain and mind to each other in contemporary cognitive neuroscience and the philosophy of mind.

## Beginnings of a Visual Rhetoric Analysis for Neuroscience

Cognitive neuroscience will continue to provide structural and functional insights into the connection between brain and mind in the near future. On the way, it will generate more brain images that require careful interpretation. Like in other natural and life sciences, a precise analysis of visual rhetoric in a novel image science is needed to raise awareness of the conditions and prerequisites of seemingly straightforward contents, which are presented as evidence.

Images are indispensable in science, taking on different grades of value in varying fields. The images in science serve many functions, and a classification helps to identify the critical issues. Based on the related alternatives of image *versus* logic (Galison 1997) and testimony *versus* arrangement (Mersch 2008), a spectrum of image types categorizes testimonial scientific images according to the relative contributions from extra-pictorial background information.

In the experimenters' laboratories, processing and analysis steps take place that are barely visible in traces, if at all, when the level of the final image as the end product is reached. In technology-intensive areas, like functional neuroimaging, a particular scrutiny is warranted to understand the interplay between analysis steps and image contents. Criticism from the neuroscientific community is exceptionally valuable to point to the crucial issues in the entanglement of various variables. The cognitive neuroscientist may then be called an "iconoclastic imager"[20]: taking images and relying on them, but also being the only one to comprehend them fully, thereby qualifying as the sole appropriate critic.

Cognitive neuroscience embarked on the endeavor to study the subjectivity of human beings as an objective science. This goal does not suffer from the requirement for massive advanced technology in functional neuroimaging. Humans do not lose their dignity by being reduced to an image in the research studies. Rather, the scientific methods enable opportunities to portray a person's inner life. While cognitive neuroscience aims to elucidate the intricate relationship between brain images and conclusions for the mind, it demonstrates the need for a novel terminology regarding the question how brain and mind are related to each other in the philosophy of mind.

## Notes

1. Regarding the term and the concept of "visual rhetoric", compare, for example, Foss (2005, 141–152) and Hill and Helmers (2004).

2. This view is particularly prevalent in the non-expert world: One "immediate problem concerns the way that brain scans are interpreted outside the neuroimaging community. [They, K.B.] possess an illusory accuracy and objectivity as perceived by the general public" (Farah 2002, 1127).

3. This is the case in, but not limited to, the academic discipline of general rhetoric, of which visual rhetoric is one specialization.

4. It is an intriguing question whether image styles will eventually take on the same relevance like verbal styles and whether similar rules apply. One preliminary attempt in this direction recommends to transfer a "not more than necessary" guideline for words to images: "Images, just like text, should not be more complicated than they need to be" (Ottino 2003, 476).

5. "Image science would have to be, and has been, a cognitive science, an empirical study of the conditions of human perception, of the centers of pattern recognition, image formation, and transformation in the brain and the mind" (Mitchell 2008, 58).

6. Regarding the multiple processing steps of fMRI images, compare, for example, Ashburner et al. (2013) and Goebel, Jansma, and Eck (2013).

7. Regarding problems with statistical analysis in fMRI, compare, for example, Bennett et al. (2009) and Bennett, Wolford, and Miller (2009).

8. This tradition values a "'golden event': the single picture of such clarity and distinctness that it commands acceptance" (Galison 1997, 22).

9. "Image machines and logic machines—each had their victories, their Nobel Prize-winning successes. At the same time, neither tradition was able to claim a privileged hold on truth for any length of time, and neither held unique sway (for long) over the physics community. . . . neither tradition has epistemic priority" (Galison 1997, 24–5).

10. "On one side of the image-logic divide stood the pure forms of image makers . . . On the other stood the pure electronic world . . . the purity of the iconoclast and iconodule was lost as hybrid instruments became the standard" (Galison 1997, 515–6).

11. The focus here is on images and their derivates. Topics that cannot be addressed include pure arrangements in science, mere illustrations by graphs and diagrams, and completely artificial images.

12. Photography by itself may certainly already be called scientific, artistic, or both (see Galison and Daston 2007). Nevertheless, the focus here is on the type of technique in the classification. It is presupposed that pho-

tography represents light information that a human observer could have indeed perceived in reality at one point.

13. One topic for a potential "image science" concerning neuroscience might be the difference between a gradual black-and-white scale *versus* color-coding. Colors in particular relate insights that language cannot easily express, and different conclusions may be derived from words *versus* grayscale images *versus* color images.

14. In other words, these hybrid types of images are truly "both material and symbolic: they integrate things with projects; they incorporate verbal references into their frames and supply scenic contexts for interpreting them" (Lynch 2006, 37).

15. This argument stems from John R. Searle (2004, 95): "The mode of existence of conscious states is indeed ontologically subjective, but ontological subjectivity of the subject matter does not preclude an epistemically objective science of that very subject matter."

16. ". . . we attempt to bring into view the subjectivity of the research subject or patient. However, we do so not to constitute this subject in a realist or humanist sense, as subjects whose humanity is left out of the laboratory picture, for example, but to emphasize the embodied presence and agency of the human subject as always present in laboratory and clinical processes. Scholarly work on MRI in sociology and anthropology has tended to focus on brain imaging, and has taken up the status of the brain as the conceptual locus of what it means to be human in the current research and popular context . . .. In the interaction we describe, however, what we see produced among practitioners is an imagined sense of the human subject as a whole body and a cognizant subject whose movements signify agency, even as the brain or spine are the isolated objects of scientific or clinical concern" (Cartwright and Alac 2008, 202).

17. ". . . 'becoming visible' is not only, and is not even primarily, connected to the faculty of sight, or to the aspect of imagination captured in the concept of mental imagery or verbal representation. Rather, making visible entails aspects of embodied feeling and enactment" (Cartwright and Alac 2008, 219).

18. Regarding embodied embedded cognition, compare, for example, Gallagher 2005.

19. The problem "Imaging or imagining?" (see Illes and Racine 2005) can indeed be addressed by awareness of the constructedness of images and by informed analysis: "Responsible and careful interpretation of data will . . . become a crucial issue as we wrestle to untangle what we image from what we imagine" (Illes and Racine 2005).

20. "At the heart of the claims about the emerging contributions of functional brain mapping is a paradox: functional imagers seem to reject representations while also using them at multiple points in their work. [There is, K.B.] a love-hate relationship between scientists and their object: the case of the iconoclastic imager" (Beaulieu 2002, 53).

## Works Cited

Ashburner, John, Gareth Barnes, Chun-Chuan Chen, Jean Daunizeau, Guillaume Flandin, Karl Friston, Stefan Kiebel, James Kilner, Vladimir Litvak, Rosalyn Moran, Will Penny, Maria Rosa, Klaas Stephan, Darren Gitelman, Rik Henson, Chloe Hutton, Volkmar Glauche, Jérémie Mattout, and Christophe Phillips. 2013. *SPM8 Manual*. London: Functional Imaging Laboratory, Wellcome Trust Centre for Neuroimaging, Institute of Neurology, UCL. www.fil.ion.ucl.ac.uk/spm/doc/spm8_manual.pdf [January 20, 2020].

Beaulieu, Anne. 2002. "Images Are Not the (Only) Truth: Brain Mapping, Visual Knowledge, and Iconoclasm." *Science, Technology, & Human Values* 27 (1): 53–86.

Bennett, Craig M., Abigail A. Baird, Michael B. Miller, and George L. Wolford. 2009. "Neural Correlates of Interspecies Perspective Taking in the Post-Mortem Atlantic Salmon: An Argument for Multiple Comparisons Correction." Abstract at the *15th Annual Meeting of the Organization for Human Brain Mapping*. San Francisco. prefrontal.org/files/posters/Bennett-Salmon-2009.pdf [January 20, 2020].

Bennett, Craig M., George L. Wolford, and Michael B. Miller. 2009. "The Principled Control of False Positives in Neuroimaging." *SCAN* 4:417–22.

Brukamp, Kirsten. 2012. "Scientific Images from Functional Brain Imaging in Contemporary Neuroscience—Complex and Problematic Processing Procedures." In *Medical Imaging and Philosophy. Challenges, Reflections and Actions*, edited by Heiner Fangerau, Rethy K. Chhem, Irmgard Müller, and Shih-Chang Wang, 75–82. Stuttgart: Steiner.

Cartwright, Lisa, and Morana Alac. 2008. "Imagination, Multimodality and Embodied Interaction: A Discussion of Sound and Movement in Two Cases of Laboratory and Clinical Magnetic Resonance Imaging." In *Science Images and Popular Images of the Sciences*, edited by Bernd Hüppauf and Peter Weingart, 199–223. New York: Routledge.

Farah, Martha J. 2002. "Emerging Ethical Issues in Neuroscience." *Nature Neuroscience* 5:1123–9.

Foss, Sonja K. 2005. "Theory of Visual Rhetoric." In *Handbook of Visual Communication: Theory, Methods, and Media*, edited by Ken Smith, Sandra Moriarty, Gretchen Barbatsis, and Keith Kenney, 141–52. Mahwah (New Jersey): Lawrence Erlbaum.

Galison, Peter L. 1997. *Image and Logic: A Material Culture of Microphysics*. Chicago: University of Chicago Press.

Galison, Peter L., and Lorraine Daston. 2007. *Objectivity.* Boston: Zone Books.
Gallagher, Shaun. 2005. *How the Body Shapes the Mind.* Oxford: Oxford University Press.
Goebel, Rainer, Henk Jansma, and Judith Eck. 2013. *Brain Voyager QX: Getting Started Guide Version 2.12 for BVQX 2.8.* Maastricht: Brain Innovation. download.brainvoyager.com/doc/BVQXGettingStartedGuide_v2.12.pdf [January 20, 2020].
Heßler, Martina, Jochen Hennig, and Dieter Mersch. 2004. *Visualisierungen in der Wissenskommunikation: Explorationsstudie im Rahmen der BMBF-Förderinitiative "Wissen für Entscheidungsprozesse."* http://sciencepolicystudies.de/projekt/visualisierung/index.htm.
Hill, Charles A., and Marguerite Helmers, eds. 2004. *Defining Visual Rhetorics.* Mahwah (New Jersey): Lawrence Erlbaum.
Hüppauf, Bernd, and Peter Weingart. 2008. "Images in and of Science." In *Science Images and Popular Images of the Sciences*, edited by Bernd Hüppauf and Peter Weingart, 3–31. New York: Routledge.
Illes, Judy, and Eric Racine. 2005. "Imaging or Imagining? A Neuroethics Challenge Informed by Genetics." *American Journal of Bioethics* 5 (2): 5–18.
Kornhuber, Hans Helmut, and Lüder Deecke. 1965. "Hirnpotentialänderungen bei Willkürbewegungen und passiven Bewegungen des Menschen: Bereitschaftspotential und reafferente Potentiale." *Pflueger's Archiv für die gesamte Physiologie des Menschen und der Tiere* 284: 1–17.
Libet, Benjamin. 2004. *Mind Time: The Temporal Factor in Consciousness.* Cambridge, MA: Harvard University Press.
Lynch, Michael. 2006. "The Production of Scientific Images: Vision and Re-Vision in the History, Philosophy, and Sociology of Science." In *Visual Cultures of Science: Rethinking Representational Practices in Knowledge Building and Science Communication*, edited by Luc Pauwels, 26–40. Lebanon, NH: Dartmouth College Press.
Mersch, Dieter. 2008. "Visual Arguments: The Role of Images in Sciences and Mathematics." In *Science Images and Popular Images of the Sciences*, edited by Bernd Hüppauf and Peter Weingart, 181–98. New York: Routledge.
Mitchell, William J. T. 2008. "Image Science." In *Science Images and Popular Images of the Sciences*, edited by Bernd Hüppauf and Peter Weingart, 55–67. New York: Routledge.
Monti, Martin M., Audrey Vanhaudenhuyse, Martin R. Coleman, Melanie Boly, John D. Pickard, Luaba Tshibanda, Adrian M. Owen, and Steven Laureys. 2010. "Willful Modulation of Brain Activity in Disorders of Consciousness." *New England Journal of Medicine* 362 (7): 579–89.
Ottino, Julio M. 2003. "Is a Picture Worth 1,000 Words?" *Nature* 421 (6922): 474–76.
Searle, John. 2004. *Mind: A Brief Introduction.* Oxford: Oxford University Press.
Soon, Chun Siong, Marcel Brass, Hans-Jochen Heinze, and John-Dylan Haynes. 2008. "Unconscious Determinants of Free Decisions in the Human Brain." *Nature Neuroscience* 11 (5): 543–45.

# 5 Using Images, Films and Colors When Communicating Neuroscientific Results

C. Giovanni Galizia

## Introduction

Neuroscientists, as all scientists, study the world—in this case the brain—and then communicate their findings. It is in communicating scientific results that rhetorical considerations—and the rhetoric of evidence—become important.

Communication can use various means to convey a message. In neuroscience, the usage of images, in particular of colored images, has seen a massive increase in recent years, both because of the availability of color print and because of the digitalization of scientific communication. The latter has also resulted in an increased availability of dynamic representations that are used to dynamically represent changes over time, for example, using movies and/or sound tracks.[1] With the increase of color usage, a critical appraisal regarding how colors are used, and what kind of information is delivered, needs to be performed. Furthermore, it is important to understand what additional information color can provide, and what information it *cannot* convey. Understanding these conditions is important for the scientist who creates the material, but equally important for the recipient to whom it is addressed, such as the reader of a scientific paper. As this paper will show, many instances of color usage in images communicating scientific results can easily be misinterpreted by an unprepared recipient. Such misinterpretations can result in two (related) consequences: firstly, the recipient might misunderstand the message; and secondly, she/he might be disappointed when realizing that the results were less significant than initially expected.

One could argue that, beginning with the raw data measured, the first step of data interpretation lies with *selecting* and *sorting* the data that is to be illustrated (looking for relevant data and focusing on it; choosing adequate thresholds etc.). Within the rhetorical *officia oratoris*, this corresponds to the levels of *inventio* and *dispositio*. After that, in a further step that can be analytically differentiated, the question as to how to color/represent the (previously selected and sorted) data/content arises (corresponding to the level of *elocutio*). The possibilities of representation are dictated/limited by the *medium* used.

To illustrate these points, I will give a few examples about the usage of color, and give examples how color choice can influence the apparent (sometimes even the real) scientific message of a figure in neuroscientific reports. I will focus on false-color coded images *sensu strictu*. False-Color coded images are those in which color is used to code for information that does not have a color itself. For example, when a weather forecast map labels cold areas in blue, and hot areas in red—these are false color maps: temperature across the country is displayed in colors, even though temperature does not have a color.[2] The choice of color is not arbitrary: we refer to blue color tones as being "cold colors," and we refer to red color tones as being "warm colors," so that the false-color coded maps (in this case the term *heat-map* is appropriate) are intuitive to the reader. They are also intuitive because they are widely used: we as recipients of such images are experienced with geographic maps that have temperature information superimposed using color.

This paper will focus on false-color codes used in images from the neurosciences. The following cases of using colors are explicitly not covered here: Colored images can be images where color depicts reality. These images display colors as they would be seen by a viewer, just like a photograph. A lot could be said about the usage of color in such photographs: choice of contrast, of color clarity, of the image itself, even of color removal by choosing black and white—all these choices influence the message delivered by an image, but I will not treat these topics here. Another category not treated here consists of images where colors are "invented," but almost real. For example, electron microscopy images are black and white as a consequence of the achromatic nature of the electron microscope. Often, however, colors are added to these images to make them more intelligible, and the color choice is generally dictated by known (or sometimes imagined) real colors of the objects. Thus, in these images, colors are "false," but realistic. These kinds of colored figures will also not be treated here.

Let me add another disclaimer: this paper is not about misuse or fraud. This is an important disclaimer, because—as we will see below—the choice of color range, color scale and threshold has an enormous influence on the information that an image conveys. Naturally, then, a scientist uses color to focus the message of a paper. I assume that this is done in a well-intentioned way—but the tools are there, and can easily be used to conceal unwanted information, or to exaggerate minimal effects. While I have occasionally seen such cases, I prefer not to use this chapter to investigate fraud, or to instruct the reader on useful techniques for it.

## Some History of Images in Neuroscience

Using different image elements for different information has a long tradition. Take, for example, one of the earliest realistic depictions of a brain in modern literature: the brain image by Andreas Vesalius, published in his influential book *De humani corpori fabrica* from 1543 and shown in figure 1.

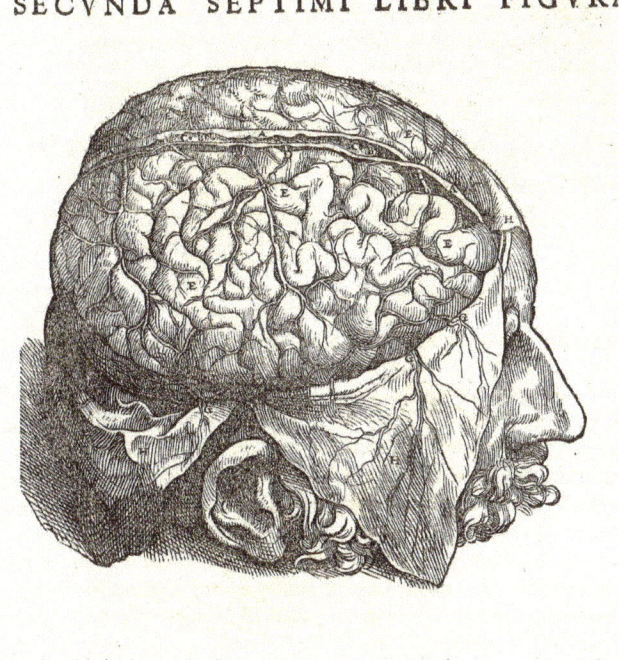

Figure 1. Depiction of the human brain by Vesalius (1543, 606). Note how the brain is shown in the context of the entire head, with face and ears clearly visible.

The brain has been exposed by removing the scull, and brain linings are shown as sheets hanging loosely to the sides. Vesalius was born 1514 in Brussels, and worked as anatomist and physician in many European cities. Adapted from http://wellcomeimages.org/indexplus/obf_images/08/29/c7b9ed48ab80dd47c7fb0e23c72a.jpg Gallery: http://wellcomeimages.org/indexplus/image/L0063890.html, CC BY 4.0, https://commons.wikimedia.org/w/index.php?curid=36231366.

The main scope of the image is to show the brain, with the blood vessels and all invaginations and brain folds. However, the image also shows a face: the face has the role to position the brain, so that it creates a reference space for the viewer. Thanks to the face, the viewer knows where the different areas of the brain are located. Thus, the image connects morphology, and a spatial reference system.

A single image can combine different visual elements to display different kinds of information. Johann Dryander gave a good example of this in a book he published in 1537 (see figure 2).

Again, you see a face, giving a spatial reference known to the reader (note the beautiful collar). The figure is about the connection between sensory input (vision, for example), and the ventricles in the brain, which were believed by Dryander to be the location of consciousness. The image is interesting because of its superposition of outer view (e.g., the face), the inner view (e.g., the nerves, the ventricles), and the externalized inner view (e.g., the brain linings hanging off the side of the head). Furthermore, depiction of reality (face) is mixed with depiction of concepts (the nerves indicate existing connections, but not their exact position). Dryander does not need any color to present all these views in one image. But an older figure, surviving in a fourteenth-century manuscript copy of Avicenna's *Liber de causis*, uses color (figure 3).

Figure 2. Dryander (1537, fol. D2ʳ), shows the presumed role of brain ventricles in the human head. The image uses the face and head as spatial reference and superimposes nerves that connect the sensory organs (eyes, mouth, skin) to the ventricles. Elements are labeled with letters for explanation in the text. Johann Dryander was born in 1500 in Wetter (today Germany) and was a physician, anatomist, mathematician, and astronomer. Image taken from the copy in the Bavarian National Library in Munich (Rar. 1467), with permission.

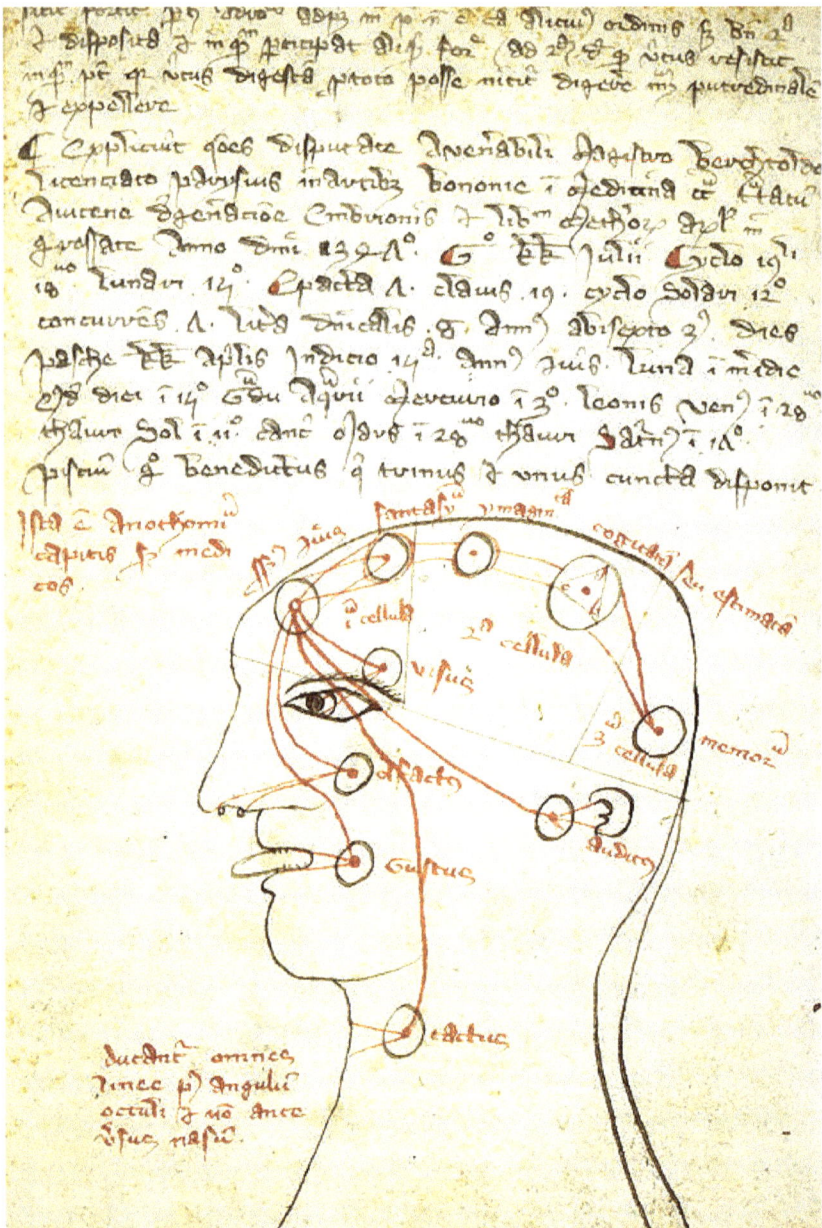

Figure 3. Avicenna (1374, fol. 64ᵛ) shows the connections between sensory organs and the brain ventricles. Avicenna, or Abū Alī al-Husain ibn Abdullāh ibn Sīnā, was a Persian physician, philosopher, mathematician, and much more who was born around 980 near Buchara (today in Uzbekistan). He worked in several cities and died in 1037 after publishing many books, some of which have been republished in Europe over the course of several centuries. Image taken from the

manuscript copy preserved in the Bavarian National Library in Munich (Clm 527), with permission.

Here, black is used for reference (the skull, the face with the location of sensory organs), while red is used for functional connections between the senses and the ventricles in the brain, and the location of functional areas, for example, memory in the occipital brain. Thus, color is used to separate two lines of communication: in broad terms, morphology (face and skull) and physiology (sensory organs and nerves).

## Brain Physiology Today

The localization of brain functions to particular areas of the brain has always been an important topic in neuroscience. Today, in many studies, brain physiology is measured spatially: electroencephalograms, magneto encephalograms, and fMRI (functional magnetic resonance imaging) images are among the most widespread. The task when visualizing research results remains similar to what Avicenna wanted to convey: show a functional content in a framework that explains the position. As for Avicenna, color is often used in a similar way: the spatial reference is given in black and white, the functional data in color.

Thus, the reason to use false-color in these images is that color allows adding a dimension of content to the data: comparable to weather maps in which color can add information about temperature to the geographic image, color can be used to add information about brain activity in a brain recording (figure 4). In this case, location is given by the color's position, and intensity is represented by its hue, in this example on a scale from black over red-yellow to white. Images like these, showing brain activity in a particular situation (e.g., "being sad," "thinking about music," or "being aggressive") have become widely distributed even in the popular press.

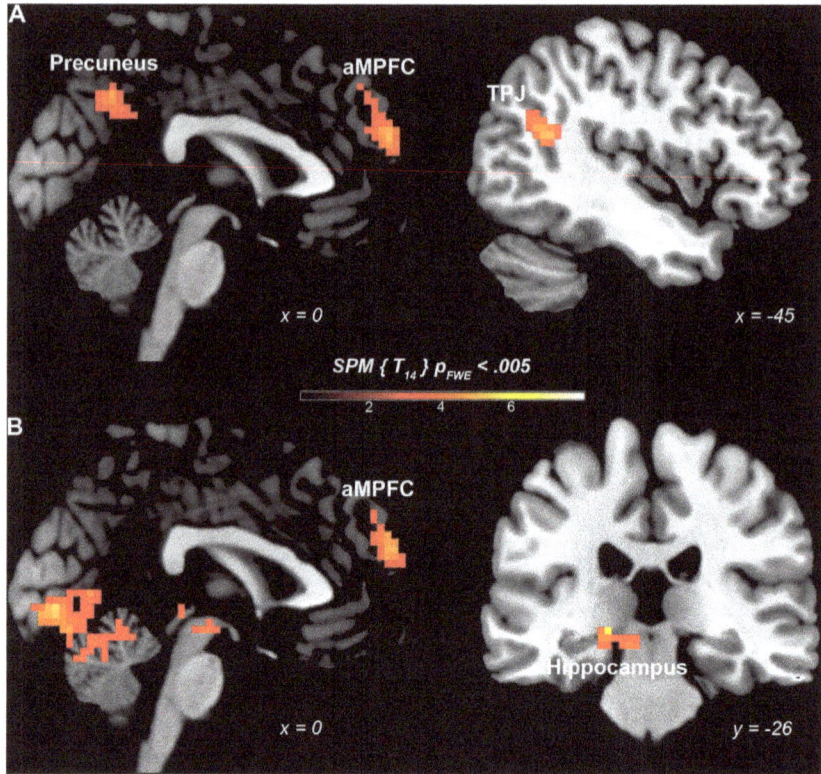

Figure 4. fMRI (functional magnetic resonance imaging) measurements of subjects in a moral judgment situation. In A, the task was presented from a first-person perspective (moral dilemma); in B, the task was in a third-person perspective (moral reaction). Both illustrations show data of significance compared to a non-moral situation. aMPFC: anterior medial prefrontal cortex. TPJ: temporo-parietal junction. SPM: statistical parametric mapping, a particular data analysis procedure for fMRI. Image taken from Avram et al. (2014), open access.

Even though these images are known to a wide public, few people realize what exactly is shown. For example, the colored pixels do not show that for a given task the brain is active *only* where the pixels are colored. They show that the brain is significantly *more* active here *as compared to* a control situation. Thus, the control situation is always part of the experiment. Furthermore, the stress should be on *significantly*, rather than on more, because the difference in activity may even be minimal—for the data shown, the important aspect is the statistical significance, not the absolute magnitude. As a consequence, two brain areas evincing hugely different levels of activity change compared to the control situation (e.g., one area being ten times more active and another area being 0.1 times more active) might both be marked with the same color—as long as the changes in both areas are of equal statistical significance. Another important point: the physiological data has a threshold. That is, areas of the brain that are not colored are not necessarily areas that do not exhibit any change in activity at all—the difference in activity is just not (mathematically) significant enough to be represented. And there is a fundamental difference between these images and the image in the Avicenna-manuscript from 1347: Avicenna showed a graphical display of what he thought about brain function in general; he used his image to illustrate an abstract concept. Brain imaging figures from fMRI studies do not show theories, they show *examples*. Often, these images are misinterpreted by the readers as being general results. Examples, however, are individual measurements (or measurement sets), that show how activity was distributed in the brain of a particular person or a standardized group of subjects. These images are easy to use for communication, and in scientific papers they are often used to explain the concepts of a study, and/or to give an example. In most cases, real data comes later in the publication, with comparisons from different groups, and quantifications, and these are generally not displayed as colored figures, but rather as statistical plots or even plain tables of numbers. For the colleagues in the field, these tables of data are the most important part of the paper, but for disseminating the results in the press and to researchers from other fields, the example—that is, the false-color-coded image of the brain—is the most effective visualization tool.

How much this visualization tool has become part of our common culture is evident when we think about sentences like, "When you see a painting, your occipital cortex lights up." There is nothing in the occipital cortex that lights up; it is the illustrations that we are given by brain imaging labs that show false-color images using colors that can be described as "lighting up" as a symbol for brain activity.

## Using False-Colors in Neuroscience: An Example

Let me take a few examples from the research in our group and give you some theoretical background in neuroscience before going into the images used for visualization. We study how brains process olfactory information, and we use insects, notably honeybees and fruit flies, as model animals. Honeybees collect nectar from flowers, learn the odor of a flower species that gives particularly good nectar, and remember that scent in order to visit similar flowers again. With as few as 160 different types of olfactory receptors, bee brains can code for thousands, maybe millions of odors (we humans have about 350 different types of receptors). How can a limited number of receptor types encode for an almost unlimited number of odors? The answer lies in the combinatorial nature of the code: the odor is not coded in a single receptor type, but in a combination of several receptor types.

In bees, odors are first detected by receptor cells that are located along the antennae. When a suitable odor hits a receptor cell, the cell will be excited and that activity is transferred to the brain via nerve fibers. The first area in the brain to receive these fibers is the antennal lobe, and all the data that I will present in this chapter is taken from recordings in honeybee antennal lobes (humans have a similar structure, called the olfactory bulb). Just as there are 160 types of receptor cells (but many cells for each type, for a total of sixty thousand cells), the honeybee antennal lobe has 160 so-called glomeruli, small spherical structures that each collect all information from a particular receptor cell type. Therefore, when an odor hits the antenna, it will activate, say, fifteen different receptor cell types, which results in fifteen activated glomeruli in the antennal lobe. The brain then recognizes this pattern as the characteristic pattern for, say, lemon tree. With 160 glomeruli, each either active or non-active, there are $2^{160}$ possible combinatorial patterns—a number that is effectively infinity.[3] How these patterns are formed for a set of odors is shown in figure 5.

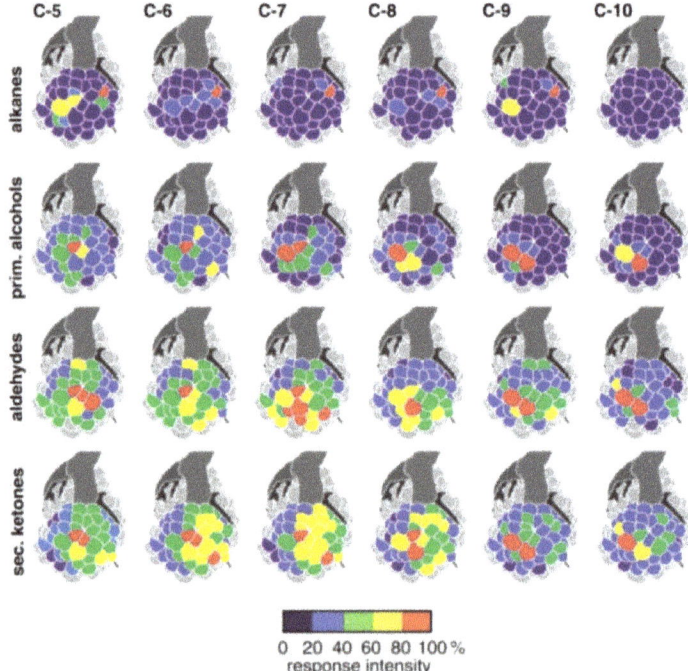

Figure 5. Spatial glomerular activity patterns for a series of odors in the honeybee antennal lobes. In this image, space is schematic, each glomerulus is indicated as

an area in a place that approximates its position in the real animal, and five different colors are used for five increasing levels of activity. The spatial nature is immediately apparent, and also that some odors elicit similar response patterns while others are clearly distinct. The odors used are monomolecular hydrocarbons, sorted by carbon chain length (C5 to C10), and chemical structure. For example, the second column shows the patterns for hexanal, 1-hexanol, 2-hexanol and hexanone. Image taken from Sachse, Rappert, and Galizia (1999), with permission.

Two major scientific question relate to the nature of the combinatorial code: (1) which patterns of glomeruli are activated by different odors, and (2) how are odor concentrations and odor mixtures represented in brain activity? To answer these questions, it is necessary to record neural activity from many, ideally all, glomeruli simultaneously, while stimulating the receptor neurons with an odor. Optical imaging techniques are suited for this purpose: the neurons are loaded with a dye that changes its color properties when the neuron is active (for example, a calcium sensitive fluorescent dye that changes its fluorescence intensity as a function of intracellular calcium concentration). Taking a movie with a camera will reveal which glomeruli are activated by a particular odor stimulus.

Figure 6 shows some examples for single odor-response recordings. Upon odor stimulation, some glomeruli are activated strongly, others less so. The image is false-color coded: strong activity is shown in yellow-red, weak activity in blue hues, following a color sequence reminiscent of rainbow colors. This is the first, and most important step in using colors when displaying neuroscience results: converting activity into a scale of colors. These colors are not in the brain—they are "false." Even though the measurements are taken with a dye that changes its color properties due to chemical effects of neural activity, the actual measurements consist in light intensity quantification; that is, they record differences in a spectrum from "dark" to "bright." Moreover, brain activity as illustrated in the false-color image does not mean "this area is bright," but rather "this area increases its brightness" (which means that calcium concentration increases). Thus, an area that is dark to begin with and increases activity may be darker when active than an area that is bright to begin with and does not change. As a consequence, in the displayed false-color image, the interest is not in the absolute recorded brightness, but in the relative change. (Relative change is often quantified as $\Delta F/F$, that is, the absolute change $\Delta F$ divided by the background brightness.) Another point is important to notice: the changes are small, and the range of brightness is large. Therefore, detectors used for these measurements generally have 4,096 intensity value as minimum (12 bit), often 65,536 intensity values (16 bit). Our eyes, however, cannot see many more than one hundred intensity values—the high dynamic range of the original measurements has to be converted into a low dynamic range image, which means that the range must be selected carefully.

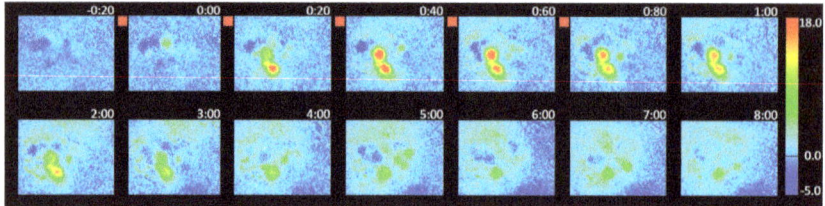

Figure 6. Example of an odor response in a honeybee antennal lobe. The odor stimulus was one second long (marked with a red square), brain activity images are shown just before odor onset, and then for the first second. The second row shows how the patterns weaken and distribute over the antennal lobe after the odor has ceased. Note that the first row is shown at higher speed (time distance between frames of 200ms), while the second row is slower (time distance between frames full seconds). Activity is false-color coded, and the color sequence is given to the right, with max and min value (ΔF/F values). Original data.

Together, these observations mean that displaying brain activity measurements in a publication cannot be done by printing a "photograph" of the situation—the data must be treated. When data is treated, the researcher must make decisions: Where should a threshold be located? Which range should be shown? Should a logarithmic or a linear scale be used? What colors are to be used? All these decisions influence the image, the content, and the message of an image, and all these decisions need to be understood by the recipient.

Take a typical situation: you want to show the activity elicited by two odors, one weak, and one strong. If you put the two images side by side, you have the choice of two very distinct scalings (in this example, I use black and white): either both images are scaled with the same mapping—in this case, one image will be totally dark, and the other will be very bright, or each image is scaled to its own minimum and maximum, in which case the two images may look very similar. In the first case, the difference between the weak and the strong odor is emphasized, but the spatial pattern of each response is lost. In the second case, the spatial pattern is emphasized, but the overall difference in intensity between the two odors is lost. It may well be that the brain "reads" the information in the antennal lobe with the same two techniques: one giving the overall response strength (to extract odor intensity), and one giving the normalized response pattern (to map the combinatorial code). Thus, these two fundamentally different ways to display the data may correspond to what the brain does, and therefore their methodical juxtaposition gains in conceptual value!

## CHOOSING THE RIGHT COLOR SCALE: EXAMPLES AND CAVEATS

Many different false-color palettes are available—among the most common ones are the rainbow palette, the thermal color palette, and the grayscale palette (figure 7). Most viewers will be familiar with these, but few realize that they have specific effects. Most importantly, the rainbow palette is the one that shows most details: the colors range from blue to green to yellow to red, allowing to encode a large dynamic range. Therefore, much more detail can be shown as compared to the black and white image—very small differences may already result in an easily detectable difference in color. However, rainbow palettes also create artificial information: our eyes create categories for the different colors, and thus a small change of intensity that leads from one hue of green to another hue of green is difficult to detect, while the same magnitude of intensity change that leads from green to yellow will have a massive impact on our visual systems. Continuous data (intensity change) is effectively coded as categorical data (blue—green—yellow—red), even though there is no scientific justification at that particular position within the scale for a category switch.

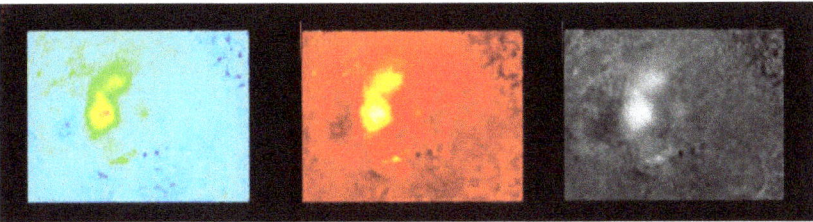

Figure 7. Spatial odor response patterns in the honeybee antennal lobe. The three images show the identical response (same measurement, same thresholds used), using different false-color palettes. Rainbow to the left, thermal color (heat map) in the center, grayscale to the right. Note how the color choice influences the impression of the results, even though at close inspection the identity of the underlying data is clearly visible. Original data.

These are problems that grayscale does not produce, but grayscale has other drawbacks. The contrast is poor, and it gets even worse when considering that many displays do not produce the necessary shadings (e.g., photocopying machines, but even printers or projectors often do not deliver the fine differences necessary to see as many gray hues as possible).

Specialized scales are created for specialized content. Neurons in the brain, for example, are often tonically active at all times, that is, they fire continuously, even if at low level. Consequently, they can go down or up in activity as a response to a given stimulus. Useful color scales for these kinds of data have a central color area that is inconspicuous, and then different colors for decreased and increased activity, for example, blue hues for negative values and yellow-red hues for positive values (figures 8 –9). Thinking about the implications reveals several aspects about data communication that are apparently trivial, but that result in considerable consequences. Most importantly, the "zero" point is crucial: the inconspicuous color should be placed in the range of background activity. Another consequence is less apparent: scaling downward may or may not be identical to scaling upward. Consider a neuron that fires action potentials (often called "spikes"), and that has an average background activity level of, say, eight spikes per second (a value often found in the brain). That neuron can decrease its activity, reaching its lowest value at zero spikes. The same neuron can increase its activity, up to two hundred or more spikes per second. In a color scale that should cover the entire dynamic range, the range from background to minimum therefore covers a dynamic range of eight spikes, while from background to maximum the range is well above one hundred. Clearly, choosing a color map here is already a first step towards data interpretation.

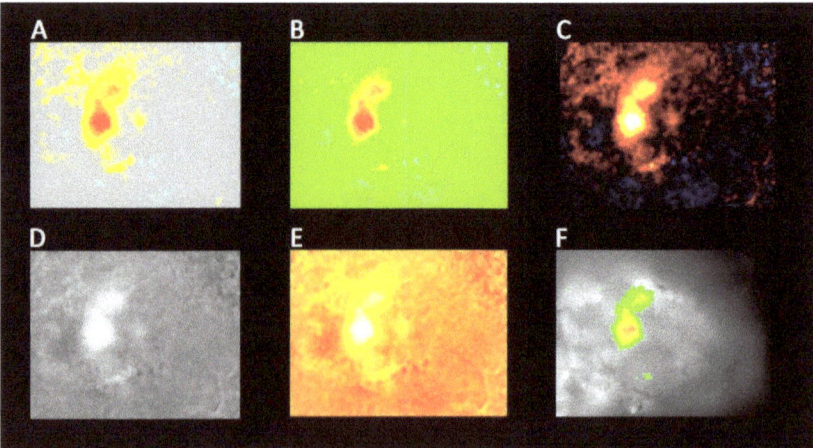

Figure 8: More examples for color scale effects. From top left, clockwise: (A) A scale with a gray center emphasizes areas of strong activity. (B) The effect is weaker with a green center. (C) A scale from dark blue to glow again changes the picture. Note that mathematically, all three images are identical, only the color mapping has changed. (D) A black and white print of the same data. (E) With a glow mapping in the upper range, the activity pattern is difficult to see. (F) Strong activity can also be emphasized by replacing weak activity areas with a morphological view of the brain. Original data.

Shifting the color scale, or extracting only a particular range, also influences the images. Technically, it is like placing a lens over a particular range—which is then visible in more detail, or even becomes visible only because a narrow range has been chosen, but at the expense of not seeing the rest of the activity range. Again, making these choices is an important aspect of data communication, and a first step towards data interpretation (because it selects which component of the data is shown, and thus deemed to be relevant). A good choice is important for good science—and knowing how that choice has been done is important for good science interpretation, that is, the recipient must be aware of the steps taken by the producer. Therefore, color scales should always also display the range numbers next to the color scale itself, and the first things to look at are the range of values that are shown and the indication within the text about how scaling was chosen: "scaled to fixed values," "scaled to its own maximum and minimum," "scaled between zero and maximum," etc.

The last aspect that I would like to cover here is not scientific with respect to the data: it is background color. The same image will be perceived differently if shown against a black, a white or (rarely seen) a colored background. The reasons for this are in part physiological (due to such effects as color constancy and center-surround color processing in our eyes), and in part psychological. Therefore, a researcher must consider the content of a figure also with respect to the background: a different color will communicate a slightly different message.

Figure 9. Using different background colors has a strong effect on the image, not only when the background corresponds to one value in the scale used. Here, black, gray, and white backgrounds are compared for three different scales. For example, black components of the scales appear less important when the background is black. Original data.

## Consequences for Science

I have reviewed different solutions about using colors in displaying brain activity measurements. Color choice is critical, because it influences what is being communicated: color scale, thresholds, dynamic range, and background color are all choices that influence the content displayed. These decisions are critical, but in most cases they follow conventions that are established in the field, so that readers and writers have no difficulty in understanding what they are communicating about.

Conventions change over time, and color language is no exception. Therefore, when reading older papers, some care is needed to make sure that false-color coded images are interpreted with the old conventions in mind. Changes in conventions may be small, or even lab-specific: some labs refuse to use false-color codes, and only adopt black and white, others prefer particular color scales.

An interesting recent example for how the use of color changes over time in scientific literature is the display of neuroanatomy data: to show how two different populations of neurons are branching in the brain, generally two separate color channels are used. Traditionally, these colors were green and red, given that the human eye has the highest color contrast in this range, possibly because human evolution has favored the detection of red fruit in green trees (though this theory is somewhat anecdotal). However, close to ten percent of the male population has some form of color blindness that affects red-green contrast (Daltonism and related conditions), and a major shift towards images in green and magenta has occurred between 2005 and 2010. Eventually, this led to a situation where red/green is very rarely used today, and green/magenta is the new standard. This shift was deliberately explicit, in that people pushed publicly towards shifting the color use: Masataka Okabe and Kei Ito (2002) published material to explain the effect of color choice on color-blind viewers and disseminated the material within the scientific community (figure 10).

Using Images, Films and Colors When Communicating Neuroscientific Results 95

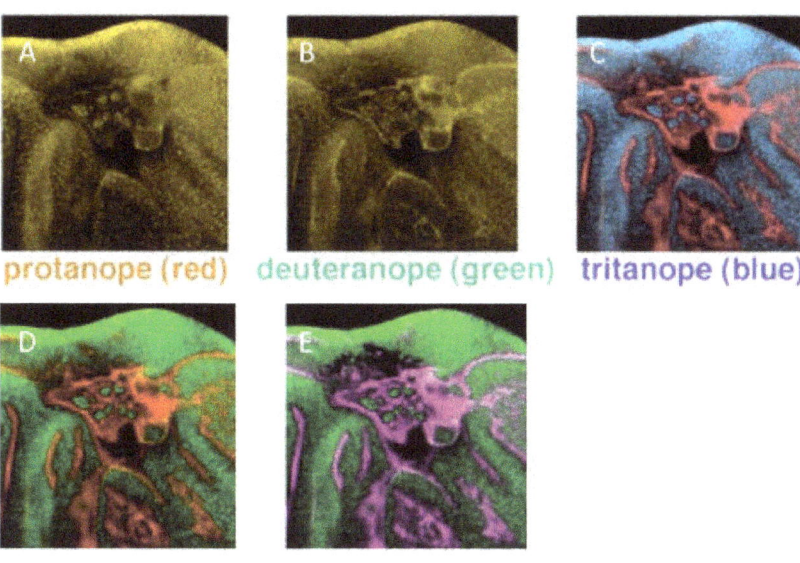

Figure 10. Examples of how colors are seen by color blind people. A, B, C: simulation of what is seen by protanope, deuteranope, and tritanope people when they look at the image shown in D. Note how the two colors red and green are lost in A and B. E shows the current consensus when using two color channels. Green and magenta can be distinguished by all color-blind subjects. Images taken from Okabe and Ito (2002), with permission.

Color codes, and the consequences of choices such as scales, need to be known to writers and to readers alike, in order to allow for efficient communication of scientific content. Generally, this communication works well within the scientific community. Misunderstandings are common, however, when the scientific community is left, and the public is addressed. How should a person, without training, read a brain scan where activity is shown in false-colored pixels? When I give talks to the general public, I am often asked questions about how the activity-sensitive dyes that we use can change their colors from blue to red, even though I give examples of different color scales and state that these colors are used for visualization only. Even more importantly, colored examples are often taken as being the data, rather than images used for visualization. In a scientific paper, often a colored figure gives a typical example of brain activity over space, using false colors. Later figures show statistical analyses across individuals: the evidence is created by these analyses. However, in a report for the public, such as in a daily newspaper, the colored figure is more useful to explain the results (see figure 4), and in the mind of the reader the chosen example will create the necessary evidence—with all the consequences regarding possible misunderstandings. In some cases, research results may even be rejected, when the single example is dismissed as being only a single observation, or when the single example is not entirely congruent with the statistical result.

Misunderstandings of these kinds are misused by people who claim that science is based on "fake news." Science communication needs to be careful in explaining its visual displays: color use (as reported in this paper), and selection of figures. Explaining how colors are used and what their choice entails will help in creating visual literacy—both in the expert audience of fellow scientists and in the lay audience of the general public. Improving visual literacy is an important step toward the rhetoric of evidence accomplishing its goal: science communication at its best. We all can gain from a rhetoric of visual evidence that uses shared understanding of the language used.

### Acknowledgments

Many thanks to all my colleagues and students in the research group, without their contribution, all the brain measurements would not have been possible. Thanks also to Tanja Klemm, who introduced me to the beautiful brain images in the fourteenth to sixteenth century. Thanks to Michael Pelzer for helpful comments and discussions.

### Notes

1. In this printed paper, the focus is on still images—simply because the medium "print" is being used. However, brain activity is dynamic, and the best way to communicate measurements is by using a medium that is inherently capable of reproducing a dimension of time, for example, movies. These use false colors in the same way as still images, and all the arguments that we will see with still images apply to movies, too. For the interested reader, I have placed a choice of example movies at http://neuro.uni-konstanz.de, to download, enjoy and use.

2. Cf. also the chapter "Communicating the Uncertainty in Weather Forecasts" by David M. Schultz in this book.

3. The calculation is simplified: on the one hand the same odor may have different patterns at different concentrations, resulting in a reduced capacity, but on the other hand the patterns are not binary since glomeruli can also be weakly active, resulting in an increased capacity.

## Works Cited

Avicenna. 1374. *Liber de causis*. Manuscript copy. Munich, Bavarian National Library, Clm 527.

Avram, Mihai, Kristina Hennig-Fast, Yan Bao, Ernst Pöppel, Maximilian Reiser, Janusch Blautzik, James Giordano, and Evgeny Gutyrchik. 2014. "Neural correlates of moral judgments in first- and third-person perspectives: implications for neuroethics and beyond." BMC Neuroscience 15:39. https://doi.org/10.1186/1471-2202-15-39.

Dryander, Johann. 1537. *Anatomiae, hoc est, corporis humani dissectionis pars prior, in qua singula quae ad caput spectant recensentur membra, atq[ue] singulae partes, singulis suis ad vivum commodissime expressis figuris, deliniantur*. Marburg: Eucharius Cervicornus.

Okabe, Masataka, and Kei Ito. 2002. "Color Universal Design (CUD)—How to make figures and presentations that are friendly to Colorblind people." Last modified September 24, 2008. http://jfly.iam.u-tokyo.ac.jp/color/index.html.

Sachse, Silke, Angelika Rappert, and C. Giovanni Galizia. 1999. "The spatial representation of chemical structures in the antennal lobe of honeybees: steps towards the olfactory code." *European Journal of Neuroscience* 11 (11): 3970–3982.

Vesalius, Andreas. 1543. *Andreae Vesalii Brvxellensis, scholae medicorum Patauinae professoris, de Humani corporis fabrica. Libri septem*. Basel: Johann Oporinus.

# 6 Communicating the Uncertainty in Weather Forecasts

*David M. Schultz*

## Introduction

Winston Churchill said, "True genius resides in the capacity for evaluation of uncertain, hazardous, and conflicting information." If that is the case, then weather forecasters must surely be some of the smartest people on the planet. Each day they go to work and make important forecasts based on imperfect information relied upon by people, government agencies, and businesses. Despite their importance, forecasters are often the brunt of jokes and scorn, and may even be fired or, in some countries, jailed for failed forecasts.

But what other discipline can promise predictions of the future with such reliability? Meteorologists must deal with the challenges of an imperfectly sampled, turbulent fluid. In contrast, astronomers making forecasts of eclipses have the relatively simple task of calculating the orbits of solid heavenly bodies. Tidal forecasts are certainly reliable, but the public would be unlikely to complain much if the tide arrived fifteen minutes too late or had less amplitude than forecast. Economists have often shown a lack of forecasting ability, particularly with the 2008 recession (see, e.g., Silver 2012). Political forecasts are often just as wrong.

Weather forecasting is one of the greatest unheralded success stories of twentieth century science. It benefits tremendously from the free exchange of meteorological data across country borders. Such exchange is one of the earliest and longest examples of international cooperation and has served as an example for other international efforts. Moreover, the first analog computer was tasked with making numerical weather forecasts (Harper 2012). As computer power has increased, computer predictions have gotten remarkably better and unforecast low-pressure systems rarely happen anymore at relatively short ranges (1–2 days).

But the utility of weather forecasts goes beyond the accuracy of the forecasts. For a forecast to be effective, it must also be communicated to the end user. Then, the forecast must be received, read, and understood by the end user. Finally, an appropriate action must be taken by the end user based on the forecast. So, effective forecasts are more than just accurate forecasts. The human element must also be involved. Thus, rhetoric—a field providing systematic approaches toward the question of how information can be effectively communicated—is especially relevant for weather forecasts. The purpose of this chapter is to discuss the uncertainty inherent in weather forecasts, demonstrating that forecasts have their most potential when a measure of uncertainty is also communicated. I also argue that improving the communication of weather forecasts will require an interdisciplinary approach.

## How Weather Forecasts Are Made

The advent of weather forecasts by computer was presaged at the beginning of the twentieth century by Cleveland Abbe (1901) and Vilhelm Bjerknes (1904), who laid out a physically based approach by which forecasts could be made. Specifically, Bjerknes said that a forecast could be created given "a sufficiently accurate knowledge of the state of the atmosphere at the initial time" and "a sufficiently accurate knowledge of the laws according to which one state of the atmosphere develops from another" (cited after the English translation, Bjerknes [1904] 1999, 1). This approach was first implemented by Lewis Fry Richardson (1922), who hand-calculated the first numerical weather forecast. Although the forecast was quite poor, it demonstrated the success of the method, a method not dissimilar from that implemented today in modern computer weather forecasts (Lynch 2006).

Consider Bjerknes's recipe for a weather forecast. Richardson first required "sufficiently accurate knowledge of the state of the atmosphere at the initial time" (Bjerknes [1904] 1999, 1). Knowing the state of the atmosphere requires global observations, not only at the surface, but aloft as well. These observations come from a variety of different observing systems: surface meteorological stations, instrumented weather balloons and aircraft, wind-profiling radars, weather buoys, and satellites. These observations are collected from around the globe and communicated internationally to numerous weather prediction centers. The observations are interpolated onto a global grid and then used to create the initial conditions for the computer models.

The second requirement to produce a weather forecast is "a sufficiently accurate knowledge of the laws according to which one state of the atmosphere develops from another" (Bjerknes [1904] 1999, 1). In reality, the physical laws that govern the atmosphere are relatively simple. They describe how the wind, temperature, and water vapor fields change. They also include the conservation of mass and water. These laws are then rewritten so that they can be programmed into computer code to create a model of the atmosphere.

With the initial conditions and the laws of physics both in the computer, a forecast can be calculated. Such forecasts are performed on supercomputers around the world by the meteorological agencies within different countries. Europe has also pooled its resources to create the European Centre for Medium-Range Weather Forecasts (ECMWF), an organization that consistently delivers some of the finest analyses and forecasts around the world.

## Why Do Good Weather Forecasts Go Bad?

If producing a weather forecast is as simple as Bjerknes's two steps, why do weather forecasts sometimes go astray? The potential problems with forecasts lie within each of the two steps, plus an inherent property within the atmosphere called chaos.

The first reason that weather forecasts go bad is an imperfect knowledge about the current state of the atmosphere. Most surface observations occur where people live. Over the oceans, few surface observations exist. Therefore, if the initial conditions are poorly known, then the resulting forecasts are likely to be less accurate. Garbage in, garbage out.

Another problem with the initial conditions is that no observations may exist of important quantities needed for forecasting. For example, knowledge of the composition of a cloud is needed to know whether that cloud will produce precipitation or not. The cloud is composed of liquid water drops of various sizes and ice crystals of different sizes and shapes. Yet, we have no direct way to measure these distributions inside clouds. Thus, we have no way to start our models with an accurate representation of the existing cloud and its properties. Instead, we must impose much simpler representations that generalize across many different clouds. Sometimes, these generalizations may be inappropriate, which may lead to imperfect weather forecasts.

The second step identified by Bjerknes is the laws of physics. These are encapsulated in our computer models, but these models are themselves imperfect. There are several reasons for this. The first is that available computer power limits our ability to make perfect forecasts. Weather predictions by computer take time because of the intensive calculations needing to be performed. In the 1970s, forecast models had grid intervals of hundreds of kilometers, so only the largest-scale weather phenomena (e.g., slowly evolving stationary high-pressure systems) could be forecast. Errors in the intensity of rapidly evolving low-pressure systems (hundreds of kilometers in diameter) were common (Sanders 1986). Presently, computers are powerful enough to model phenomena just a few kilometers in scale, meaning that these computers can resolve individual convective storms. Second, although the laws of physics for the motion of the atmosphere are well known, physical processes acting on smaller scales may not be precisely known and must be handled by a process called parameterization (Stensrud 2009). Consider what is going on inside the cloud, for example. Ice crystals inside clouds can take a number of different shapes: needles, columns, plates, and dendrites. Modeling these behaviors in forecasting models has only recently been attempted because of the difficulties of understanding how quickly they grow and interact with each other.

The third reason why weather forecasts go wrong is due to an inherent property of the atmosphere: chaos (Lorenz 1998). Chaos in the atmosphere was discovered by Edward Lorenz of MIT in the early 1960s while running a very simple atmospheric model (Lorenz 1963). He found that small differences in the initial conditions—the size of the internal round-off error in the computer's memory—led to large changes in the outcome later in the forecast. Even with as perfect an initial condition as is possible and a perfect model, Lorenz later estimated that such small-scale errors would grow large enough by two weeks to swamp any utility for the forecast. Thus, Lorenz declared that the practical limit to weather forecasting was two weeks, a value that has been confirmed more recently using different methods. (Note that this is different than seasonal or climate forecasting which is interested in the average weather and its variability, not the specific conditions at a future time and place.)

These three limitations to *creating* weather forecasts inevitably lead to problems with *communicating* these forecasts, as we will see in the next sections.

## Communicating Uncertainty

Because good forecasts can go wrong, there is little point in forecasters providing absolute statements about the forecast, what meteorologists refer to as *deterministic forecasts* (e.g., "The high temperature tomorrow will be 25°C."). Instead, forecasts should express not only the uncertainty due to the output from the computer forecast models, but also the uncertainty due to the human forecaster's confidence in the forecast (National Research Council 2006). One example is *probabilistic forecasts* (e.g., "a forty percent chance of rain tomorrow"). Yet, as described by Jodie Peachey et al. (2013), there are at least two reasons why adoption of probabilistic forecasts has been limited. The first is a view by reluctant meteorologists that the public misunderstands or misinterprets probabilistic forecasts. The second is the possible negative feedback from the public. For example, the Plain English Campaign awarded the UK Met Office a Golden Bull award for one of 2011's "'best' examples of gobbledygook." The award citation read, "for empowering people to make their own decisions by using the technical systems for the probabilities of precipitation" (Plain English Campaign 2012).

These concerns need to be addressed. Evidence suggests that the public does reasonably well in understanding probabilistic forecasts (e.g., Peachey et al. 2013; and references within), although further education would improve the situation. Thus, meteorologists need to accept that all weather forecasts are uncertain and communicating that uncertainty really does empower individuals to make smarter decisions for themselves. Yet, there are many ways to communicate uncertainty information in forecasts. What follows is a short list of the ways that meteorologists are using uncertainty information in producing and communicating forecasts.

## Ensemble Forecasts as a Means to Communicate Uncertainty

*Ensemble forecasting* is a way to address the issue of uncertainty head-on by acknowledging the difficulty of producing a deterministic forecast (e.g., Callado et al. 2012). Rather than starting with one initial condition and using a single model, ensemble forecasting embraces chaos as an inherent part of its DNA. An ensemble is a collection of forecasts using (1) a variety of different (but plausible) initial conditions, (2) a variety of different model configurations, or (3) both. Because each forecast will evolve slightly differently, a range of possible outcomes can be created.

One of the first ways that the uncertainty from ensemble forecasts was displayed was through *postage-stamp plots* (figure 1). These show the individual outcomes of each of the forecasts after a certain fixed time. In the case of figure 1, fifty-two different forecasts are displayed. Fifty of these forecasts are produced by running a forecast model from slightly different initial conditions. Two deterministic runs are also included. The resulting fifty-two forecasts at seventy-two hours are then presented in snapshots (called postage stamps for their smallness and similar shape). Although all members of the ensemble have a low-pressure center over northern Scandinavia, the intensity of the low varies from member to member. Although quite effective at showing all the possibilities in the ensemble, such a diagram is difficult to interpret. Cluster analysis can be employed to identify the most common evolutions and any members that may produce especially extreme weather.

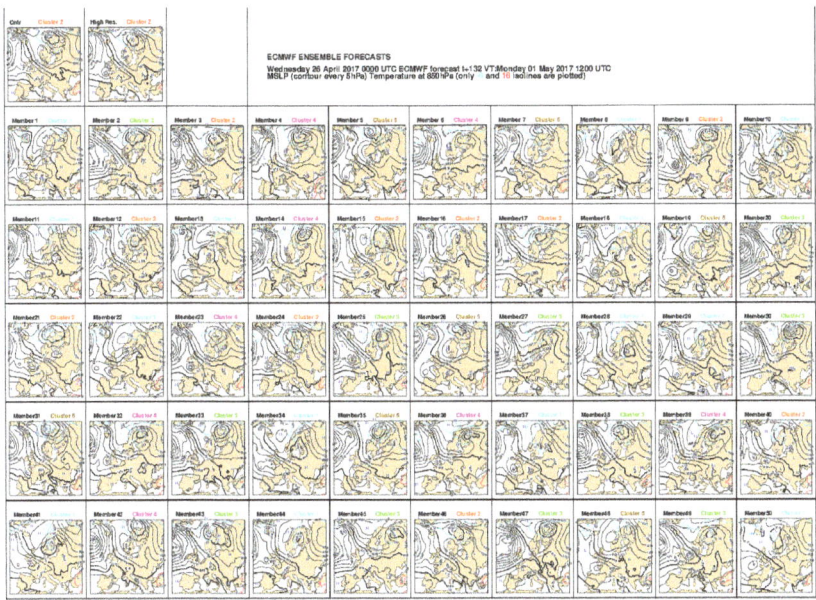

Figure 1. Postage stamp plots of sea-level pressure (contoured every 5 hPa) from a seventy-two-hour forecast from the European Centre for Medium-Range Weather Forecasts (Figure courtesy of ECMWF).

*Spaghetti plots* take one or more contours on a map and plot them from all members (figure 2). Contour lines being close together indicates more certainty in the forecast than lines farther apart. Figure 3 shows two contours of the height of the 500-hPa surface over central and eastern North America and the North Atlantic Ocean. These contours indicate the approximate path of the jet stream at 5.5 km above the surface of the Earth. Although spaghetti plots consolidate the information from postage-stamp plots onto a single graphic, the information can be difficult to interpret if too many lines are plotted. For fields with more detail such as precipitation, spaghetti plots would be too messy to interpret.

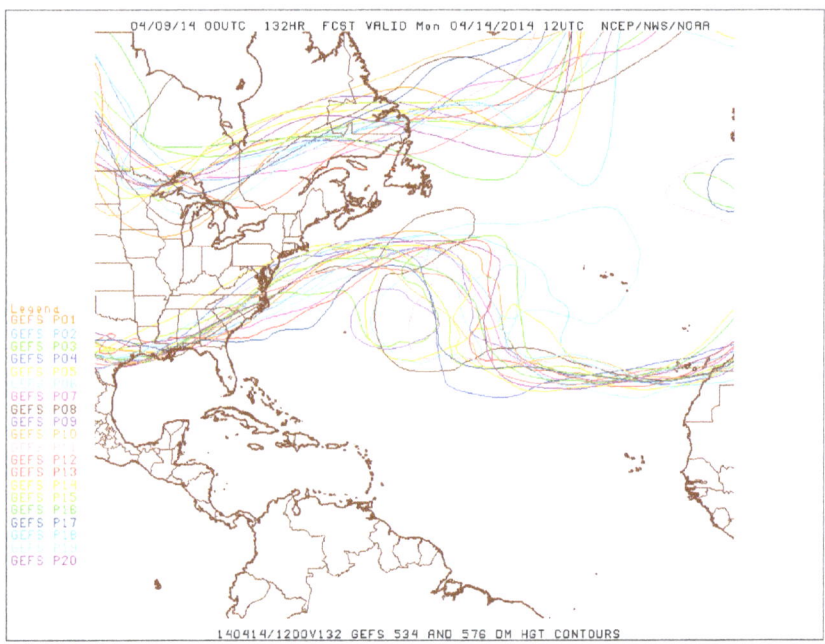

Figure 2. Spaghetti plot of two contours of the 500-hPa surface (534 and 576 dam) from the US Global Ensemble Forecast System (http://mag.ncep.noaa.gov/model-guidance-model-area.php).

To make postage-stamp and spaghetti plots more amenable to quantification, fields of probabilities can be constructed. For example, an experimental product that the UK Met Office produced during the 2012 Summer Olympic Games was derived from their ensemble system (figure 3). This graphic represents probabilities plotted directly from the model output (i.e., if three out of ten ensemble members predicted rain, then the probability would be thirty percent). At this time, the Met Office ensemble system is not being used to provide public forecasts in this graphical format, although probabilities can be found for a specific location at a specific time elsewhere on their website.

*Communicating the Uncertainty in Weather Forecasts* 105

19/09/12 13:00 — 20/09/12 07:00 BST

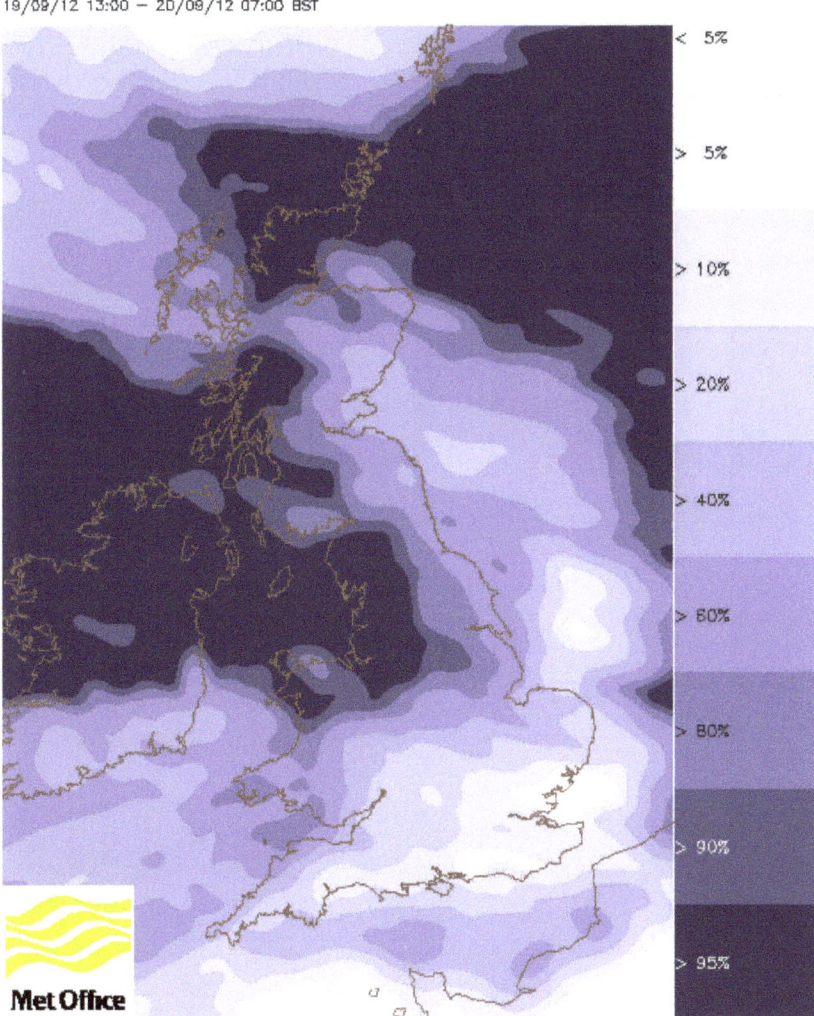

Figure 3. UK Met Office experimental forecast product during the 2012 Summer Olympic Games. Shaded are the probabilities that rain (>0.2 mm h$^{-1}$) will fall sometime within an eighteen-hour period (Crown copyright).

*Box-and-whisker plots* are another way that the uncertainty can be displayed, this time at a single point over the duration of the ensemble forecast (figure 4). In the case of figure 4, output from the ECMWF ensemble is used to calculate statistics on the distribution of cloud cover, precipitation, surface wind speed and surface temperature. Consider the temperature forecast, which shows that the range of forecast temperatures is within a few degrees until about five days into the forecast when the range jumps to about seven degrees Celsius. The range is a measure of uncertainty in the forecast, which increases with time. A benefit of box-and-whisker plots is that actual statistical information from a point in time and space can be determined, but a disadvantage is that the presentation of the data can be difficult for a nonspecialist to interpret without some guidance.

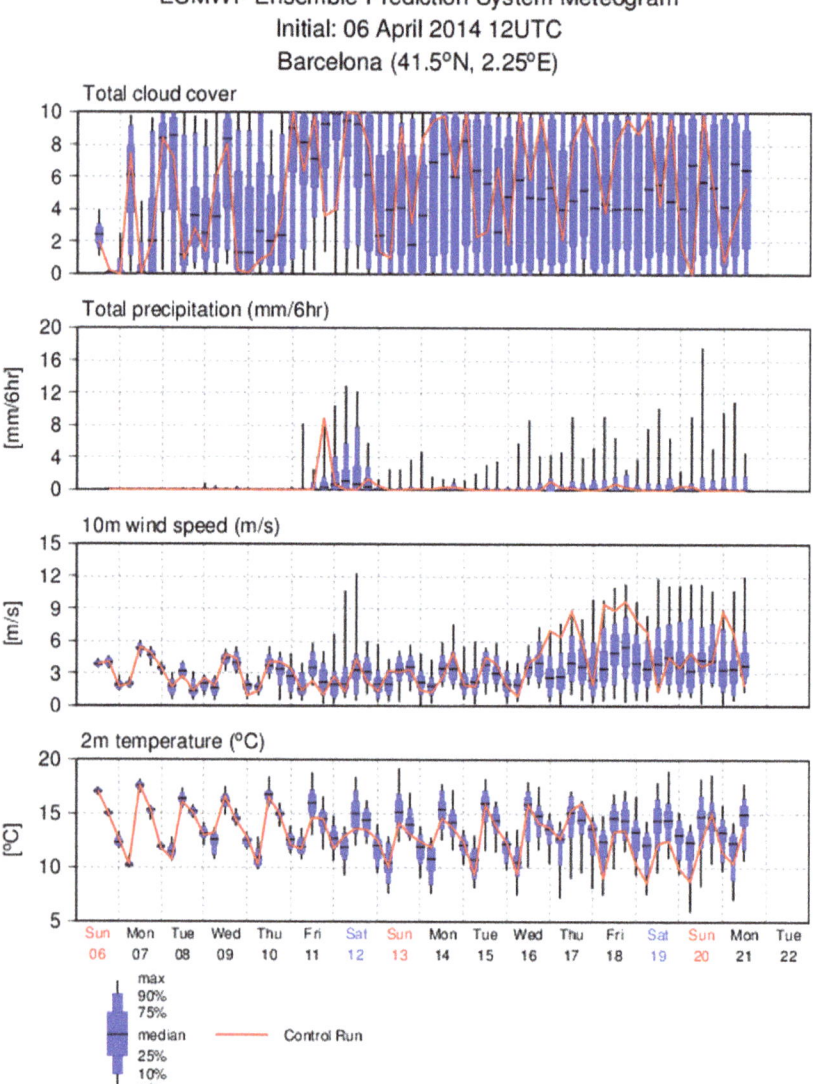

Figure 4. Box-and-whisker plots of cloud cover, precipitation, surface wind speed, and surface temperature in the ECMWF ensemble (figure courtesy of ECMWF).

An approach to communicate the uncertainty in the movement of specific weather phenomena is the *cone of uncertainty*. The US National Hurricane Center introduced the cone of uncertainty in 2002 to express the uncertainty in the movement of tropical cyclones (figure 5). Kenneth Broad et al. (2007) and Michelle Saunders and Jason Senkbeil (2017) argue that misinterpretations of these graphics are common, and they encourage more social science research to improve the effectiveness of such graphics in the future.

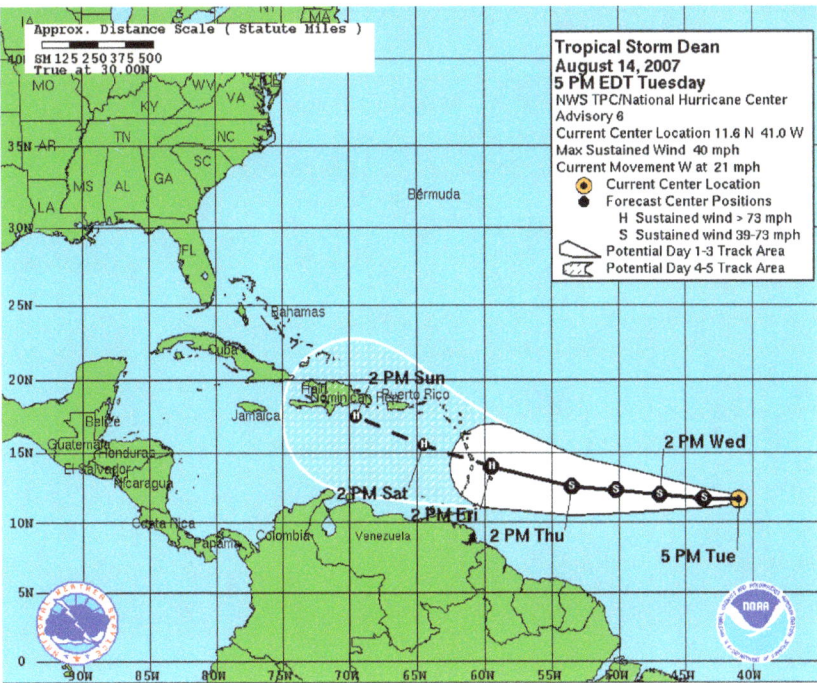

Figure 5. Cone of uncertainty from the US National Hurricane Center for Tropical Storm Dean (http://www.nhc.noaa.gov/aboutcone.shtml).

Finally, a goal of the US National Weather Service is *Warn on Forecast* (Stensrud et al. 2009, 2013; see figure 6). Currently, warnings for severe weather such as thunderstorms or tornadoes are issued once the storms that produce the weather have already formed. To increase the lead-time available to the public to prepare, warnings would have to be created from short-term computer forecasts, a feat that, because of the small scale of convective storms, would require exceptionally accurate initial conditions from which to create an ensemble. Should such efforts succeed, then probabilistic forecasts of tornado occurrence, damaging hail, lightning, or flooding rains could become a reality. Yet, how the public reacts when they have one to two hours of lead time for forecasts of such severe weather events is unclear (Hoekstra et al. 2011). Thus, much more work is needed on the human dimension and effective communication of forecasts in such time-sensitive weather situations.

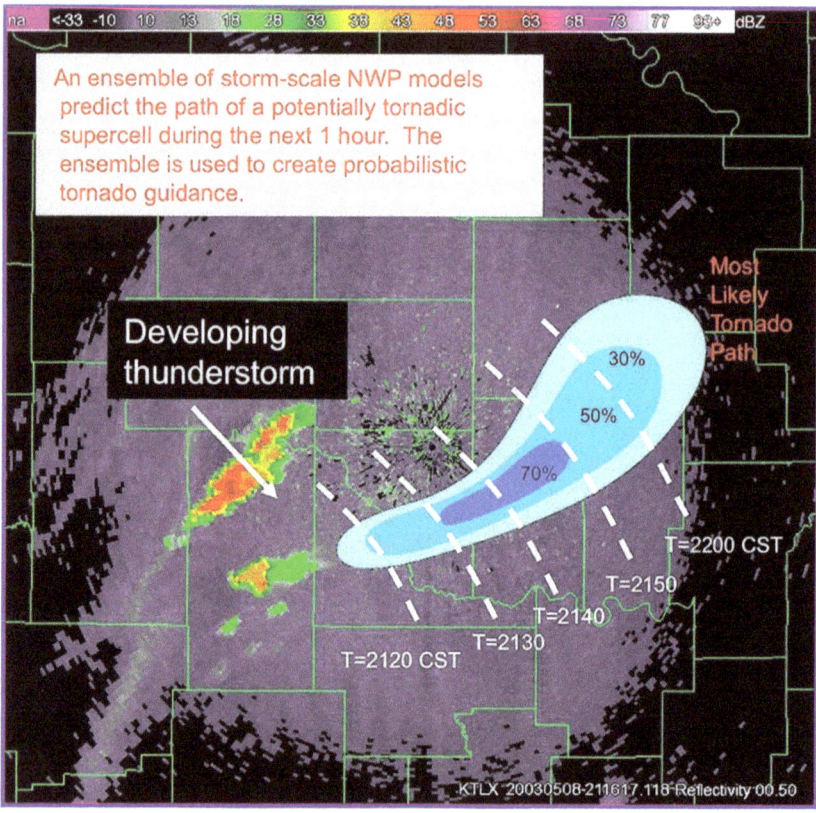

Figure 6. The *Warn on Forecast* concept from the U.S. National Weather Service (http://www.nssl.noaa.gov/tools/forecast).

## Communicating Weather Forecasts Online

My PhD advisor Lance Bosart often said that we meteorologists know more than we tell the public. Twenty years ago when only two- and three-day weather forecasts were reliable, the forecast could be easily communicated via written text (e.g., in newspapers). Now that forecasts are often communicated out to five to ten days and more precision is possible (i.e., postcode forecasting), text is largely inadequate to convey daily information in a concise way. So, providers of weather forecasts use icons to communicate the forecast (figure 7).

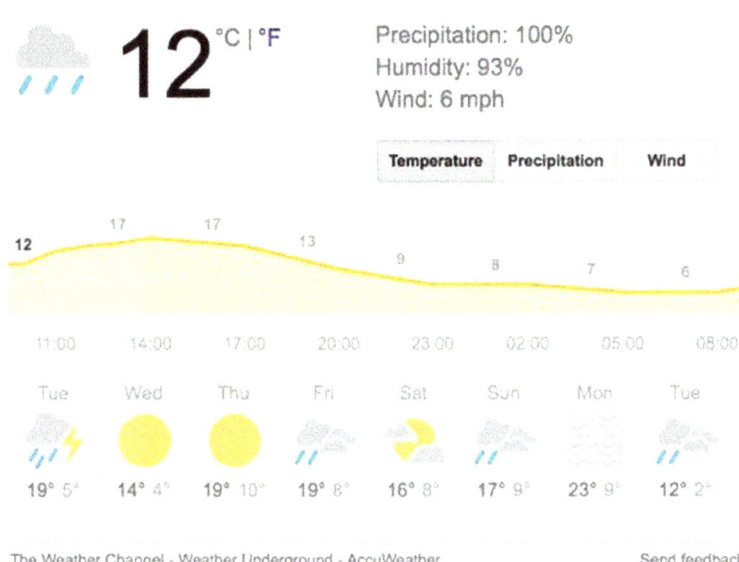

Figure 7. An example of weather icons from Google.

These icons have the benefit of communicating a lot of information in a concise format, but they have three problems:

1. Icons are not precise nor detailed representations of weather. If Saturday's forecast were represented by a cloud with two raindrops, does that mean it will rain all day? Or will the rain represent the worst possible weather for the day? How can the complexity of the weather within an individual day be represented within a single icon?
2. These icons often do not express uncertainty of the forecasts, leaving readers with a false sense of confidence in the forecasts.
3. Readers are left with the impression that the value of the forecasts are all the same (i.e., a five-day forecast is as accurate as a one-day forecast).

What is needed are some professionals outside of meteorology to work with meteorologists to produce better ways to communicate a detailed forecast concisely and accurately to the public. Whether they are psychologists or graphic designers, their input is needed to improve this situation.

## What Is an Effective Weather Forecast? The Example of Hurricane Katrina

Even if all these issues with producing and communicating the best forecast are addressed, there is still the recipient of the forecast to account for. Charles A. Doswell III (2005) has argued that effective weather forecasts go beyond creating the most accurate prediction. To be effective, users of weather forecasts must also receive it, understand it and its implications, know what actions to take based on the forecast, and then take the appropriate action. Thus, the entire chain must be operating to achieve maximum impact.

Hurricane Katrina was an example where the threat to New Orleans had been well known for years. The forecasts were eerily accurate and adamantly clear, yet more than 1800 people died because they failed to receive the warnings, believe them, or—even after hearing the forecasts—failed to take the appropriate action and evacuate. Specifically, the National Hurricane Center issued a hurricane watch for New Orleans two days before landfall. Twenty hours before landfall, the National Weather Service issued a forecast that included the following language:

> . . . Devastating damage expected . . .
>
> Hurricane Katrina . . . a most powerful hurricane with unprecedented strength . . . rivaling the intensity of hurricane Camille of 1969.
>
> Most of the area will be uninhabitable for weeks . . . perhaps longer. At least one half of well constructed homes will have roof and wall failure. [. . .]
>
> Airborne debris will be widespread . . . and may include heavy items such as household appliances and even light vehicles. Sport utility vehicles and light trucks will be moved. The blown debris will create additional destruction. Persons . . . pets . . . and livestock exposed to the winds will face certain death if struck.
>
> Power outages will last for weeks . . .as most power poles will be down and transformers destroyed. Water shortages will make human suffering incredible by modern standards. (National Weather Service 2005)

This forecast was unprecedented in the history of the National Weather Service because it not only conveyed the weather that would occur as in their everyday forecast, but because it conveyed the dismal situation that would occur.

Yet, the deaths from Katrina were largely preventable. A Bipartisan Select Committee of the United States Congress investigating the preparation and response to Katrina concluded,

> Many of the problems we have identified can be categorized as "information gaps"—or at least problems with information-related implications, or failures to act decisively because information was sketchy at best. Better information would have been an optimal weapon against Katrina. Information sent to the right people at the right place at the right time. Information moved within agencies, across departments, and between jurisdictions of government as well. Seamlessly. Securely. Efficiently. (Select Bipartisan Committee to Investigate the Preparation for and Response to Hurricane Katrina 2006)

Specifically, state and local officials delayed issuing mandatory evacuation warnings until nineteen hours before landfall, despite receiving warnings fifty-six hours before landfall. The President received inadequate advice from a senior disaster official, with the federal government failing to be proactive. State and federal government resources were ill-prepared and failed to implement existing protocols. In hindsight, many of the problems were associated with communication and the lack of it. Again, accurate forecasts are no good if they are not received, understood, and acted upon (Schmidlin 2006).

## Conclusion

Frank Herbert in the *Heretics of Dune* wrote, "People generally prefer the predictable. Few recognize how destructive this can be, how it imposes severe limits on variability and thus makes whole populations fatally vulnerable to the shocking ways our universe can throw the dice." The backlash by the Plain English Campaign against the introduction of probabilistic forecasts in the UK supports Herbert's point. What is needed is a public education campaign to show the benefits of using probabilistic forecasts, a more sensible way to communicate the uncertainty within weather forecasts, and the help of social scientists to craft concise but accurate representations of the forecast. Such collaborations could result in accurately painting the uncertainty in weather forecasts and could help the public to see not only their limitations, but the tremendous value that such added information content provides.

Beyond the specific aspects of uncertainty and its communication, there is a range of opportunities for meteorologists to collaborate with communication experts from other fields. For specific graphics in communicating uncertainty, what are the best graphics to use when communicating with the public? In the case of Katrina, there are the issues of how those in leadership roles make decisions in a crisis and communicate those decisions. Even when those who receive the orders for evacuation (albeit at a late stage before hurricane landfall) don't respond, we need to understand why. What ways can information be communicated to ensure action is taken? As a popular sign at the recent March for Science read, "At the start of every disaster movie, there's a scientist being ignored." Perhaps it's not the scientist, but the message that is being ignored.

## Acknowledgments

This work is partially funded by the UK Natural Environment Research Council through grants Diabatic Influences on Mesoscale Structures in Extratropical Storms (DIAMET, NE/I005234/1), Precipitation Structures over Orography (PRESTO, NE/I024984-1), Tropopause Folding, Stratospheric Intrusions and Deep Convection (TROSIAD, NE/H008225/1), and The Environments of Convective Storms: Challenging Conventional Wisdom (NE/N003918/1), the Risk Prediction Initiative of the Bermuda Institute of Ocean Sciences through grant RPI2.0-2016-SCHULTZ, as well as grants from the Geography, Earth, and Environmental Sciences Subject Centre of the Higher Education Academy.

## Works Cited

Abbe, Cleveland. 1901. "The Physical Basis of Long-range Weather Forecasts." *Monthly Weather Review* 29 (12): 551–61.

Bjerknes, Vilhelm. 1904. "Das Problem der Wettervorhersage, betrachtet vom Standpunkte der Mechanik und der Physik." *Meteorologische Zeitschrift* 21:1–7.

—. (1904) 1999. "The problem with weather forecasting as a problem in mechanics and physics." In *The Life Cycles of Extratropical Cyclones.*, edited by Melvyn A. Shapiro and Sigbjørn Grønås. Boston, Mass.: American Meteorological Society, 1–4. Orig. German version first published in 1904 (see above).

Broad, Kenneth, Anthony Leiserowitz, Jessica Weinkle, and Marissa Steketee. 2007. "Misinterpretations of the 'Cone of Uncertainty' in Florida during the

2004 Hurricane Season." *Bulletin of the American Meteorological Society* 88 (5), 651–67.
Callado, Alfons, Pau Escribà, José A. García-Moya, Jesús Montero, Carlos Santos, Daniel Santos-Muñoz and Juan Simarro. 2012. "Ensemble forecasting." In *Climate Change and Regional/Local Responses*, edited by Yuan zhi Zhang and Pallav Ray. DOI: 10.5772/55699, https://www.intechopen.com/books/climate-change-and-regional-local-responses/ensemble-forecasting.
Doswell, Charles A. III. 2005. "Progress toward Developing a Practical Societal Response to Severe Convection (2005 EGU Sergei Soloviev Medal Lecture)." *Natural Hazards and Earth System Sciences* 5 (5): 691–702.
Harper, Kristine C. 2012. *Weather by the Numbers: The Genesis of Modern Meteorology*. Cambridge: MIT Press.
Hoekstra, Stephanie, Kimberly E. Klockow, Rachel Riley, Jerald A. Brotzge, Harold E. Brooks, and Somer A. Erickson. 2011. "A Preliminary Look at the Social Perspective of Warn-on-Forecast: Preferred Tornado Warning Lead Time and the General Public's Perceptions of Weather Risks." *Weather, Climate, and Society* 3 (2): 128–40.
Lorenz, Edward N. 1963. "Deterministic Nonperiodic Flow." *Journal of the Atmospheric Sciences* 20 (2): 130–41.
Lorenz, Edward N. 1998. *The Essence of Chaos*. Seattle: University of Washington Press.
Lynch, Peter. 2006. *The Emergence of Numerical Weather Prediction: Richardson's Dream*. Cambridge: Cambridge University Press.
National Research Council. 2006. *Completing the Forecast: Characterizing and Communicating Uncertainty for Better Decisions Using Weather and Climate Forecasts*. Washington, DC: National Academies Press.
National Weather Service. 2005. "Urgent—Weather Message." Issued August 28. Archived at https://web.archive.org/web/20080120002429/http://www.srh.noaa.gov/data/warn_archive/LIX/NPW/0828_155101.txt.
Peachey, Jodie A., David M. Schultz, Rebecca E. Morss, Paul J. Roebber, and Robert Wood. 2013. "How Forecasts Expressing Uncertainty are Perceived by UK Students." *Weather* 68 (7): 176–81.
Plain English Campaign. 2012. "Golden Bull awards 2011." http://www.plainenglish.co.uk/campaigning/awards/2011-awards/golden-bull-awards.html. Accessed February 2, 2022.
Richardson, Lewis Fry. 1922. *Weather Prediction by Numerical Process*. Cambridge: Cambridge University Press.
Sanders, Frederick. 1986. "Explosive Cyclogenesis over the West-Central North Atlantic Ocean, 1981–1984. Part II. Evaluation of LFM Model Performance." *Monthly Weather Review* 114 (11): 2207–18.
Saunders, Michelle E., and Jason C. Senkbeil. 2017. "Perceptions of Hurricane Hazards in the Mid-Atlantic Region." *Meteorological Applications* 24 (1): 120–34.
Schmidlin, Thomas W. 2006. "On Evacuation and Deaths from Hurricane Katrina." *Bulletin of the American Meteorological Society* 87 (6): 754–56.

Select Bipartisan Committee to Investigate the Preparation for and Response to Hurricane Katrina. 2006. *A Failure of Initiative*. Washington, DC: US Government Printing Office.

Silver, Nate. 2012. *The Signal and the Noise: Why So Many Predictions Fail—But Some Don't*. New York: Penguin.

Stensrud, David J. 2009. *Parameterization Schemes: Keys to Understanding Numerical Weather Prediction Models*. Cambridge: Cambridge University Press.

Stensrud, David J., Louis J. Wicker, Kevin E. Kelleher, Ming Xue, Michael P. Foster, Joseph T. Schaefer, Russell S. Schneider, Stanley G. Benjamin, Stephen S. Weygandt, John T. Ferree, and Jason P. Tuell. 2009. "Convective-Scale Warn-on-Forecast System." *Bulletin of the American Meteorological Society* 90 (10): 1487–99.

Stensrud, David J., Louis J. Wicker, Ming Xue, Daniel T. Dawson, Nusrat Yussouf, Dustan M. Wheatley, Therese E. Thompson, Nathan A. Snook, Travis M. Smith, Alexander D. Schenkman, Corey K. Potvin, Edward R. Mansell, Ting Lei, Kristin M. Kuhlman, Youngsun Jung, Thomas A. Jones, Jidong Gao, Michael C. Coniglio, Harold E. Brooks, Keith A. Brewster. 2013. "Progress and challenges with Warn-on-Forecast." *Atmospheric Research* 123:2–16.

# 7 THE COMMUNICATIVE CONSTRUCTION OF EVIDENCE: PRESENTATIONAL KNOWLEDGE IN COMPUTATIONAL NEUROSCIENCE

*Hubert Knoblauch, Eric Lettkemann, and René Wilke*

## INTRODUCTION

Calling for evidence is not only a basic demand made of (and in) science, it is also a demand made by our courts. Of course, it is commonly known that in the law, evidence takes a different form than it does in science.[1] While this observation is known in the study of rhetoric, it is also one that is systematically investigated in the sociology of knowledge. Non-sociologists may readily assume scientific knowledge differs from jurisprudential knowledge and therefore find it plausible to assume evidence in these two realms differs as well. But is this due to different forms of knowledge? Would one have to then assume there are different forms of evidence in other social realms, such as in politics or in the market?

The philosopher Edmund Husserl, who influenced our contemporary notions of what evidence is, argued strongly against such a view. To him, a sentence that was thought or expressed had a meaning corresponding to the perception of the senses. So, if I say, "that house is green," and I perceive a green house in front of me, then I have the correspondence Husserl called evidence. While this sounds similar to the logical positivist argument that scientific truth is established through *Beobachtungssätze* (observational statements) about empirical perceptions (Carnap [1928] 1998), Husserl's notion of evidence is far more radical. To him, scientific evidence is not grounded, as it were, in itself but instead has a pre-scientific basis in the *Lebenswelt* (the lifeworld) (Husserl 1977, 111). This idea of the lifeworld was subsequently adopted and adapted in the sociology of knowledge, most prominently by Alfred Schütz, Peter Berger, and Thomas

Luckmann. In their view, knowledge, much like evidence, was based on a person's reflective consciousness, which meant individuals could turn to their experience *as* experience: "The man in the street . . . 'knows,' with different degrees of confidence, that this world possesses such and such characteristics" (Berger and Luckmann [1966] 1991, 13).

From the sociological point of view, however, knowledge by definition is not confined to the individual but is "socially constructed," as Berger and Luckmann put it in their by now classic 1966 work. As they showed, it is not just worldviews; ideologies; or the higher forms of knowledge in the visual arts, music, or literature (together with their imaginary components) that are social. Much more fundamental categories of thought, perception, and corporeality are also socially constructed, including syllogisms, conceptions of linear time, or binary gender identity and sexuality. These are the kinds of things the sociology of knowledge focuses on.

Berger and Luckmann's thesis also led to debates about the extent of this social construction (Knoblauch and Wilke 2016). For example, radical social constructionists feel everything can be constructed. Recently, the new realists have opposed this view. But actually, Berger and Luckmann themselves already argued that social construction is based on objectivations that could not be ignored because they give shape to the "objective reality."

Wherever one finds oneself in this debate, it directly touches on the question of evidence. For evidence cannot be embedded, as it were, in the perceptions or experiences of an individual untouched by society or culture. Rather, our subjective knowledge is more or less completely transmitted from an already constructed society. The thesis here is of a sociality of evidence, of evidence embedded in society and social structure.

This thesis has not only to do with the origin or sources of evidence, but thanks to the study of rhetoric, the idea of the sociality of knowledge can also be applied to the evidence that experience provides us with. In fact, rhetoric assumes evidence follows certain fixed forms,[2] and its core interest lies in examining the form communicative acts take between humans. In that sense, the interests of rhetoric overlap with a second aspect of the sociality of knowledge, or evidence, that the sociology of knowledge investigates, namely the construction of evidence in the context of social conduct. Against the backdrop of the contemporary debate about constructivism, one should note that such constructs must in essence occur communicatively. Regardless of whether one assumes human experience transcends culture (because one believes it is based on nature, or on body physiology, or on mental capacity) or assumes it is decisively socio-culturally shaped or even determined, the evidence in any case must be communicated to others—and that includes meaningful and sensory references to what is supposed to be evident (Knoblauch 2014).

The assumption that processes of social construction make empirical reference to communicative action is also called communicative construction (see Knoblauch 2011; 2020). In important ways, this overlaps with theories of communication and of communicative action in the study of rhetoric (see Knoblauch 2000). Yet, the scope of sociological investigation is considerably broader; rhetoric confines itself to situations in which at least one of the actors communicating intends to persuade or convince. By contrast, the sociology of knowledge understands communicative construction as applying to all situations. In fact, it goes further by starting from a hypothesis that though not all forms of experience are socially shaped, all forms of action are. Even action in isolation from others is regarded as derived from social action—which seems confirmed by conversations one has with oneself or when one seeks support for what one has seen (see Mead 1967).

Aside from the fact that communicative action is not confined to rhetorical situations, it also is not limited to verbal acts, though in its interest in "visual rhetoric" (see, e.g., Hope 2006), the study of rhetoric has increasingly taken that which is not verbalized into account. Communicative action also includes objectivation, which can include signaling, such as pointing gestures made to, or diagrams on, PowerPoint slides (see Knoblauch 2008), or it can involve objects such as a hammer, or houses, or dogs. Much like embodiment, signals and objects are something like the materialization of meaning (Wilke and Hill 2019).

In science, these materializations play an important role. Other than in mathematics and in logic, the sciences—and even literature or art—are always concerned with objects that possess constitutive materiality. It is this materiality that forms the basis of the kind of evidence both Husserl and Rudolf Carnap meant (see Carnap [1928] 1998).

Such evidence is transmitted in a dual manner. On the one hand, it is transformed in a manner referred to as representations. Whether it is samples prepared in a laboratory, objects collected at an archeological dig, illustrations of neurons, or statistical curves, in each case, evidence is generated in a discipline-specific manner. This is seen in a particularly striking manner in Computational Neuroscience (henceforth: CNS), our case study, a field that generates computer models and computer simulations inspired by processes in the nervous system. On the other hand, the processes themselves are already (*re-*)*presentations* generated by the researchers (more on this below), but researchers also *present* the objects of study verbally and visually to make them understandable. In each case, as we wish to demonstrate, evidence is a form of communication.

In the following empirical section, we provide examples of the form evidence takes in communicating science in CNS. Science communication, in the sense of communicative construction, is not just an abstract term that involves the transfer of knowledge, using a simple sender-and-receiver model. Nor does it resemble products of the media labelled as communicating science. Rather, our interest is in the performative processes (in real time and embodied) in actually communicating science, specifically in the form of the argument used. Argument provides the framework, but not in the sense of a monologue; here, disagreement plays a key role in generating evidence, and by it we mean the cooperative collaboration of actors. In communicative sequences of successive speech acts (called expansion) as in a lecture or talk, disagreement triggers an argumentative episode. It is in this argumentative episode, in which something is stated as a justification, that one finds what one can call a piece of evidence. In the sequential order of an argument, evidence is that which closes out the rhetorical sequence, in a manner similar to the punchline of a joke that similarly ends it (see Luckmann 1995).

In addition to the structural role it plays in argument, evidence of course also has content. The first aspect of this is the medium, the materials, and, in the case we examine here, the visual aspects used to transmit what is to be made evident. It also concerns the level of knowledge of the participants: in our case study, this is quite varied. Though we can treat the complex structure of knowledge among participants only in passing, it should be clear that evidence takes a particular communicative form that must not only be generated by the actors but whose form also must be recognized as such. Second, the evidence is characterized by the objectification of something that can be detected before the (quite different) background of knowledge as common. The generation of commonality is carried out by the participating actors through the use of communicative forms which do not just represent knowledge but that, through organized cooperation, generate *presentational knowledge*.

Before we address the institutional context and historical development of CNS, we would like to first briefly discuss the peculiarities of scientific knowledge as well as be more specific about presentational knowledge. Then we give an example of what we regard as typical for the generation of evidence in CNS. In the conclusion, we place our findings within the broader theoretical context.

## Presentational and Representational Knowledge

While the sociality of knowledge is a classic sociological topic, it has only been since the 1930s that research has focused specifically, if gradually, on scientific knowledge (for an overview, see Knoblauch 2010, 234–56). Since the 1970s, the investigation of the social construction of scientific knowledge has broadened out to become the field of Science and Technology Studies (henceforth: STS).

STS brings together sociologists, historians, philosophers, and representatives from other fields, often in the cross-disciplinary context of STS institutes, STS conferences, and STS publications. It shares the assumption common among sociologists of knowledge that scientific research and technological development are at heart social processes, and hence accessible to the kinds of methods used in the humanities and social sciences (for an overview, see Hackett et al. 2008). Inspired by the work of Ludwik Fleck and Thomas Kuhn on the communal structures employed in research, STS regards "thought collectives" or "epistemic (knowledge) cultures" as its central unit of investigation (Knorr-Cetina 1999). An important characteristic of these units, in their communicative contexts, is their focus on their own objects of knowledge and the claim that they themselves have the power to interpret these objects (see Rheinberger 1997). Such objects of knowledge can be treated "objectively" through language, through formal systems of signs as in mathematics, or through other means: as a rule, these are referred to as representations.[3]

Representations can, for example, be natural objects that have been worked on in the laboratory and transformed into signs, and in this manner made communicable between the members of an epistemic community (see Amann 1994). But representation can also be analog or digital images generated in other ways, as in the illustrations used in science talks that we present here (see the contributions in Lynch and Woolgar 1990 and Coopmans et al. 2014).

For the communication of science, representation, as the objectivation of a methodologically controlled generation of knowledge, is a key form of evidence. Particularly in those sciences with a positivistic orientation, this kind of evidence is regarded as transcending cultures and in principle as capable of being universal and therefore also objective. Lorraine Daston and Peter Galison, by contrast, have shown how this notion of objectivity in the natural sciences has changed over the course of the last three centuries.

Following Daston and Galison (2007), we can distinguish between three epochs in which differing visual and representational orders dominated. Each order was characterized by specific criteria for evidence, or, as the authors call it, different "epistemic virtues" (39). In the early modern period, through the selection and synthesis of natural exemplars that were recorded in ideal-typical drawings, erudite savants defined "truth to nature" (55–113). The skepticism of the Enlightenment soon rose up against the epistemic authority of these learned men, and by the nineteenth century, this order was increasingly pushed to the margins by the rising "virtue" of a kind of "mechanical objectivity" (115–90). The new virtue demanded of scientists was that they rely on automated instruments for their observations of nature to systematically exclude their own subjective selves from the observations. Yet, doubts and unease soon emerged whether photographs or other recording instruments were depicting nature in a genuinely undistorted manner. The "trained judgment" (309–61) became increasingly regarded as a virtue in the twentieth century, which facilitated people's ability to recognize artifacts being produced by the recording instruments or to recognize recurrent patterns in images. Here, experts might use color to highlight individual details on an image or add markings, enhancing and commenting on their instrument-generated recordings based on their theoretical knowledge and technical experience.[4]

Daston and Galison (2007) show how the notions of objectivity, and hence also the criteria for evidence, have shifted both historically and socially. However, it should be kept in mind that earlier criteria for evidence may persist in one epistemic culture even as they have already changed in another. What is regarded as evident, and how evidence itself is generated, therefore strongly depends on the knowledge culture in a given area of research (see Engelen et al. 2010).

At the end of their treatise, Daston and Galison (2007) note a very recent shift—one of considerable importance for our own investigation—in some sciences to a form of objectivation of knowledge for which the term representation is no longer appropriate. Rather than providing exemplars from the real world, simulations, in particular, create a new class or type of virtual knowledge objects. As a result, Daston and Galison speak of presentations rather than of representations. *Presentational knowledge*, then, is no longer oriented towards depicting the epistemic object. Instead, presentations display knowledge much more in a manner of allowing it to be *used* by others: "image-as-evidence" becomes "image-as-tool" (see Daston and Galison 2007, 363–415).

## THE EMPIRICAL FIELD OF COMPUTATIONAL NEUROSCIENCE

The term *computational neuroscience* was first used in 1985 at a conference organized by Eric L. Schwartz in Carmel, California, designed to bring those interested in the theory of brain function together with computer scientists. This is a research area in which simulation and models even today play a key role in creating common points of reference between various knowledge cultures. For our own investigation, in fact, it is relevant that the knowledge order remains fuzzy in this area of research. Indeed, one of our research questions about the communication of science (which we cannot pursue at appropriate length here) is whether CNS has developed a largely independent, if hybridized, research culture by now or whether it only has a kind of "trading zone" (see Galison 1996) in which the representatives of heterogeneous research cultures exchange bits and pieces of knowledge.[5]

The digital revolution of the 1980s was one technical precondition for this new field—for, at the time, computers were only beginning to be introduced on a large scale for laboratory work. One early self-description of CNS noted that:

> [T]echnical achievements in designing fast, powerful, and relatively inexpensive computing machines have made it possible to undertake simulation and modeling projects that were hitherto only pipe dreams. (Churchland, Koch, and Sejnowski 1993, 47)

Since the 1980s, CNS has dreamt of realizing two complementary goals. The first is to better understand the neurobiological foundations of the brain with the help of computer analogies. The translation of the insights into the brain back into simulation imagery makes this analogizing interesting for the clinical users of neurobiological knowledge, as well as for neurobiologists themselves. The second goal CNS researchers are pursuing is to reconstruct the performance of the brain in machines. In that sense, CNS is a branch of artificial intelligence research, though one inspired by neurobiology.[6] As a result, CNS is internally differentiated along two axes, with researchers oriented to a greater or lesser extent to one of these two goals.

Interestingly, neither approach is concerned with depicting, or *re*-presenting, actually existing brains in simulations. Instead, *presentational knowledge* is in the foreground, meaning aspects of technical efficiency as well as the possibilities for the experimental use of simulations. Even the interest of experimenters, whether clinical or neurobiological, in computer analogies stems more from a desire to learn from the differences between idealized simulation images and laboratory objects. In other words, the simulation images used in CNS are exemplars of the kind of presentational knowledge Lorraine Daston and Peter Galison described.

While Daston and Galison were only able to reconstruct practices derived from this knowledge based on historical documents, we investigate communicative action *in situ*. Our empirical object of research is the actual manner in which presentational knowledge is demonstrated in CNS. To investigate this, we carried out a focused ethnography (Knoblauch 2005) in CNS, some of whose results we present now.[7]

## The Evidence Episode During the Group Talk

Knowledge production in CNS is not only highly interdisciplinary but it is also very individualized. Researchers mostly work on their own, at their own computers, on data, programs and visualizations.[8] Precisely because the production of knowledge takes place in such comparative isolation, the occasions when members of a CNS research group discuss their work take on a particular significance. It is thus not surprising that a particular kind of scientific discourse (see Günthner and Knoblauch 2007), the group talk (Wilke 2022), has established. While it is yet unclear how distinctive this kind of discourse is for this field, it is nevertheless clearly one of the central intersections at which representatives of the various knowledge cultures meet. The particular case we examine is a weekly meeting of a CNS working group that doctoral students, post-docs and professors from physics, biology, computer science, and psychology attend.

As a rule, a group talk is a contribution to a scientific colloquium where various members of the research group (and occasionally outside guests) present the preliminary results of their work and their thinking about it. The talk itself is always a PowerPoint[9] presentation, a strongly visualized form. The term *lecture* is not appropriate, since what is special about these group talks is their decidedly argumentative and dialogic character. Comments, questions, and interjections from the audience are explicitly called for, and structure the talk in a dialogic manner that no longer corresponds to the notion one has of a typical—and monologue-like—lecture.[10]

The talks we will discuss in the following analysis were given in a small seminar room at a German university department where the research group has its home. The seating arrangement corresponds to that of classical frontal instruction, with the speaker facing the audience. The wall of the room is at his back, serving as the surface to project his PowerPoint slides onto (on the spatial, temporal, and technical framing of PowerPoint presentations, see Knoblauch 2013). The audience of about twenty researchers sits in three rows at typical seminar room tables, and as many are not German, the group talk takes place in English. The participants come from Asia, South America, and Europe, but no one is a native English speaker. We have selected certain segments of a typical event to investigate more closely specific argumentative episodes, transcribing them (see below) from the videotape we made.[11]

The speaker in the sequences we analyzed is a computer scientist who concerns himself with a particular problem in artificial intelligence research. Hereinafter, we call him Axel. As the result of his long-lasting research, he created new algorithms on his own. His aim during the group talk is to make the algorithms evident as efficiently capable to solve particular problems of artificial intelligence research. However, during his introduction he has got to handle a further communicative problem, because from the title of his talk alone, it was by no means clear—in this heterogeneous disciplinary context—to everyone listening what exactly the problem is that he was addressing. Axel himself made this clear by his use of analogy right at the beginning, exemplified in the form of two visualizations on his first slide (see figure 1). The analogy to be considered (by the audience) is the technical performance of a computerized traffic monitoring system (represented by the top diagram in figure 1) and the human perceptual capacity in carrying out, or playing, a strategy-oriented computer game (represented by the screenshot of a computer game in figure 1, bottom diagram).

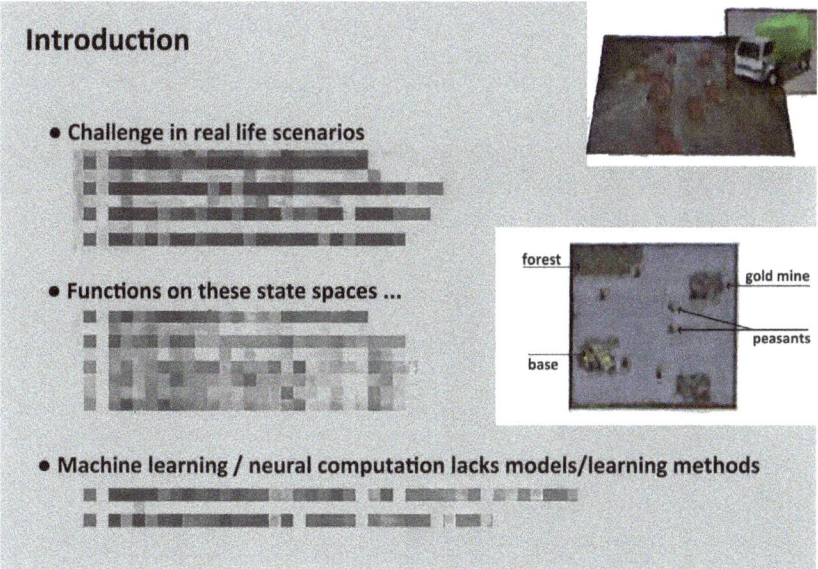

Figure 1. The introductory slide with bullet points (left) and virtual images (right) (for anonymization reasons, text elements have been concealed). Two diagrams can be seen that the lecturer uses to illustrate an analogy: a computerized traffic

monitoring system (above) and a screenshot of a computer game (below) that is a type of simulated economy.

> Axel: just for now, take this as an analogy. i mean, there is <u>no</u> particular knowledge that ((pointing *to the diagram in the upper right corner of figure 1*)) <u>this car here</u> is driven by mister müller. <u>it is just a car</u>, it has some (…) properties like size, speed, lane, whatever, but it's not – it does not have in any way a particular <u>identity</u> that you could recall immediately.

Here Axel describes the basic theoretical considerations underlying the use of his analogy. On the one hand, he regards traffic situations, like computer games, as complex state spaces. On the other hand, in neither case could an individual event, such as a car driving by (figure 1, top diagram) or a virtual computer figure ("peasant") interacting with a human player (figure 1, bottom diagram), have a specific identity. The referring statements (above) lead us to our first example and thereby to the point of disagreement.

## Disagreement

The particular form of the group talk is evident in the fact that one of the listeners (Will)—without any particular ritual prefacing[12]—interjects:

> Will: but they have some number plates.
>
> Ern: ye::ah.

Will's formulation, which is seconded by another member of the audience ("yeah"), is apparently with reference to identifying the individual character of events Axel questioned, since number plates make this possible. This interpretation is also confirmed by Axel who asks a rhetorical question in return:

> Axel: ((a little annoyed)) do you see any license plates here?
>
> Audience: ((general laughter))

That this question is rhetorical can be seen in the fact that Axel only provides an explanation after the general laughter from the audience. With reference to his previously formulated "analogy," this laughter can be seen as a reason given for the lack of difference he claimed:

> Axel: °i take this as an analogy too.° of course, in reality no two cars are the same. but sometimes you can't identify them really quick. and in this case it is actually the case? every peasant here is

exactly the same. i mean, >they follow the same computer code, they use the same pixel representation on screen, they have the same internal statistics.< everything is exactly the same.

As the general laughter accompanying the objection and the rhetorical counter-question subsides, Axel explains that the chosen examples are also "an analogy." With reference to the real-world situation ("in reality") and in the visualization of traffic monitoring (figure 1, top diagram), he admits that there are idealizations ("in reality no two cars are the same"). At the same time, by using the laser pointer on the slide to accompany his words (underlining), he emphasizes the adequacy of the analogy (figure 1, bottom diagram) in that part that refers to human perception in playing computer games: "in this case it is actually the case: every peasant here is exactly the same."

This excerpt shows how a group talk takes place, not as a monologue but in the form of turn-taking (by changing speakers).[13] These changes in who speaks can take the simple form of pair sequences, as in fact occurs immediately after the sequence just described. After Axel describes the statement he has just made in mathematical terms, accompanied by his closing words, he reaches with his hand to his laptop to change slides (figure 2):

Figure 2. The speaker wants to change the slide when he is again asked about his introduction.

>Axel: so these are the kind of functions I like to talk about
>((stops while he is about to change the slide)).

Before he can change his slide, the same colleague (Will) asks Axel a question:

>Will: axel, practically speaking, what do you want to do? do you want to navigate that space?
>[from one thing to the other without bumping into an-

Axel: [°no, i want,° ((turning away from the laptop))

Will: ything?

While the speaker has now heard the end of the question, he walks, shaking his head, to his questioner and tries to explain in the context of a small expansion:

Axel: ((shaking his head and turning to Will)) >i want to learn something very, very basic<. and this is, (.) °i want to do regression, basically.°

One can see that the answer is divided. It contains something very general ("I want to learn something very, very basic.") as well as a very specific formulation. This is, thus, also a formal answer to the particular form in which Will puts the question: a question and the paraphrase of a question, where a specific question follows a very general one (Bergmann 1981). Axel in turn replicates this order such that his second answer ("I want to do regression, basically.") can be understood as an answer to the question: "do you want to navigate that space?" But the sequence is not finished, and instead Will continues by stating:

Will: NO, practically speaking. in eng:::lish.

With his "no," Will makes clear that he is not satisfied by Axel's answer. While he very pragmatically ("practically speaking") wants to know what the procedure Axel suggests can be used for, Axel says that he "basically" wants to do a regression, a standard statistical procedure, to test his model. But Will flags something one needs to stress: his "no" clearly contradicts Axel, and is thus a disagreement.

Even though theories of consensus and of argument often empirically assume that what is the problem or topic in disagreement is obvious, one should not forget that it is a thoroughly interactive phenomenon we are familiar with from everyday communication. This also means that disagreement has a sequential structure, as Jeff Coulter (1990) clearly showed:

First move:             declarative assertion

Second move:       disagreement token/counter-assertion

It is noteworthy that the first assertion need not be a contention; it is more the case that it becomes a claim only once the counter-assertion is made. But even this second move is not enough to establish disagreement; it requires both moves. This shows disagreement to be an interactive phenomenon, which can also be seen in the fact that what the problem is—in classic terms, the *quaestio*—does not simply lie in the assertion made in the second move. Rather, the problem is generated as well by the way the disagreement is formulated.

In our case, this is quite clear, for Will does not only use one disagreement token. Instead, he adds a "practically," which grammatically refers to Axel's "basically" assertion. This not only names the subject of the disagreement, but the choice of these adverbs also points to professional competencies. Axel is a computer scientist, and in the context of the CNS group talk, inhabits the role of the provider of basic scientific knowledge; Will, by contrast, is a biologist interested in the practical application of computer science modelling.

A further characteristic of disagreement is that it leads to consequences and a kind of decoupling. Scott Jacobs and Sally Jackson (1981) speak of a conversational "expansion":

> A: statement
>
> B: disagreement
>
> expansion

What happens after the disagreement can be called an "embedded sequence" (see Goffman 1981; also see note 11). Whatever happened before the disagreement is now interrupted, and a return to the discourse only takes place once the expansion has concluded. Who is responsible for the expansion can be ignored, but to omit an expansion can have serious consequences and is a structural precondition for the transition to an argument or a dispute (see Knoblauch 2009).

This structure is momentous because it provides a guide to comprehension since everything that follows the disagreement is, *ceteris paribus*, understood just for structural reasons, as argument. This is exactly what happens in our case: Axel seems entirely conscious of the need not to continue on with his topic but instead—after acknowledging the dissent with an "okay"—proceeds with a kind of justification:

> Axel: OKAY. (2.0) °i give you ((pointing finger at Figure 1, top diagram)) this image° > (.) or a series of this images<, a::nd you give me (.) if this traffic-light should be red or green. this is °what i want to learn.°

By saying "you," Axel is apparently referring to Will; his statement then very "practically" refers to what he wants from Will and what he specifically gives to him. With this, the speaker is also formally trying to bring the disagreement to an end by picking up, with his final formulation, what Will initially posed as a general question:

Will: What do you want to do?    Axel: This is what I want to learn.

THE EXPANSION OF THE ARGUMENT

However, with this the argument is by no means concluded. Instead, Axel then provides his audience with a slide, a visual schematic containing biological images (a brain analogy), a depiction of an informatics process (a computer analogy), as well as mathematical operators (elements of the basic mathematical model), which not coincidentally correspond to the heterogeneous knowledge order in CNS. Yet this visual schematic again triggers disagreement. The leader of the research group (Wolf) asks repeated questions about the specifications of the mathematical elements: (Wolf: "sorry, i don't understand this. i thought you compose a function as a linear combination of phis?").

After a few minutes and various follow-up questions, Axel decides to bring up a new slide that shows a series of mathematical functions and equations:[14]

> Axel: ((changes to the slide with the equations)) °maybe i give you the equation first°. so, maybe this is a little bit more, it's really simpler. ((The new slide shows mathematical equations. In one of the equations, Axel now circles around a mathematical term.)) what you have here is an input, this is the x(a). ((circles another term)) this is like the functional expanding of it. ((circles another term)) this is the matrix, that makes ((circles another term)) these psis out of it. but now all of these psis are pointwise for each (.) each function in psi is pointwise multiplied with all the different (.) ((circles another term)) over all the alphas.

After he switches to the slide with the equations, he goes through the individual mathematical elements found on it, in verbal conjunction with the schematics shown in figure 3. In doing so, he uses the laser pointer and gestures to draw attention to the (as yet) underdetermined mathematical symbols in the equations. These are given indexical verbal labels, such as "this" and "here" in connection with their closer specification as elements of the schematic depiction (such as "the $X_a$," "the functional expanding of it," or "the matrix"), and only then and thus are given the additional meaning Axel is referring to.

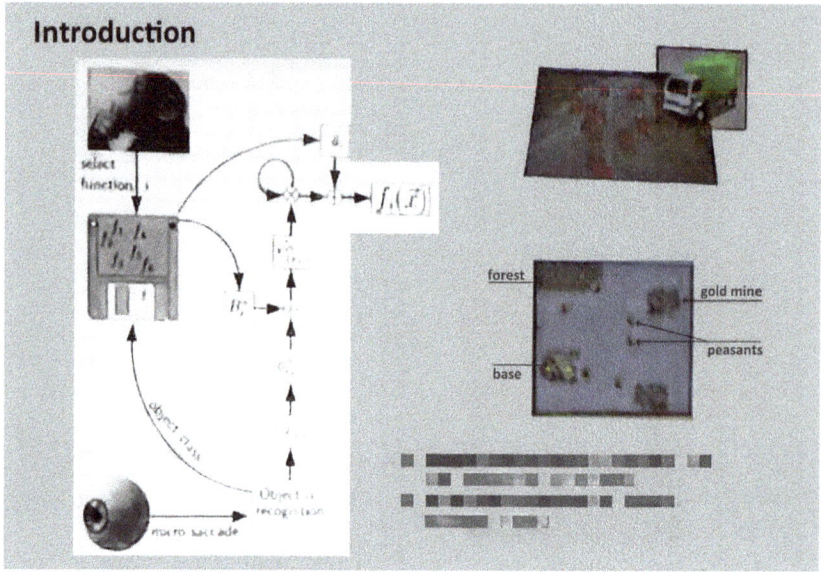

Figure 3. On the left, a schematic depiction of the model patterned on cybernetics. It includes biological (ape and eye), informatics (arrows to symbolize data processing) and mathematical elements (arithmetic operators and functions). On the right, the diagrams shown in figure 1.

It is only after this visual presentation and verbal explanation (as well as the connection between the two established by the speaker's performance) that the first markers of consensus are heard:

Wolf: ah – okay.

Axel: so – it's like you have a couple of – so this is like n-<u>dimensional</u> and you always have like – remains    [(…).

Wolf:              [(…) psi as a function of $X_1$ times psi as a function of $X_2$ times psi – so it's pointwise.

Axel: ja, exactly.

Wolf: okay.

Wolf expresses a marker of approval ("ah—okay") that can certainly be understood as assent and offers a closing that picks up on a formulation by

Axel. It is not only Axel who agrees ("ja, exactly"), but Wolf also explicitly ratifies this approval ("okay").

## The Evidence

We have only indicated in passing what role the differences in knowledge play in the communication that has transpired in the example we analzed, nor have we discussed the contribution the visual presentations make. Yet, both play a decisive role in the last part of this episode. After the first markers of approval have been expressed, Axel, using standard visualizations, is able to make his main argument evident, namely that his algorithms work. We want to examine this more closely, because based on the examples we have analyzed, it is clear that the structure of the argument does not fundamentally differ from that found in everyday conversations.[15] How the PowerPoint presentation proceeds is by no means specific to its use in a scientific talk. What does seem particular here, though, is *how* the argument—one only roughly sketched out here—comes to an end. It is the manner of ending the argumentative episode, both with respect to how it is (visually) experienced and with respect to the particular nature of knowledge employed (in this case, presentational), that deserves the term *evidence*. To illustrate, we want to familiarize the reader, at least in broad strokes, with the kind of knowledge and its visualization that occurs in this last sequence:

> Axel: these are the results. so these are like the classical value functions that i am always dealing with. so they are really like something that i want. (…) so this is the original function. ((Pointing to the diagram in the upper left corner of figure 4)) these are the first twelve features that my algorithm ((points to the twelve smaller diagrams in the middle/above of Figure 4)) my compression algorithm finds. and this is the linear combination of those twelve features. ((points to the upper right of figure 4)) the l-square-error is somewhere in the range of ten to minus nine or so. it is really, really close. and when you really compare those things here (…) there is really – you can't find a difference with the eye between those two functions anymore.

In this excerpt, one finds Axel's concluding, monologue-like, contribution, one sequentially distinguished by the fact that no one contradicts him. Here—generally speaking—what is at stake is to find an approximating algorithm for particular functions that are difficult or impossible to calculate. Hence, the question is how to *approximate* one function with the help of other functions that, ideally, have especially simple construction features and particularly good numerical qualities (a realistic amount of computing time, a small amount of memory capacity needed, etc.). Axel presents a method in which the corresponding function is approximated by a special class of functions. His remarks, however, are not made in reference to the stated task of approximation but rather with reference to the demonstration, namely that the functions used have particularly good compression qualities.

The compression of functions is a mathematical procedure that can be understood as a reduction in the information the corresponding function transmits. If the compressed function approximately corresponds to the original function, it means that "the algorithm really extracts something that is underlying the data . . ., not the representation of the data," as Axel puts it.

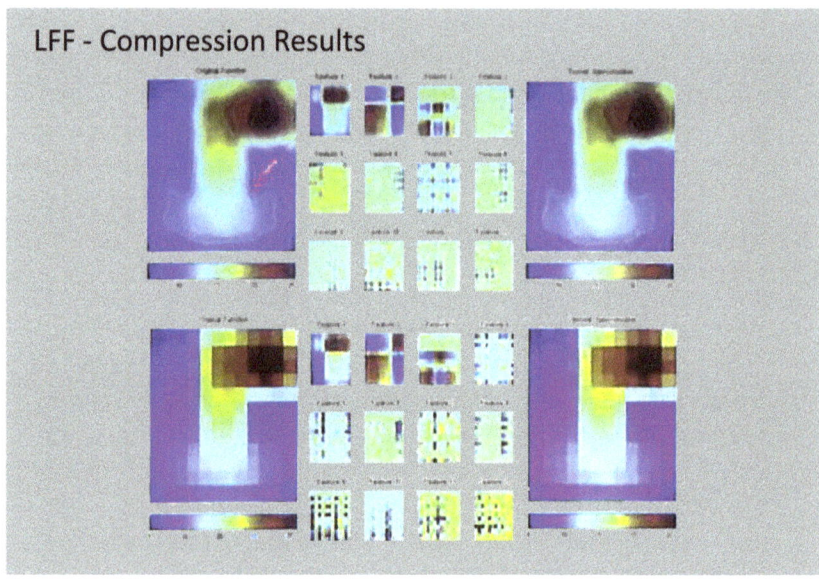

Figure 4. The visualization used by Axel. In the upper left corner, one has an image of the original function; in the middle, this compression function is disaggregated into twelve basic elements; the upper right corner displays the compression function.

This closing argument is not only presented verbally, But also visually as Axel refers in various ways to the slide being displayed (figure 4). One can note that it is divided into upper and lower halves. The upper half, which is relevant here, has three parts. On the left, one sees a single square heat diagram;[16] in the middle one finds twelve small, and differing, heat diagrams; and on the right again a single square heat diagram. Through gestures and their accompanying verbal commentary, we learn that the single diagram on the left shows the original function, the middle diagrams are the individual components of the compression, and the single diagram on the right is the aggregation of these individual components and thus the calculated compromised variant of the original function.

Axel interprets the quality of the function selected, to begin with, in terms of the visual (and referential) concordance of two images, the single square diagrams on the left and on the right, and thereby turns it into an issue of visual evidence. He also makes strategic use of the visual and sensory character of the slide images when he challenges his audience to compare with their own eyes and be convinced: "There is really—you can't find a difference with the eye between those two functions anymore."

To be able to speak of evidence, however, sensory visuality is not enough. What is important in this situation is that the images used can only be understood in light of particular knowledge. Indeed, the images displayed are themselves models of formulae and not images of actual objects; what we have here is presentational knowledge. These visualizations are created by the actors themselves (in this case, by Axel), and the quality of the approximation approach cannot be established only based on a context-free comparison of images or diagrams. This is made clear, for example, in Axel's remark before inviting his audience to see for themselves and compare the diagrams: "The L-square-error is somewhere in the range of ten to minus nine or so. It is really, really close".

The images to be compared are the output and result of software immediately linked to a well-established program. This program, in turn, carries out particular mathematical functions (at a certain quality level), in this case the calculation of a mean square error between the original and the compressed function. It is precisely the knowledge of this numerical estimate of error—in the range of $10^{-9}$—that validates the research result achieved by Axel and that provides the basis for the visual evidence. Evidence arises here, and this is the decisive point, from the intertwining of two different levels of knowledge, namely the immediate graphic image and the formalism of the mathematical and the calculated, which seems typical of the presentational knowledge employed in CNS. Unlike the two previous episodes, this last section is characterized by a type of seeing that is guided by specific (or specifically) scientific knowledge.

Such knowledge is not only embodied by Axel. Rather, it is precisely the kind of knowledge demanded, by disagreeing and dissenting, by the audience. Of course, at this point one would have to ask what stocks of knowledge participating researchers possess, and where they differ.[17] Our case indicates that participants understand the representation of the calculating of a mean square error as the display of the image of a heat diagram—and even understand the equivalence between the calculation being represented and the image that represents it. As we showed, however, evidence is not at all only the result of connecting the contents of a visual and sensory presentation to specialized knowledge the audience possess. Whether the participants can actually reproduce the evidence in detail is less important in terms of its social consequences than the fact that this evidence is what rounds out and ends an argumentative episode generated by a dissent.

## Conclusion

The final visualization appeared as a form of evidence that supported the assertion of the speaker that his approximation function yielded the desired result. The slide clearly served as the materialization of appearances, of that which, within the heterogeneous knowledge culture of the discussants, is shared. The fact that we are dealing with very exclusive and specialized knowledge indicates that connecting visualization and presentational knowledge in a CNS group talk provides what can be regarded as evidence in this field of work. One can also suspect that it serves as a kind of basic idiom, one that is necessary for these forms of heterogeneous scientific research.

Evidence, we argue, is part of a communicative form, which in our case is dialogical. One could certainly also examine forms of monologues and suspect that evidence is presented in a different manner there. But in fact, rhetoric provides numerous examples of such monologue situations. Still, there are good reasons to assume that an argumentative role of evidence is exemplified by, and rooted in, the dialogic situation. One need only recall Jürgen Habermas's pragmatics, which places the yes/no answer to a statement as the starting point for claiming universal validity (see Habermas 1987). Habermas feels the validity claim can be affixed to the verbal form of the statement in question, but we think it more appropriate to assume that the argumentative issue is signaled (and negotiated in the subsequent moves) by the interactive formulation of disagreement.

The formulation of disagreement not only is the interactive starting point for the argument, but it also is the catalyst for an episodic sequence that—after the disagreement—calls for a third speech move or other communicative acts in which a justification may sequentially follow. As we have seen, such a justification need not necessarily be evidence. It is also questionable whether what serves as argumentative explanation can be said to have a universal function, in the manner Stephen Toulmin recommends, as "backing" or "warrant" (see Toulmin [1958] 2003).

In contrast to Habermas's assumption, it could certainly be the case that these third moves (and their later expansions) may not be verbal at all but may be filled instead by gesturing at something that then serves as evidence. Interestingly, it is precisely these non-verbal signs that appear, in the interactive position of serving as justification, that seem to be the closest to what one could call evidence. It is worth noting that here it is not about the representation of objects but instead about the visualization of something that itself is a visual product of action, and that is placed in the context of an instrumental action—in short, presentational knowledge.

## Acknowledgments

We would like to take this opportunity to thank Lisa-Marian Schmidt for her valuable preliminary work, and John Bendix for translating this chapter. We also thank our colleagues in the unit of general sociology at the Technische Universität Berlin for suggestions they made in our common meetings to analyze the videotaped data. Our special thanks go to Christian Kiesow, Miira Hill, Anja Schünzel and Jakob Gerber.

## Notes

1. In the philosophy of science, the term evidence refers to proof of the correctness of a hypothesis that is based on methodologically guided observations (e.g., empirical evidence). However, evidence is understood differently in Anglo-American law and in continental European law. In German law, the term *Offenkundigkeit* (obviousness) designates all that which does not require proof, while in Anglo-American law, the law of evidence has developed into its own complex jurisprudence that regulates not only which material is admissible in ascertaining the facts of a case but also the manner in which such material may be presented to the court. Evidence in the Anglo-American sense corresponds to what is called *Beweis* in German law: that which is submitted to the court by the parties in dispute. If this is ruled admissible by the court, it is regarded as proof of fact (see Kemmann 1996).

2. Evidence in classical rhetoric is regarded as a generic term for a whole series of techniques of "placing-before-the-eyes" that can be disaggregated into "procedures of vivification" (*Verlebendigung*) and "providing details" (*Detailierung*) (see Kemmann 1996, 1).

3. Particularly in science, the neutral term *objectivation* suggests what is to be treated as a "knowledge object" (see Berger and Luckmann 1991).

4. Michael Lynch and Steve Woolgar argue that no binding order for depiction exists anymore and that current practices for generating and utilizing representation are a *bricolage*. See their preface to their edited volume Representation in Scientific Practice (Lynch and Woolgar 1990, vii).

5. In terms both of history and personnel, CNS overlaps with computer engineering fields such as neuroinformatics and machine learning as well as with the more mathematically-oriented branches of systems biology or educational psychology.

6. In this, it is in competition with the more established and less biological approaches used in computer engineering research on machine learning, which tends to be more oriented to symbolic AI. For a sociological treatment of the controversy between symbolic AI and the more biological and neural net approach see Olazaran (1996).

7. The data collected is in the context of the "Bildkommunikation in der Wissenschaft am Fallbeispiel der Computational Neuroscience" (Imagery Communication in Science, Illustrated by the Case of Computational Neuroscience) research project funded by the German Science Foundation (DFG) from 2013 to 2017. The authors control the rights to the images used here. The names of the persons referred to in the transcripts were changed for reasons of data protection. For further information see Lettkemann and Wilke (2016) and Wilke and Lettkemann (2018).

8. On knowledge production in neuroinformatics, see Schmidt (2013); on the role of computer-generated images, see Lettkemann (2013).

9. We use the term PowerPoint as a synonym for computer-supported visual presentations.

10. The monologue-like scientific lecture has been far more studied than the more dialogically-structured group talk. For example, see Goffman (1981, 60–69).

11. Methodologically, we follow the approach used in videography, described in detail in Knoblauch, Tuma, and Schnettler (2014). There, one can also find explanations relevant to transcription. To understand the transcripts provided in this contribution, the following conventions have been used:

| | |
|---|---|
| Axel: | lecturer (computer scientist) |
| Will: | biologist from the working group |
| Wolf: | head of the working group |
| (…) | unintelligible (unsure transcription) |

| (( )) | gesture |
| [ | simultaneous acts |
| ____ | emphasis |
| (1.0) | 1-second pause |
| (.) | short pause |
| ? | rising intonation |
| , | sligthly rising intonation |
| : | stretch |
| >< | faster |
| °° | calmer |
| SO | louder |

12. On the ritual framings for initiating audience interaction in PowerPoint presentations, see Knoblauch (2013, 125–135).

13. For our analysis of the sequences of turn-taking, we turn to conversation analysis; more on this in Sacks, Schegloff, and Jefferson (1974).

14. Parenthetically, R's deictic references mean this slide is not simply a "linear" continuation of the previous slide but is instead an explication of the flow diagram shown in figure 3. On the circumventing of the supposed linearity of PowerPoint slides, see Knoblauch (2013, 71–77).

15. Whether this is true for all types of group talks remains to be investigated.

16. In a heat diagram, different function values of a function f (as in $R^2 \to R$, for example a temperature distribution in a two-dimensional region) are depicted as different values on a color scale: higher values normally correspond to lighter colors and lower values to darker ones.

17. This question remains to be investigated, and differences in fields or disciplines as well as the positions held and individual biography play a role. Through their interaction, in the area of research examined here, and particularly in the group talks, participants are socialized into linking differing forms of visual and formalized quantitative verification, as well as learn the skills of negotiating and legitimizing their work.

## Works Cited

Amann, Klaus. 1994. "Menschen, Mäuse und Fliegen." *Zeitschrift für Soziologie* 23 (1): 22–40.

Berger, Peter L., and Thomas Luckmann. (1966) 1991. *The Social Construction of Reality: A Treatise in the Sociology of Knowledge*. London: Penguin Books.

Bergmann, Jörg R. 1981. "Frage und Frageparaphrase: Aspekte der redezuginternen und sequenziellen Organisation eines Äußerungsformats. " In *Methoden der Analyse von Face-to-Face-Situationen*, edited by Peter Winkler, 128–42. Stuttgart: Metzler.

Carnap, Rudolf. (1928) 1998. *Der logische Aufbau der Welt*. Hamburg: Meiner.

Churchland, Patricia S., Christof Koch, and Terrence J. Sejnowski. 1993. "What is Computational Neuroscience?" In *Computational Neuroscience*, edited by Eric L. Schwartz, 46–55. Cambridge, MA and London: MIT Press.

Coopmans, Catelijne, Janet Vertesi, Michael Lynch, and Steve Woolgar. 2014. *Representation in Scientific Practice Revisited*. Cambridge, MA: MIT Press.

Coulter, Jeff. 1990. "Elementary Properties of Argument Sequences." In *Interaction Competence*, edited George Psathas, 181–203. Washington, DC: University Press of America.

Daston, Lorraine, and Peter Galison. 2007. *Objectivity*. Brooklyn, New York: Zone Book.

Engelen, Eva-Maria, Christian Fleischhack, C. Giovanni Galizia, and Katharina Landfester. 2010. *Heureka—Evidenzkriterien in den Wissenschaften. Ein Kompendium für den interdisziplinären Gebrauch*. Heidelberg: Spektrum Akademischer Verlag.

Galison, Peter. 1996. "Computer Simulations and the Trading Zone." In *The Disunity of Science: Boundaries, Contexts, and Power*, edited by Peter Galison and David J. Stump, 118–57. Stanford, CA: Stanford University Press.

Goffman, Erving. 1981. "The Lecture." In *Forms of Talk*, 160–96. Oxford: Blackwell.

Günthner, Susanne, and Hubert Knoblauch. 2007. "Wissenschaftliche Diskursgattungen—PowerPoint et al. " In *Reden und Schreiben in der Wissenschaft*, edited by Peter Auer, and Harald Beßler, 53–66. Frankfurt am Main and New York: Campus Verlag.

Habermas, Jürgen. 1987. *Theory of Communicative Action*. Vol. 2 of *Lifeworld and System: A Critique of Functionalist Reason*, translated by Thomas McCarthy. Boston, MA: Beacon Press.

Hackett, Edward J., Olga Amsterdamska, Michael Lynch, and Judy Wajcman. 2008. *The Handbook of Science and Technology Studies*. 3rd edition. Cambridge, MA and London: MIT Press.

Hope, Diane S. 2006. *Visual Communication: Perception, Rhetoric and Technology*. Cresskill, NJ: Hampton Press.

Husserl, Edmund. 1977. "Die Krisis der europäischen Wissenschaften. " In *Die Krisis der europäischen Wissenschaften und die transzendentale Phänomenologie: Eine Einleitung in die phänomenologische Philosophie*, edited by Elisabeth Ströker. Hamburg: Meiner.

Jacobs, Scott, and Sally Jackson. 1981. "Argument as a natural category: The routine grounds for arguing in conversation." *Western Journal of Speech Communication* 45 (2): 118–32.

Kemmann, Ansgar. 1996. "Evidentia, Evidenz. " In *Historisches Wörterbuch der Rhetorik*, vol. 3, edited by Gert Ueding, 37–38.. Tübingen: Niemeyer.

Knoblauch, Hubert. 2000. "Die Rhetorizität kommunikativen Handelns." In *Rhetorische Anthropologie: Studien zum Homo rhetoricus*, edited by Josef Kopperschmidt, 183–204. Munich: Fink.
—. 2005. "Focused ethnography." *Forum Qualitative Sozialforschung / Forum: Qualitative Social Research* 6 (3), Art. 44. Accessed: October 09, 2021. http://dx.doi.org/10.17169/fqs-6.3.20.
—. 2008. "The Performance of Knowledge: Pointing and Knowledge in PowerPoint Presentations." *Cultural Sociology* 2 (1): 75–97.
—. 2009. "Kommunikative Lebenswelt, die Kunst des Widerspruchs und die Rhetorik des Dialogs in informellen Diskussionen. " In *Rhetorik im Gespräch: ergänzt um Beiträge zum Tübinger Courtshiprhetorik-Projekt*, edited by Joachim Knape, 149–75. Berlin: Weidler.
—. 2010. *Wissenssoziologie*. 2nd ed. Konstanz: UVK.
—. 2011. "Relativism, Meaning and the New Sociology of Knowledge." In *The Problem of Relativism in the Sociology of (Scientific) Knowledge*, edited by Richard Schantz, Markus Seidel, 131–56. Frankfurt am Main, Paris, and Lancaster: Ontos.
—. 2013. *PowerPoint, Communication, and the Knowledge Society*. Cambridge: Cambridge University Press.
—. 2014. "Communication, Culture and PowerPoint." In *Culture, Communication, and Creativity. Reframing the Relations of Media, Knowledge, and Innovation in Society*, edited by Hubert Knoblauch, René Tuma, Marc Jacobs, 155—76. Frankfurt am Main: Peter Lang.
—. 2020. *The Communicative Construction of Reality*. London and New York: Routledge.
Knoblauch, Hubert, René Tuma, and Bernt Schnettler. 2014. *Videography*. Bern: Lang.
Knoblauch, Hubert, and René Wilke. 2016. "The Common Denominator: The Reception and Impact of Berger and Luckmann's the Social Construction of Reality. *Human Studies* 39: 51—69.
Knorr-Cetina, Karin. 1999. *Epistemic Cultures: How the Sciences Make Knowledge*. Cambridge, MA, and London: Harvard University Press.
Lettkemann, Eric. 2013. "Die Beobachter der Beobachtungsinstrumente. Elektronenmikroskopische Laborarbeit vor und nach der digitalen Revolution." In *Visuelles Wissen und Bilder des Sozialen: Aktuelle Entwicklungen in der Soziologie des Visuellen*, edited by Petra Lucht, Lisa-Marian Schmidt, and René Tuma, 193–212. Wiesbaden: Springer VS.
Lettkemann, Eric, and René Wilke. 2016. "Kommunikationspraktiken. Wissenskommunikation im Group Talk." In *Wissen–Organisation–Forschungspraxis. Der Makro-Meso-Mikro-Link in der Wissenschaft*, edited by Nina Baur, Cristina Besio, Maria Norkus, Grit Petschick, 447–79. Weinheim, Munich: Juventa.
Luckmann, Thomas. 1995. "Interaction planning and intersubjective adjustment of perspectives by communicative genres." In *Social Intelligence and Interaction:*

*Expressions and implications of the social bias in human intelligence*, edited by Esther N. Goody, 175–86. Cambridge, MA: Cambridge University Press.

Lynch, Michael, and Steve Woolgar. 1990. *Representation in Scientific Practice*. Cambridge MA: MIT Press.

Mead, George H. 1967. *Mind, Self and Society from the Standpoint of a Social Behaviorist*. Chicago: The University of Chicago Press.

Olazaran, Mikel. 1996. "A Sociological Study of the Official History of the Perceptrons Controversy." *Social Studies of Science* 26 (3): 611–59.

Rheinberger, Hans-Jörg. 1997. *Toward a History of Epistemic Things: Synthesizing Proteins in the Test Tube*. Stanford: Stanford University Press.

Sacks, Harvey, Emanuel A. Schegloff and Gail Jefferson. 1974. "A simplest systematics for the organization of turn-taking for conversation." *Language* 50 (4): 696–735.

Schmidt, Lisa-Marian. 2013. "Sehen und gesehen werden. Visualisierungen in der Neuroinformatik." In *Visuelles Wissen und Bilder des Sozialen. Aktuelle Entwicklungen in der Soziologie des Visuellen*, edited by Petra Lucht, Lisa-Marian Schmidt, and René Tuma, 175–92. Wiesbaden: Springer VS.

Toulmin, Stephen E. (1958) 2003. *The Uses of Argument*. Cambridge, UK, and New York: Cambridge University Press.

Wilke, René 2022: *Wissenschaft kommuniziert. Eine wissenssoziologische Gattungsanalyse des akademischen Group Talks am Beispiel der Computational Neuroscience*. Wiesbaden: Springer VS.

Wilke, René, and Eric Lettkemann. 2018. "Bewältigung interdisziplinärer Wissenskommunikation. Bausteine einer wissenssoziologischen Gattungsanalyse des Group Talks in der Computational Neuroscience." In *Knowledge in Action: Neue Formen der Wissenskommunikation*, edited by Eric Lettkemann, René Wilke, and Hubert Knoblauch, 73–107. Wiesbaden: Springer VS.

Wilke, René, and Miira Hill. 2019. "On New Forms of Science Communication and Communication in Science: A Videographic Approach to Visuality in Science Slams and Academic Group Talk." *Qualitative Inquiry* 25 (4): 363–78.

# 8 Narrative, Rhetoric, and Science: Opportunities and Risks

*Jenny Rock and Julia Siebert*

We are experiencing a time in which everyone is keen on story in science, whether in press release or curriculum, popular documentary or even the annals of peer reviewed publishing. This is not surprising as the way stories are told within science has a great effect on how people engage with science. But the storytelling is not one-way; the way that science is encapsulated in story is also affected by the way people want to see science and how they want to understand the world. These expectations can have a deep impact on the conceptions of the single scientist and on scientific development more generally. In this chapter we dive into the internal structures of scientific knowledge gain as well as the perception and communication of scientific results. The aim is to critically reflect how these processes are occurring within the scientific community and also with the broader public, examining some wide-spread narratives and assumptions. Nevertheless, we clearly reject any attempt to use our work to fuel general distrust in science or to categorically question scientific evidence. Scrutinizing and enhancing the scientific process must occur within the framework of science.

Being a scientist is not simply about generating and disseminating results, but about packaging them in a story to make one's work and its implications evident for other scientists and a broader public (including users, stakeholders, and future funders). In addition to empirical evidence, scientists also depend on the successful rating of their achievements (see Kemmann 1996) and need to apply rhetoric for creating such evidence (Latin: *evidentia*). Indeed, rhetoric provides a conceptual framework for analyzing different ways of creating evidence and represents a powerful device which, in addition to opening up manifold opportunities, also carries a high risk of obscuring scientific knowledge and scientific processes. We will explore examples of these opportunities and risks in the following sections, depicting how scientific results (in this case from the field of biology) are embedded in persuasive structures to achieve evidence. The current popularity of story as a means of communicating science brings again to the fore the importance of understanding the role of narrative and rhetoric in science.

## The Role of Rhetoric in the Reciprocal Interaction Between Science and Society

Since Thomas S. Kuhn's (1962) seminal theory about the structure of scientific revolutions, the idea that science in practice is not simply the rational application of neutral testing of logical arguments has become well accepted (see, e.g., Lakatos and Musgrave 1970; Fleck 1979; Latour and Woolgar 1986). The contemporary understanding of the social process of science acknowledges that it is affected by complex human interactions and aesthetic factors. For many (and at varying proximities to science) this idea enriches the concept of science, for others, however, it remains threatening. At the least, recognizing the two-way relationship between science and society opens a door to useful exchange of analytical tools and philosophical insights between science and the humanities. For instance, science includes a multitude of communication structures that can be analyzed and understood from the perspectives of rhetoric, sociology, and psychology. When communicating with the public, scientists will use rhetoric and narrative structures to explain their results and to arouse public interest. However, these same persuasive structures also shape and propel the paradigms operating within science and forge substantial—though often unnoticed—two-way interaction between science and society.

The circle of reciprocal interaction between science and society can be found at multiple levels: with the individual scientist, within the scientific community, and with the public. These parties interact with each other in complex ways, and their roles can transition in different contexts (e.g., a scientist is part of the public in most contexts). To contribute to the additive, self-correcting process of science, scientists require a structured environment ordered by a given hierarchy of accepted ideas. Thus, they will often identify with a distinct set of scientific theories and paradigms to establish a clear self-conception and to promote acceptance of their work. At a slightly broader level, scientific communities also align their collective work within prevailing paradigms. Indeed, the scientific community acts and behaves like most social groups—they put pressure on their members by creating ingroup-outgroup thinking, which disadvantages non-conformists and is accompanied by various self-reinforcing processes (see Sherif 1935; Eagly and Chaiken 1993; Myers 2005). Scientists, as individuals within a scientific community, are encouraged to act strategically to get support for their research, for instance by deliberately analyzing and meeting the expectations of the public. This public collectively judges and evaluates scientific results based on popular value systems, forcing the scientist and the scientific community to do the same.

The public desires ground-breaking results, in line with their world view, and packaged in fascinating stories. It also wants its money spent on exciting and productive things. There is no interest in science following a hypothesis that proves false, an elimination process often interpreted as failure. Scientists know this and behave accordingly.

> If anyone tried to publish a story more like real life, in which hypotheses were dropped for lack of support, apparatuses couldn't be made to work within the parameters of the original experiment, and so on, it would be turned down. Journals do not publish inconclusive work. . . . Science must present a smiling face both to itself and to the world. (Harré 1990, 87)

The easiest way for a scientist to "stay smiling" is to support the prevailing (successful) paradigm, since that has proved a recipe for achieving evidence. This means that the strategic scientist often feeds the public with exactly the kind of results it wants to receive (Kuhn 1962, 23–35), using rhetoric the public wants to hear and supporting paradigms that allow for stable identification with a suuccessful perspective.

The rhetoric of science thus involves the risk of leading the public to become further entrenched in a paradigm, as critical thinking is constrained and it becomes increasingly difficult to move away from a particular position. As self-reinforcement this also makes it more difficult for the scientist and the scientific community to recognize and support the need for a new paradigm shift. With time (and often technological and/or socio/political change), science eventually will gain critical mass for a paradigm shift; however, it then might find the public resistant to the concept of such change in science. Although there is much complaint from within the scientific community regarding the public's expectations of a static science (that produces stable truths), there is little acknowledgement that the rhetoric employed routinely during Kuhn's periods of "normal science" is in fact part of the cause. By acting along the lines of public expectations, the scientist is partly responsible for the difficulty in changing a public opinion once it has been established (Kuhn 1962, 76–78). Reviewing some principles of rhetoric, such as persuasion and identification, allows us to better understand this complex relationship between science and society and its role in producing evidence in the ever-persistent rivalry for scientific appreciation.

### Persuasion and Identification in Rhetoric and Science

The act of persuasion is inherent in the process of rhetoric; persuasive structures are a general character of language that are particularly flexible and responsive to different contexts. Indeed, rhetoric can be understood as functional communication during which the main interaction can be observed between people and their environment (Bitzer 1980, 21, 23–25), and it results in a rhetorical situation that is in no way rigid or predictable. Persuasion depends on a flexible, complex, and changing context that always requires a new analysis to act efficiently. Thus, a coherent logical structure alone is not enough to ensure successful persuasion (as it is highly depended on context variables). Although it is recognized that some tactics of persuasion may be based on *logos* (logical-referential level of approach), the other approach is based on *ethos* and *pathos* (at the personal-affective level) (Ogden and Richards 1923; Richards 1965). Because the rhetorical situation revolves around the social background of the recipient and the audience, this implies that it is always easier to persuade if the argument is consistent with the belief system (e.g., paradigm) already generally accepted (Johnstone 1965; Bitzer 1980).

Persuasion plays a major role in defining the beliefs of the strategically acting individual scientist, as well as that of the greater scientific community, in terms of which paradigm is considered to be correct. "Scientists are not persuaded by *logos* alone; science is no exception to the rule that the persuasive effect of authority, of *ethos*, weighs heavily" (Gross 1990a, 12–13). Indeed, words do not have one distinct meaning but different interpretations depending on their context (which itself is dependent on the recipients and their backgrounds) (Kuhn 1962, 125–27). So, communicators must use certain linguistic means (vehicles) to create a certain connotation (tenor) in order to make their own beliefs comprehensible for the recipient: "only through persuasion are importance and meaning established" (Gross 1990a, 4). Persuasive efforts then contribute to these beliefs being regarded as direct proof, by both the scientific community and the public. Thus, rhetoric can be used to enhance acceptance for a scientist's work within science as well as to convince the public by making its merits particularly evident and difficult to ignore. Although some of the aforementioned use of persuasion is intentional, persuasive effects may also arise inadvertently. Even though effort is continually made within science to find a neutral language to objectively describe its findings, language itself is laden with expectations, assumptions and constraints that often reflect prevailing paradigms. Indeed, language has a metaphorical character that further constrains science to contingent, non-neutral communication (Kuhn 1962, 125–27) (e.g., innumerable analogies originated from the world of computers and machines, and now both inform and constrain our understanding of neurobiology [Hildt and Kovács 2009]).

Due to the impossibility of a neutral language, scientific communications can be rhetorically analyzed like any other text, and this reveals that they contain many standard persuasive and strategic elements regarding language usage and stylistic devices. These elements are often hard to detect, because scientists make every attempt to frame their experiments and observations from an objective stance of representing factual reality (Gross 1990a, 4–7; Gross 1990b, 91–92). Indeed, one of the most notorious examples of rhetoric in scientific prose (Gross 1990a, 69–73) is the use of the passive (third-person) voice, in which the actions and decisions of the scientist are presented as a minor role in the process of science. Not only does this produce text that is awkward to read and understand, it constructs a facade of physical scientific results resolving themselves untarnished by human influence. Another rhetorical technique is to use a collective "we" to impart on the audience the impression that they are included in a part of the story, somehow contributing to the scientific achievements. As a pleasant side effect of this "ephemeral special relationship" (Harré 1990, 85), narrative strategy keeps the audience from questioning the presented story.

The use of concise terminology is another rhetorical technique in science with complex repercussions. Scientific results, once verified, are quickly aligned with a terminology that is precise and specific (i.e., linked with highly complex definitions that have accepted, distinct context and interpretation). This is an essential precondition for becoming part of the construct of ideas of theoretical knowledge. After achieving this important "inclusion through alignment" with such categorized knowledge, a contrary tendency can be observed. At this point, scientists willingly release the hard-earned scientific terminology to make room for generalizations that are easier to communicate widely, but in so doing lose association with their specific contexts. Summary texts, graphics, and tables often play a significant role in decontextualizing science; instead of illustrating complex and variable circumstances, more often they simplify by emphasizing idealized causalities between components. Central quantifiable aspects are encapsulated in familiar key words, while simplistic explanations become the evidence fueling the formation of scientific norms that subsume important details, aberrations and contextual complexity (Gross 1990a, 69–75; Harré 1990, 86–87).

The structural format of scientific papers presents further rhetorical effect. Within the "introduction," the focus on referencing previous studies ensures that the presented experiment is part of a bigger validated research agenda, while the "material and methods" section extends the protocol for results to be repeatable (contending that not the scientist but the characteristics of reality are the cause of the observed results). This purpose leads to the presentation of far more background information than is necessary to provide explanation of the single experiment (arguably a breach of Gricean maxims of quantity and relevance). The "discussion" finally is written on the assumption that there are universal laws that can be deduced from the experimental data, even if there are some discrepancies that need to be rationalized away. To this end, the experimental data and the conclusions arise from different sources—the former from the laboratory, the latter from nature (Grice 1989; Gross 1990a, 85–91).

The rhetorical concept of *identification* is closely related to the aim of persuasion, as identification is arguably the precondition for every successful act of persuasion. The recipients must first identify themselves with the communicators and their message: "You persuade a man only insofar as you can talk his language by speech, gesture, tonality, order, image, attitude, idea, identifying your way with his" (Burke 1969, 55). This implies that it is mainly the recipient who orients the direction of the persuasive effort made by the communicative actor. The recipients then build evidence from the impression that they have experienced the story told—emotively connected through perceived experience, the conclusions of a story are then unquestionable.

Identification can occur at a very fundamental stage in general language structure (e.g., time structure, sayings, and the availability of words for linguistic expressions to describe circumstances), and we also identify with certain language usages. In every social group, specific linguistic usages emerge that are accompanied by the establishment of specific meanings with determined connotations and expectations (Turner 1987, 22–23). It is mostly by using familiar and accepted text structures (e.g., an introduction–pro/contra–conclusion scheme, or enumerations always using three examples) and stylistic devices (e.g., metaphors) that persuasion can be achieved. In so doing, our symbolically charged language is itself turned into action, as it already defines our perception of reality (i.e., we are always dealing with an interpretation of reality rather than with one objective reality; see Burke 1969). Identification is also associated with another powerful component of rhetoric—that of the narrative structure of story.

## Narrative in Science

Narrative devices represent an inherent part of rhetoric, with *narratio* being the second stage of the classical oration (*exordium, narratio, argumentatio, peroratio*), and understood as a subjective illustration of circumstances (see Quintilian *Inst.* 4.2.31) that can be used as a basis for the whole speech (see Cicero *De or.* 2.330). To make one's own point of view most persuasive, factual elements are selectively shaped, emphasized, modified or even removed (Quintilian *Inst.* 4.2.67). Story is often broadly described as the way we make sense of our lives and the surrounding world, allowing us to construct greater meaning from a collection of events. A narrative shapes how we understand concepts and place knowledge in contexts of time and space. Indeed, stories stay with us from childhood, becoming the format by which we expect to understand everything, from conflict motifs of contemporary news, to the hero's quest or rags-to-riches journeys of political campaigns. Like the previously described rhetorical techniques, devices, and structures, the ways stories are told thus affect the making of meaning and the way the audience achieves understanding (the point when identification processes are initialized). It is an inherent characteristic of stories to make their content evident by creating lively images and evoking emotions that make it easier to identify with a particular plot. This process of creating evidence holds also true for scientific communications.

The story structure of scientific studies also follows certain rules to invite attention and to obtain acceptance. Rhetorical methods of narrative shape the way in which scientists conceptualize and communicate their work. Scientists benefit from the use of stories to improve their communication success with the public and within their own scientific community (whether narratives are used consciously or unconsciously). Indeed, a welltold story brings significant advantages for the scientist, since admiration for the story itself is also transferred to the scientist, lending authority, esteem, and persuasive power (Terrell 1990, 8; Aristotle *Rh.* 1356a). This is linked to a phenomenon called "normative social influence" in social psychology, which explains conformity by the intense subconscious gain of removing risk of unexpected rejection and gaining social recognition within the scientific community in which the scientist requires acceptance (e.g., Festinger 1957; Eagly and Chaiken 1993; Myers 2005, 622–35). Thus, social admiration for a scientist's storyline will further instill the storyline as normative in the scientist's operating paradigm. As a result, narratives are prevalent in multiple aspects of science, from processes within the scientific community to communication both internal and external to science. But the influence of narrative runs even deeper. Our expectations and aesthetic awareness for certain types of narrative influence our expectations of the world, including natural phenomena described by science. Thus, the paradigms of science are not just framed in accepted story structures, but these structures actually form the expectations and predictions of the paradigms. Essentially, paradigms are the acting narratives of science. Reviewing the basic components of narrative theory and linking these devices with their implications allows us to see how they can shape our understanding of science, paving the way for any persuasive effort in making circumstances evident.

There are multiple narrative structures, or ways to tell stories, but most of the ones we are most familiar with group events into cause and effect or action and inaction, and they are organized tightly within time and space. Society has been conscious about the common structures of stories and their use for a long time; the observation that narrative structure often revolves around a beginning, middle, and end has existed for several thousand years, and certainly since Aristotle (*Poet.*; cf. also figure 1). The classic five-stage narrative structure has also been widely acknowledged, moving from *exposition* (setting of scene and character), to *development* (of situations and additional characters), to *complication, climax* (decisive moments) and *resolution*, or according to Gustav Freytag (1894): Introduction, Rise, Climax, Return or Fall, and Catastrophe. Guided by their fundamental understanding of stories, people expect to find the same unchangeable order also in scientific stories, with information arranged to fit into a certain framework.

> Using a story format to report historical facts and figures may encourage us . . . to believe that the past was patterned in other ways, too: perhaps as a tale of growth or decline, improvement or devolution, or a movement from homogeneity to heterogeneity, from early simplicity to later complexity. History may, of course, have such patterns. But patterns like these must be seen, so to speak, not merely presumed. (Terrell 1990, 19)

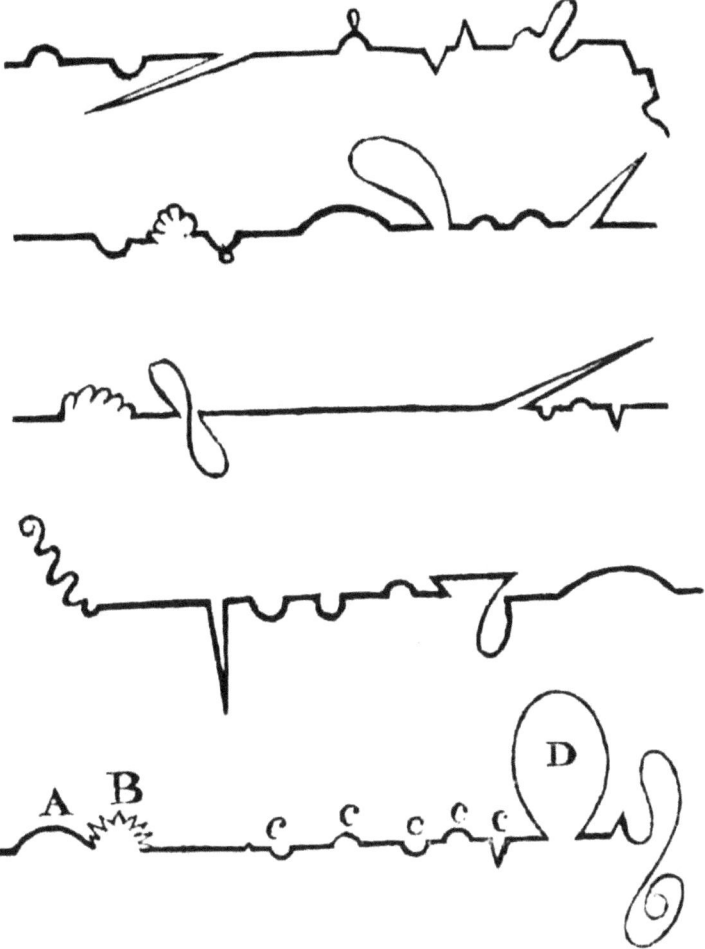

Figure 1. A Visualization of narrative techniques in Laurence Sterne's *Tristram Shandy*. Although Sterne's sketches depict narrative deviations in a well-told story, his examples are all linear. The image depicted above combines the sketches found on two consecutive pages in many editions (here Sterne 1849, 386–387; copyright expired).

Narratives impose not just ordered sequences but cause and effect relationships. Narrative structures move us from one stage of equilibrium (initial state of "balance" between potentially opposing forces) to another, when *resolution* returns us to a new state of equilibrium, after some necessary disruption from the *complication*, which the protagonist confronts and wins over, thus restoring order and balance again (Todorov 1969). The ubiquity of these structures is reflected in the strong belief that it is always possible to detect causal relations in the observed phenomenon and that they are clearly recognizable, being the stage described before the cause in the linear story line. "We usually expect a well-told story to make sense not only as a meaningful totality that leads to some kind of resolution or conclusion but also as a developing, coherent whole—a well-crafted sequence of events and episodes without extraneous characters, useless detail, unexplained happenings, or loose ends" (Terrell 1990, 17).

As we are always expecting causal relations, we also infer causality within scientific studies, even if there is no obvious reason to do so (Terrell 1990, 7). What emerges is not only the expectation of a linear improvement in stories about natural processes, but also an expectation of a reliable and continuous progress that is cumulatively reaching higher organization in a step-by-step process. This is the kind of assumption biologists like Ernst Mayr and Stephen J. Gould long fought, arguing that biology does not function with a causality like physics or chemistry. There is no predefined goal or inherent linear improvement in nature (or even a reliable prediction one could refer to, provided that we take the impact of emergence seriously). In fact, the entire theory of evolution is contrary to the belief of a pre-existing goal, yet the adaptationist regime lives on beneath its elaborate spandrels (Mayr 2004, 21–66; Gould and Lewontin 1979; cf. figure 2).

Our thinking is bound to these ideas, driven by the popular narrative of order, hierarchy, purpose, and progress (Grobstein 2005, 12). Beliefs like these often lead to fixed inductive categories of evidence that are difficult to change. This is reminiscent of the controversy between Kuhn and Popper in which Kuhn tries to demonstrate that new scientific theories and paradigms are not better but very different (in fact incommensurable) compared to the old, rejected ones. According to Kuhn (1962, 1–2, 198–222), there is no linear improvement in science at all.

*Narrative, Rhetoric and Science* 151

Figure 2. Spandrels. The beautiful and often ornamented spaces between arches and ceiling are architectural artefacts, but, as for many biological forms, we mistakenly view them as purposeful. The picture above shows a detail of Nidaros Cathedral's sanctuary, Trondheim (by Concierge.2C; licensed under the Creative Commons Attribution-Share Alike 3.0 Norway license).

Valuing hierarchy and order (balance) has contributed to the paradigm of a steady state in natural sciences that has led to multiple misinterpretations of biology. It has contributed to the idea of mammalian physiology associated with endothermy as being more advanced (e.g., more complex than that of "lower" ectotherms). This "advancement" is assumed to arise from a greater separation from environmental vagaries through maintenance of a "higher" steady-state condition—when there is no biological or ecological imperative for this reasoning. A preoccupation with change over time as a linear process leading to progress also became manifest in the idea of environmental stability being achieved through graded linear progression to higher order stability. These formed central components of ecological theory in the twentieth century such as trophic levels, carrying capacity, equilibrium, and succession. "The concept of natural communities as cooperating wholes may simply be a hopeful anthropomorphism based on socioeconomic structures of Greek city states" (Drury 1998, 20). Although complexity theory is now shifting the paradigm to include non-linear dynamics and non-equilibrium systems, many aspects of successionist climax theory persist in ecology and conservation biology. Expected narratives of progress and change also help explain why "living fossils" remain popular aberrations as organisms that are supposedly enduring in a primitive form across evolution. While one or more of their traits may remain conserved, many more will be vastly different from their ancestral state, and as organisms and lineages living fossils have of course changed along with their environments and ecosystems (cf. figure 3). However, science and the public alike refuse to let go of their storyline of surviving ancient relicts understood to be "frozen in time."

Requiring a final resolution from beginning to end is also a problematic expectation for stories in science, as science is inherently unresolved. A narrative focus on resolution teaches us the wrong expectations of the process of science. Requiring a plot with a climax and an obvious arc of suspense, conflict, and confrontation is also problematic to a realistic understanding of the collective process of scientific endeavor. Many narrative arcs impose the assumption of the existence of a predetermined goal whose existence has always been clear for the scientists, such that they only had to find the right way to reach an end already teleologically determined. This runs counter to the self-correcting flexibility of science in practice, where a hypothesis for testing is often refined after many results have already been acquired (see Terrell 1990, 17–19; Harré 1990, 88).

Figure 3. The paradigm of primitive. Supposedly "less advanced" ectotherms, like the tuatara reptile, are arguably misunderstood as primitive on many counts. This collagraph print references the fact that fossils of its lineage are found all over the world and argues for reconceptualizing it as adaptive and dominant rather than a "living fossil" relict (copyright permission from artist Jenny Rock).

The popular narrative device of conflict between binary oppositions is a driver of many stories, and again can be particularly problematic in science. Claude Lévi-Strauss (1955) suggests that narratives revolve around dichotomies such as good vs. evil, humans vs. aliens (known vs. unknown), and past vs present. Directed to make sense of the world this way (by dividing it into clear dichotomic categories), we expect a right-vs.-wrong clearcut resolution to stories in scientific inquiry. By expecting fixed categories of interaction, we also expect to reach a solution in the end that is equally clear and reliable, not just one possibility of many, or one based on complex probabilities. Further, once we have a solution, which we expect to be akin to the "right" or "winning" paradigm, we try to keep it as long as possible as a basis for our thinking, understanding, and as an important point of reference (Kuhn 1962, 77). This fixation on dichotomies explains, for example, why the "nature vs. nurture" debate will not die, although there is long-standing evidence for highly integrated interplay between both genetic and epigenetic mechanisms in every aspect of biology.

While some narrative modes focus on a narrative of events (a chain thereof, with cause and effect), others dwell on the narrative of drama (in which few events happen but there is much in the drama surrounding a character). Vladimir Propp (1968) identified a suite of character roles within a variety of narrative functions including: the villain, hero, donor, helper, princess (sought-for person/reward for hero/victim of villain's schemes), king (rewarder of hero), dispatcher, and false hero. Propp suggested that certain types of characters shape certain kinds of narratives and identified thirty-one possible stages or functions of any narrative that might be present in a story (and which are ordered in an invariable sequence of occurrence). Joseph Campbell (1968) developed this further by suggesting that narrative structures generally followed common archetypes of set characters in set situations, such as the hero quest/journey, initiation, fall or death/rebirth.

> Stories usually have . . . heroes and scoundrels, triumphs and defeats, trials and tribulations, conquests and achievements, winners and losers. There is likely to be at least one critical turning point somewhere in the middle of a story . . . . The end may be tragic, romantic, comic, ironic, or heroic. Often, too, stories conclude with ethical lessons or judgments of the principle characters as good or bad, better or worse . . . . (Terrell 1990, 4)

In the stories of scientific achievements, equivalents of the character roles are enacted. For example, scientific breakthrough is often presented as a narrative of a scientist's trials/quest. This perspective explains the expectation of change during research and scientific development. Not only are we expecting the scientists to meet a challenge within these changes (acting like the hero who has been chosen to enable the new state of equilibrium), but we also wait for betterment throughout the story (Kuhn 1962, 1–2, 152–59). Due to the specific character roles and order of events befalling them, our attention is drawn to certain aspects of the story while others remain unnoticed. Our focus dwells on the singular hero in science for longer than it is useful to science. This may help rationalize how, for instance, the central dogma of DNA as central controller persists in the face of overwhelming evidence for complex feedback loops of silencing and enhancement through RNA-mediated regulation (cf. figure 4).

Narrative, Rhetoric and Science 155

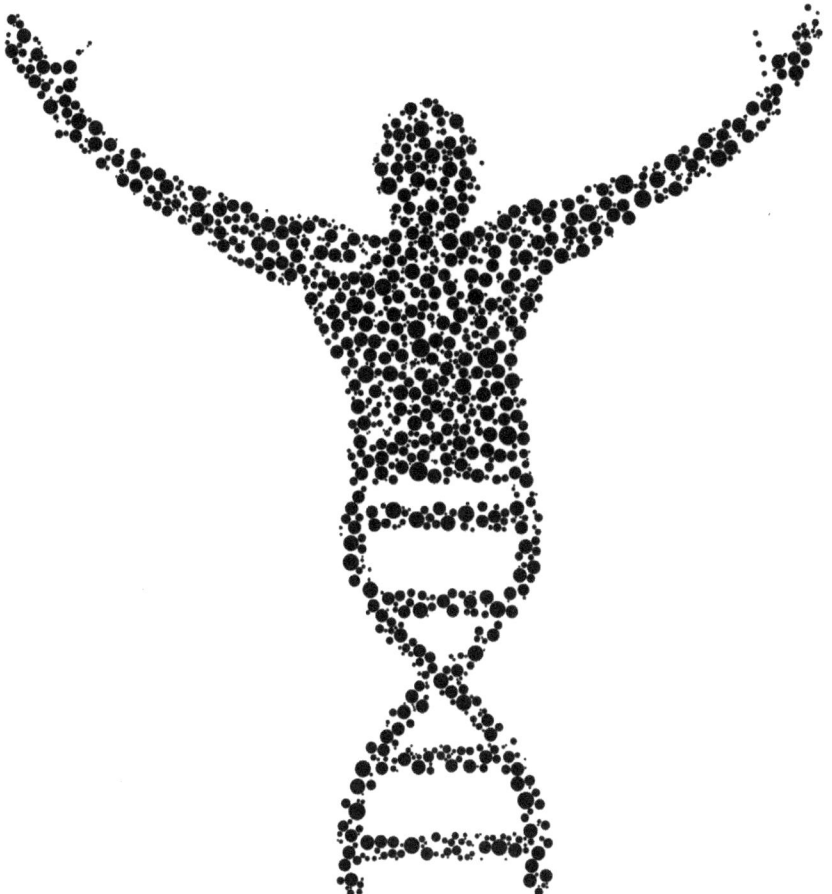

Figure 4. Biological Man. Our fixation on the gene as a central controller undoubtedly links to the hero motif in genetic determinism as well as the aesthetics of a double helix conformation (image sourced from https://openclipart.org/detail/277335/biological-man-circles; CC0 Creative Commons).

Narrative structures can help communication, making it easier for the audience to absorb the given information. The danger is that the audience—other scientists and the public alike—is often not able to distinguish between their expectations of a storyline delivered and the actual attributes and relationships of the scientific elements. In other words, they may not realize which are the crucial aspects leading to the successful achievement of evidence they are experiencing. Story can impose false relationships and hide or inflate the roles of various elements. Thus, when communicating science, story can in many instances confuse the original meaning or even misrepresent it. At worst, it offers opportunities for the scientists to conceal gaps and shortcomings within their theories and presentations; holes in data or gross uncertainties can be covered by a good story line, giving the impression that there is nothing unconvincing at hand. Scientific results can be charged with significance, and causal relations can be implied by a narrative device that makes it much easier to infer far-reaching conclusions (Terrell 1990, 7). The story convinces not only the public audience—it will convince the teller as well, whether it be the individual scientist or the collective scientific community substantiating its popular paradigms. However, varying interpretation of data is of course central to the scientific process. Progress is achieved by shifting explanations and focus (paradigms) and this is a key danger of narrative—its compelling aesthetic to set story structure has the power to stall the healthy paradigm shifts and cycles of evidence building that are so fundamental to science.

## Conclusion

Unable to communicate without using the structures of rhetoric, we are always thinking and acting within patterns and conditions that significantly affect the messages and information we aim to share. We are well advised to identify and consider these effects especially within the scope of science. Everyone, from scientists to members of the public to professional communicators, must be vigilant to the effects of these structures of persuasion and narrative in science. This understanding calls rhetoric into specific action as a discipline that offers a wide variety of instructions for language usage that could also lead to greater clarity in science communication. Indeed, rhetoric can offer both—methods to achieve desired communication effects and guidance on how to keep their affect clear and conscious (Kemmann 1996, 39). An increased awareness of rhetoric, including various narrative techniques and devices, can help to detect these persuasive structures at multiple levels of science. Awareness may act to improve the communication structures between scientific communities, or between science and the public, and to reduce misunderstandings. But more importantly, it opens our eyes and increases our appreciation for the diverse drivers of science. Understanding the influence of history and aesthetics on paradigms does not undermine science—it enriches our view and lends far greater accuracy to our comprehension. Indeed, from a rhetorical perspective the legitimacy of every single paradigm can be called into question—nothing remains unchallenged, even established positions must be declared again and again to justify their dominance and validity. This leads to a more flexible and changeable basis for scientific development.

Undoubtedly, it is useful to employ persuasive structures like narratives and other rhetorical devices to attract attention to scientific achievements, to gain an evident depiction and to optimize persuasiveness. For scientists and members of the public alike, there is great power in an understanding of the underlying processes that shape the interaction between science and society, and a consciousness of scientific process as always influenced by persuasive efforts. Though it grants no Archimedean point from which we can compare different theories or paradigms with complete neutrality (as every position carries particular premises whose acceptance is necessary to follow the scientific approach), with greater consciousness scientists might be able to step back and view the efforts of their community from a distance, to recognize alternate possibilities. A wider understanding of the processes that shape the interaction between science and society also recasts the audience as no longer a passive recipient but an active participant in evaluating scientific results (Fröhlich 2008, 452). This may not only broaden the scope for evaluation, but also allow a wider participation in the scientific process itself. The resulting richness of hypotheses is influenced by the number of different stories and the breadth of story motifs (see the "candidate stories" and "repertoire" in storytelling styles identified by Grobstein 2005, 11).

For those external to science but communicating its stories to the public, further care must be taken to acknowledge that narrative structures are already at work in the rhetoric and paradigms of science itself—even before one starts to build another interpretative layer of evidence. Perhaps the biggest challenge, however, for science communicators both inside and outside of science is to be careful regarding what kind of story they tell (and how they present it). At the same time, it is crucial for the public to be aware of what kinds of stories they are demanding, as, collectively, we can all be held responsible for entrenching scientific paradigms or facilitating healthy and productive flexibility and change in the discourse and functioning of science. It is particularly useful to remind ourselves of such interactions as we revel in the modern rebirth and ascendancy of narrative in science.

## Works Cited

Aristoteles. 1982. *Poetik*. Translated and edited by Manfred Fuhrmann. Stuttgart: Philipp Reclam jun.

Aristoteles. 1999. *Rhetorik*. Translated and edited by Gernot Krapinger. Stuttgart: Philipp Reclam jun.

Bitzer, Lloyd. 1980. "Functional Communication: A Situational Perspective." In *Rhetoric in Transition. Studies on the Nature and Uses of Rhetoric*, edited by Eugene E. White, 21–38. University Park, PA: Pennsylvania State University Press.

Burke, Kenneth. 1969. *A Rhetoric of Motives*. Berkeley: University of California Press.

Campbell, Joseph. 1968. *The Hero with a Thousand Faces*. Princeton: Princeton University Press.

Cicero. 2007. *De Oratore*. Translated and edited by Theodor Nüßlein. Düsseldorf: Artemis & Winkler Verlag.

Drury, William H. Jr. 1998. *Chance and Change: Ecology for Conservationists*. Berkeley: University of California Press.

Eagly, Alice H., and Shelly Chaiken. 1993. *The Psychology of Attitudes*. Fort Worth: Harcourt Brace Jovanovich.

Festinger, Leon. 1957. *A Theory of Cognitive Dissonance*. Stanford: Stanford University Press.

Fleck, Ludwik. 1979. *Genesis and Development of a Scientific Fact*. Chicago: The University of Chicago Press.

Freytag, Gustav. 1894. *Freytag's Technique of the Drama: An Exposition of dramatic Composition and Art*. Translated by Elias J. MacEwan. Chicago: Griggs & Company.

Fröhlich, Sandra. 2008. "Rhetorik und Wissenschaft: Von einer rhetorischen Erkenntnistheorie zur Wissenschaftskritik der Social-Text-Affäre. " *Rhetorica: A Journal of the History of Rhetoric* 26 (4): 439–53.

Gould, Stephen J., and Richard C. Lewontin. 1979. "The Spandrels of San Marco and the Panglossian Paradigm: A Critique of the Adaptationist Programme." *Proceedings of the Royal Society of London. Series B, Biological Sciences* 205 (1161): 581–98.

Grice, Paul H. 1989. *Studies in the Way of Words*. Cambridge: Harvard University Press.

Grobstein, Paul. 2005. "Revisiting Science in Culture: Science as Story Telling and Story Revising." *Journal of Research Practice* 1 (1): Article M1. http://jrp.icaap.org/index.php/jrp/article/view/9/17.

Gross, Alan G. 1990a. *The Rhetoric of Science*. Cambridge: Harvard University Press.

—. 1990b. "The Origin of Species: Evolutionary Taxonomy as an Example of the Rhetoric of Science." In *The Rhetorical Turn: Invention and Persuasion in the Conduct of Inquiry*, edited by Herbert W. Simons, 91–115. Chicago: University of Chicago Press.

Harré, Rom. 1990. "*Some* Narrative Conventions of Science Discourse." In *Narrative in Culture: The Uses of Storytelling in the Sciences, Philosophy and Literature*, edited by Christopher Nash, 81–101. London: Routledge.

Hildt, Elisabeth, and László Kovács. 2009. *Was bedeutet genetische Information?* Berlin: De Gruyter.

Johnstone, Henry W. Jr. 1965. "Some Reflections on Argumentation." In *Philosophy, Rhetoric and Argumentation*, edited by Maurice Natanson and Henry W. Johnstone, Jr., 1–9. University Park: Pennsylvania State University Press.
Kemmann, Ansgar. 1996. "Evidentia, Evidenz." In *Historisches Wörterbuch der Rhetorik*, edited by Gert Ueding, 33–47. Tübingen: Niemeyer Verlag.
Kuhn, Thomas S. 1962. *The Structure of Scientific Revolutions*. Chicago: The University of Chicago Press.
Lakatos, Imre and Alan E. Musgrave, eds. 1970. *Criticism and the Growth of Knowledge*. Vol. 4. Cambridge: Cambridge University Press.
Latour, Bruno, and Steve Woolgar. 1986. *Laboratory Life: The Social Construction of Scientific Facts*. Princeton, NJ: Princeton University Press.
Lévi-Strauss, Claude. 1955. "The Structural Study of Myth." *The Journal of American Folklore* 68 (270): 428–44.
Mayr, Ernst. 2004. *What Makes Biology Unique?: Considerations on the Autonomy of a Scientific Discipline*. Cambridge: Cambridge University Press.
Myers, David G. 2005. *Psychologie*. Heidelberg: Springer Medizin Verlag.
Ogden, Charles K., and Ivor A. Richards. 1923. *The Meaning of Meaning: A Study of the Influence of Language upon Thought and of the Science of Symbolism*. London: Routledge & Keagan Paul.
Propp, Vladimir. 1968. *Morphology of the Folktale*. Austin: University of Texas Press.
Quintilian, Marcus Fabius. 1988. *Ausbildung des Redners: Zwölf Bücher. Erster Teil: Buch I-VI*. Translated and edited by Helmut Rahn. Darmstadt: Wissenschaftliche Buchgesellschaft.
Richards, Ivor A. 1965. *The Philosophy of Rhetoric*. New York: Oxford University Press.
Sherif, Muzafer. 1935. *A Study of Some Social Factors in Perception*. New York: Columbia University Press [Archives of Psychology 187].
Sterne, Laurence. (1759–67) 1849. *The Life and Opinions of Tristram Shandy, Gentleman*. Leipzig.
Terrell, John. 1990. "Storytelling and Prehistory." *Archaeological Method and Theory* 2:1–29.
Todorov, Tzvetan. 1969. *Grammaire du Décaméron*. The Hague: Mouton.
Turner, John C. 1987. *Rediscovering the Social Group—A Self-Categorization Theory*. Oxford: Blackwell.

# 9 Humans after *Heidelbergensis*: The Spirited Rhetoric of Paleoanthropology

*Jeffery Gentry*

## Introduction

Although paleoanthropologists concur that humans evolved by natural selection, their agreement nearly ends there. The leading view holds that *Homo sapiens* emerged from an earlier species known as *Homo heidelbergensis*, within Africa, roughly 200,000 years ago and replaced all other contemporaneous human populations (such as the Neandertals in Europe and *Homo erectus* in Asia). However, a minority of scientists views humanity as a likewise singular but far-flung species going back nearly two million years. The fundamental divide among equally qualified experts suggests that the rhetoric of science provides a rich foundation for research in twenty-first century persuasion.

The present chapter offers a rhetorical analysis of the debate between the recent African origin model (RAO) versus multiregional evolution (MRE). After reviewing salient literature, the rhetorical situation is considered, including arguments and evidence supporting the two competing theories. Next, two methods of rhetorical criticism are described: the classical neo-Aristotelian approach and the narrative paradigm of Walter Fisher. Finally, RAO and MRE are critiqued to discern which human-origins theory produces the greater rhetorical effect.

Science as an object of twenty-first century rhetorical inquiry has been confined to two approaches. Either the author describes rhetorical elements without issuing a critique (e.g., Jack 2010), or, if a critique is provided, the topic of scientific controversy is one-sided, usually a debate between science and pseudo-science (e.g., Paroske 2009). Legitimate scientific controversies swirl around the twenty-first century academy and are ripe for analysis, but only if scholars are willing to engage them. This chapter provides a framework and example for such rhetorical criticism, using as its case study the primary controversy within human-evolution theory.

Science is rhetorical. In some circles, this claim is self-evident. In others, not so much. Celeste Condit (2008) rightly assails scientists who claim that evidence generated by their methods is purely objective:

> Scientific knowledge and understanding can only be constructed through words, symbols, and the associated diffuse interactions commonly called their "meanings" or "ideas." Words and symbols are inherently value laden because they are embedded as structures of relation in interest-laden biological beings. (390)

Condit observes that not only did science gerrymander facts for political aims in the past; today's scientists are just as human as their predecessors, and their inferences should not be considered any less value-laden than those of earlier eras (389). Condit is a rhetorical scholar in a department of speech communication. Yet, paleontologist Milford Wolpoff (1976) foretells her later thesis when noting that scientific controversies will continue regardless of the facts, "because science is a human activity" (95).

Wolpoff (1976) scolds scientists who claim that data should be left to speak for themselves. Sounding like a teacher of argumentation, he teases, "I, for one, will freely admit that I have never heard paleoanthropological data speak. Data, in my view, cannot exist outside of a theoretical framework, and the relation of data to such a framework lies in their potential power of refutation" (95). The married team of anthropologists Rachel Caspari and Milford Wolpoff (1997) note, "Science by its very attempts to explain things is not evenhanded" (30). (Dr. Wolpoff soon returns to star in our featured debate.) Chad Wickman (2012) likewise affirms that the process of scientific inquiry is rhetorical and epistemic, yielding new knowledge in its very communication (22). Understanding that science is inherently rhetorical, we may turn our attention to scholarship in the genre.

TWENTY-FIRST CENTURY STUDIES IN THE RHETORIC OF SCIENCE

As noted above, many studies in the rhetoric of science are either highly descriptive, thus lacking a critique, or the controversies are one-sided. Fisher (1984) describes the dual strands of rhetoric as typically studied in the fields of speech communication versus English, respectively: "the argumentative, persuasive theme and the literary, aesthetic themes" (2). The literary/aesthetic approach is favored by English scholars such as Jordynn Jack (2010), who holds that the main task of rhetorical studies on science is to illuminate the use of symbolic and linguistic resources (210). This approach provides value, but scholars in rhetorical criticism, housed in the field of speech communication, go beyond illumination by evaluating the advocate's rhetorical effect (cf. Brock and Scott 1980, 17). Effect involves judging, for example, whether the speaker achieved her persuasive goals with the immediate audience or produced rhetoric that will have a lasting impact on society. Rhetorical criticism is thus a qualitative research method used to discern the impact of persuasive discourse.

When recent rhetorical studies of science do venture into considerations of effect, the result is often a one-sided polemic. For example, Condit's (2008) study condemns research by geneticist Bruce T. Lahn. Lahn had suggested that a gene related to enhanced brain size was distributed unevenly among different races. From the outset Condit emphasizes that scholars "rapidly and unanimously discredited Lahn's claim of a genetic connection between race and intelligence" (Condit 2008, 384). By the time of Condit's study, Lahn had given up on such research to focus on other subjects. Perhaps a more fruitful rhetorical criticism would tackle a *legitimate* scientific controversy, that is, one that is not immediately obvious but dwells in the realm of the contingent (cf. Aristotle *Rh.* 1.1–3).

Other rhetorical critiques of science read much like Condit's, as their purpose seems to be to refute unenlightened scientific or pseudo-scientific claims. Marcus Paroske (2009) condemns former South African president Thabo Mbeki's argument that the HIV virus does not cause AIDS. Valerie Rohy (2012) exposes flaws in the Religious Right's claim that homosexuality cannot be natural or else gays would be able to reproduce. Leah Ceccarelli (2011) takes to task three "manufactured" scientific controversies: AIDS dissent (again featuring Mbeki), global warming skepticism, and intelligent design versus evolution. The final study uses terms like "appalling," "self-interested obstructionists," and the anti-scientific yet well-worn phrase "overwhelming scientific consensus" (bandwagon fallacy) on one page alone (Ceccarelli 2011, 196). Each of these subjects is an easy target, with the world's intellectual community solidly on one side of the supposed controversy. But traditional rhetorical criticism grants the speaker her motives. Rather than simply discredit one side, critics provide greater value when they offer a reasonably even-handed analysis of salient rhetorical elements.

It would appear from the studies above that the only controversies in science are manufactured by malevolent forces or by pseudo-scientists. Are there no legitimate scientific controversies in the twenty-first century? None that occupies Aristotle's realm of the contingent? According to an editorial on paleoanthropology in the prestigious journal *Nature*, science thrives on debate: "In contrast, a field in which everyone blandly agrees with everything is a field in stagnation" (Rude Paleoanthropology 2006, 957). Rather than being above debate, science is at its best (and most stimulating) when embroiled in it, in which the facts themselves are in dispute as well as the inferences drawn from those facts. A collection of such studies could even develop into a new critical genre (cf. Campbell and Jamieson 1978), which we could term the *rhetoric of legitimate scientific controversies*.

Even one of the scientific controversies cited above can, with a little effort, be viewed as providing two legitimate sides. The thesis of anthropomorphic climate change has met skepticism among well-qualified solar scientists (e.g., Bilali, Patterson, and Prokoph 2013). Other legitimate scientific controversies may be worthy of study, such as whether earth can sustain a population above eight billion, or if Pluto should be considered a bona fide planet. In contrast to the polemical studies noted above, a traditional rhetorical criticism that provides a fair or dispassionate analysis of effect may produce a compelling critique.

## Methods

Jack (2010) provides criteria for studies of rhetoric in science, but not on scientific controversies. For this model, we may turn to Wickman (2012), who touts classical rhetorical criticism (a.k.a., traditional or neo-Aristotelian) to discern the effect of scientific discourse. Although his case study limits itself to illumination like Jack's (2010), Wickman recommends stasis theory, artistic and inartistic proofs, the canons of rhetoric, and the topoi. Similar to Jack (2010), Wickman (2012) touts rhetorical methods as "a way to contribute our own disciplinary expertise to the broader field of science studies" (38). We may add the importance of refutation, as the advocate rebuts her opponent's constructions while extending or rebuilding her own original arguments. Finally, classical rhetoric recommends a consideration of the three artistic modes of proof: ethos, pathos, logos (see Aristotle *Rh.* 1.2).

In addition to classical rhetoric, Fisher's (1984) narrative approach provides tools for the rhetorical analysis of scientific controversies. Borrowing the linguistic style of anthropologists like Wolpoff, Fisher (1984, 1) conceives of human beings not as *Homo sapiens*, but "Homo narrans"—the storytelling person. Like Wolpoff (1976) and Condit (2008), Fisher challenges the idea that rhetoric is confined to expressly persuasive discourse, but permeates all communication, including science. His approach holds that so-called distinctions between informative and persuasive communication are artificial and illusory (2). People naturally tell stories that influence one another, and they possess an inherent ability to understand and judge the stories of others. Stories that provide good reasons for their claims carry influence.

Fisher upholds narrative as a philosophical paradigm, one that challenges the rational-world paradigm centered on logic and the leading role of experts in adjudicating good arguments (cf. Aristotle *Rh.*). Therefore, scientific elites do not solely own the rhetoric of legitimate scientific controversies. In a narrative universe their competing stories about science and nature will be judged by opinion leaders, educators, media, and the public in a long-term struggle for influence. As Fisher (1984) notes, "the world is a set of stories which must be chosen among to live the good life in a process of continual recreation" (8). A compelling story is more convincing than simply amassing a preponderance of evidence.

Olaf Kramer's application of narrative theory in chapter 3 of this volume analyzes micronarrative storytelling in Hans Fallada's novel *Every Man Dies Alone*. This chapter, in contrast, applies Fisher's theory to the complex and argumentative story of human evolution. Kramer's analytical focus lies on stories that create common ground and "reduce resistance, because they are more open and inclusive than rational arguments," whereas this chapter considers "rational arguments, which rely on the choice between limited and clearly marked alternatives" (cf. chapter 3). Kramer emphasizes *aesthetic* storytelling in the direct form of a novel. This chapter emphasizes *forensic* storytelling, more like a criminal suspect's "story," or claim of innocence. Both chapters use narrative theory to illuminate meaning-rich discourse.

The narrative approach contains two stock issues for audiences to consider: "their narrative probability, what constitutes a coherent story, and their constant habit of testing narrative fidelity, whether the stories they experience ring true with the stories they know to be true in their lives" (Fisher 1984, 8). The former principle, narrative probability (or coherence), will prove particularly useful in the present study. It considers how well the story hangs together, or avoids internal contradictions (see logos). Theory-building in science attempts to construct a story, or satisfying explanation, that remains consistent with the known facts. Although the facts themselves are often in dispute, any disconnect between the facts and the theory expose its weaknesses and can be exploited. If the facts more consistently support an alternate theory, it will gain in influence.

Narrative fidelity refers to whether the story rings true or prompts immediate face validity and consistency with what the hearer already knows or believes to be true. Fidelity refers to the facts themselves, and whether hearing them leaves the listener satisfied, as opposed to experiencing cognitive dissonance. This could include the effect of visual rhetoric, as will be shown below. Thus, narrative theory is well suited to testing the rhetorical effect of scientific discourse. In the case of competing scientific theories, the question is which provides the more rational arguments (Aristotle *Rh.*) and the more compelling narrative (Fisher 1984). Select elements from both theories will be applied in this case study on the rhetoric of legitimate scientific controversies.

## HUMANS AFTER *HEIDELBERGENSIS*: RAO AND MRE

After nearly forty years, two leading narratives in paleoanthropology continue to vie for prominence among scientists, the media, and the attentive public. These theories are the recent African origin model (RAO) and multiregional evolution (MRE). The notion of a singular and recent origin of humans in Africa (e.g., Tattersall and Schwartz 2009) enjoys a status close to that of the perceived "consensus" of anthropomorphic climate change touted by Ceccarelli (2011, 195), with most paleoanthropologists on board. On the other hand, multiregional evolution (MRE) is championed by Milford Wolpoff of the University of Michigan (e.g., Caspari and Wolpoff 2013). Many of MRE's strongest supporters tend to be Wolpoff's own former students. After describing each narrative, we can observe the points of agreement and disagreement, and then offer a rhetorical critique.

The words "recent African origin" describe a time and place when the human race is thought to have begun (e.g., Tattersall and Schwartz 2009). According to the RAO story, also known as "Out of Africa II," "the replacement hypothesis," or the "Garden of Eden" theory, today's humans arose in Africa roughly 200,000 years ago and later colonized the rest of the world. An earlier hominin had left Africa about 1.8 million-years prior. It evolved into *Homo erectus* and Denisovans in Asia, Neandertals in Europe, and Homo floresiensis in the East Indies, with all sub-species thriving for tens of thousands of years. But Homo erectus, Denisovans, Neandertals, and Homo floresiensis died out after contact with Homo sapiens, who had evolved independently in Africa and then expanded into Europe and Asia less than 100,000 years ago (thus, "Out of Africa II"). The now-extinct branches of the *Homo* species handed down little or no lineage to present-day people, either because any mixed offspring with Homo sapiens were infertile or debilitated, or because the respective subspecies did very little mingling to start with. These branches are indicative of the phylogenic-branching model (see figure 1), in which only Homo sapiens survived to the present.

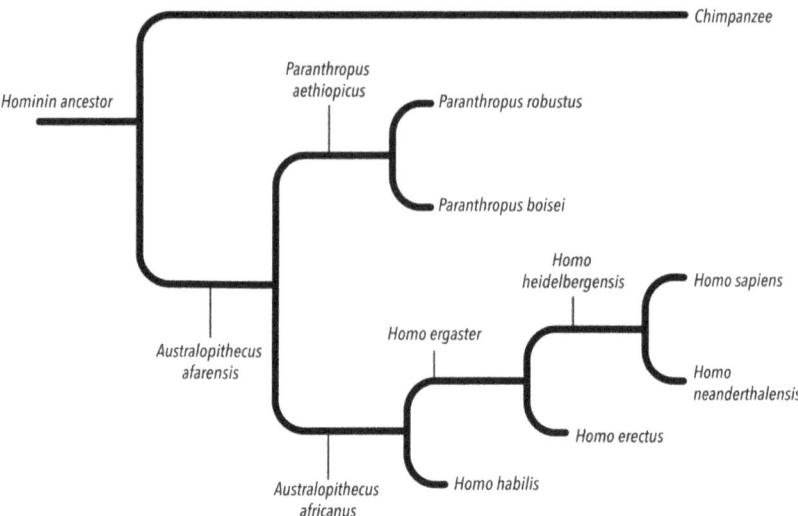

Figure 1. Example RAO Phylogenic Branching Model. Graphic design by Jessica Gerlach.[1]

In contrast to discredited polygenic theories of the early twentieth century, which had suggested humans evolved independently into five modern subspecies, RAO holds that all living people share highly similar genetics due to their recent, singular African origin. This singularity was caused by one or more evolutionary bottlenecks that rendered all other *Homo* species extinct, possibly influenced by the eruption of the Toba volcano seventy thousand years ago. Superficial physical differences among modern populations are merely recent adaptations to diverse environments and do nothing to change the singularity of the human race.

RAO works as a satisfying narrative due to its effectiveness in upholding Fisher's (1984) twin stock issues of narrative fidelity and narrative coherence. Entirely consistent with evolution by natural selection, RAO raises no red flags unless the hearer rejects "evolution" reflexively. Twenty-first-century scientists test its hypotheses via archaeological, fossil, and genetic evidence. So, the theory rings true as consistent with Darwinian principles. A second case of narrative fidelity is that RAO entails a single human race, supplying an empirically testable rejection of hateful nativism, or notions of any race being superior. Racism falls flat when all of us alive today are very near cousins, with demonstrably less genetic variation than all other primate species and most other mammals. It even works well within the framework of the world's great monotheistic religions. This is because RAO (a.k.a., the Garden of Eden theory or Out of Africa II) has demonstrated that all humanity can be traced back to a single woman, known to anthropologists as mitochondrial Eve, just 160,000 years ago (see figure 2). This new species, with its uniquely sophisticated brain, outcompeted all others to become the last humans standing.

Figure 2. *The Temptation of Eve*, painting by Jean-Baptiste Marie Pierre (eighteenth century, public domain work).

Narrative coherence is an even greater strength of the recent African origin model. It hangs together as a plausible explanation for present-day humanity for several interconnected reasons. First, humans around the world are a closely matched species, proven by our universal fertility. For example, England and Australia are nearly as far apart as two places on earth can be. Yet Evonne Goolagong Cawley, who contains a blend of "English" and "Aboriginal" genes, became the number-one women's tennis player in the world. In fact, humans endemic to all regions have no difficulty producing healthy children with each other (see figure 3).

Figure 3. Inter-racial American family from European, African, and Middle Eastern descent. Photograph by Cynthia Gentry. With permission.

The genes of humans around the world are all nearly one hundred percent traceable to recent Africa, which is why there is more genetic diversity within the continent than outside of it. Genetic mutations, most of which are neutral, accumulate fairly consistently over time; and African genes contain more of them than anywhere else in the world. This makes perfect sense if Africa is the birthplace of all humanity. Physical differences among modern "races" are only superficial physical adaptations to different world environments that took hold very late in the human era. Finally, our sophisticated use of stone tools and other modern behaviors likewise appeared in Africa long before anywhere else.

An alternative to the RAO narrative is multiregional evolution (MRE) (e.g., Caspari and Wolpoff 2013). In this story, the human race arose in Africa about two million years ago. Humans expanded into Asia and Europe soon after, with all populations evolving together. Continual genic transfers across regions of the old world were balanced by a degree of regional continuity. This narrative does not view *Homo erectus* and Neandertals as distinct species or subspecies from Homo sapiens. Instead, these terms merely refer to *populations* of Homo found in different regions during the Pleistocene epoch (2.6 million B.P. to 11,700 B.P.). Nor does Wolpoff accept the term *anatomically modern human* (AMH) to exclude Neandertals from Cro-Magnons, which RAO scientists hold to be the original *Homo sapiens* in Europe. Therefore, humans are a single, global species with a faint degree of old, localized natural selection. Homo erectus and Neandertals never went extinct but live on in today's Asians and Europeans. The physical differences found across continents, a.k.a. their regional continuity, are mere remnants of early human variation and adaptation.

Despite its incompatibility with RAO, the story of multiregional evolution (MRE) likewise provides narrative fidelity and narrative coherence. Similarly based on Darwinian evolution by natural selection, MRE undergoes hypothesis testing under the same scientific method that all paleoanthropologists aspire to uphold. Its narrative fidelity further derives from modern science's abhorrence of the notion of genetic superiority. MRE begins with the notion that humanity has always been a single multiregional species, therefore no population group can claim to be the prototype or zenith. Like RAO it is built on analyses of archaeological, fossil, and genetic evidence.

MRE provides narrative coherence in its internal consistency. For example, it provides a plausible explanation for the racial diversity seen in people today without the taint of ugly eugenic implications. Caspari and Wolpoff (1997) state, "We have to consciously think of races as dynamic, changing entities with temporal depth because they are not the diverging branches on an evolutionary bush but the constantly separating and merging channels in a stream" (356). The small but enduring physical differences among races are holdovers from up to two million years before the present, as populations across the old world evolved as one species but retained physical continuities within their home regions in Africa, Europe, Asia, and Oceania. Once a mutation was selected as beneficial in one region, it quickly spread to the others, partly because human mores favoring exogamy (anti-inbreeding, itself a positively selected behavioral trait) prompted inter-marriage with groups downstream or across the valley. MRE is represented by a trellis model of human evolution, in which populations across the Old World continually "stayed in touch" genetically (see figure 4).

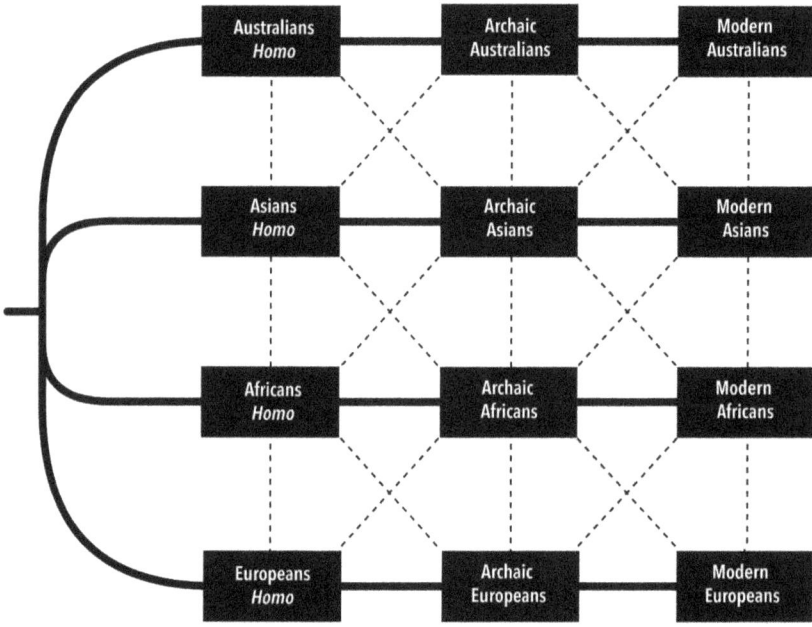

Figure 4. Example MRE Trellis Model. Graphic design by Jessica Gerlach.

Only moderate levels of human migration were needed to launch positively selected mutations thousands of kilometers within a few generations. Neandertals and Homo erectus were merely localized populations of Homo sapiens. Along with the more populous African Homo sapiens, they evolved together via continual genic transfer across the Old World, all the while retaining some of their older distinct features.

## Comparing the Theories

One can readily note the similarities and differences between the two leading theories of human evolution (see Tables 1 and 2). In the descriptive section above, I took care to avoid argumentative claims, instead expressing each theory on its own terms as though there were no controversy.

Table 1. Similarities Chart: Recent African Origin (RAO) and Multiregional Evolution (MRE). Graphic design by Jessica Gerlach.

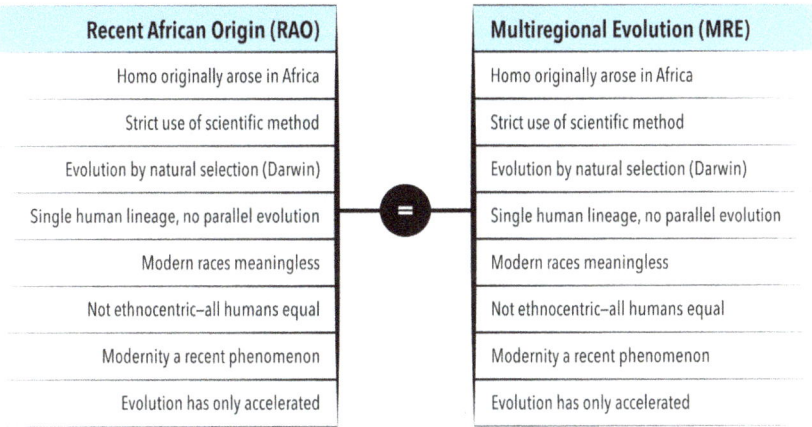

Table 2. Differences Chart: Recent African Origin (RAO) and Multiregional Evolution (MRE). Graphic design by Jessica Gerlach.

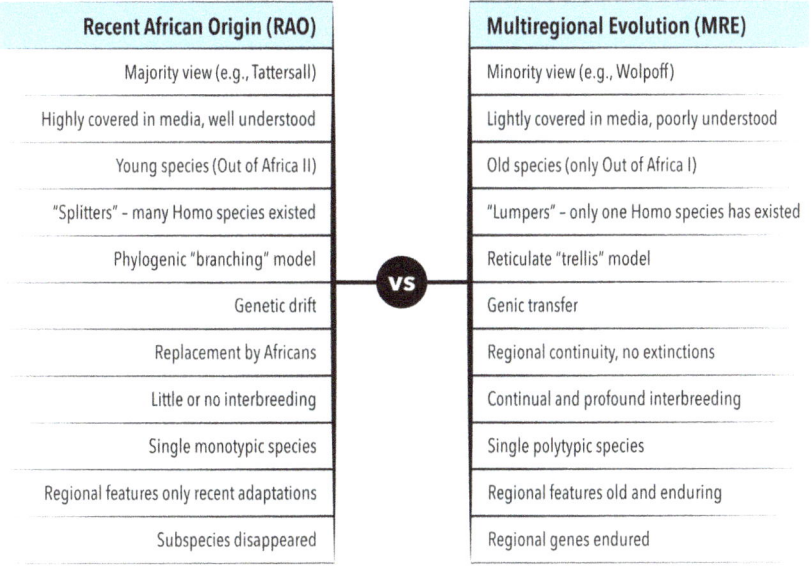

Controversy abounds, however. Table 2 summarizes the main points of contention between the two leading theories of paleoanthropology. The most obvious difference: RAO entails that humans are a relatively new species whereas MRE places our origin ten times deeper into the past. Humanity's superficial racial differences are new in RAO, old in MRE. However, some scholars view the two theories as compatible, resulting in several assimilation models (e.g., Stringer 2012). In this view, humans are *principally* African; yet modern Europeans, Asians, and Australasians of the old and new world retain a trace amount of deep regional ancestry. Rather than compromise, however, Caspari and Wolpoff (2013) reject assimilation as a legitimate position (364). They argue that any degree of assimilation constitutes multiregionalism entirely, relegating RAO as an extreme view.

Despite a constant flow of new evidence and theoretical refinements, the heavyweight battle in human evolution remains RAO versus MRE, and their debate provides the focus of this rhetorical investigation. Unlike the purely descriptive or one-sided studies cited previously, this debate involves enough light, heat, and unknowns to provide an argument-rich environment for analysis.

The arguments contested by RAO and MRE range from polite scholarly disagreement to uncontained food fight. On key points of disagreement, they seek to poke holes in the narrative coherence of the other theory. Although the debate is many decades old, it ignited in the late 1980s when breakthroughs in mitochondrial DNA research seemed to confirm a recent African origin for humanity (Cann, Stoneking, and Wilson 1987). RAO immediately captured the public's imagination, with numerous cover stories in major news magazines declaring that the Garden of Eden had been found in time and space (Caspari and Wolpoff 1997, 43). The time was 160,000 years before the present (YBP). The place was Africa. Quickly, paleoanthropologists who had been on the fence or even opposed to RAO began lining up behind it. A decade later, Tattersall and Schwartz (2009) claimed, aside from Caspari and Wolpoff, "there is more or less complete consensus among paleoanthropologists that Homo sapiens originated relatively recently, somewhere in Africa" (82). In contrast, Caspari and Wolpoff (2013) asserted that a new consensus exists on *their* side, but the authors cite no actual source except a puzzling reference to a 1963 work by Ernst Mayr.

The mitochondrial DNA evidence for RAO is a narrative unto itself. The world's most satisfying stories have a clear beginning. At only 160,000 YBP compared to the planet's age of 4.3 billion years, RAO gives humans the impressive status of nature's "best new idea." At the same time we are left in humble awe at our fleeting existence compared to creatures like sharks, which have patrolled the oceans a thousand times longer (i.e., greater than 160 *million* years). By counting the random accumulation of mutations in humans around the world, Rebecca Cann, Mark Stoneking, and Allan Wilson (1987) can point the way back in time six-thousand-plus generations to Mitochondrial Eve, a real African woman who is literally the mother of all people alive today. In this view, Homo neanderthalensis was an evolutionary dead end (see figure 5).

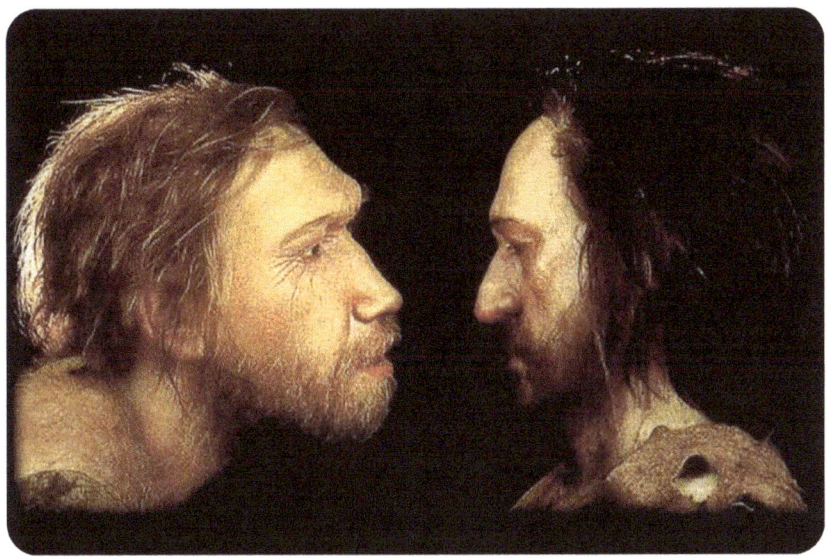

Figure 5. Neandertal/Cro-Magnon. Detail from the Cover of *Neandertal/Cro-Magnon: La Rencontre* (Arles: Éd. Errance, 2014) by Belgian scholar Marcel Otte. With permission.

RAO's popularity completely overshadowed the multiregional view led by Milford Wolpoff, Xinzhi Wu, and Alan G. Thorne (1984), who would fight and fail to convince the media to grant the MRE side an equal hearing. Wolpoff had completed his multiregional model just three years before the world met mitochondrial Eve. Ever since, the two theories have battled in a zero-sum game. For years the predominance of RAO left the multiregional view characterized less by its own narrative than as a refutation. It did not help MRE that many anthropologists conflated it with the discredited candelabra model of parallel evolution (cf. Fagan, 1990, 20–21), including its sordid linkage to racist eugenics theory. Thus, the two theories are best analyzed in competition, their pattern of argument-refutation-rebuttal recalling an old-fashioned high school debate.

To this day Wolpoff remains unconvinced by Cann's DNA evidence. His objection to her inferences about mitochondrial DNA lay in the interpretation of the time frame. It is clear that African genomes contain the majority of routine mutations, but with no way of knowing which ones occurred when, it is impossible to say exactly when "Eve" lived. So, for any realistic estimate of her age, scientists must assume that these inconsequential mutations occur fairly regularly, like clock-work. Cann estimates that they occur at a rate to place Eve at 160,000 YBP. Wolpoff disputes this estimate, arguing that mutations accumulate more slowly. So slowly, in fact, that he places mitochondrial Eve deeper in time by nearly a factor of ten: to 1.4 million YBP. This date fits nicely into MRE's timeline of an old species evolving as one across multiple regions, thus no "Out of Africa II." However, Wolpoff made little headway with these arguments among his peers, as the bogeyman of "overwhelming consensus" anointed RAO as untouchable and left MRE irrelevant. His idea that there has only been one Homo species on earth is dismissed by Tattersall and Schwartz (2009) as tautological:

> The practice of cramming all of this material into a single Old World-wide species is highly questionable. Indeed, the stuffing process has only been rendered possible by a sort of ratchet effect, in which fossils allocated to Homo erectus almost regardless of their morphology have subsequently been cited as proof of just how variable the species can be. (71)

After the turn of the twenty-first century the multiregional view seemed consigned to oblivion, even as holdout Milford Wolpoff entered his seventies in 2012. The only DNA that could be analyzed was from living humans, and it seemed to support only RAO. Wolpoff's claim that the blood of Neandertals and Homo erectus still flows in contemporary humans remained frustrated by a lack of evidence. But improvements in the extraction of ancient genetic material from human bones, developed by the Max Planck Institute in Germany, came to the rescue (Yong 2011, 34). Suddenly, RAO was on the defensive. Just a few months before, scientists assumed that ancient DNA from Neandertals and Homo erectus was too degraded for genomic testing. Wolpoff was elated to learn that not only could the full Neandertal genome be mapped, but that some one to four percent of the DNA of living Europeans and Asians could be linked to them. Moreover, genomic testing of an ancient human from Denisova cave in Siberia found DNA links between this hitherto undiscovered population—the Denisovans—and living Melanesians and native Australians (Yong 2011). A logical inference is that Homo sapiens is a hybrid of ancient humans from multiple regions. This would mean no replacement of ancient populations by Africans.

As one might guess by the pitched battle of human origins, RAO did not surrender in the face of the new genomic research. Trenton W. Holiday, Joana R. Gautney, and Lukáš Friedl (2014) argued that population densities were far too small to permit the worldwide genic transfers needed for MRE to explain today's universal human fertility. Anders Eriksson and Andrea Manica (2012) point out that the common DNA between modern non-Africans and Neandertals may simply be the remnant of a common African ancestor to both. That ancestor was likely Homo heidelbergensis. They conclude that "evidence for such admixture events is inconclusive at best. Future tests, to be convincing, will need to show that the genetic patterns used to invoke hybridization cannot be explained by [underlying] population structure" (Eriksson and Manica 2012, 13958). Ed Yong (2011) agrees, saying these may be phantom signs of mixed DNA that are not real (36). Even so, some scientists have recently edged toward the MRE camp (i.e., assimilation theory), including a previous champion of RAO, Chris Stringer (2012) of London's Natural History Museum.

The RAO and MRE perspectives clash over more than DNA. Bones and behavior provide the other main areas of clash. These arguments are less explosive than the DNA debate, with the two sides quibbling over finer interpretations of fossils and stone tools. The essence of the fossil clash is that Wolpoff finds few differences among the skeletons of Neandertals and Cro-Magnons (the earliest modern humans in Europe according to RAO), whereas Tattersall and the majority view these physical differences as profound. This is the phenomenon of "lumpers" (Wolpoff) versus "splitters" (Tattersall).

The eye sockets of Neandertals are huge, they have sloping foreheads and horizontal braincases rather than vertical ones like ours, the occipital bun at the backs of their heads is unique, and their forward-thrust faces mean they have no chin. (We are the only animal on Earth with a chin.) Neandertal bones are far thicker than Homo sapiens, and their large ribcages are shaped like bells. Caspari and Wolpoff (2013, 363) dismiss these differences as within the normal range for neighboring Cro-Magnons of the day. Comparisons should be made contemporaneously, they argue, not between ancient Neandertals and today's humans.

Regarding behavior, Wolpoff perceives the stone tools of the two European populations as nearly identical, consistent with the fact that Neandertal brains were just as large as the Cro-Magnons. Tattersall counters that the Neandertals simply copied the Cro-Magnons' superior technology. Arguments like these are so subjective as to be impossible to resolve. Further studies suggest the Neandertals' large eye sockets meant oversized eyes and superior vision, requiring more of the brain to be devoted to the visual cortex (Marshall 2013). This left less grey matter available for higher-level human communication and symbolic thinking. This conclusion fits RAO, with Homo sapiens outcompeting Neandertals for resources due to greater reasoning and communication faculties. Wolpoff counters that the Cro-Magnons were more like Neandertals than we are. They merged with each other and with Africans, Homo erectus and Denisovans: each group contributing valuable genes that make humans the global success we are today.

## Rhetorical Criticism: RAO vs. MRE

The richness of the RAO vs. MRE debate lies in the many points of clash. But which side produces the greater rhetorical effect? Neo-Aristotelian criticism and narrative theory provide vehicles for such a critique. In the narrative section above each theory provides narrative fidelity in its respective explanation of how modern humans came to be. Both stories are entirely plausible and consistent with evolution via natural selection. Table 1 likewise endorses fidelity in how they corroborate each other to a point, as well as their mutual support for a single human race of equals. The conflicts mainly arise in narrative coherence, as detailed in the section immediately above. Here the two sides have attempted to expose contradictions between what the opposing theory says versus the known facts. We may turn now to the neo-Aristotelian modes of proof, issues of presumption, and the effect of each side's discourse.

### Observation 1: A Clash of Egos, Not Ethos

Ethos is the persuasive appeal of the speaker. In paleoanthropology, ethos is replaced by egos. The editorial noted above in *Nature* terms the debate in paleoanthropology positively "splenetic" (Rude Anthropology 2006, 958). In such a high-status field as paleoanthropology (name a more important scientific question than who we are and where we came from), perhaps it is inevitable that personalities will clash. As the highly identifiable, sometimes solitary champion of MRE, Milford Wolpoff has a right to his ego-involvement. He has had to fight his way into the top conferences, sometimes losing (Wolpoff 1995, 185), and MRE is often ignored in textbooks and media coverage.

The debate has frequently become personal. Ann Gibbons (2011) quotes RAO star Christopher Stringer as saying, "attention to inconvenient details has never been part of the Wolpoff style," as well as Wolpoff referring to an RAO chart as "Stringer's desperate argument" (392). Wolpoff, Hawks, and Caspari (2001) accuse their detractors of posturing and spin-doctoring. When Wolpoff seemed vindicated by evidence that Neandertals may contribute up to four percent of the nuclear DNA of modern Europeans, he gushed, "It's hard to explain how good I feel about it," as the evidence exceeded his wildest expectations (Gibbons 2011, 393–94). Wolpoff (1995) once even claimed that one of his opponents "promised to accept the Multiregional explanation if we promise to stop writing about it" (186).

## Observation 2: A Dose of Humility Is in Order

There is good reason that subjectivity and personal clashes have plagued paleoanthropology. The evidence in this field is so frustratingly fragmentary and subject to wide interpretation that universal agreement on all but the most basic points is impossible. This leads to tautological thinking, as scholars rely on their pre-existing stories (theories) to fill in the huge gaps in evidence. Think about it: an entire species/population of humans, the Denisovans, were theorized on the basis of a few bone fragments from four individuals—all fortuitously noticed in a Siberian cave during the past decade (Slon et al. 2017).

Not only is the evidence sketchy in this debate, it is indecisive. John H. Relethford (1998) tested both RAO and MRE and found them lacking. The genetic evidence is indeterminate; so much so that "our analyses are not often likely to tell us which underlying model is correct" (Relethford 1998, 5). The tick-tock of mitochondrial DNA is likewise unknown, with mitochondrial Eve dating anywhere from forty thousand YBP to 1.4 million YBP. That range encompasses both theories completely.

It is ironic that *immediately* after asserting an almost universal consensus for RAO, Tattersall and Schwartz (2009) lament, "but the sketchy nature of the fossil record currently at hand makes it possible to glimpse only very dimly the context out of which our species emerged" (83). The two statements make no sense when viewed together. For their part, Wolpoff and Caspari (2012, 4) use the word "certainty" to describe the truth of MRE. This claim may be true, but only if they are allowed to paint their opponents into a corner. They hold that RAO is wrong unless it is proven that humans trace their ancestry *"exclusively* back to a *small* African population that expanded and *completely* replaced archaic human species, without *any* interbreeding" (Wolpoff and Caspari 2012, 4; emphasis mine). His use of the word "certain" does not prevent Wolpoff (1999) from complaining about overly authoritative, "firm-sounding pronouncements" by his opponents (278).

Some humility *can* be found in the words of eminent geneticist Mark Stoneking of the Max Planck Institute. Stoneking had helped lead-researcher Rebecca Cann and their mentor Allan Wilson (1987) discover Mitochondrial Eve and thus establish RAO's dominance. In reference to the lack of evidence in human origins, Stoneking (2008) aptly cites a quotation from American author Mark Twain: "There is something fascinating about science. One gets such wholesale returns of conjecture out of such a trifling investment of fact" (S50). Likewise noting that nature can only laugh at humanity's so-called scientific knowledge, the brilliant American inventor Thomas Edison said, "It's obvious that we don't know one millionth of one percent about anything" (Pichtel 2007, 327). Paleoanthropologists can take heart that they probably do understand one millionth of one percent about human origins. They just don't know *which* 0.000001 percent it is.

## Observation 3: Science Is Rhetoric, Indeed

Associating science with rhetoric does nothing to diminish science as a valued human enterprise (emphasis on human). Far from it. This chapter should instead elevate the reputation of rhetoric, which merits rehabilitation in the twenty-first century intellectual community. In the popular mind rhetoric occupies a low status, as in the phrase "empty rhetoric." A healthier attitude toward the role of rhetoric in science can help scholars craft more coherent theories. Rhetoric is produced when fact claims beget value claims, in turn resulting in policies, which are then tested by new facts. Hopefully, this process results in an upward spiral of human advancement. Similarly, science happens when facts inform hypotheses, begetting theories, which are then tested by new facts: again, hopefully, resulting in scientific advancement (see figure 6). Rather than merely be considered "rhetorical," science may prove itself to be a form of rhetoric itself. An awareness that science and rhetoric occupy two sides of the same coin can reinvigorate our policy debates in which science plays a central role.

The idea that the natural world is sacrosanct, justifying the censorship of any opposition to "settled science," has polarized key policy issues such as climate change, science education, and environmental protection. Robust exchanges on these issues are impossible when advocates engage in name-calling and marginalizing opponents over a bogus "scientific consensus." We need a healthier attitude toward rhetoric to reinvigorate discourse at conferences, parliaments, and the media. A received view perpetuated by science elites should never chill the research of equally qualified, minority-viewpoint scientists whose findings produce contrasting inferences. Placing science above rhetoric only stifles debate, turns off the public, and may lead to poor policy decisions. Nor should the public leave science policy strictly to the "experts." As Fisher's narrative perspective affirms, the universal audience is essential to effective decision-making in free societies.

If leaders cannot communicate their priorities effectively, new leadership may be needed.

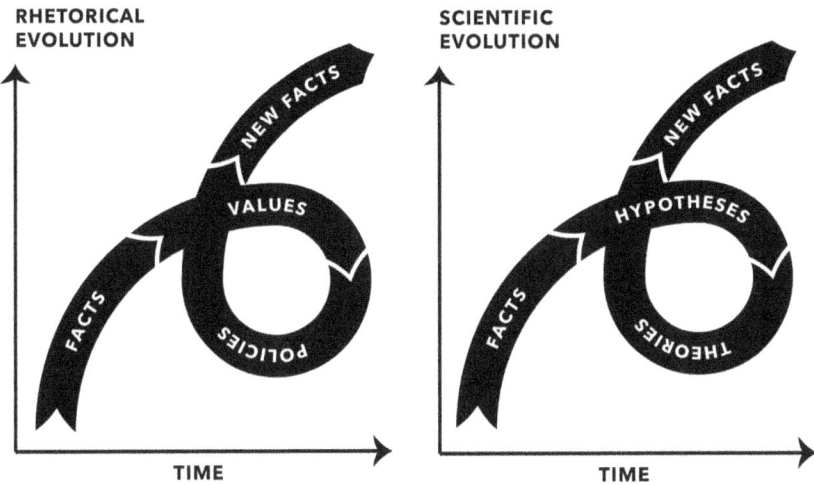

Figure 6. Rhetorical and Scientific Advancement. Graphic design by Jessica Gerlach.

## Observation 4: Legitimate Scientific Controversies Are Repellant to Nonscientists

As noted in the review of literature, rhetorical scholars have eschewed legitimate scientific controversies in favor of pseudo-controversies. Likewise, journalists tend to ignore the heated debates among anthropologists, treating the RAO model as simple fact *even when* describing elements of MRE approvingly. The special case of view-point conformity regarding science, at a time when popular culture thrives on socio-political controversy, is puzzling. Media members, scholars, and other elites seem to share an aversion to legitimate controversies in science, but why?

Perhaps science occupies a special place among non-scientists: a refuge from the confusion and doubt that permeates the rest of society. Leon Festinger's (1957) cognitive dissonance theory holds that humans abhor dissonance and will go to great mental lengths to maintain cognitive consistency. As science ostensibly exists in the sphere of fact rather than opinion, it offers a safe haven from subjective viewpoints. Science gives answers, solutions. Science provides clarity, not dilemmas. It enjoys an elevated status of intellectual virtue, unlike the dirty sphere of politics. Politics occupies Aristotle's realm of the contingent (which entails dissonance), thus it is constantly in need of deconstruction. Science is supposed to be above deconstruction in the popular imagination.

The intolerance for ambiguity in science may explain why cultural elites go apoplectic when anyone questions anthropomorphic climate change. For example, environmental lawyer Robert F. Kennedy, Jr. says skeptical politicians and scientists "should be enjoying three hots and a cot at the Hague with all the other war criminals" (Cooke 2014, par. 8). So, when Cann, Stoneking, and Wilson (1987) made their worldwide splash with mitochondrial DNA evidence supporting RAO, the popular mind closed the book on human evolution. Dr. Wolpoff has been playing catch-up ever since.

## Observation 5: Wolpoff as Hard-core Contest Debater

The consensus that Africa produced Homo sapiens very recently is repeated as fact by commercial media and textbooks, leading to gross misunderstandings of the theory of multiregional evolution. Wolpoff constantly has to correct his critics on the very basics of MRE, including paleoanthropologists who should know better. As noted above, Brian Fagan (1990), an otherwise brilliant anthropologist, dismissed MRE as a candelabra theory, in which different races would have had to evolve separately and simultaneously (20–21). This straw-person argument is unrealistic on simple evolutionary grounds, and if accurate would also leave the theory vulnerable to attack as racist. If Africans, Asians, and Europeans evolved independently for two million years they would indeed be separate subspecies. Such species cannot independently evolve to become the same. Gross teleological thinking is required, in which destiny drove multiple diverse species in a straight line to modernity. Yet, Wolpoff has struggled to impart the real MRE even to anthropologists, prompting Fagan to maintain that "out of Africa" (RAO) is "almost universally accepted" (personal communication, 13 December 2013).

Like Fagan (1990) popular accounts of MRE conflate it with the candelabra model. Even when news articles endorse Wolpoff's theory, RAO assumptions find their way into the text with no awareness of the fundamental contradictions. For example, William K. Stevens (1992) writes in the *New York Times* about Wolpoff and MRE: "Dr. Wolpoff, on the other hand, says Neanderthals were ancestors of modern Europeans, *although* the evolving Europeans of that era may have interbred with their counterparts in other regions" (C-1; emphasis mine). This false view of MRE casts it in contradiction with itself. Time after time, Wolpoff has to defend his theory against mischaracterization.

Who is to blame for the miscasting of MRE as a separate evolution of the races? Perhaps it lay at the door of Dr. Wolpoff himself. The phrase "multiregional evolution" represents a serious problem of semantics, or Aristotle's notion of language style. The word multiregional suggests multiple evolution events occurring in separate regions, when MRE is really a singular model with no speciation events. A better name for the theory would be "Afro-Eurasian evolution," "single-Homo evolution," or "pan-Pleistocenic evolution." The name "Afro-Eurasian" would distinguish it from RAO's Africa-only perspective and unify the single, large region (not separate regions) in which human evolution took place. "Single-Homo evolution" would make clear that there has only been one human (Homo) species, capitalizing on the theory's parsimony. Thus, terms like Homo habilis, Homo erectus, Homo heidelbergensis, Homo neanderthalensis, and Cro-magnon are more clearly cast as misnomers. They are only different populations, not species. "Pan-Pleistocenic evolution" would signify the long-arc of single-species human evolution, with a two-million-year phase rather than RAO's timeline that is ten-times shorter. Each of these labels would be clearer than MRE and add a degree of persuasion.

Clearly, multiregional evolution is an ineffective name for a worthy alternate narrative to RAO. Taking a cue from Disney, "The small world hypothesis" would even be better than "multiregional evolution." Its flawed semantics may explain some of the confusion and underrepresentation of the theory, whether in anthropology, the mass media, or the public imagination. Despite his respect for the power of rhetoric in science, for twenty-seven years Wolpoff failed to convince either anthropologists or the media that his theory had merit. Only when geneticists came to the rescue by cracking the code of Neandertal DNA would MRE emerge from the wilderness.

Dr. Wolpoff uses combative language in reference to his opponents, which Caspari and Wolpoff (2013) euphemize as simply direct. In addition to referring to opponents as "desperate," "posturing," and "spin-doctoring" (noted above), we can add Wolpoff's language choice when describing a single skeleton that seemed to suggest a Homo sapiens and Neandertal hybrid: "This find should be devastating to the Out of Africa people. It shows their theory doesn't work, at least in Europe" (Wolpoff 1999, 1). Sounding even more like a debater, he claims that a "refutatory approach" is an effective if off-putting means of testing a competing hypothesis (Wolpoff 1999, 278). If humor is needed, Wolpoff is prepared. When an opponent dismissed his theory as largely bankrupt, he replied, "In America, bankruptcy is a temporary condition, and only stays on your credit record for ten years" (Wolpoff 1999, 283).

The other element of Wolpoff as contest debater involves his seizing of presumption in addressing the assimilation model. Wolpoff, Hawkes, and Caspari (2000, 134) hold that RAO and MRE are mutually exclusive, with no compromise position possible. One theory is right and the other is wrong. In argumentation theory, the status quo enjoys presumption, and the challenger is burdened to prove his case. Wolpoff, Hawks, and Caspari (2000) claim presumption by asserting that all assimilation models are subsumed entirely under MRE (134), relegating RAO to an extreme position (see figure 7).

| Multiregional Evolution | Recent African Origin |
|---|---|

High admixture/genic exchange    Moderate admixture    Complete replacement

Figure 7: Wolpoff's Seizure of Presumption. Graphic design by Jessica Gerlach.

They claim that even if recent Africans constitute the majority of the current gene pool in East Asia (which it does by far), multiregional evolution would still be correct (131). MRE's breadth accounts for all evidence except for one hundred percent recent African ancestry of one hundred percent of all living humans. Any admixture whatsoever, even 1/10 of one percent means a complete vindication of MRE in their view. But they go further, stating, "multiregionalism could be a valid explanation for human evolution even if every Neandertal became extinct without issue. No human populations persist endlessly or continuously through time; all either become extinct, or merge with other populations" (Wolpoff, Caspari, and Hawks 2000, 132). This statement truly is a vivid case of hedging one's bets (see figure 7). Like the others above, it clearly supports the proposition that paleoanthropology and rhetoric are inextricably linked.

## Conclusions

After reading hundreds of pages of scholarship and media on paleoanthropology's spirited rhetoric, one can begin assessing the league tables, known in speech communication as the rhetorical effect. In human evolution the critic is left to choose a young, singular species from Africa taking over the world (RAO) or an old, singular species where diverse populations evolved together via genic exchange across a huge geographic area (MRE). For RAO to work, several intelligent Homo species had to split off from one another, with all but one of them later dying out. On the other hand, if genic transfers constantly swept through the Old World for two million years, the multi-regional model is correct.

RAO says we are the only Homo species left standing. Then why did Homo neanderthalensis, the second most intelligent creature that ever lived, just go "poof"? Why should they have disappeared in a world where migrating lemmings stupidly drown trying to swim across large bodies of water, yet *their* species persists? Why is human evolution best described by a tree model when our mating patterns are naturally exogamous? As Wolpoff, Hawks, and Caspari (2000) point out, reticulate evolution—the trellis model of MRE—is completely unaccounted for in branching models like RAO. And what about the fossil finds of Dmanisi, Georgia, suggesting that humans in the same breeding population were as diverse as several different Homo species (Zorich 2014, 26). RAO cannot explain these facts.

The indictment of RAO above does not leave MRE in the clear. To the multiregional position the critic asks, why do Africans supply one hundred percent of the uncontested genes in humanity across the globe? If MRE occurred with *mutual* genic exchange, why are no endemic European or Asian genes found in Sub-Saharan Africa? Caspari and Wolpoff (2013) inexplicably claim that this is because Africa is at the "center" of the human population range, and the center will contribute more genes than it receives. They call this the "center and edge effect" (356). Although Africa had higher population densities than Europe and Asia at that time (unlike now), any glance at a world map shows Africa surrounded by the sea on *three sides*. It is not the center of anything (see figure 8). Instead, Africa lies at the southwestern "edge" of the Old World (a.k.a. Afro-Eurasia), where MRE supposedly worked as a melting pot across the expanse of tens of millions of square kilometers. At least ninety-five percent, and possibly one hundred percent of the human genome comes from a small population of recent Africans. The utter lack of non-African genes in Sub-Saharan Africans presents a serious problem for MRE.

Figure 8. Center and Edge Construct. Graphic design by Jessica Gerlach.

Another maddening element of MRE's center-and-edge effect is the claim that Africans have the most robust skeletons of modern humans, and that the farther from Africa one goes the more gracile people are. Any look at modern Africa finds no such correlation. Many of the incredibly-diverse ethnicities across this enormous continent feature tiny frames, such as certain tribes in Ethiopia and Kenya that produce many of the world's great distance runners—all of them highly gracile. Powerlifting Germans and Japanese sumo wrestlers are anything but small boned. The center-and-edge effect falls flat.

Tattersall and Schwartz (2009) compared the average number of mitochondrial DNA differences among randomly selected modern humans (eight) with the average human-Neandertal difference of twenty-six, "taking the Neanderthals well outside the modern human envelope" (81). Moreover, they found that Neandertals were no closer to modern Europeans than to other modern populations. Dr. Wolpoff is right to say that Neandertals shouldn't simply be compared genetically and morphologically to modern humans; they should be compared with contemporaneous Africans. Unfortunately for MRE, Weaver and Roseman (2005) report negative results: "All the Neandertals and none of the ancient modern humans yielded sequences similar to previous Neandertal sequences" (680).

In the case of Asia, Tattersall and Schwartz (2009) argue that no fossil evidence links Homo erectus in Asia to modern humans, as the few fossils that appear to show continuity are poorly dated (77). As for Stringer, the former champion of RAO hasn't budged much in minimizing the importance of the Neandertals, and thus negating MRE: "Instead, we see Neanderthals going up to around thirty thousand or forty thousand years ago and then disappearing. They've passed some DNA on but that didn't change their evolutionary history" (Yong 2011, 35).

From a narrative fidelity point of view, just looking at a Neandertal skull next to a Cro-magnon/modern human's is shocking (see figure 8). The Neandertal face is pulled so far forward that their chin disappears and their brain case takes a different shape. They have a sloping forehead and horizontal (not tall, round) heads. Their brow ridges and other bones are far thicker and stronger than ours, and their jaws are enormous. It is difficult to imagine this creature as a fellow Homo sapiens despite the diverse Dmanisi fossils (Zorich 2014). As Jean-Jacques Hublin (2005) points out, "If any living Neandertals had come to the conference dressed in a suit and tie, they still would have stood out" (62). Although they lasted much longer than we have so far (viz. RAO), Neandertals contributed at most four percent of the DNA of modern Europeans, and no Neandertal contributions are found in the mitochondrial DNA of anyone living today (Weaver and Roseman 2005, 682).

Just as African genes overwhelmed all competitors (c.f. Hublin 2005), so has RAO swamped MRE rhetorically. The numbers of public scientists, journal articles, and popular media supporting RAO dwarf those favoring the second theory. An RAO-bias even permeates articles trumpeting that Europeans and Asians are part Neandertal, referring to Neandertals and Homo erectus as extinct species. The only problem is that RAO is probably wrong, too. Yet, on both sides humility, like the fossil record, is in short supply.

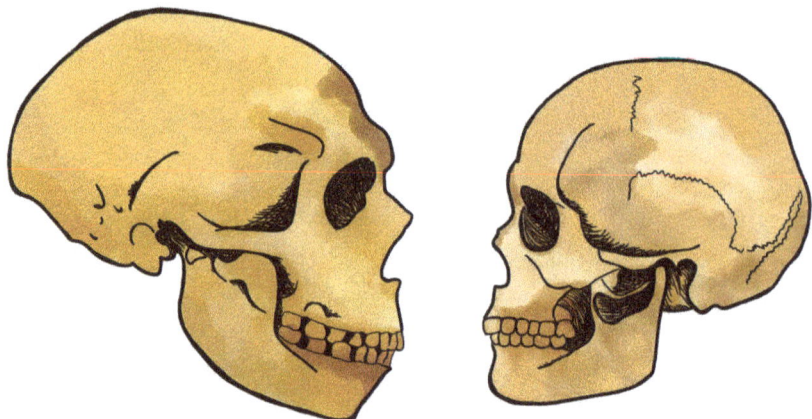

Figure 9. Neandertal and Cro-magnon Skulls. Graphic design by Jessica Gerlach.

Principally, the decades-long debate with human evolution presents a problem of evidence. Unlike Aristotle's day, the twenty-first century critic values inartistic proofs (evidence, data) over the artistic (ethos, pathos, logos). If facts do not align with the theory, then something is wrong with the theory. Assimilation likely best narrates the facts, but the morphological and even genetic evidence remains so scanty that a completely different theory may be needed to explain the origin of humans on planet Earth. Until then, the pitched battle of paleoanthropology goes on.

Rather than occupy opposite ends of an intellectual continuum, science and rhetoric are complementary human enterprises. Science is meaningless until it is communicated, communication being an inherently subjective human enterprise. Therefore, Wolpoff is right: facts can never speak for themselves, even in the production of inferences about the natural world. Those who hide behind this myth, or behind fallacies like the bandwagon "scientific consensus," should instead develop a stronger argument.

The fundamental question of our paleoanthropological debate is this: how old is the human race? When one side claims 160,000 years and the other says two million, we have barged-in on a stark and salient dispute about the nature of humanity. Either humans and Neandertals split 500,000 years ago, as two offshoots of Homo heidelbergensis, or we are the same species still. We evolved either on one continent or across three. The yield of this study suggests that legitimate scientific controversies provide a rich source for twenty-first century rhetorical criticism. Soon more "open questions" of science may avail themselves to qualitative analysis, instead of the usual polemical exercises that critics deliver when science and pseudo-science collide.

## Notes

1. I would like to thank Jessica Gerlach of the University of Arizona for creating the graphic design on figures 1, 4, 6, 7, 8, and 9 as well as tables 1 and 2 in this chapter.

## Works Cited

Aristotle. 1924. *Rhetorica*. Edited and translated by William Rhys Roberts. Vol. 11 of The Works of Aristotle, edited by W. D. Ross. Oxford: Clarendon Press.

Bilali, Hafida, R., Timothy Patterson, and Andreas Prokoph. 2013. "A Holocene Paleoclimate Reconstruction for Eastern Canada based on 180 Cellulose of Sphagnum Mosses from Mer Bleue Bog." *Holocene* 23 (9): 1260–71.

Brock, Bernard and Robert Scott. 1980. "An Introduction to Rhetorical Criticism." In *Methods of Rhetorical Criticism: A Twentieth-century Perspective*, edited by Bernard Brock and Robert Scott, 9–22. Detroit: Wayne State University Press.

Campbell, Karlyn and Kathleen Jamieson. 1978. *Form and Genre: Shaping Rhetorical Action*. Falls Church, VA: The Speech Communication Association.

Cann, Rebecca, Mark Stoneking, and Allan Wilson. 1987. "Mitochondrial DNA and Human Evolution." *Nature* 325:31–37.

Caspari, Rachel and Milford Wolpoff. 1997. *Race and Human Evolution*. New York: Simon & Schuster.

Caspari, Rachel, and Milford Wolpoff. 2013. "The Process of Modern Human Origins: The Evolutionary and Demographic Changes Giving Rise to Modern Humans." In *The Origin of Modern Humans: Biology Reconsidered*, edited by Fred H. Smith and James C.M. Ahern. 2nd ed., 355–91. Hoboken, NJ: Wiley.

Ceccarelli, Leah. 2011. "Manufactured Scientific Controversies: Science, Rhetoric, and Public Debate. " *Rhetoric & Public Affairs* 14 (2): 195–228.

Condit, Celeste M. 2008. "Race and Genetics from a Modal Materialist Perspective." *Quarterly Journal of Speech* 94 (4): 383–406.

Cooke, Charles C.W. "Robert Kennedy, Jr.: Aspiring Tyrant." *National Review Online*. Accessed September 22, 2014. http://www.nationalreview.com/article/388595/robert-kennedy-jr-aspiring-tyrant-charles-c-w-cooke.

Eriksson, Anders, and Andrea Manica. 2012. "Effect of Ancient Population Structure on the Degree of Polymorphism Shared Between Modern Human Populations and Ancient Hominins." *Proceedings of the National Academy of Sciences of the United States of America* 109 (35): 13956–60. DOI:10.1073/Pnas.1200567109.

Rude Paleanthropology. 2006. "Rude Paleoanthropology." *Nature* 442: 957–58.

Fagan, Brian. 1990. *Journey from Eden: The Peopling of Our World*. London: Thames & Hudson.

*Festinger*, Leon. 1957. *A Theory of Cognitive Dissonance*. Stanford, CA: Stanford University Press.

Fisher, Walter R. 1984. "Narration as Human Communication Paradigm: The Case of Public Moral Argument." *Communication Monographs* 51 (1): 1–22.

Gibbons, Ann. 2011. "A New View of The Birth of Homo Sapiens." *Science* 331 (6016): 392–94.

Holiday, Trenton W., Joanna R. Gautney, and Lukáš Friedl. 2014. "Right for the Wrong Reasons: Reflections on Modern Human Origins in the Post-Neanderthal Genome Era." *Current Anthropology* 55 (6): 696–724.

Hublin, Jean-Jacques. 2005. "The New Neandertal." *Archaeology* 58 (4): 61–66.

Jack, Jordynn. 2010. "Object Lessons: Recent Work in the Rhetoric of Science." *Quarterly Journal of Speech* 96 (2): 209–16.

Marshall, Michael. 2013. "Neanderthals' Big Eyes Came at a Big Cost." *New Scientist* 217 (2908): 8.

Paroske, Marcus. 2009. "Deliberating International Science Policy Controversies: Uncertainty and AIDS in South Africa." *Quarterly Journal of Speech* 95 (2): 148–70.

Pichtel, John. 2007. *Fundamentals of Site Remediation: For Metal-and Hydrocardon-Contaminated Soils*. 2nd ed. Lanham, MD: Government Institutes.

Relethford, John H. 1998. "Genetics of Modern Human Origins and Diversity." *Annual Review of Anthropology* 27 (1): 1–23.

Rohy, Valerie. 2012. "On Homosexual Reproduction." *Differences: A Journal of Feminist Cultural Studies* 23 (1): 101–30.

Slon, Viviane, Bence Viola, Gabriel Renaud, Marie-Theres Gansauge, Stefano Benazzi, Susanna Sawyer, Jean-Jacques Hublin, Michael V. Shunkov, Anatoly P. Derevianko, Janet Kelso, Kay Prüfer, Matthias Meyer, and Svante Pääbo. 2017.. "A Fourth Denisovan Individual. *Science Advances* 3, no. 7 (July): e1700186.

Stevens, William K. 1992. "Neanderthals: Dead End or Ancestor?" *New York Times*, February 4, Sec. C-1.

Stringer, Chris. 2012. "What Makes a Modern Human." *Nature* 485: 33–35.

Stoneking, Mark. 2008. "Human origins. The molecular perspective." *EMBO Report 9* (Suppl 1): S46–S50.

Tattersall, Ian, and Jeffrey H. Schwartz. 2009. "Evolution of the Genus Homo." *Annual Review of Earth and Planetary Sciences* 37: 67–92.

Weaver, Timothy D., and Charles C. Roseman. 2005. "Ancient DNA, Late Neandertal Survival, and Modern Human-Neanderthal Genetic Admixture." *Current Anthropology* 46 (4): 677–83.

Wickman, Chad. 2012. "Rhetoric Techne, and the Art of Scientific Inquiry." *Rhetoric Review* 31 (1): 21–40.

Wilford, John Noble. 1999. "Discovery Suggests Humans are a Bit Neanderthal." *New York Times*, April 25, 1-1.

Wolpoff, Milford. 1976. "Data and Theory in Paleoanthropological Controversies." *American Anthropologist* 78 (1): 94–96.

Wolpoff, Milford. 1995. "Untangling the Issues: A Reply to Dr. Stringer." *American Journal of Physical Anthropology* 96 (2): 185–88.

Wolpoff, Milford. 1999. "Paleoanthropology: Controversy without End or an End without Controversy?" *Reviews in Anthropology* 28 (3): 267–88.

Wolpoff, Milford, John Hawks, and Rachel Caspari. 2000. "Multiregional, not Multiple Origins." *American Journal of Physical Anthropology* 112 (1): 129–36.

Wolpoff, Milford, and Rachel Caspari. 2012. "How Did Modern Humans Originate." *General Anthropology: Bulletin of The General Anthropology Division* 19 (2): 1, 4–6.

Wolpoff, Milford, Xinzhi Wu, and Alan G. Thorne. 1984. "Modern *Homo sapiens* Origins: A General Theory of Hominid Evolution Involving the Fossil Evidence from East Asia." In: *The Origins of Modern Humans: A World Survey of the Fossil Evidence*, edited by F. H. Smith and F. Spencer, 411–83. New York: Liss.

Yong, Ed. 2011. "Our Hybrid Origins." *New Scientist* 211 (2823): 34–38.

Zorich, Zach. 2014. "Homo Erectus Stands Alone." *Archaeology* 67 (1): 26.

# 10 Civic Science: Applied Rhetoric as a Facilitator of Scientific Knowledge

*Colleen E. Kelley*

## Introduction

It has been argued, albeit tongue-in-cheek, that "even bacteria communicate better than earth scientists" (Hooke 2011, 2). The focus of this paper is both a serious challenge to this assumption as well as a deconstruction of the mediated reality of American science as discourse situated in, experienced by and, ultimately, argued through an interface between expert and lay opinion. In short, science communication is not working well in the United States, a serious failure because the public must have experts available with whom to discuss their assumptions and "truths" about science through audience and "other" oriented-specific discourse. As the COVID-19 pandemic began to spread in 2020, so too did the mass mediated proliferation of relevant as well as misleading information, much of the latter including potentially dangerous health-related narratives with potentially significant repercussions for individual and public health worldwide (Lavorgna and Myles 2021; see also Strazewski 2020). The crucial question addressed therefore becomes not whether public involvement in science should occur but how, with what impact, in what areas, and with what level of trust and precision. At the intersection of art and science— bridging a willingness to be mindful with the knowledge of the diverse lenses through which people configure science—an opportunity exists to discursively create a deeper, richer, and more culturally embedded sense of the value of science (Lindenfeld 2018, 10).

In this view, the truth of science is only partially told by experts inside labs or behind conference podiums. Rhetoric may secure the public's affirmation after scientists' claims have been credentialed as "true" within their own professional communities. And rhetorical literacy empowers scientists to successfully and publicly communicate their research and so facilitate scientific literacy. Experts' communication of science and technology is increasingly at odds with public consumption and comprehension of that same science and technology. The disconnect between twenty-first century American scientists and the publics upon whom their science depends may be more substantial and potentially serious than those of previous decades. This argument will be examined in greater detail later in the chapter. It has been suggested that the battles astronomer and science advocate Carl Sagan engaged in during the 1980s over Ronald Reagan's "Star Wars" program and "nuclear winter" were "dress rehearsals" for the politicization of science over issues like climate change (Mooney 2013). The essential existence and future of American science depends in part on public funds and cultural legitimation secured through appeals to community and not by the facts that exist independently of the rhetors (Harris 2005, 254; see also Paul, Charney, and Kendall 2001; Wells 1996). Science becomes "truths" intersubjectively created through language and situated within particular contexts, addressed to particular audiences. While the arguments in this chapter pertain specifically to enactments of civic science within the United States, they also inform similar practices globally in that the future of human society may depend, at least in part, on an essentially universal mandate for rhetorically competent scientists.

## The Public Sphere and Science

Controversies over scientific truth may be framed as a struggle over knowledge and whose version of truth will be accepted (see Fennell 2009). Everyday understanding of the natural world is often at odds with scientific conclusions (see Roth 2014). Consequently, many experts frame the general public as illiterate or non-scientific, and some scientists have "gone on the defense," particularly against those who collapse science in with other cultural traditions as "just another way of knowing" (Shermer 2010).

The public understanding of science by lay people is often about stories that involve complex technical knowledge. These narratives coalesce into interpretive spaces within which non-experts may deliberatively communicate about the meaning of science (Majdik 2009). In this way, those without professional expertise determine a validity, if not a "truth" of science, which may be contraindicated by the scientists themselves. In a sense, scientific findings may be ejected in unscientific ways. When asked, the public frequently indicates they like and admire science. However, the evidence also shows that they do not know much about it and poorly understand the methods science uses to pursue the truth about nature. Findings of science are under attack from a wide variety of audiences, informed by social, political, and cultural forces that dismiss, deny, denigrate, and distort legitimate results of scientific research they construe as unwelcome or uncomfortable (Frazier 2009, 9; see also Giubilini et al. 2021).

It appears, then, that scientific texts alone will not usually persuade non-technical audiences. This disconnect emerges from seemingly irreconcilable visions of two primary publics. The first favors action in response to empirical evidence. The second refutes the former's position with evidence substantially grounded in political and personal ideology rather than in scientific analysis. The problems relate to framing the issues, or rather, allowing the opponents of the science to frame them (Banerjee 2012). According to Honey Rand (1998), the public—viewers, readers, listeners, taxpayers in the United States—fund most of scientific research. As a result, when the public expects to be involved in such public policy development, a singular and particularly rhetorically strategic communication behavior emerges as the singular skill scientists need to explain their work and so gain a competitive edge with the public.

Public narratives that counter, and on occasion dismiss, intersubjectively agreed upon scientific "truths" are often successful because they frame such conclusions as political truths or issues and so transform them into "something other than science," for the inexpert communities. Such recurring stories within the popular public sphere include dismissing the value of vaccines, that evolution is not a scientific fact and that the earth is flat. As a result of such "rhetorical transformations," the outcomes are judged by different, often non-technical and/or non-scientific rules of assessment of the truth value of the statements. The burden of proof for persuading the public to embrace the workable truths of the scientific/technical community rests with scientists who must rhetorically interface with the public/lay community to persuade the public that what scientists do and what scientists believe is directly beneficial to that public (Prelli 1989, 235). Scientists "do" science for other scientists. They must converse about science with non-scientists. Sarah R. Davies (2008) contends that the primary traditional purposes of public science communication—to educate, to inspire and to recruit—are informed by a linear discursive construct that frames communication as a negative and one-way process with no exchange of knowledge. Public voices are often silent and the concept of two-way communication "othered" and made invisible. To illustrate, Leah Ceccarelli (2001, 319) argues that scientific texts are not transparent but account, at least in part, for the difficulty some scientists encounter when telling their "truths" to a public who does not share them. In sum, the enactment, comprehension and perhaps substance of science is rhetorically constituted and, as a result, communication-based. As a result, academic and professional communication scholars are instrumental in promoting "inclusive and informed public rhetoric about science and technology in classrooms, communities, and personal lives, as well as in the public sphere" (Keranen 2019, 24).

## Rhetorical Scientists

As with other kinds of discourse (e.g., political or religious), scientific claims are made and judged on the basis of formal logic and reasonableness, but also according to criteria unique to their disciplines of science—such as what constitutes reasonableness of premises, relevance of data, precision of measurements, and warrantedness of conclusions. Scientific argument is not only a matter of demonstration and truth (Kuhn 1966), rather it communicates a truth that must be argued for and that emerges only through discussion and debate, grounded in community values and agreements (see Perelman 1982). The burden inherent in making a scientific theory persuasive is that it must be more than appealing on its own terms but regarded as consistent with other things known.

The public understanding or misunderstanding of science is based more in factors such as social access, trust, and negotiation, rather than intellectual ability or "imposed authority." Should witnessing audiences understand that science is *unfolding argumentation*—whatever else it may be—they would not necessarily be frustrated by controversial scientific claims (Prelli 1989, 265–66). For example, modern science results are typically storied in the language of statistics and probabilities, particularly in scientific studies of complex phenomena, such as climate science. However, this hallmark of much science has led some less familiar with technical argument to interpret uncertainty as evidence for a *major scientific controversy*, often when there is none within the scientific sphere.

As a result, science must incorporate extra-scientific narratives, themes and materials to enhance interest and promote understanding to lay persons. The dynamics of scientific controversy are linked by narrative, the attempt on all sides to create the more plausible story that must, at least, be credibly argued. Each side challenges the story of the others, adducing facts and arguments in its favor. Closure or the securing of the other's adherence to the argument is achieved only if one story achieves consensus. In the American public sphere, this consensus grounds social policy in public knowledge, sometimes in opposition to scientific conclusions (cf. Gross 1990).

## Public Framing of Science

The "imperfect fit" between the domains demarcated in science in general and, for example, evolutionary theory in particular, illustrates the rhetorical/persuasive limitations of technical expertise as it is articulated before nontechnical audiences/publics. The rationality of American public deliberation is based on choosing relevant experts without granting authority to expertise simply because it is expert. As such, the public demarcation rhetorics of the scientific community require astute analysis, because nontechnical audiences may craft oppositional discourses to deal with what they perceive as the unnecessary extension of expertise in the domain of public authority. Such "oppositional discourses" emerge from concerns such as those regarding evolution and climate change.

To illustrate, Missouri legislators have recently called for laws that would require schools to notify parents if the theory of evolution by natural selection was being taught at their child's school and give them opportunity to opt out of the class. The bill is one of several anti-evolution proposals that have been introduced across the United States that range from presenting a debate between evolution and creationism to mandates for the teaching of the theory of intelligent design in biology classes (Scott 2014; see also Missouri House Bill No. 911 2003).

Critics of the teaching of evolution as part of the required science curriculum in American public schools have been gaining ground by linking global warming and evolution, arguing that opposing views on both areas of science should be taught in public classrooms. For example, a bill was introduced in the Kentucky Legislature which would mandate that the controversies—the "advantages and disadvantages of scientific theories" including "evolution, the origins of life, global warming, and human cloning"—be taught to children in science. Laws were passed in 2008 that allow the Louisiana state board of education to "assist" teachers in promoting "critical thinking" on all of those subjects. The Texas Board of Education has required that "all sides of the evidence on evolution and global warming" be taught (Kaufman 2010) and, most recently, blocked the teaching of CRT in public schools (Kaufman 2010; Lopez 2021). In addition, an increasing number of American parents in more than half of states are opting out of school vaccines for their children, many because of fears that vaccines cause autism (see "More Skip Vaccines" 2011).

Oppositional discourse narratives counter human sexuality researchers and therapists who have reached a near consensus that homosexuality is a natural orientation, mainly caused by genes. Many religious conservatives in particular believe that homosexuality is an unnatural, abnormal lifestyle, mainly caused by inadequate parenting and/or sexual molestation during childhood; they argue that it is chosen and can be "cured" (Pollack 2001; see also Tsang and Rowatt 2007).

Climate change is another paradigm scenario that illustrates the outcomes of oppositional discourse. For example, a 2013 report from the United Nation's Intergovernmental Panel on Climate Change concludes with ninety-five percent certainty that humans are mostly to blame for temperatures that have dramatically climbed planet-wide since 1951 (Borenstein 2013). Yet, the number of Americans who believe global warming isn't happening has risen to twenty-three percent, up seven percentage points since April 2013 (Pappas 2014). The situational constraints that influenced COVID oppositional discourse in the United States included a resurgence of the virus across conservative and right-leaning southern states, with multiple governors and a sitting American president supportive of the protestors. By the fall of 2020, the anti-science movement directed against vaccines and COVID-19 moved into Europe. To illustrate, far right anti-COVID vaccine protestors in Germany created "Trump, Please Help" posters, while others joined QAnon conspiracy theorists in praising prominent anti-vaccine advocate Robert F. Kennedy Jr. while condemning Bill Gates's prioritizing of COVID-19 interventions (Hotez 2020, 506).

Ceccarelli (2011, 198, 218) considers these scenarios "argumentative traps" that constrain mainstream scientists as they produce "stumbling responses" as attempts to defend scientific consensus and deflect "manufactured controversies." It does appear that science communication as it is generally enacted is not working particularly well for scientists or the public in the United States. Often, the messages are not being received or comprehended as scientists expect, and the public is not benefiting from substantial vital scientific knowledge. Regardless of what purpose a science inquiry may serve, if someone in the public has a question, someone representing the science community must communicate an answer (Science's Nature 2007). Rhetoric, in theory and practice, is the frame within which to most effectively situate this discourse. Science becomes a symbolic construct and series of mediated controversies. Most recently, such mediation was evident through the informal discourse of a COVID-19 denial movement that initially presented itself in the Spring of 2020. Reconfigured as strategies to simultaneously protect public health and freedom, oppositional discourses emerged that opposed testing, contact tracing, government-mandated social distancing and vaccinations (Hotez 2020, 505).

The oppositional discourses of science and religion are informative here. Nearly seventy percent of American adults self-report being very or moderately religious (Newport 2012). Alva Noë (2013) argues that the tension between science and other modes of conscious life, including religion, is real and open to resolution. In the case of science, it is possible to verify what one trusts is so, by the accumulation of predictions tested by experiments that generate results predicted by models. Conversely, the notion that faith can be buttressed by evidence is the difference between science as a human enterprise, a "faith" and other faiths that depend on equally strong certainty emerging from within, but not testable by evidence (Pollack 2001).

To illustrate, belief systems undergirding creation science and intelligent design do not accept the scientific explanation of the theory of evolution. Intelligent design holds that, while the creation of the earth and the universe did not literally happen in six days, neither was it blind chance. Intelligent design proponents argue these concepts as a *big tent*, suggesting that people opposed to the theory of evolution get over their differences and focus on general and quasi challenges to scientific theories. This view leads to the framing of natural sciences, along with theories generated by them, as false (Vasas 2013).

The facts of science, by exposing the absence of purpose in the laws governing the universe, force taking responsibility for the welfare of self, species, and planet. For the same reason, they undercut moral or political systems based on mystical dialectics. Therefore, the stories scientists need to tell about climate change or evolution or genetic research require creative and audience specific communication strategies. As the latest science controversies demonstrate, inexpert publics can withhold recognition of specific disciplines (evolutionary biology) or contest specific claims (regarding climate change) when these conflict with popular narratives or particular interests. Upon closer inspection, the "scientific method" has proven to be, at least on occasion, an oversimplification of the negotiations that characterize the actual conduct of inquiry (Rehg 2009, 288–89).

Fundamentalism in particular has evolved into a discursive framing of contemporary post-modern culture as undermining America's Christian and biblically anchored foundations of civilization. So, a dominant theme of American fundamentalism is the tension between trust and distrust of the intellect including an unwillingness to accept principal narratives of science (Marsden 2006).

Clearly, there are significant limits to relying on technical expertise as the sole evidence for successfully arguing science. For example, although the explanatory and heuristic value of Darwinian evolution and its more recent progeny has been demonstrated in a wide variety of disciplines, experts have yet to breach the gulf between their conclusions and that of many in the American public that "evolution" and "intelligent design/

creationism" are theories of equal scientific merit. The rhetorical view of science is anchored on the premise that science is not the "world" or "nature" itself but a strategic representation. Data is not meaningful without context. In Cezar M. Ornatowski's (2007, 2) view, speaking people face such problems as what to say (invention), to whom (audience), with what purpose (argument), how (arrangement and style), and in what manner or medium (delivery)—"the major dimensions of any act of human communication and the fundamental concerns of rhetoric." It follows that human knowledge is rhetorical and involved with language and narrative in ways that go beyond presentation. Discourse also creates emerging knowledge as it embodies combined perspectives, values and norms. As a result, knowledge does not exist apart from knowers (Ornatowski 2007, 3).

Ceccarelli (2011) configures the oppositional discourse of climate change denial, the "teach the controversy" rhetorics, and AIDS dissent as manufactured to derail mainstream science. Such arguments rely on "appeals to open-mindedness freedom of inquiry, and fairness" so the "defenders of the scientific mainstream cannot refuse to debate without seeming dogmatically unscientific and opposed to democratic values" (198). This chapter contends that these arguments may be countered through empowering those "trained in science" with rhetorical competency.

## Intelligent Design and Evolution

Since the nineteenth century, evolution as configured by scientists generally requires neither a "reason" nor a "reasoned being" for its existence. Yet, more than forty percent of Americans espouse "young earth creationism," an ideology anchored in Biblical inerrancy, which asserts "science changes, but the word of God never changes" (All About Adam 2013). A June 2014 Gallup poll revealed forty-two percent of Americans still believe God created human beings in their present form less than ten thousand years ago (cited in Werleman 2014). Such "biblical biology" was the dominant theme in a recent Texas State Board of Education hearing keynoted by speakers who urged the SBOE to adopt textbooks that reflect "biblical principles" of evolution. Claims included that the evidence supporting evolution is so "incredibly weak" that it strains popular common sense (Jones 2013). It is simply difficult to believe that life emerged out of the original disorder of the universe. As such, a "common sense" invites people who look at "starry skies above and the moral law within" to believe that a personality, rather than blind chance, must have arranged them (Marsden 1991, 167). The length of time it would take for the present order of life to arise from disorder is staggering and stretches popular conceptions of probability. So, a commonsense story, an anti-supernaturalistic evolutionary scientific narrative, is far less compelling than the old argument from design (Marsden 1991, 167). Michael J. Behe's (1996, 111) "Black Box" argument, that because of its failure to explain the "irreducibly complex systems" of evolutionary biochemical cellular processes, "the Darwinian theory of evolution" is invalid, rings true for many.

This tension is significant because it has existed between fundamentalists and mainstream science in the United States for decades. Religions are not theories that explain or predict. The value of religious texts does not derive from being verified through methods of natural science (Noë 2013). An alternative—or additional—explanation for such challenges to mainstream science may be that arguments grounded in faith rely on different concepts of evidence to secure acceptance of their premises. Science and faith are different tools that generate different results because they start from different premises (Pollack 2001).

According to American courts, creationism has been demarcated from science. However, this does not change the fact that creation stories have been sanctioned as reasonable by members of many audiences. This fact reflects the reality that different intellectual communities use different arrays of logical tests for what is reasonable (Prelli 1989, 235). These arguments, that failed to convince legal and scientific experts to include creationism in science curricula, were still good reasons for many political and religious audiences. Situational constraints, personal contexts, and beliefs influence and validate the judgments made. In this way, scientific results have multiple meanings that may lead people with the same data to different but equally reasonable decisions (Majdik 2009).

## Rhetorical Ecology

Contemporary American science would benefit from the creation of an interface between the technical/professional and the public/lay spheres. It is a distinctly rhetorical challenge in that each sphere is defined by unique discourses. The traditional objectivist model of scientific communication is not generally consistent with contemporary understanding of the science and communication interface because such a configuration is grounded in the assumption that correct scientific conclusions are directly inferable from empirical data, and that nonscientific values and purposes have no role in the selection theories, and that scientists can be dispassionate about their own ideas while objectively evaluating other proposals (Czubaroff 1989, 45–46).

This rhetorical vision departs from previous attempts to demarcate a single border between science and "non-science." It illustrates how competing traditional research communities build such boundaries to advance their "proprietary interests." An "ecosystem" metaphor clarifies this argument:

> Containing numerous constituents, an ecosystem recognizes the primacy of certain species within their ecological niches. That primacy, however, comes not as a function of one species' isolation from others, but from the ecosystem's profound interconnectedness. The more or less peaceful and balanced coexistence of multiple species is the goal toward which we ought to strive [and work] for a recognition of the inescapable symbiosis of what traditionally we have called the technical and the public, the internal and the external, or the natural and the cultural (Taylor 1996, 7–9).

In this vision, science is not a stand-alone component of the physical world but constructed through humans to emerge at some point as yet another construct. Rhetoric's traditional identification as public, communal discourse suggests that a rhetorical perspective on demarcation must begin with some conception of science as a communal enterprise. An essential characteristic of rhetoric is that it is addressed discourse, concerned with the persuasion, intentional or otherwise, of an audience. As a result, the "rhetorical inducement of scientific audiences succeeds or fails depending on whether scientific rhetors render their narratives as reasonable according to the judgments of their situationally constrained audiences" (Prelli 1989, 217–18).

Just as the well-being of both expert and inexpert sectors benefit through developing discourse communities with permeable boundaries, so too might scientific and oppositional discourse communities benefit from participating in intercommunity narratives of science in the United States.

When one turns from general theory to ask what the pattern of rhetorical invention is for scientific communication, the postulates of general rhetorical theory become more precise. One cannot think about purposing in precisely the same way as one moves from theological to political to legal to scientific subjects and audiences. The interests, values, and logical requirements of each community prescribe and so limit what can be legitimately purposed, designate what will be the significant points at issue, and specify the range of appropriate lines of argument.

To illustrate, categorical statements dichotomizing emotionality and rationality as well as credibility and rationality may be misleading. To that end, Taddicken and Reif (2020) suggest the traditional rhetorical proofs of ethos and logos, so often dismissed in the theories and practice of science communication, as lucrative research areas that may inform effective narratives with which to counter anti-science discourses.

In addition, to better understand the dynamics of non-science-based health practices and possibly think of more productive harm mitigation strategies, it is crucial to better understand (rather than overlook or simply dismiss) the epistemological dimension of certain communities, identifying and analyzing their beliefs and contextual practices.

For example, future research might consider that initiatives to understand a rhetoric of science denial based on methodological and conceptual frameworks from the Global North alone can cause wrongful conclusions. As a case in point, comparisons of COVID vaccine hesitancy between the Global South (e.g., Africa and Latin America) and the Global North (e.g., Europe and North America) might factor in context-specific issues, such as ease of access, ethnic and religious issues, reactions to governments, reactions to recent episodes of vaccine tests on populations, and reactions to pasts of colonial violence (Matos et al 2021).

Finally, further research might examine the tenets of this interactive public space through a discussion of its attributes and channels as well as scientists' perceptions of it. In addition, the symbiosis between non-technical (or "lay") audiences and scientific texts could be considered as well as the core narratives of technical truths that emerge within such public spaces as science is rhetorically enacted.

## Civic Science

In 2019, the WHO listed vaccine hesitancy as a global health priority, driven by a rhetoric of oppositional discourse, exemplified most recently by refusal of COVID-19 inoculations ("Ten Threats" 2019). In particular, a discursive movement originating in the United States has emerged into a multi-national phenomenon of toxic narratives that could decelerate already established protocols for combating COVID-19, a virus that has spread world wide in a matter of months (Hotez 2020, 507).

Multiple discourses have coalesced to challenge the science that addresses this phenomenon, foregrounded by a global vaccine hesitancy, comprised of prominent PACs, the ascension of nationalistic tendencies and communities on "dark web" sites that are not easily searchable (506). Combating or defusing this triumvirate will require extensive rhetorical interaction between scientists and the public.

One of the results of this rhetoric and science interface becomes the collaborative endeavors of civic scientists, experts who communicate with broad audiences and bring knowledge and experience into the public through channels ranging from traditional to social media to political and religious institutions and structures (Clark and Illman 2001, 6). Such individuals are, in a rhetorical sense, quintessentially persuaders. Peter Pockley (2001) suggests that trust in science and technology can only be achieved with the public if scientists engage in interactive communication with non-technical audiences. The central question becomes how to forge a more sustainable dialogue between science and society, and the many different publics whose assent ultimately is needed if these oppositional or argument traps are to be re-configured into reasonable and applied discourses of science. Hotez (2020) argues global narratives that challenge the science behind COVID interventions coincide with a triad of other factors to complicate discursive mediation of such unproductive discourse. These include global mass-mediated digital campaigns that weaponize health communication through the promotion of conspiracies platformed by bots and trolls into organized disinformation campaigns (507).

In sum, this chapter configures a rhetorical vision of American science as multiple-voiced contextualized narratives. Within this shared discursive space, research crucial to resolving crises such as the COVID pandemic becomes a cooperative endeavor and so more highly valued by those whom science informs and serves. It is when this assent occurs that the claims of scientists may achieve the status of communal knowledge. And it is this process that evidences science itself as rhetorical invention.

## Works Cited

"All about Adam." 2013. *The Economist*, November 23, 2013. Accessed November 14, 2017. https://www.economist.com/news/united-states/21590475-furiousand-politicaldebate-about-origins-mankind-all-about-adam.

Banerjee, Neela. 2012. "Climate Change Skepticism Seeps into Science Classrooms." *Los Angeles Times*, January 16, 2012. Accessed November 14, 2017. http://articles.latimes.com/2012/jan/16/nation/la-na-climate-change-school-20120116.

Behe, Michael J. 1996. *Darwin's Black Box: The Biochemical Challenge to Evolution*. New York: The Free Press.

Borenstein, Seth. 2012. "Mumbai, Miami on List for Big Weather Disasters." *Yahoo! News*. Accessed November 14, 2017. https://www.yahoo.com/news/mumbai-miami-list-big-weather-disasters-150359548.html.

Broad, William. 2020. "Putin's Long War Against American Science." *The New York Times*, April 13. Accessed October 15, 2021. https://www.nytimes.com/2020/04/13/science/putin-russia-disinformation-health-coronavirus.html.

Ceccarelli, Leah. 2001. "Rhetorical Criticism and the Rhetoric of Science." *Western Journal of Communication* 65 (3): 314–30.

—. 2011. "Manufactured Scientific Controversy: Science, Rhetoric, and Public Debate." *Rhetoric and Public Affairs* 14 (2): 195–228.
Clark, Fiona, and Deborah L. Illman. 2001. "Dimensions of Civic Service: Introductory Essay." *Science Communication* 23 (1): 5–27.
Czubaroff, Jeanine. 1989. "The Deliberative Character of Strategic Scientific Debates." In *Rhetoric in the Human Sciences*, edited by H.W. Simons, 28–47. London: Sage.
Davies, Sarah R. 2008. "Constructing Communication: Talking to Scientists About Talking to the Public." *Speech Communication* 29:413–34.
Fennell, Dana. 2009. "Marketing Science: The Corporate Faces of Genetic Engineering." *Journal of Communication Inquiry* 33 (1): 5–26.
Frazier, Kendrick. 2009. "Introduction." In *Science Under Siege: Defending Science, Exposing Pseudoscience*, edited by K. Frazier, 9–16. Amherst, New York: Prometheus Books.
Giubilini, Alberto, Francesca Minerva, Udo Schuklenk, and Julian Savalescu. 2021. "The 'Ethical' COVID-19 Vaccine is the One that Preserves Lives: Religious and Moral Beliefs on the COVID-19 Vaccine." *Public Health Ethics*. July 19, 2021. Accessed October 31, 2021. DOI: 10.1093/phe/phab018.
Harris, Randy A. 2005. "Reception Studies in the Rhetoric of Science." *Technical Communication Quarterly* 14 (3): 249–55.
Hooke, William H. 2011. "Communication Researchers as Pygmalion: Turning Earth Scientists into Sparkling Conversationalists." *Spectra* 47 (4): 2–6.
Hotez, Peter J. 2019. "Anti-Science Extremism in America: Escalating and Globalizing." *Microbes and Infection* 22 (10): 505–7.
Jones, Robert. 2009. "Changing What Science Is and How It's Done." *American Physical Society March Meeting*, March 16–20, abstract #K1.153.
Keranen, Lisa. 2019. "Science, Rhetoric and the Public Good." *Spectra* 54 (3): 21–25. Accessed October 30, 2021. https://www.natcom.org/sites/default/files/NCA_Spectra_2018_September.pdf.
Kuhn, Thomas S. 1996. *The Structure of Scientific Revolutions*. 3rd ed. Chicago: The University of Chicago Press.
Lavorgna, Anita, and Heather Myles. 2021. "Science Denial and Medical Misinformation in Pandemic Times: A Psycho-Criminological Analysis." *European Journal of Criminology*. January 22. Accessed October 20, 2021. https://journals.sagepub.com/doi/full/10.1177/1477370820988832.
Lindenfeld, Laura A. 2018. "Wide Open, Messy Opportunities: On the Art of Science Communication." *Spectra* 54 (3): 8–12. Accessed October 30,2021. https://www.natcom.org/sites/default/files/NCA_Spectra_2018_September.pdf.
Lopez, Brian. 2021. "The Law That Prompted a School Administrator to Call for an 'Opposing' Perspective on the Holocaust is Causing Confusion Across Texas." *Texas Tribune*. October 15, 2021. Accessed October 20, 2021. https://www.texastribune.org/2021/10/15/Texas-critical-race-theory-law-confuses-educators/.

Majdik, Zoltan P. 2009. "Judging Direct-to-Consumer Genetics: Negotiating Expertise and Agency in Public Biotechnological Practice." *Rhetoric and Public Affairs* 12 (4): 571–605.

Marsden, George M. 2006. *Fundamentalism and American Culture*. New York: Oxford University Press.

Matos, Camila Carvalho de Souza Amorim, Bruna Aparecida Gonçalves, and Marcia Thereza Couto. 2021. "Vaccine Hesitancy in the Global South: Towards a Critical Perspective on Global Health." *Global Public Health*. Accessed October 22, 2021. DOI: 10.1080/17441692.2021.

McLaughlin, Danielle M., Jack Mewhirter, and Rebecca Sanders. 2021. "The Belief That Politics Drive Scientific Research and Its Impact on COVID-19 Risk Assessment." *PLOS ONE*. Accessed October 30, 2021. https://doi.org/10.1371/journal.pone.0249937.

Missouri House Bill No. 911. 2003. "House Bill No. 911, 92nd General Assembly." Missouri House of Representatives. December 19. Accessed November 26, 2017. http://www.house.mo.gov/content.aspx?info=/bills041/biltxt/intro/HB0911I.htm.

Mooney, Chris. 2013. "Could Carl Sagan Have Defeated Climate Denial?" *Mother Jones*. November 13, 2013. Accessed November 14, 2017. http://www.motherjones.com/politics/2013/11/carl-sagan-climate-seth-macfarlane.

"More Skip Vaccines." 2011. *Erie Times-News*. November 11, A3.

Newport, Frank. 2012. "Seven in 10 Americans are Very or Moderately Religious." *GALLUP Politics*. December 4. Accessed November 14, 2017. http://www.gallup.com/poll/159050/seven-americans-moderately-religious.aspx.

Noë, Alva. 2013. "Science and Its Reality: Take 2." *NPR*. December 6. Accessed November 14, 2017. http://www.npr.org/sections/13.7/2013/12/06/249029985/science-and-its-reality-take-2.

Ornatowski, Cezar M. 2007. "Science and Rhetoric: A Changing Relationship." *The Writing Instructor*. September, 2007. http://www.writinginstructor.com/ornatowski.

Pappas, Stephanie. 2014. "Climate Change Disbelief Rises in America." *Live Science*. January 16, 2014. Accessed November 14, 2017. http://livescience.com/42633-climate-change-disbelief-rises.html.

Paul, Danette, Davida Charney, and Aimee Kendall. 2001. "Moving Beyond the Moment: Reception Studies in the Rhetoric of Science." *Journal of Business and Technical Communication* 15 (3): 372–99.

Perelman, Chaïm. 1982. *The Realm of Rhetoric*. Notre Dame, IN: University of Notre Dame Press.

Pockley, Peter. 2001. "Public Dialogue, Not Monologue, Science Leaders Urge." *Australasian Science* 22 (10): 11.

Pollack, Robert. 2001. "Roundtable: Science and Faith." *PBS*. Accessed November 14, 2017. http://www.pbs.org/wgbh/evolution/religion/faith/discuss_01.html.

Prelli, Lawrence J. 1989. *A Rhetoric of Science: Inventing Scientific Discourse*. Columbia, SC: University of South Carolina Press.

Rand, Honey. 1998. "Science, Non-science and Nonsense: Communicating with the Lay Public." *Vital Speeches of the Day* 64 (9): 282–84.

Rehg, William. 2009. *Cogent Science in Context: The Science Wars, Argumentation Theory, and Habermas.* Cambridge, MA: The MIT Press.

Roth, Wolff-Michael. 2014. "*Nacherzeugung, Nachverstehen*: A Phenomenological Perspective on How Public Understanding of Science Changes by Engaging With Online Media." *Public Understanding of Science* 23 (7): 850–65. Accessed November 17, 2017. DOI: 10.1177/0963662513512441.

Science's Nature. 2007. "Science's Nature Requires Purpose to Be Explained." *PRweek*, Feburary 1. Accessed November 14, 2017. http://www.prweek.com/article/1259090/sciences-nature-requires-purpose-explained.

Scott, Dylan. 2014. "Unprecedented Attack on Evolution 'Indoctrination' Mounted in Missouri." *Talking Points Memo.* February 14, 2014. Accessed November 14, 2017. http://talkingpointsmemo.com/news/missouri-anti-evolution-law-parent.

Strazewski, Len. (2020). "How Science Communication Is Failing During COVID-19." *AMA.* Accessed October 26, 2021. https://www.ama-assn.org/delivering-care/public-health/how-science-communication-failing-during-covid-19.

Taddicken, Anne, and Monika Reif. 2020. "Between Evidence and Emotions: Emotional Appeals in Science Communication." *Media and Communication* 8 (1). Accessed October 17, 2021. DOI: https://doi.org/10.17645/mac.v8i1.2934.

Shermer, Michael. 2010. "Norman Jay Levitt 1943-2009." *Skeptic* 15 (3): 65.

Taylor, Charles A. 1996. *Defining Science: A Rhetoric of Demarcation.* Madison, WI: University of Wisconsin Press.

"Ten Threats to Global Health in 2019." 2019. The World Health Organization. Accessed October 20, 2021. https://www.who.int/news-room/spotlight/ten-threats-to-global-health-in-2019.

Tsang, Jo-Ann, and Wade C. Rowatt. 2007. "The Relationship Between Religious Orientation, Right-wing Authoritarianism, and Implicit Sexual Preference." *International Journal for the Psychology of Religion* 17 (2): 99–120.

Vasas, Emily. 2013. "Messiah Professor Discusses Debate of Bible vs. Biology." *Etownian* 110, no. 4 (October): 6.

Wells, Susan. 1996. *Sweet Reason: Rhetoric and the Discourses of Modernity.* Chicago: The University of Chicago Press.

# Rhetorics of Evidence in Media and Culture

# 11 Beyond Literalism: Reality and Imagination in the Public Image

*Robert Hariman and John Louis Lucaites*

The claim that documentary photographs—or any photographs, for that matter—are incontrovertible evidence has long been a powerful conceit, its epistemological status evoked by the aphorism passed down from one generation to the next that "seeing is believing."[1] The importance of this vernacular assumption is highlighted by Errol Morris's (2011) attempt to discipline it in his book *Believing Is Seeing*. The tension between these two claims—"seeing is believing" and "believing is seeing"—frames a series of important questions that complicate the ways in which we understand the capacity of photography to mediate one's relationship with the world. In short, what is the relationship between photography and knowledge? Is the photographic image a source of knowledge, or merely a mode of presentation? Does it provide objective information, or does it depend on contextual assumptions? Is it a trace or an artifact? Index or symbol? These are not chicken-and-egg questions, but rather examples of how different conceptions of photography, and of knowledge, can lead to more or less productive uses of visual media.

Attention to questions of referential objectivity, reliability, and accuracy are important for any medium of communication, and they acquire specific application within any domain of use: for example, the criminal justice system, scientific research, advertising, and snapshot photography each observe and (to various degrees) discuss and refine specific techniques and standards of visual representation. Much of the time, the process is relatively smooth: new technologies or other changes can of course provoke controversy, but a great deal of ordinary practice in the courts, in the lab, in the studio, or on Facebook is relatively self-evident: the photograph, already produced according to current technical and stylistic conventions, becomes transparent enough to serve as evidence, that is, as a reliable indication of an actual set of circumstances. Of course, when controversies about an image, archive, or technology occur, they are by definition significant moments for reconsideration and change, but soon enough the specific community of practitioners stabilizes around another set of assumptions. Indeed, that may be one of the features of most domains of knowledge production: the use of any medium is largely instrumental. The more circumscribed or expert the domain, the more it can seem to provide a model of reliable communication.

But what about the public media? What should count as evidence in the news media and in related forms of exposition and advocacy by citizens, governments, and others competing for attention in the public sphere? What should be the standards for reliable communication, and who should make those decisions? Committed to reason but having no specific expertise or shared objective, the public is by definition profoundly pluralistic, and public media and audiences are infamous for their susceptibility to emotional appeals, ideological biases, and other invitations to error. Photography plays a particularly characteristic role in this ongoing drama: it is suspect as supposedly being non-verbal, emotional, and manipulative, yet also valued in specific cases for its capacity to expose reality and provoke collective moral response. Specific media typically are judged more "popular" and less authoritative based on the extent and manner in which they deploy images, yet the public itself is increasingly defined by conditions of common spectatorship (see, e.g., Green 2010). Is the public's dependence on visual images evidence that it is grounded more in opinion than knowledge, or do those images provide a basis for a distinctively public knowledge of the world?

We address this problematic by advancing the claim that the evidentiary value of photography eludes simple conceptions of information and objectivity and resides instead in understanding how seeing is an active engagement with the world. From this perspective, strictly epistemological questions can be misleading: the knowledge produced by the photographic event can be more than determinations of fact or agreement about explanatory claims. These achievements are not ruled out of bounds, but they operate as part of a larger process of co-orientation. Photographic reportage is a way of seeing that articulates a way of being in the world that is both *referential* and *relational*, both about something that exists objectively in front of the lens of the camera and something that is addressed to an audience. To become evidence of what is, what is probable or possible, or what should be done, the photograph has to provide image and optic, both a record of what is and a way of seeing with others. This dual articulation, we argue, requires both realistic and imaginative modalities of response. In advancing this claim, we hope to advance a rhetorical conception of the photographic image that accounts for how photojournalism operates as a public art. By simultaneously recording reality and engaging the imagination, photojournalism can communicate profound truths about the human condition while also calling people into democratic community.

## Realism and Imagination

Photography is defined as a medium by its relationship to reality, and defined as an art by its relationship to the imagination. These distinctions have shaped the discourse of photography from its inception, and each successive reformulation of the discourse involves a new understanding of how reality and the imagination might be entangled together in the still image.

Perhaps the most succinct formulation was provided by the film theorist Siegfried Kracauer, who was trying to identify how "each medium has a specific nature that invites certain kinds of communications while obstructing others."[2] Kracauer (1960, 11–12) defined photography as being shaped by two generative principles: "there is on the one side a tendency toward realism culminating in records of nature, and on the other a formative tendency aiming at artistic creations." We might call this model the photographic matrix. Every photograph will consist of both a referential and an imaginative orientation. Any photograph is both more or less a record of what happened, and more or less an artistically enhanced experience; both more or less empirical, and more or less interpretive; both more or less accurate, and more or less suggestive.

These two principles do not have equal status, however. As Kracauer correctly observed, the media specificity of photography comes from the primacy of the realistic principle. Although "a minimum requirement," it is almost absolute: photographs are expected to show something that was in front of the lens prior to the creation of the image (Kracauer 1960, 13). That said, Kracauer (1960, 16) recognized that the imaginative and realist principles don't have to conflict: indeed, the formative tendency "may help substantiate and fulfill" the realist tendency.

What might seem like a minor caveat is in fact a radical insight that speaks directly to photography's role as a mode of evidence: *realism has to be the first principle of photographic art, but it cannot be achieved completely without imaginative presentation and response.* The camera records the surface of the world like no other instrument, but the truth of what is shown can be *realized* only through an act of imagination. Stated otherwise, the photograph is inherently not reducible to a single principle of representation, and instead is a "heterogeneous object" where different sources of meaning intersect, and the intersections are lodged in the formal design and explored through interpretation.[3]

Failure to appreciate photography's dual nature as record and artifact has led to a serious disconnect between theory and practice. As Patrick Maynard (1997, 86) has summarized, "both among theoreticians and in the popular mind . . . industrial technologies (quaintly associated with our 'needs')" were defined in contrast to the fine arts, with "imagination as the very antithesis" of industrial production. Instead of considering the imagination to be "a crucial practical skill," and photography to be a technology for amplifying imaginative powers, the separation of mechanical reproduction from aesthetic experience became conventional wisdom (Maynard 1997, 83–85). More recently Jae Emerling (2012, 15) has concluded that the "contemporary impasse of photography is, in large part, a result of this rejection of aesthetics, something that one finds throughout its discursive history." This separation and a corresponding skepticism regarding mass culture have long been the dominant attitudes in academic, professional, and public commentary. One result has been puzzlement or embarrassment regarding the continuous stream of images having both representational validity and imaginative power, not to mention popular appreciation. Another result, we believe, has been widespread acceptance of a tame conception of photographic realism—what we will label "literalism"—and with that, a weakening of the political imagination.

It should be clear that we are not insisting on a single definition of either realism or reality. As noted above, the habitus of photography contains varied conceptions of how photographs do or do not provide a veridical record of what was before the lens. Those differences reflect everything from pragmatic variations in use, to philosophical debates about representation, to fine art experiments with the conventions of visual perception, to journalists' debates about artistic manipulation in digital processing, to professional and public controversies about photoshopping the news, and so on. Fortunately, engaged spectatorship does not require a comprehensive theory or professional doctrine, while it benefits from making specific aesthetic and political commitments against a background of plural perspectives. We believe that the camera's capacity to directly and inexpensively produce reliable pictures of the world remains an essential technology for democratic societies, but the full benefit will be realized only through imaginative interpretation of the public image. Such spectatorship attempts to develop the full richness of the image and the archive, to place the viewer in an engaged relationship with the real world and those who live there. To do that, each generation will have to work through the fundamental tension between trace and artifact, reality and imagination. Unfortunately, the current legacy has left us with too weak a sense of both art and representation.

## From Realism to Literalism

The invention of photography was a profound and yet curiously pleasing shock to modern habits of representation. In retrospect, the effect seems to have been one of receiving a large and unexpected inheritance. By so perfectly and easily capturing the observable world, this obviously modern technology offered a new, more immediate, unbiased, and comprehensive relationship to reality itself. In fact, the removal of human mediation was thought to be the supreme achievement of the technology, an idea captured by Henry Fox Talbot's ([1844–46] 2010) label, the "pencil of nature." Louis Daguerre ([1838/39] 2008) had already gone one better, claiming that the daguerreotype was "not an instrument to be used to draw Nature, but a chemical and physical process which gives her the ability to reproduce herself." Reality now could communicate directly, without need of or distortion by human artistry. A French journal (*Cosmos*) summed up the matter succinctly: "We can hardly accuse the *sun* of having an imagination" (quoted in Jammes and Janis 1983, 247).

Photography's exclusion from the fine arts followed directly from this statement of the obvious: photography was not an art, could not become an art, and any attempt to do so could only corrupt both art and photography. Charles Baudelaire got closest to the problem with his disdainful account of how the new medium was changing the public and, with that, the artists who would pander to the sensationalism of the real. Thus, "progress" was decline—"by progress I mean the progressive domination of matter"—as photography drove the artist to paint "not what he dreams, but what he sees." Because the camera was aligned with both the material force of matter and "this great industrial madness of today," it was driving out the imagination, leaving a void sure to be filled only by banality, mediocrity, and sentimentality (Baudelaire 1980, 85, 88, 89). What actually was happening, of course, was that the definition of art was changing radically due to the pressure of photography's mimetic power and widespread circulation, and by being freed from the imitation of nature, modern painters unleashed one of the most significant bursts of creativity in the history of art. Even so, Baudelaire was prescient in recognizing that photography was distinguished not merely by a close fit with nature but also by its industrial production, and that a major effect was the change in public spectatorship.[4]

Despite the strong separation of reality and imagination in these early debates, other voices were developing a more nuanced view of the technology, one that recognized artistic potential beyond veridical representation. Oliver Wendell Holmes was an avid promoter of photography and also one of its most insightful commentators. His account of the medium includes a phenomenology of seeing whereby "the mind feels its way into the very depths of the picture"; a sense of "inexhaustible" complexity where "there will be as many beauties lurking, unobserved, as there are flowers that blush unseen in forests and meadows"; and, perhaps most important, the idea that "form is henceforth divorced from matter" and thereby something that can be reproduced, shared, studied, and enjoyed easily (Holmes 1859). As these and other quasi-artistic experiences were being explored in practice, the trafficking between photography and the imagination became a busy street corner where eccentrics, charlatans, artists, and journalists worked side by side. Victorians indulged an appetite for photographs of fairies and other traces of a spirit world; Surrealists redefined the camera as an instrument for artistic experimentation; and photographers such as Alfred Stieglitz, Edward Weston, and Henri Cartier-Bresson developed the idea of photographic artistry as an important, though carefully circumscribed marker of professional value.

Much else happened as well, but by the middle of the twentieth century, photography had achieved a complacent stasis in respect to both reality and the imagination. It was solidly institutionalized as a modern recording technology that served science, industry, advertising, art, and most notably the press, but always in a subordinate role. *Life* magazine and *National Geographic* epitomized this cultural consensus: the photographs were taken by highly skilled photographers for an audience that wanted to be both informed and entertained. In sum, the photographic image was securely ensconced as the instrument of accurate observation, and some photographs were valued for how well they enhanced the viewing experience. Along the way, the discourse on photography had become largely dormant: beyond the technical manuals, there wasn't much sense that the medium might exemplify important problems in modern culture. Perhaps for that reason, both realism and the imagination had been tamed.[5] Photography had become part of a standard world whose only horizon was one of continued progress. Although described by some as a Golden Age of photojournalism, in fact the time had come for someone to upend the table.

More than one critic stood up, but none with more success than Susan Sontag, who convinced her readers that photography was both characteristically modern and deeply problematic: "the quintessential art of affluent, wasteful, restless societies—an indispensable tool of the new mass culture."[6] Equally important, she changed the relationship of photography both to reality and the imagination. The key restatement is this:

> Photographs are, of course, artifacts. But their appeal is that they also seem, in a world littered with photographic relics, to have the status of found objects—unpremediated slices of the world. Thus, they trade simultaneously on the prestige of art and the magic of the real. They are clouds of fantasy and pellets of information.[7]

Sontag has defined photography along Kracauer's two axes: its relationship to reality and to the imagination. The photograph is simultaneously artifact and fact, fantasy and information, an imaginary world and a small piece of the actual world. So far, so good. That colorful vacation photo, that astronaut on the moon, demonstrators shouting across a police line, a starving woman holding a starving child: each depicts a tiny slice of what was there then, and also activates visions of leisured happiness, technological progress, political action, and ethical community. This framework doubles as a highly concise critical method: for any photograph, one can ask how it is too small—too selective—as a record of the event or process, and how it appeals to the spectator's desires, not least as these have been shaped by larger practices of cultural domination.

The problem is in the specific inflection given to each of the two generative principles of the photographic art. Sontag's formulation is radically reductive, and doubly so as both representation and imagination are recast in their least adequate forms.[8] The photograph's relationship to reality is reduced to mere information, and in the most demeaning sense that can be attributed to that term. "Pellets" denotes the product of an industrial process, one that produces endless numbers of small, identical objects. The photograph is seen through Baudelaire's eyes: fused with the most alien aspect of reality, its sheer materiality, devoid of consciousness, and with the most impersonal and powerful form of modern society, its relentless industrialization.

The damage done to the imagination is at least as bad. Information is legitimate and legible in a modern society, but fantasy is a cheap thrill at best. As before, however, Sontag does have one leg to stand on: the substitution of fantasy for imagination rightly has been identified as a recipe for bad art. If photography replaced imagination with fantasy, that could be an example of cultural decline (compare even today the relative status of "literature" and "fantasy literature"). And some photography certainly will indulge fantasy, not least if one looks to advertising, travel photography, and other commercial practices.[9] More generally, the distraction (and easy path) of fanciful artistry is a constant temptation for audiences and artists alike in any art or other area of creative work, and no small number of bad poems, novels, films, buildings, cars, and clothes are evidence of that. However, Sontag has claimed that a negative tendency in any imaginative process is an essential condition of photography. Photography cannot be imaginative, yet it is an artifact, therefore it must be merely fanciful. Which, not surprisingly, would seem to explain why it would be so appealing to the mass culture audience.

This model became the foundation of the late-twentieth century discourse on photography. Note, for example, the double denigration in John Tagg's assessment of the New Deal's Farm Security Administration (FSA) photography project:

> We cannot be innocent of the values which inhere in the 'realism' of these photographs . . . . We may live the space of the picture, its 'reality,' its ideological field. But as the picture draws us in, we are drawn into its orbit, into the gravitational field of its 'realism' . . . . We seem to experience a loss of our own reality . . . we are invited to dream in the ideological space of the photograph. (1993, 182–83)

He concludes by quoting Freud: "'When the work of interpretation has been completed, we perceive that a dream is a fulfillment of a wish'" (Tagg 1993, 182–83). The supposedly realistic image is a fabrication that takes the spectator away from reality and substitutes instead a dream world. Photography misleads because of both how it shows the world and how it invites imaginative response to what is shown.

From this platform and through the application of semiotics, rhetoric, psychoanalysis, and other critical technologies, the two principles of realism and imagination were each subjected to withering attack.[10] On the one hand, photography did not provide adequate representation of the real world. Instead of being a transparent window on the real, the photograph was an artifact, a designed object that shaped perception according to technological or ideological imperatives. Instead of being directly apprehended, it was essentially meaningless until provided with contextual information. Instead of recording exactly what happened, it offered only the thinnest sliver of any event, a tiny fragment of time with no sure indication of what happened before or afterwards. Instead of being the objective result of a mechanical process, the photograph was the product of desires and conventions that affected every element of its existence and use. Instead of providing veridical evidence of actual events, the images of the world were being used to make social hierarchies appear natural. In Martin Jay's (1993, 130) succinct summary, "by the late twentieth century the realist paradigm was practically obliterated."

On the other hand, photography also was faulted for being incapable of artistic extension into the more creative and critical modes of perception. Instead of being oriented toward the imagination, photography was doubly banal: a cheap, disposable object documenting the most ordinary circumstances, people, and events of everyday life. Instead of being used to think critically, it was taken by the public to be merely descriptive, informative, factual. Instead of elevating thought, it was a relentless mixer and leveler that fueled popular culture while making amateurism into a virtue. Instead of channeling the emotions to break through convention and complacency and motivate action, it substituted faux experiences of empathy and other bourgeois sentiments. Instead of enhancing perception, it "aestheticized" reality, prettifying the ordinary and converting horror into perverse fascination. Instead of providing a bracing encounter with the unknown, it encouraged voyeurism, tourism, and other irresponsible habits that converted people into images for consumption. By the early 1990s Fredric Jameson (1992, 1) could pronounce the sweeping verdict on modern visual experience: "The visible is *essentially* pornographic: which is to say that it has its end in rapt, mindless fascination."

Most people don't talk like this, but the critical discourse has seeped into public consciousness. Nor is this a mysterious process: the discourse became the lingua franca of higher education and other cultural institutions, and the criticisms were identifying real problems: it becomes widely evident in a media-intensive society that representation is both unstable and powerful, and this combination is a pervasive source of anxiety. People want to be grounded in reality, not reality effects, and they want to control their lives, not be controlled. Nor is renunciation a viable option: it is difficult to be employed or be a parent or enjoy one's leisure time without using modern media. Not surprisingly, the media institution attuned to public opinion has developed a means for coping with photography's uneasy combination of reality and imagination. In place of a strong sense of either photographic realism or photographic art, the default mode now is a commitment to literalism.

According to this model of visual literacy, the news photograph is taken to be a veridical record of reality, but only if it is presented and interpreted in strict accord with neutral determinations of fact. The photograph is literally true, or disqualified if found to be altered, but that is all. No other kind of speech acts are recognized: photographs state what is, but they do not explain, predict, judge, confront, suggest, plead, or otherwise call for a response. Photographs do all those things, however, so exceptions have to be accounted for. First, some photographs are acknowledged to work on a higher plane: iconic photos are the leading example (Hariman and Lucaites 2007). These moments of visual eloquence are admittedly exceptions, however; ordinary images are supposed to be seen and not heard. Second, all the aesthetic, emotional, symbolic, moral, or other resonances are limited to private, subjective experience: these are individual reactions, but they obviously do not have the same public status—the same common recognition—of ordinary perception. Even those photos that shock the viewer only activate subjective reactions; they provide no moral knowledge that might be shared.

The staying power of this discourse is suggested by how it prevails in Sontag's revisionary codicil to her earlier work; a work often cited as if it represented a significant break toward appreciating photography's capacity for moral witness. Although she conceded that aesthetics and morality can work together and that photography need not lead to compassion fatigue, moral reflection (e.g., on the spectator's complicity in the structure of violence) "is a task for which the painful, stirring images supply only an initial spark" (Sontag 2003, 103). Likewise, "such images cannot be more than an invitation to pay attention, to reflect, to learn, . . . with the understanding that moral indignation, like compassion, cannot dictate a course of action" (Sontag 2003, 117). Thus, the only real change is granting that shock value may persist rather than lead to numbness; otherwise, photographs retain the essentialist definition of her earlier work: "The limit of photographic knowledge of the world is that, while it can goad conscience, it can, finally never be ethical or political knowledge. The knowledge gained through still photographs will always be some kind of sentimentalism, whether cynical or humanist. It will be a knowledge at bargain prices—a semblance of knowledge, a semblance of wisdom" (Sontag 1977, 23–24). Images, like the emotions they invoke, are only prompts to reflection, while moral knowledge and action absolutely require the rational deliberation that is supposedly found in writing but never in visual media. Once these shallow binaries between reason/emotion, text/image, and acting/seeing are accepted, it becomes easy to compare photography with voyeurism and pornography, and not with more public ways of knowing and being in the world.

As this hermeneutic dominates professional journalism and public discussion, literalism becomes appealing because it intuitively responds to the critical deconstruction of both the referential and the artistic dimensions of the image.[11] Is reality constructed? Well, then we will insist on the most basic model: the who, what, where, when of each single event. Can artistry divert or enthrall? Well, then we will relegate such reactions to private experience: they will not have the status of public acknowledgment. So it is that the press promises unaltered images, photographers or editors provide relatively neutral captions, commentators state that their opinions are their own and not those of their organization, and the public discussion includes continual fretting about digital manipulation. Admittedly this helps one avoid both flights of fantasy and errors of fact. (Make no mistake, these are important concerns for both the press and the public.) Literalism also is legible, as anyone can identify some fantasies and various facts, whereas the intermediate realm of beliefs and values is harder to pin down, much less lead to agreement. Unfortunately, the easier path leaves spectators ill equipped for critical discussion or democratic solidarity.

## From Literalism to Realism

Whatever the cultural domain, literalism is not far from fundamentalism. One sticks to the letter of the text or the law or scripture to stay close to the essential elements of a doctrine. In the case of photography, the doctrine is the modernist commitment to objectivity on behalf of rational deliberation. If the image is found to be too artistic, emotional, or suggestive, these are biases that pitch it away from its referential or evidentiary function and toward fantasy and political manipulation. The knowledge that perfect objectivity may be impossible is not a deterrent, but instead cause for increased vigilance. For example, the popularity of digital cameras and amateur photo-manipulation has only heightened anxieties about the reliability of the image, rather than becoming evidence that the question of literal accuracy might be merely a preliminary basis for understanding the photographic encounter.

Photographic literalism has received additional promotion through Errol Morris's *Believing is Seeing*, which followed from his essays at the *New York Times* on visual truth and deception. The book provides an engaging set of detective stories, what Morris refers to as the "Mysteries of Photography" in the subtitle of his book. As others have noted, Morris is a careful (and appropriately obsessive) Sherlock Holmes as he interrogates the facts of the matters before him: Can we determine where and when a photograph was taken? What is the order of photographs in a sequence of images? Is the placement of objects in a scene empirically verifiable? As these and similar questions are answered, it becomes clear that the mysteries of photography are altogether secondary to Morris's primary concern, which, as Kathryn Schulz (2011) has observed, is epistemology. The goal is knowledge, and at the cost of bracketing from consideration everything that cannot be demonstrated conclusively in respect to the specific circumstances of image and event.

This shift from photography to epistemology is exemplified by the first half of Morris's title: *Believing is Seeing*. His phrasing reverses the terms of the cultural aphorism, "seeing is believing." This is not just a stylistic affectation. The more common phrase calls attention to the activity of "seeing" as the source of belief. As such, it carries an assumption about how we come to be (and to believe) in the world. As Aristotle remarked in his *Metaphysics* ([1941, trans. Ross], 980a), "For not only with a view to action, but even when we are not going to do anything, we prefer seeing (one might say) to everything else. The reason is that this, most of all the senses, makes us know and brings to light many differences between things." To "see" is more than just to "look" at or to "gaze" upon; to see the world is to be in it and to be of it; it is to understand the world actively. This sense of active discernment is captured metaphorically by the phrase, "I see what you mean." By reversing the terms, Morris prioritizes "belief" as the active agent that controls seeing, and in the process he reduces the later term to a condition of passivity.

To privilege belief in this way underscores a narrow definition of truth and what counts as evidence to establish truth. For example, Morris attends to two famous Roger Fenton photographs from the Crimean War. In one photograph the road is covered with cannonballs. In the other photograph the cannonballs are on the side of the road. For Morris there are two mysteries: what accounts for the movement of the cannonballs from one location to the next? And which of the photographs was shot first? The first mystery is never fully solved, though Morris does ultimately provide a solution to the second. But what, really, does it tell us about the truth of the matter? Or more to the point, the truth that it uncovers seems ultimately trivial when measured over and against the horrific conditions of the war and the suffering that it caused—a truth that doesn't change if the cannonballs actually landed on the road or not.[12]

This is another way of saying that one very quickly gets to the limits of literalism. The epistemological questions can never be answered in full (as in philosophy proper), while they displace other substantive questions. The literalist asks whether the photo is accurate, but not what other statements it might be making. Although the displacement of all social, cultural, moral, and political questions is hardly Morris's intention, one can see exactly that use of literalism in ordinary commentary on photography. Such commentary regularly insists that a disturbing or challenging photograph can only support the most minimal account of the event, or that since it is not perfectly reliable it cannot support an interpretation.

Underscoring the limits of literalism is not to deny the importance of detailed observation and media reliability for evidentiary purposes, whether in a court of law or the court of public opinion. There are times that the stakes are very high and all can turn on the veracity of the literal image. As was noted, however, almost all photography is accurate enough for the purposes to which it is put. From tourism to scientific research, the cameras and images in use have been selected because they are sufficiently reliable for the task at hand. The problem is that literalism elevates an occasional concern into a preoccupation. Discussions of photography that focus on questions of whether the image was digitally manipulated, are comparable to literary criticisms that focus exclusively on questions of plagiarism. In each case one might conclude that we are hearing about an interesting problem but still fall well short of taking the measure of the art.

Literalism includes a general suspicion of both aesthetics and rhetoric—and for good reason, as they invariably dismantle the assumptions necessary for believing in the inerrancy or objectivity or neutrality of literal statements. They also contrast with literalism's own, implicit aesthetic norms, which typically involve some minimalism, iconoclasm, or other aversion to excess in representation and response. From this perspective, the imagination is by definition excessive and unlikely to keep an audience adequately tethered to text or reality. Thus, when realism is reduced to questions of referential accuracy about "pellets of information," imagination has to follow a corresponding redefinition as "clouds of fantasy" providing willful, superficial enchantment.

To challenge this reduction, one might recall Samuel Taylor Coleridge's ([1817] 1975, 50, 167) distinction between imagination and fancy. Imagination is the vital ability of the mind to see its way into new perceptions, new creations, new syntheses; it is the human ability to create ideas, images, and relationships that had never existed before, and to do so in a way that brings us closer to the real nature of things. Fancy, by contrast, is merely the mind at play with things it already knew: it is the mechanism by which we assemble and reassemble memories without regard for reality in order to pander to our desires.

To bend these ideas in the direction of photography, we might think of imagination as a way of extraordinary seeing: that is, how one sees beyond the horizon of ordinary observation or conventional belief. Astronomy, for example, is an incredible act of imagination: by looking at a pale disk and points of light in the sky, people came to understand that the earth is a planet, and by looking at telescopic photographs and other electromagnetic traces we have learned that the universe consists of billions of galaxies that will never be visible to the naked eye. Likewise, photography has been a remarkable exercise in imagination, for by showing distant people, places, and events, it has brought spectators around the globe to realize that they are part of a common humanity living in a myriad of different cultures that no one will actually see together (Sliwinski 2011). In both cases, moreover, the mode of extraordinary seeing brings the viewer closer to reality, and to a larger reality, not farther away from it.

Stated otherwise, a photograph is always both image and optic: a reproduction of some part of reality, and a way of seeing that reality more extensively. Just as we can say that the photo shows more than one thing, or that it can mean different things to different people, so can it contain multiple optics. Thus, in looking at the iconic photograph of a man standing before a row of tanks near Tiananmen Square, one might see Cold War geopolitics, democratic revolution, liberal individualism, global citizenship, and other perspectives as well, including the Chinese government's focus on the restraint of the tank driver, as well as high-modernist aesthetic simplification that reinforces "seeing like a state" (Hariman and Lucaites 2007, 208–42). Most important, each perspective is simultaneously grounded in the particular event being depicted and extended beyond that moment to other actual or potential events that are part of some larger pattern; put differently, an image is intelligible only because of implicit continuities with other images within the same optic. So, for example, one sees a man pitching over a cliff and imagines him falling. If the man is wearing a swimsuit and gracefully arching toward water, the viewer sees a dive instead of an accident. Additional cues and inferences can cohere into an image of an exotic vacation, extreme sport, idealized youth, or artful suicide. The optic has to have some purchase in the event that the viewer can recognize or it won't be activated at all, and it has to imply additional extension if the event is to have any significance. Seeing is believing, but belief must be activated by the imagination, which draws on what we know to create a possible future.

The imagination is not an innocent place, of course, but rather one traversed by vectors of power and colonized by societies and their institutions. Thus, critical awareness must be brought to bear, both when imagination is stunted or co-opted by the powers that be, which happens all too often, and when mere fantasy can mislead those who have few resources to waste. Imagination is a political resource—including fantasies of power by both the strong and the weak (Scott 1990), but much more as well—and it needs to be used.

One of the functions of journalism is to report reliably on what is actually happening so personal and institutional responses can be grounded in reality. Another is to create the imaginative space of the public sphere—a space in which citizens have the freedom to consider alternatives to the status quo while oriented toward both reality and each other.[13] Professional journalism has described itself as if a carefully managed literalism is sufficient to serve the public interest. It is not sufficient, and fortunately journalism's actual practice has exceeded its disciplinary norms, not least because of photojournalism. What still is needed, however, is a stronger understanding of photojournalism as a public art—that is, an understanding that returns from literalism to a more complex and nuanced mode of spectatorship.

## Reimagining Spectatorship

If photography's relationship to reality is to be more than either factual or fraudulent, then the audience has to matter. Referential meaning still is needed, but it no longer is limited to questions of accuracy or authenticity. Instead, questions of relevance (Does the projection tell us what we need to know?), resonance (Does it connect with other sources of insight and value?), engagement (Does it pull us out of our ordinary indifference?), confrontation (Does it challenge conventional wisdom or denial?), and other measures of participation come to the fore. The key is to see such questions as integral to the meaning of the image, and not supplemental or extrinsic considerations. The public image is already part of a social imaginary, and it already has received significant social investment. As John Roberts (1998, 4) argues, this conception of the medium acknowledges that photographs provide practical knowledge for negotiating the contradictions of social organization while calling for (rather than presuming) democratic community.

The status of the realistic photograph as a mode of evidence is thus doubled, functioning both as a recording of specific facts and an act of imagining a world. The chief dimension of meaning is the one that is promoted by the epistemological conventions and media institutions of modernity, and much has been gained from that. There are costs, however: First, the world that is reproduced most of the time is a standard world, a world determined by the forces and agents recognized as authoritative. Second, when the image does provide additional resources for living well in that world or changing it for the better, those resources often are not recognized, or they are felt or are honored only in exceptional cases. So it is that we have photographic icons: those moments when eloquence is acknowledged, albeit as an exception from the ordinary image world. What is needed is a more continuous engagement with images that push us to think more widely and creatively about what the world might be. One might imagine that captions would serve that function, at least in part, and there is little question that they are central to the visual hermeneutic that governs the "reading" of documentary photography and of photojournalism in particular—and the literature here is extensive.[14] We are making a different point, however, for even as a caption contributes to this or that bias, the conventions of captioning can activate a visual literalism and a minimalist, unimaginative aesthetic to reinforce the assumptions that representation of the news should be apolitical and that spectatorship should be passive.

Two examples can help to clarify the problems of an overly vigilant literalism and the possibilities of a more active spectatorship that engages with the complexity of the public image. Literalism holds the spectator close to the habits of ordinary perception, and as such it is a doctrine of stasis, of adhering to fixed things, and that can be costly to those experiencing either domination or change. Two aspects of the literalist optic are particularly telling in this regard. The first is the focus on a narrow conception of epistemology that displaces ethical and political questions to the margins. The second is a reductive, typifying optic that lends itself to oversimplification rather than complexity and abstraction rather than engagement. In every case, the mentality extends across *both* image and caption; more precisely, the news image begins as an imagetext in which a photograph of a specific event has been framed by an accompanying verbal description.

Consider figure 1, which appeared in *Time* magazine and was captioned as follows: "April 30, 2013. Israeli security forces arrest a Palestinian man during clashes with Jewish settlers, left background, near the Jewish settlement of Yitzhar, near Nablus" (Time Lightbox 2013). Whoever wrote the caption was playing by the conventional rules, carefully identifying who, what, when and where in sufficient detail to place the photo within the event being covered. Given either forensic or historical questions, these could be crucial details.

Those are not the only questions that apply, however, for there are also political and moral questions that need to be considered. In respect to those questions, two very significant actions have not been identified by the caption. The first missing detail is that the settlers were rioting: they were attacking Palestinian people and property in revenge for an allegedly criminal act (a stabbing) (Ma'an News 2013). To be sure, the stabbing of a settler should lead to an arrest, but don't police usually respond to rioting, whatever the provocation, by arresting the rioters? In the scenario near Nablus, instead of Jewish settlers violating the rule of law and attacking innocent people, the police treat the Palestinian as the sole lawbreaker.

Figure 1. Nassar Ishtayeh/Associated Press; April 30, 2013.

The second omission is more telling, as it contradicts evidence in the image itself. The man is doubled over in pain while trying to get something out of his eyes. He is a large, well-muscled man yet unable to resist the two soldiers grabbing him, so the pain must be debilitating. Now look closer: the two soldiers have been or are still trying to spray something into his face. The one soldier was or is spraying—you can see that he is holding a spray canister with his finger in the firing position, and the white blur could be the foam or mist being sprayed. The other soldier was or is trying to hold and turn the man so that the first could hit him directly in the face. Without a second image, we don't know if the soldiers are moving back from the man or continuing to assault him, but it is clear that he has been sprayed once and that he may be about to get a second dose.

The caption did not say, "April 30, 2013, Israeli security forces try to force a second dose of pepper spray into the eyes of a Palestinian man during rioting by Jewish settlers." That probably would be a more specific, more accurate description of what is being shown. It also would shift the political and moral resonance of the image: instead of a man being "arrested" as a criminal, we have Israeli soldiers siding with the settlers who were attacking his community. Instead of soldiers attacking a wounded man to deliver a second dose of punishment, we have merely an arrest.

Any caption tells you both what to see and what to ignore in the photograph. In this case the reportage is showing the violence, but it also is coaching the viewer in how to look past it, minimize it, pretend that even though nasty things happen on behalf of security, one really doesn't have to *say* what happened. By adhering to the supposedly neutral protocol of supposedly literal description, the captioning enforces two sets of rules: the rules that guide reporting of what is supposed to be said, and the rules that ensure that some things are not said. By focusing on what are the minimal details for a stock description, such purportedly neutral descriptions are persuading us to *not* see, *not* check, and *not* ask about what actually happened, and especially about what relations of power are exposed in that moment. To the credit of the news organizations, the actual behavior often is shown, but it is not mentioned as often as it is shown. That strategy probably is safer for the news organizations—they are less likely to be accused of being "political," or of having their photographers beaten. But the omission is not just a prudent division of labor: it schools the public in seeing and not saying. In short, it encourages the worst form of bystander behavior.

Of course, we had to make some suppositions here that may well be mistaken; the significant point, however, is that this is a result of the caption not supplying key information. And more, it underscores how language traffics in abstractions and stock typifications that influence what is seen, what is remembered, and how it is used. Photographs are hardly immune to typifications themselves, but they also feature the particularity that can counter abstractions, and those surface details of the image are precisely what can activate the imagination and invite consideration of the complexity, relationality, and multiple perspectives attendant to this or any "event." By inviting imaginative extension of the rich particularity of the image to place what is happening in relation to larger social and political practices, the still photograph can expose the truth of an event. Or at least it does so if and when we are willing to recognize a more capacious sense of what the photograph might evidence and to see it as such.

A more lyrical example, figure 2, makes the point a bit differently.

Figure 2. Josh Newton/Associated Press; June 7, 2014.

The Associated Press caption says that "Newlyweds Michael Wolber and April Hartley pose for a picture near Bend, Ore., as a wildfire burns in the background" (*Time* 2014). Romance often burns like a wildfire, and so the photograph in figure 2 would not surprise us in the least if it showed up as an advertisement for the latest fashions in wedding attire. After all, fashion photography traffics quite comfortably in the world of fantasy, and the photograph was taken by a wedding photographer. But this photograph showed up in any number of slide shows and soft news stories. As with figure 1, in the typical reportage something evident was *not* being said, but this time despite an adequate caption. One might ask, if a stock image of a romantic ideal is in the foreground, what else, along with the unnamed fire, is in the background?

While wildfires are overrunning different parts of the world and in ways that are completely out of synch with normal weather patterns, surely it cannot be that one more photograph of a wildfire is adding probative evidence to make a claim about matters of fact. That is, does anyone really question whether these wildfires exist, and is there a need for one more picture of a wildfire to make the case that such fires are potentially catastrophic? Yet, the mash-up of genres—photojournalism and wedding photography—is being used to offer something that is newsworthy. But what?

One answer is that it offers evidence of a pervasive attitude that takes such wildfires for granted, treating them as something like the "new normal." The fire was close enough that the minister performed a shortened ceremony so that the wedding party could be safely transported elsewhere for the reception, but then again it was not so close that the couple seems distracted. The fire in this photograph is, after all, little more than a dramatic backdrop to the foregrounded nuptials. What better way to secure one's wedding vows—"for better or for worse, through sickness and in health"—than to locate the beginning of one's life-long future with another person against a conflagration that also promises to be there forever? As *The Oregonian* put it, the fire gave the couple "the photograph of a lifetime," and a Smithsonian educational website asked, "Did the fire make or break the wedding?" (Smithsonian 2014). Thus, as the image circulated, the threat of the wildfire was displaced into stories about the photograph and the wedding, and, with that, a process of denial. So it is that the image extends beyond the mere facts of the specific situation (one couple, one fire) to point toward conditions that encompass both the subjects in the photograph and its spectators. The photo is literally about two people, and imaginatively about the public; literally about a wedding, and imaginatively about global warming; literally about posing for a dramatic photograph; imaginatively about denying the obvious.

The irony within the frame is both rich and astonishing, but what is most important is how it stands as evidence of how a modern society that should know better can domesticate even the most tragic and potentially catastrophic of events. Admittedly, we have made assumptions in our reading of the image that are activated by the imagination. The irony could just as easily cut in a different direction if we were to assume that these newlyweds are actually dedicated environmentalists and that they are using the occasion of their union to call attention to the inanity of such ceremonies when the world is ablaze. Perhaps in the next moment (or after their reception) they peeled off their wedding vestments and donned the attire of activists concerned to alert the world of the need to address the problem. Whether read as "active" or "passive," however, the image provides a formal affordance for a political imagination capable of addressing a global catastrophe.

However one reads the photograph—whatever attitude or potential action one sees—it evidences the likelihood of a troubling future, *if we are willing to see it*. By our reading, it points to a tragic outcome, particularly if we persist in accepting the background of the photograph as just another dramatic setting for our everyday activities. The global fires, after all, will only continue to burn brighter and get closer. Indeed, when on the verge of catastrophe, photojournalism can provide evidence of a sort that might be perfectly suited for public knowledge: *it can reveal that we are denying what we already know*. We saw as much with the photograph from Palestine, and it is evident again in the photograph from Oregon. By the imaginative fusion of objective reportage with the obviously idealized genre of wedding photography, a public image exposes how public knowledge depends on a will to know, and how private and public life can be complexly intertwined for better and worse, and how photojournalism, therefore, is always a means for the public to know itself.

Indeed, photography provides evidence that the imagination is necessary across the board. Snapshots celebrate ordinary people, but so does democratic politics; entertainment traffics in desire, but so does social justice; advertising pitches spectatorship toward the future, but so does institutional planning; the arts depend on imaginary relationships, but so does the public sphere. Photography in each domain is providing images of vernacular life that require various modes of visual literacy. The importance of recognizing this richer, imaginative and evidentiary conception of the photograph was captured by the poet William Carlos Williams (1994, 19):

> It is difficult
> to get the news from poems
> yet men die miserably every day
> for lack
> of what is found there.

One might say that there is precious little poetry in the news, but we suggest that actually there is quite a bit there, present but unrecognized. The poetry in this case is the artistry available in photojournalism. Because it is a public art, however, it is caught between appearing merely quotidian, as it often is, and having the special powers of insight and engagement that are attributed to art. By learning to read this richer sense of the news, one might do as Williams urges, that is, acquire ways of knowing, feeling, imagining, and associating with others that could be used to change a civilization's habits of human sacrifice. That's a pretty good definition for what an "art" can do, and it suggests why photojournalism should be understood as a public art. Although there still is value in striving for an objective "window on the world" where truth is a simple matter of presenting the facts, photojournalism offers instead a way of being in the world that relies on the medium's unique capacity to integrate reality and the imagination. When that happens, knowledge can become a basis for living with others, and images can become evidence of what is already visible but not seen.[15]

## Notes

1. Joel Snyder (2004) traces out the history of the photograph as "direct testimony" grounded in legal proceedings of the eighteenth century.

2. Kracauer (1960, 3). Today many speak of media constraints and affordances to make the same point.

3. The term is from Rosalind Krauss (1999). We also follow the maxim by William J.T. Mitchell (2005, 343) that "all media are mixed media." The full extension of the heterogeneity argument denies that photography is a medium at all; see Pirenne and Streitberger (2013). That work is centered on art photography, whereas our interest on public communication is better served by staying with the more familiar concept of relatively discrete though intertwined media. Our sense of heterogeneity also includes the multiple "semiotic transcriptions" that are layered within any image and throughout its reception; see Robert Hariman and John Louis Lucaites (2007, 34–35). Contra the insistence in modernism on the optimization of the unique features of each medium in isolation from all other practices, this approach can acknowledge some media specificity but as part of more comprehensive processes of social interaction. As Mary Ann Doane (2008) has demonstrated, media specificity itself can change with other developments in technology and historical context. See also Joel Snyder and Neil Walsh Allen (1975), who conclude with an eminently clear and sensible brief for critical pluralism.

4. Baudelaire was mistaken, however, regarding the richness and effects of the French public's delight in photography and other media that combined appeals to both realism and amusement. For an excellent account of the role of public displays in the development of modern mass culture, see Schwartz (1999).

5. Roland Barthes (1981, 119) recognized as much. "Mad or tame? Photography can be one or the other: tame if its realism remains relative, tempered by aesthetic or empirical habits (to leaf through a magazine at the hairdresser's, the dentist's); mad if this realism is absolute and, so to speak, original, obliging the loving and terrified consciousness to return to the very letter of Time."

6. Sontag (1977, 69). Sontag was not the most nuanced, rigorous, or original of the authors of the critical discourse on photography, but she remains the leading representative in the United States, and the only prom-

inent writer on photography to acquire the status of a public intellectual there, not least due to her gift for bold statements—and overstatements.

7. Sontag (1977, 69). Note the Platonic tinge: hierarchy ("prestige") is a given while ordinary life is an enchanting ("magic") distraction from the ideal.

8. Patrick Maynard (1997, 14–15) aptly summarizes the discourse of "reputable opinions" by Sontag, Berger, and other representative figures of the mid-century critical paradigm as geared toward reification, dualism, and essentialism: "the conception of a topic in terms of substantives, 'things'—in fact, two kinds of things . . . on one side there is 'the photograph' (click); on the other 'reality' (THUD) . . . [and then] a search for the essences (drawn from impressions of a few instances) of one or the other member of this pair of things, as well as for an essential relationship between them, from which perceptions are to flow."

9. The relationship between advertising and other photography is in fact crucial, and a sure test of one's attitude toward the medium as a whole. As Paul Frosh (2003, 99) explains, the stock images of advertising work precisely by blending realism and imagination, to move from "the conventional reproduction of the *actual*—whose temporality is past continuous, invoked as experience, habit, and memory—with the persuasive simulation of the *possible*—whose temporality is future, invoked as dream and desire." They can do this, however, because they are amplifying a capacity of all photography and other media as well.

10. Note that we are not critical of these methods and movements *tout court*, which have been vital sources for our own work. The critique here is that a historically specific development in respect to photography produced both fifty years of important work and serious misrecognition of how photography functions as a public art. To make a long story short, that hermeneutic did what it could do and now needs to be changed, even as all its methods will continue to be available in the new constellation that eventually emerges (see Hariman and Lucaites 2016).

11. Sontag (2003, 47) suggests that it is the default mode for all photographic spectatorship: "Everyone is a literalist when it comes to photographs."

12. See Phelan (2009, 374–76). Liam Kennedy (2016, 165) points out that "Morris's argument that 'believing is seeing' has value in foregrounding the role of ideological dispositions." One can indeed use it that way, although that is not the route taken by the literalist.

13. For development of this argument in terms of photography, see Azoulay (2012).

14. For the general consensus on the role of captions and how they function see Hall (1981); Skow and Dionisopoulos (1997); Perlmutter (1998, 143–44); Zelizer (1999, 112–13); Anden-Papadopoulos, (2008); Griffin (2010, 17); Greenwood and Jenkins (2013).

15. This chapter includes work that also was published in Hariman and Lucaites (2016).

## Works Cited

Aristotle. 1941. *Metaphysics*. In *The Basic Works of Aristotle*, translated by W. D. Ross. New York: Random House.

Anden-Papadopoulos, Kari. 2008. "The Abu Ghraib Torture Photographs: News Frames, Visual Culture, and the Power of Images." *Journalism* 9 (1): 5–30.

Azoulay, Ariella. 2012. *Civil Imagination: A Political Ontology of Photography*. London: Verso.

Barthes, Roland. 1981. *Camera Lucida*. New York: Hill and Wang.

Baudelaire, Charles. 1980. "The Modern Public and Photography." In *Classic Essays on Photography*, edited by Alan Trachtenberg. New Haven: Leete's Island Books.

Coleridge, Samuel Taylor. 1975. *Biographia Literaria: or Biographical Sketches of My Literary Life and Opinions*. New York: E.P. Dutton & Co.

Daguerre, Louis Jacques Mandé. (1838/39) 2008. "Daguerréotype," translated by Beaumont Newhall. http://www.daguerreotypearchive.org/texts/M8380001_DAGUERRE_BROADSIDE_FR_1838.pdf.

Doane, Mary A. 2008. "Indexicality and the Concept of Medium Specificity." In *The Meaning of Photography*, edited by Robin Kelsey and Blake Stimson, 3–14. Williamstown, MA: Clark Art Institute and New Haven: Yale University Press.

Emerling, Jae. 2012. *Photography: History and Theory*. New York: Routledge.

Frosh, Paul. 2003. *The Image Factory: Consumer Culture, Photography and the Visual Content Industry*. New York: Berg.

Green, Jeffrey E. 2010. *The Eyes of the People: Democracy in an Age of Spectatorship*. Oxford: Oxford University Press.

Greenwood, Keith, and Joy Jenkins. 2013. "Visual Framing of the Syrian Conflict in News and Public Affairs Magazines." *Journalism Studies* 16 (2): 207–27.

Griffin, Michael. 2010. "Media Images of War." *Media, War & Conflict* 3 (1): 7–41.

Hall, Stuart. 1981. "The Determination of News Photographs." In *The Manufacture of News*, edited by Stanley Cohen and Jock Young, 226–41. Beverly Hills, CA: Sage.

Hariman, Robert and John Louis Lucaites. 2007. *No Caption Needed: Iconic Photographs, Public Culture, and Liberal Democracy*. Chicago: University of Chicago Press.

Hariman, Robert, and John Louis Lucaites. 2016. *The Public Image: Photography and Civic Spectatorship*. Chicago: University of Chicago Press.

Holmes, Oliver Wendell. 1859. "The Stereoscope and the Stereograph," *The Atlantic Monthly* 3: 738–48. http://www.theatlantic.com/magazine/archive/1859/06/the-stereoscope-and-the-stereograph/303361.
Jameson, Fredric. 1992. *Signatures of the Visible*. New York: Routledge.
Jammes, André, and Eugenia Parry Janis. 1983. *The Art of French Calotype*. Princeton: Princeton University Press.
Jay, Martin. 1993. *Downcast Eyes: The Denigration of Vision in Twentieth-Century French Thought*. Berkeley: University of California Press.
Kennedy, Liam. 2016. *Afterimages: Photography and US Foreign Policy*. Chicago: University of Chicago Press.
Kracauer, Siegfried. 1960. *Theory of Film: The Redemption of Physical Reality*. New York: Oxford University Press.
Krauss, Rosalind. 1999. "Reinventing the Medium." *Critical Inquiry* 25 (2): 289–305.
Ma'an News. 2013. "PA official: Over 20 Injured as Settlers Riot Near Nablus." *Ma'an*, April 30, 2013. http://www.maannews.net/eng/ViewDetails.aspx?ID=590837.
Maynard, Patrick. 1997. *The Engine of Visualization: Thinking Through Photography*. Ithaca: Cornell University Press.
Mitchell, William J. T. 2005. *What Do Pictures Want? The Lives and Loves of Images*. Chicago: University of Chicago Press.
Morris, Errol. 2011. *Believing is Seeing: Observations on the Mysteries of Photography*. New York: Penguin Press.
Perlmutter, David D. 1998. *Photojournalism and Foreign Policy: Icons of Outrage*. Westport, CT: Praeger.
Phelan, Peggy. 2009. "'In the Valley of the Shadow of Death': The Photographs of Abu Ghraib." In *Violence Performed: Local Roots and Global Routes of Conflict*, edited by Patrick Anderson and Jisha Menon, 374–76. New York: Palgrave-Macmillan.
Pirenne, Raphaël and Alexander Streitberger, eds. 2013. *Heterogeneous Objects: Intermedia and Photography after Modernism*. Leuven: Leuven University Press.
Roberts, John. 1998. *The Art of Interruption: Realism, Photography, and the Everyday*. New York: St. Martin's Press.
Schulz, Kathryn. 2011. "Errol Morris Looks for the Truth in Photography." *New York Times Sunday Book Review*, September 1. http://www.nytimes.com/2011/09/04/books/review/believing-is-seeing-by-errol-morris-book-review.html?_r=2&.
Schwartz, Vanessa R. 1999. *Spectacular Realities: Early Mass Culture in Fin-de-Siecle Paris*. Berkeley: University of California Press, 1999.
Scott, James C. 1990. *Domination and the Arts of Resistance: Hidden Transcripts*. New Haven: Yale University Press.
Skow, Lisa M. and George N. Dionisopoulos. 1997. "A Struggle to Contextualize Photographic Images: American Print Media and the Burning Monk." *Communication Quarterly* 45 (4): 393–409.

Sliwinski, Sharon. 2011. *Human Rights in Camera*. Chicago: University of Chicago Press.
Smithsonian. 2014. "Wildfire Creates a Once-in-a-Lifetime Wedding Photo." *Tween Tribune*, June 12, 2014. https://www.tweentribune.com/article/tween56/wildfire-creates-once-lifetime-wedding-photo/?page=2.
Snyder, Joel. 2004. "Res Ipsa Loquitur." In *Things That Talk: Object Lessons From Art and Science*, edited by Lorraine Daston, 195–221. New York: Zone Books.
Snyder, Joel, and Neil Walsh Allen. 1975. "Photography, Vision, and Representation." *Critical Inquiry* 2 (1): 143–69.
Sontag, Susan. 1977. *On Photography*. New York: Picador.
Sontag, Susan. 2003. *Regarding the Pain of Others*. New York: Picador.
Tagg, John. 1993. *The Burden of Representation: Essays on Photographies and Histories*. Minneapolis: University of Minnesota Press.
Talbot, William Henry Fox. (1844–46). 2010. *The Pencil of Nature*. Project Gutenberg, August 16, 2010. http://www.gutenberg.org/files/33447/33447-pdf.pdf.
Time. 2014. "Here's an Amazing Photo of a Couple Marrying as a Wildfire Rages On." June 10, 2014. https://time.com/2852109/heres-an-amazing-photo-of-a-couple-marrying-as-a-wildfire-rages-on/.
Time Lightbox. 2013. "Pictures of the Week: April 26-May 3." *Time Lightbox*, May 3, 2013.
Williams, William Carlos. 1994. "Asphodel, That Greeny Flower." In *Asphodel, That Greeny Flower and Other Love Poems*.
Zelizer, Barbie. 1999. "Form the Image of Record to the Image of Memory: Holocaust Photography, Then and Now." In *Picturing the Past: Media, History and Photography*, 98–121. Champaign: University of Illinois Press.

# 12 "The Journalism of Tomorrow." Medium-Specific Evidence in Nineteenth-Century Illustrated Magazines

*Anne Ulrich*

In 1886, the French magazine *Le Journal illustré* published a special issue entitled "L'art de vivre cent ans. Trois entretiens avec monsieur Chevreul photographiés à la veille de sa cent et unième année"[1] (Nadar and Nadar 1886). It featured the renowned French chemist Michel-Eugène Chevreul in a highly inventive way. The eight-page interview included thirteen photographs, or more precisely, photo engravings, the first covering the entire front page, with the other photographs organized in fours on three pages. The issue is widely considered to be the first photo interview in history (see Gernsheim and Gernsheim 1969, 453). Conceived and executed by the famous portrait photographer Gaspard-Félix Tournachon (also known as Nadar) and his son Paul, the piece points far beyond the then common journalistic and photographic practices. It is not surprising that scholars have treated it with great interest—be it as a milestone in the history of photography, of the illustrated press, and of the journalistic interview, as an extraordinary example of scientific faith in the waning nineteenth century, or as an exponent of naturalism (see Auer 1999; Bigg 2007; Gervais 2009; Reynes 1981; Ruchatz 2014, 173–179). Moreover, it anticipates our modern notion of the scientific personality (Bigg 2007, 162–63) and of "the audio-visual" in general (Reynes 1981, 155).

It is in this spirit that I read the Nadar-Chevreul interview as a medium-specific form of rhetorical *evidence*.[2] "L'art de vivre cent ans" foreshadows the instantaneousness, vividness, visual intensity, and credibility of "liveness," an evidential effect closely connected to broadcast television and news journalism. Thus, this chapter undertakes a close reading of the interview against the backdrop of media history, journalism history, and photographic history to shed light on the medium specificity of *evidence* and the rhetorical paradox it entails. In the end, it reveals the inherent illusiveness of our contemporary notions of liveness.

## Detailing and Vivification—A Conversation in "Real Time"

The term *evidentia* was first coined by Cicero as a translation of the Greek word *enárgeia* to describe an obvious, concrete, and plausible verbal utterance (Cicero *Luc.* 17). Its etymology reveals a prioritization of visual perception (Walde 1965, 423) provoked by the use of verbal language. The speaker strives for a description so vivid, clear, and concrete that he or she enables his or her audience to "see" the depicted object, person, or action for themselves (Kemmann 1996, 33).[3] Even this basic definition, however, points to an underlying paradox: How can the audience "see" for themselves if their imagination relies on the picture the speaker paints for them (see Müller 2007, 61)? How can the speaker "produce" evidence if it can only be realized by the audience? Rhetorical evidence takes place within the framework of *dissimulatio artis*, that is, the art of concealing the art. It relies on a tacit mutual agreement between the speaker and the audience that enables the speaker to artfully stimulate the audience's imagination and enables the audience to believe in the immediacy and originality of their imagination. If this effect is successfully achieved, evidence "epitomizes the highest level of persuasiveness" (Kemmann 1996, 39). In this sense, as we will see in the conclusion to this chapter, the Nadars certainly go to great lengths to dissimulate their persuasive goals in front of their audience.

Ancient rhetorical tradition distinguished between *enárgeia* and *enérgeia*, the first describing an act of detailing, the latter an act of vivification (Kemmann 1996, 40; see also the introduction to this volume). Both rhetorical techniques are used to simulate clarity in a given situation where no such clarity exists. They therefore transcend the limits or the very mediality of language. This exact notion resonates in "L'art de vivre cent ans." The photo interview transcends the limits of the written word and the printed photoengraving in order to animate the conversation between Chevreul and Nadar before the reader's eyes, thus eliminating the need for "further coaxing" (Kemmann 1996, 39, own translation).

"L'art de vivre cent ans" was published as a special issue of the *Journal illustré* to celebrate both the birthday of the well-known chemist and the young *Troisième République*, which had chosen "progress" as one of its distinctive values (Bigg 2007, 159). The issue starts with a photographic portrait of Chevreul that fills the whole front page and mentions Chevreul's date of birth in the caption: "Born on the 31$^{st}$ of August, 1786, in Angers" (Nadar and Nadar 1886, 281, see figure 1). The next two pages display the written editorial remarks and the first sections of the verbal interview arranged in three columns and a small font. The verbal interview comprises seven topical sections: "On the secret of longevity" (282), "On diet" (282–83), "Hygiene and philosophy" (283), "On photography" (283, 286), "On balloons" (286), "On colors" (286–87), and "Spiritualism" (287). The first double page of eight photographs is "inserted" in the section on photography (284–85), the second photo page constitutes the last page of the special issue (288). Additionally, there are some small advertisements in the central and right columns on page 287.

To capture what is so extraordinary about the interview it is necessary to consider the production set-up as well as the arrangement of the photographs and their captions on the printed pages. Félix Nadar used his skills as a writer and journalist (see Prinet and Dilasser 1966, 203), whereas the photos were taken by Paul Nadar, to whom Félix Nadar gradually passed his business. According to the introductory remarks by "the editors" of the magazine (most probably Félix Nadar himself; see Bigg 2007, 164) and to later statements by both father and son, the interview was only supposed to be a first essay, to be followed by a book publication with over eighty photographs under the same title, which never materialized (see Reynes 1981 and Bigg 2007, 163; some of the photographs were also traded as cabinet photographs, see Gosling 1977, 22–24). All in all, Félix Nadar had at least three separate conversations with the famous chemist (see Reynes 1981, 157).

Paul Nadar claims that it was his idea "to add the photographic camera to the phonograph and to execute a couple of images of the illustrious old man during his conversations with my father. But because Edison, who is said to have since picked up this idea, had not yet supplied the phonograph commercially, I put a stenographer in charge of simultaneously gathering the pronounced words" (Nadar 1892, 285–86).[4] Thus, the entire set-up follows the idea of "recording" the conversations both verbally and visually, which is why Geneviève Reynes has called the photo interview the "first audio-visual document" (Reynes 1981, 155 and 183).

Figure 1. The photoengraving of Chevreul covers the front page of "L'art de vivre cent ans" (Nadar and Nadar 1886, 281). Public domain work, Bibliothèque Nationale de France, Paris.

While the result was not really audio-visual, of course, the piece was, as Jens Ruchatz (2014, 177) puts it, certainly "conceived audiovisually." This impression of audio-visuality *avant la lettre* is achieved by the genre convention of the interview as a conversation in "real time," and by the serial presentation of the photographs. Each photo page features four photographs that are consecutively numbered. This "sequentiality" is further underlined by the serialism of the photographs themselves.

Figure 2. Synchronization of words and images in "L'art de vivre cent ans" (Nadar and Nadar 1886, 284). Public domain work, Bibliothèque Nationale de France, Paris.

On page 284, for example, all four photographs show Chevreul sitting behind a table with an open autograph album in front of him (figure 2). Chevreul is apparently involved in a conversation with an invisible person on his right. Paul Nadar must have pressed the shutter button virtually every other second to capture Chevreul's gestures and facial expressions without changing the position of the camera. Only Chevreul's movements change from photo to photo, "animating" the sequence before the reader's eyes. In the first photograph, Chevreul is obviously talking to his invisible interviewer, displaying an interrogatory facial expression. In the next, Chevreul pauses, looking the spectator in the eye. In the third, he holds a fountain pen in his right hand, ready to write something in the album, but still wondering what to write—his eyes staring over the rim of his glasses into space. The fourth finally shows him bent over the album, writing his dedication.

The virtual "emergence" of the scene is further underlined by the captions, which translate as follows: "1. '—And what do you want me to write in your album?'"; "2. '—I see Mr. Pasteur's name on this page. I will put my name under his. Mr. Pasteur is one of the greatest geniuses of our time . . .'"; "3. '—I'll write my first philosophical principle. I did not formulate it myself, it was Malebranche. I have searched well; I have not found any better." The fourth caption then features a facsimile of the signature itself: "One should strive for infallibility without claiming to have achieved it (Malebranche). E. Chevreul" (Nadar and Nadar 1886, 284).

The Nadars apparently strove for an effect of "audio-visual liveness" by "synchronizing" the photographic moments with the exact words of Chevreul. According to Charlotte Bigg (2007, 164), "co-ordination between the recording of sound and image was effected by the calling of numbers, making it possible to match the photographs closely with the words spoken at the time of exposure." The thoughtful linear arrangement of the synchronized photos and captions "animates" the entire scene before the reader's eyes. The unusually vivid effect is not only based on verbal language, as common in the rhetorical tradition, but on the mixed semiotic modalities that were typical for illustrated journalism at the time.

## Photographic enárgeia in the *Journal illustré*

The *Journal illustré* was founded in 1864 as a competitor to the British penny press (Bacot 2004). It was very popular in France, and from its very beginning relied heavily on images. In its first issue, the journal wrote, the "engraving speaks all languages, it is understood by all nationalities. It is the authority that captivates; and the text, whatever it is, must be but its very humble servant" (*Le Journal illustré*, February 14, 1864; quoted in Crowley and Jobling 1996, 25). The weekly magazine specialized in the quality and timeliness of its engravings. It was addressed to a popular audience, which it sought to both educate and to entertain (Bacot 2004, 59–60). In 1886, it had a circulation of 105,000 copies and was still sold at the cut-rate price of fiftene centimes (Gervais 2009, 16). According to Reynes (1981, 156), the magazine was not only an expert in engravings, but also, "one of the specialists in the reproduction of photographs."

Charlotte Bigg (2007, 161) describes magazine journalism at the time as an important "locus for experimentation, creativity, and renewal in matters of representation." The title of the special issue at hand indicates that the photos in the magazine were in fact photoengravings produced by Stanislas Krakow, an artisan who managed to produce very good results even on the relatively bad paper of the *Journal illustré* (Gervais 2009, 18–19). This astonishing quality can be clearly seen on the front page of the special issue on Chevreul. In his drafts for the book publication, Félix Nadar described the face of the old man like a landscape: "Out of the scattered white and long spikes of his dense and stubbly beard, there appears, notching the razor, a dermis that is devastated by eczema. There are only scales and fissures, scum, stains, blackheads, and cysts" (quoted in Reynes 1981, 158). In ancient rhetoric, such descriptions are examples of *enárgeia*, the technique of detailing. In the *Journal illustré*, this technique was transposed to photography. Thanks to the quality and the size of the photoengraving, readers can discover all these details, and maybe even more, by studying the face of the centenarian themselves. Here, photo technological *enárgeia* takes effect. Famously described by Roland Barthes ([1968] 1986, 141–48) as the "reality effect," it makes use of seemingly "useless details" to provoke a feeling of "the real."

Whereas Nadar focused on Chevreul's face, the readers can decide for themselves what to look at: his clothing, his hair, his facial expression, his eyes that are focused directly at the camera, or his scales and fissures. The "vivification" of evidence, that is, its transposition from written language to "audio-visual" representation, gives the magazine editors more possibilities to shape their journalistic credibility and to attract the readers' attention.

## Transitions from "Telling" to "Showing"

Although the photographs play a crucial role in the construction of evidence, we have to be careful not to overlook other realizations of rhetorical evidence in the *Journal illustré*. Additionally, not every photoengraving in every illustrated magazine is evidential *per se*. We, thus, must acknowledge that evidence is only a constituent *part* within a persuasive context, where it represents the functional equivalent of proof or, in Aristotle's words, of a "nonartistic" proof.[5] Or, as Bill Nichols puts it with regard to the documentary genre:

> Though frequently necessary, inartistic proofs still have to be incorporated into a discourse where they would become convincing. Alone, the inartistic proofs might be necessary but hardly sufficient. Only when such proofs took on their second life as evidence inside a body of signification—discourse—did it become possible for a convincing argument to emerge. How inartistic proofs become incorporated into the discourse thus matters more than what these proofs reveal in and of themselves. (Nichols 2008, 32–33)

For Nichols, discourse is a "body of signification" that represents a form of public discourse. Rhetorically speaking, the term *discourse* can also refer to the speech—or, in our example, the magazine issue—as a whole. This narrow definition implies that we should be able to identify evidential elements within a non-evidential work, that is, nonartistic proofs within an artful argumentation or narration.

The act of applying evidence to a situation has been called the "evidentiary process" ("Evidenzverfahren," see Jäger 2005; Campe 2004). Although the understanding of the term in German research remains relatively obscure, we use it in two respects: first, to emphasize the discursive dimension of rhetorical evidence, considering evidence to be an effect that should appear in the mind of the audience *after* a rhetorical operation has been successfully executed. Second, to stress the mutual transcription and remediation that is involved in the operation of evidence (Jäger 2005, 10–11; see also Nohr 2004, 9). If evidence is conceived of as a "nonartistic proof" that is embedded in a rhetorical form of discourse, then we can identify it by looking at transitions between different discursive modes, semiotic codes, or even different media. In Wayne C. Booth's theory of narratology, such transitions are described as changes of mode from "telling" to "showing."[6] Here, the narrator changes from the narrative mode to the 'evidentiary" mode by verbally putting something before the audience's eyes, filling a scene with enormous vividness. The change of mode happens within the same medium: language. While it can be difficult to recognize, the transition is marked by the rhetorical figure of hypotyposis, where the narrator recedes into the background in favor of the events being presented (Booth 1983, 3–20; see also Jäger 2005, 10).

But within a more complex medium such as the illustrated magazine, we find a much wider variety in the discursive marking of evidence. The transition may even involve different media. Therefore, the photo interview in the *Journal illustré* is a medium-specific example of evidence, using the layout of the magazine to incorporate non-artistic proofs into its "discourse" by switching between different modes of written word and photography.

THE INTERVIEW AND THE PROMISE OF ACCURATE REPRODUCTION

Although "L'art de vivre cent ans" was first and foremost praised for its innovative use of photography, it also applied an innovative written form of evidence that is often overlooked: the interview. This newly invented journalistic genre was a reaction to the rapidly growing demand for both information and celebrities in the waning nineteenth century (Ruchatz 2014, 39–70). The French magazine used the English term, putting it in quotation marks to underline its innovation and foreignness.[7] Unlike a common interview of the time, where a journalist could only rely on his "easily mistaken ear and his treacherous memory," the *Journal illustré* preferred a more precise method, clearly outlined in the introductory remarks by the authors themselves: "only science can provide a solution to this problem of inaccuracy, which is easily committed even with the best will, and give the reader 'the proof' of the veracity of the reproduced conversation" (Nadar and Nadar 1886, 282).

Firstly, accuracy was apparently equated with exact reproduction, which the Nadars claimed to achieve by using a human stenographer (as the phonograph was not yet available). Secondly, the editors interestingly put the word "proof" in quotation marks. This curiosity is also found in Félix Nadar's drafts (as quoted in Gervais 2009, 14). He laments a weakness "in the results of this creation of modern journalism" and enquires about the "guaranties" of the interview: "What control? What corroborating evidence? . . . where is 'the proof'?" In his opinion, journalism needs the accuracy of science to provide proof without quotation marks: a method, a set-up, and quasi-mechanical tools. All of this underlines the growing importance of objectivity and impartiality in news discourse of the time (see also Gervais 2009, 14).

In the 1960s, Everett Hughes pointed out that journalists follow "ritualistic procedures in order to deflect potential criticism" (Tuchman 1972, 661). The main techniques are, among others, the "presentation of supporting evidence," the "structuring of information in an appropriate sequence" and "the judicious use of quotation marks" (664–671). Although the *Journal illustré*, as a weekly magazine aimed at informing and entertaining, its readership was not exposed to the same demands as newspaper journalists in the 1960s; one can easily see early forms of such procedures in "L'art de vivre cent ans." This is even more noticeable as it was, at the time, rather unusual, sometimes even frowned upon, to take notes during an interview. The conversations were afterwards written down from memory and often printed with little or no direct quotation at all (Schudson 1996, 80–83). The Nadars, however, chose a verbatim delivery of the interview and announced this decision explicitly with the following line, which serves as a transition from telling to showing—and therefore as a marker of evidence: "We now textually reproduce the dialog between M. Chevreul and M. Nadar" (Nadar and Nadar 1886, 282). Then there is a colon, a subheading, and the interview begins with a dash and Félix Nadar's first question. The idea of the sound recording is referred to by sporadic insertions in parentheses, such as, "low-pitched" (Nadar and 1886, 287). Thus, every effort was made to create an impression of objectivity and scientific procedure.

The photo interview was considered so innovative at the time that it was promoted in another illustrated journal, the *Petit Journal*, a few days before its release. The author, Thomas Grimm, there briefly praised the innovative method and claimed: "With Nadar's system there is no interpretation: it's the exact reproduction with all the incidents, all the interruptions of the phrase, all the suspensions that the conversation allows. We have a document of an absolute historical accuracy" (Grimm 1886, 1; see also Gervais 2009, 35). This strategic refusal of interpretation declared by Grimm equates the production of "nonartistic" proof and represents another reason to read the interview as an extraordinary example of rhetorical evidence. Or in Ruchatz' (2014, 178–179, own translation) words: the technical process of "authentication" has been "refined semantically." The readers were supposed to believe that the human stenographer executed his task with quasi-mechanical objectivity, and certainly delivered an accurate reproduction of the conversation.[8]

## A New Understanding of Instantaneousness

Let us return to the proto-liveness of "L'art de vivre cent ans." As already seen, innovation was a crucial element in this specific instance of rhetorical evidence. The whole session would not have been possible without the newly developed Eastman films, which allowed much shorter exposure times. According to the editors, "we are now far from the time when Niépce and Daguerre needed fifteen minutes of posing, in the sun, to obtain an image; with Eastman, photography now is able to capture images in two thousandths of a second" (Nadar and Nadar 1886, 282).[9] These technical possibilities created an important potential for the rhetorical realization of evidence, enabling the effects of "instantaneousness" and "real time" to form a kind of "proto-liveness." In an age of increasing acceleration in general (see Rosa 2013), the photos were perceived as an "instantaneous" reproduction of the facial expressions and attitudes of the centenarian as they changed under Nadar's photographic gaze (Nadar and Nadar 1886, 282).[10] As Thierry Gervais (2009, 15) has pointed out, 1886 was also the year when Albert Londe, a pioneer in photography, published his book *La Photographie instantanée. Théorie et pratique*, in which he coined the term, *instant photography*.

This idea of literally "capturing" the moment created a whole new understanding of immediacy, and this interview can be considered to be a prototype of *audio-visual liveness*, which has often been closely linked to the televisual image. Television scholar Herbert Zettl (1981), for example, has stated that such images, "can detect, clarify, and intensify the energy and quality of the moment" (130). We can see such potential inherent in these photographs of the famous chemist: they have the air of a "snapshot," showing us a "real" conversation and not a staged one. Among others, Susanne Holschbach has emphasized that Chevreul's gestures don't look like poses, but like natural expressions accompanying a lively discussion. Chevreul's poses, she says, "stand as examples for the advance of photography in the realm of bodily expressions that go beyond the conscious theatrical pose for the camera. Twentieth-century photography will accumulate immense archives of frozen gestures that it wrests from 'real life'" (Holschbach 2006, 94; see also Prinet and Dilasser 1966, 204 and Ruchatz 2014, 176).

This idea of naturalness also corresponds to the setting and habit that are shown on pages 285 and 288 (figure 3) of "L'art de vivre cent ans." We see both Chevreul and Félix Nadar sitting at a table that has been covered with a rustic tablecloth. There are several carelessly outspread carpets on the floor—only the background, so it seems, has been "staged," sort of "neutralized" for the interview by placing a huge cloth behind the scene. Charlotte Bigg (2007, 163) describes it aptly as "a very plain setting" where Chevreul seems "to have made himself comfortable, shedding his top hat, tie, and even his shoes, swapping them for slippers." Félix Nadar also comfortably holds his head in his hand, resting his elbow on an album that lies on the table. Thus, the readers see a very lifelike scene that contains a lot of seemingly unnecessary details—which allows them to believe the visual "reproduction," and its depiction as both vivid and immediate. This immediacy is used to shape both Chevreul's and Nadar's personalities and, insofar, represents a very early form of visual "personalization."

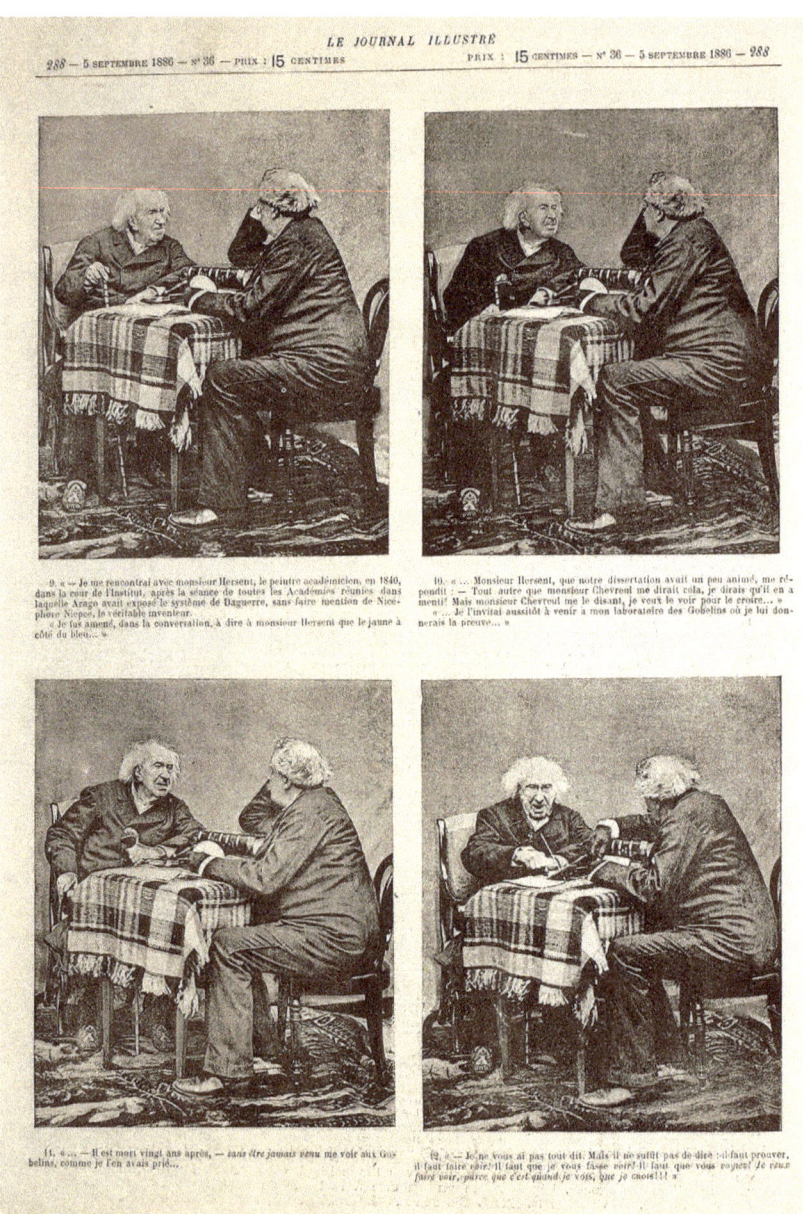

Figure 3. The final quartet of photos in "L'art de vivre cent ans" (Nadar and Nadar 1886, 288). Public domain work.

To understand this, we must return to the innovations that took place in photography at the time, specifically chronophotography, which created an important framework for both the set-up and presentation of the photo interview (Bigg 2007, 166). This method was primarily developed by Eadweard Muybridge and Étienne-Jules Marey, both photographic pioneers and interested in studies of animal motion. Chevreul even mentions Marey explicitly in the interview with Nadar (in the section "On photography"), referencing his inventions in the same breath with Eastman's. In his autobiography, *Quand j'étais photographe*,[11] Nadar remembers being fascinated by the chronophotographic images of flying birds, and praises Marey in the highest possible tones as an "invaluable" photo pioneer, particularly for his scientific accuracy (Nadar [ca. 1900], 251).

The printed juxtaposition of Marey's images emphasized their serialism and drew the viewer's attention to the tiny differences in the animal's movement from photo to photo. This principle was applied in the interview in the *Journal illustré* as well. Here, viewers were also invited to perceive the movements and (in Chevreul's case) expressions to "animate" the photo sequence in their imagination. Chronophotographic images were also composed temporally, not spatially, to present a proto-film sequence. Nadar described this process in his memoirs as well:

> In the world of photography, we have not forgotten the excitement caused by the first instant prints that arrived from San Francisco. Muybridge captured twenty-four positions of a galloping horse. Arranged in a zoetrope, the father of the cinematograph, these twenty-four takes of a periodic action achieved the movement itself as a gyrating illusion for the eyes. Muybridge will always have this honor. (Nadar [ca. 1900], 259)

There is a temporal dynamic inherent to these chronophotographic images that anticipates the vividness and timeliness of the moving image. The "vivification" must have been both fascinating and moving for viewers at the time who took great pleasure in the perfections of optical illusion. Current video documentaries about "L'art de vivre cent ans" cannot resist the temptation to use a "flipbook" effect and thus "animate" the conversation between Chevreul and Nadar by presenting the photographs successively and not side by side.[12] The proto-filmic aesthetic even led an Australian TV network to literally re-enact the interview (see Tupicoff 2011). There are even GIFs that display an animated loop in the conversation of Chevreul and Félix Nadar based on the photographs on page 285 in the *Journal illustré*.[13]

## Disclosure of a Private Self

Charlotte Bigg (2007, 167) has claimed that "L'art de vivre cent ans" represents a "transposition of chronophotography to the realm of personality." The readers of the magazine were supposed to get the impression of a lively and "real" debate whose authenticity was based on the instantaneousness of the photographs. The famous sociologist Erving Goffman, studying human interaction in the 1960s, coined the distinction between "expression" and "communication." Goffman understood "expression" as everything people exhibit about themselves with their facial expressions, gestures, intonation and other nonverbal expressions, while "communication" referred to the conscious delivery of a verbal message (Goffman 1969, 4–11). Television critic Joshua Meyrowitz has fruitfully adopted this distinction to better make sense of the "personalization" of television:

> [I]n terms of this distinction, one can start and stop communicating at will, but one cannot stop expressing. Communications are consciously given, but expressions are unconsciously "given off." Expressions are constant and much less controllable than communications. Further, while communications can be about anything, expressions, in one very important sense, are always "about" the individual giving them off. Expressions are personal and idiosyncratic; we look to them to discover how a person feels and what he or she is "like." (Meyrowitz 1985, 94)

The interview with Chevreul can thus be understood as a very early example of this "personalization strategy" in journalism, that is, drawing the attention away from the topic of the conversation and towards the character and the personality of the interviewee (see also Sennett 1986, 150–52). This interpretation is also supported by the fact that the conversation tends to focus on personal characteristics. The first section of "L'art de vivre cent ans" does not deal with Chevreul's scientific achievements at all, focusing instead on the "secret" of his age, which was, of course, the reason for the interview in the first place. The second section then treats his diet, focusing on his habit of eating at the exact same hour every day, chewing his food carefully and completely, and his abstinence from wine and tobacco. Another quote from this section (Nadar and Nadar 1886, 285) is also the caption of photograph number 5: "I have always only drunk water, yet I am the president of the Anjou Wine Society—but honorary president only!" It seems quite obvious that the interviewer, not only a famous photographer, but also an experienced writer and caricaturist, intended to entertain his readers by disclosing the seemingly trivial but amusing facts of Chevreul's everyday life.[14] It's not until the third section of the interview that scientific topics are even touched upon.

The "disclosure" of Chevreul's personality and his private self is a phenomenon Meyrowitz considered typical for electronic media—and not for print media (see Meyrowitz 1985, 94–95). This emphasizes once more the avant-garde character of a photo interview preferring expressions over communications, entertaining its audience with insights into Chevreul's private self and his everyday habits, rather than informing them on the nature of his scientific achievements.

## ". . . It Is When I See That I Believe"

The famous photographic interview is evidential not only due to its immediacy and vividness, but also because of its potential to turn its readers into pseudo-eyewitness. Nadar definitely had this effect in mind. In his drafts, he wrote: "For the first time the reader becomes the spectator . . . . For the first time, he does not need anyone to listen and to see for him: it is he, he himself, who sees, who listens" (cited in Bigg 2007, 164). Turning one's audience into witnesses is an important feature of rhetorical evidence (see Lausberg 1960, §810). Doing it in an illustrated magazine reveals a medium-specific form of rhetorical evidence: the act of concealing the process of medialization itself. Although the magazine was neither able to display moving images, nor to instantly deliver the chronophotographic images to their viewers, both the presentation of the interview and its set-up bring audio-visual liveness to mind. The interview offers an incredible timeliness (Gervais 2009, 16), anticipating a central feature of news journalism.

According to John Ellis (2000, 11), "to treat the audio-visual as a form of witness is to realize that it offers a distinct, and new, modality of experience." Readers of illustrated magazines are used to finding out about current events through typical genres of print journalism such as the report or the commentary. In Ellis's sense, the photo interview offers a new modality of experience. Readers are given the impression of "*happening* to events we know have *already* happened" (Friedman 2002, 143). The photo interview is produced and presented to readers in a way that transcends the temporal and spatial limitations of the printed magazine. Especially the set-up of the photo interview parallels the set-up for a live production in the TV studio. Both utilize a stage and one (or more) permanently installed cameras with fixed perspectives and angles. The apparatus—or dispositif, as Jean-Luc Baudry (1986) and Knut Hickethier (1995) would say—is entirely adjusted to the recording and accurate reproduction of everything that happens on the stage. In this way, it resembles the set-up of scientific experiments;

paralleling the epistemic production of evidence (see also, for example, Campe 2006, 26–32).

As noted above, *scientificness* was a key concept in the Nadar/Chevreul interview. Not only was a scientist selected for the interview to emphasize the seriousness of the undertaking (Reynes 1981, 156), science was also an important framework explicitly referred to by both of the Nadars, and by Chevreul himself. By emphasizing the immense value of observation, of the sense of vision and the "rhetoric of mechanical objectivity," the photo interview punctuated its own plausibility and veracity (Bigg 2007, 167). Interestingly, the concept of *science* was juxtaposed with the concept of *rhetoric*, which had only negative connotations in the interview. This is clear from page 285, where the picture on the upper right shows Chevreul with a skeptical expression. The caption reads: "This is the nuisance of this *philosophie du jour*, this philosophy of rhetors, of great sayers of nothing. We are satisfied with words and empty rhetoric" (Nadar and Nadar 1886, 285).

Chevreul explicitly distanced himself from the insufficient persuasiveness of the word, getting excited in the next picture with the following words: "Notice that I am far from condemning what I cannot explain; but I will say that you have to prove it to me, that I have to see" (Nadar and Nadar 1886, 285). The compelling credibility of the visual is further underlined in the caption to the final of the twelve photos in "L'art de vivre cent ans" (Nadar and Nadar, 288): ". . . it's not enough to say that you have to prove, you have to show! I have to make you see! You must see! I want to show, because it is when I see that I BELIEVE!!!" The photo shows a determined Chevreul, pounding his right hand firmly on the table. As the final photograph, and thus the conclusion of the interview, this expression of the famous aphorism "seeing is believing" is heavily emphasized and can thus be understood as an outstanding marker of evidence.

## The Evidentiary Paradox

But can we believe what we see (and read) in "L'art de vivre cent ans"? Does the photo interview keep its promises of immediacy and accuracy? Certainly not. The genre of the interview, the order of the interview sections, the photographs, and even the captions were willfully arranged, most likely by Félix Nadar. Geneviève Reynes has carefully studied the drafts of both the interview and the unpublished book to reconstruct the exact order of the interviews, which took place in at least three different places (see also Auer 1999, 8). She concluded that the captions "were randomly distributed: Chevreul makes one statement in one; in the next photo we find remarks that were said another day on another topic." Also, different versions of the same photo were provided with different captions, or vice versa (Reynes 1981, 156). In the captions, Chevreul's thoughts were pulled out of context, shortened or even modified—in brief: "these interviews with Chevreul were rewritten by Nadar." Moreover, Nadar "endeavored to render the real more real" (Reynes 1981, 157). In other words: Nadar strategically manipulated both the interview and the photo pages and their captions to provide a seemingly un-manipulated, immediate experience. He therefore used rhetorical means to create supposedly "nonartistic" proofs. The guiding principle here was the already mentioned dissimulation of the art, the crucial framework for rhetorical evidence.

In editing and staging the interview to create the effect of rhetorical evidence, Nadar offered readers several ways to read and view the interview. The audience might choose to look first or even exclusively (as most of the studies on "L'art de vivre cent ans" have) at the visual images, the captions, and, perhaps, at some of the introductory remarks. Anticipating this possibly rather distracted mode of reading, the editors chose to follow possible reader expectations and open the photo article with a big, conventional portrait of Chevreul. Then, the first photo series (described earlier) serves as an aesthetically appealing introduction to both Chevreul's personality and the idea of chronophotography. The other two pages focus on the conversation between Chevreul and Nadar, showing them both sitting at a table, involved in a lively discussion that is mostly carried by Chevreul. The choice and the composition of the captions are a testament to Nadar's talent as an "entertainer." Some of them deal with the age and the diet of the centenarian, his personal encounters and, in passing, with only one of his diverse scientific achievements: the laws of the contrast of colors. Four of the captions deal with the "seeing is believing" aphorism in different forms, emphasizing the epistemic dimension of evidence and, self-reflectingly, the importance of the photographs themselves. They are in no way a "proportional" representation of the whole interview. Instead, the captions represent a careful selection of both amusing and impressive arguments for the originality of the interview.

On the other hand, the audience might choose to closely follow the written order of the article. Within this rather "concentrated" mode, readers would begin with the introductory remarks, which focus on the exceptional and historical nature of the interview. They would continue with the verbal interview, read Chevreul's opinion on photography—one he remarked many times since Daguerre's and Niepce's invention of photography, and that Eastman's current developments allowed for much shorter exposure times (Nadar and Nadar 1886, 283). Turning the page, they would find the first two "audio-visual" sequences based on this "instant photography"; then be brought back to the photography section of the interview. They would continue reading until Chevreul's concluding words: "Look, look well, look again, you'll finally see it too" (Nadar and Nadar 1886, 287),[15] before once again turning a page and regarding the last four photos, the last caption with another bow to the "seeing is believing" doctrine.

It is now clear that the published interview was not dictated by the events themselves,[16] but rather by an editor who left nothing to chance. Everything has been carefully staged: the transitions from "telling" to "showing," the switches from written word to photographs and back again, and even the turns of the pages.

Additionally, Nadar's article extensively prepared its audience for how to experience this innovative journalistic genre. There is significant effort to establish the evidentiary claim. The introductory remarks to the interview in the *Journal illustré* promote it as "a new, unforeseen work that will stand out in the annals of human discoveries." Félix Nadar refers not only to the present, but also imagines a future with instant audio-visual transmission: "To sum up, it can be asserted that we will transmit, optically and acoustically, and in all their successive manifestations, every action, every scene that is of public or private interest to future generations" (Nadar and Nadar 1886, 282). In his drafts of the interview, Nadar uses the expression "journalism of tomorrow" (quoted in Reynes 1981, 155), envisioning broadcast television and audio-visual live streaming, as we might now assume.

The advance article in the *Petit Journal* also participated in the myth-making process by pointing out the originality of the undertaking.[17] Its author, Thomas Grimm (1886, 1), claimed to be "very happy to be the first" to read the interview and predicted an "immense success" for the issue of the *Journal illustré*, placing it in the history of photography and of journalism.[18] The extensive (self) marketing may also be one of the reasons why this interview is often referred to as a predecessor for so many media genres and effects. Yet, Nadar also wrote that the published interview was nothing but "the first *improvised* attempt"—compared to the book publication, the interview would certainly be fascinating, but not yet perfectly accomplished (Nadar and Nadar 1886, 282). By sounding this "humble" note, Nadar probably sought to take the wind out of possible critic's sails, knowing that the promise of "pure" and immediate evidence is one that cannot be kept. Nevertheless, this small statement did not change the impact of the overall evidentiary claim. Instead, it merely reveals the inherent paradox in rhetorically claiming the immediacy and reality of a heavily mediated, edited, and staged interview.

In summary, Ruchatz (2014) has rightly remarked that "Nadar thus did not start a 'revolution of the interview'; he did not create something radically new. Instead, he clairvoyantly captured the medial and cultural dynamic that is inherent in the interview" (179). "L'art de vivre cent ans" thus represents an important transitory form rather than a founding document. In its portrayal of a centenarian, especially in its depiction of his old-fashioned language, it reached far back into the nineteenth century. By using the latest in photographic and printing technology, however, it was also very state of the art, practically breathing the *zeitgeist*, which fostered acceleration and progress, personalization and commercialization. In anticipating the instant transmission of both sound and images, it transcends its own temporal—and medial—limitations, providing a hint of liveness and audio-visuality long before its invention. It unites both the worlds of the past and of the future by staging a spectacular journalistic 'event' of the present.

## Notes

1. The title translates to "The Art of Living a Hundred Years. Three Conversations with Mr. Chevreul Photographed on the Eve of his Hundred and First Year."

2. I use the term *evidence* as a translation of the German term *Evidenz*, but Evidenz does not exactly mean evidence in the sense of "proof." Instead, as I will further elaborate, it refers to the artful process of attributing the characteristics of "nonartistic proofs" to representations. German research has discussed both the term and the phenomenon extensively, also exploring the rather close connections between Evidenz and rhetoric (see, e.g., Blumenberg 1981, 104–36; Campe 1997, 2004, 2006; Cuntz et al. 2006; Müller 2007; Nohr 2004).

3. See also Cicero *De or.* 3, 202: "For instance, dwelling on a single point makes a very strong impression, as do lucid exposition and laying things almost before people's eyes, as if they are actually taking place; this device is very powerful both in lending brilliance to our account, when we are setting forth the case, and in amplification, in order to make what we are amplifying seem to our audience as important as our speech can make it" (trans. James M. May and Jakob Wisse, Cicero 2001).

4. Here and in the following, I provide English translations from French or German for the sake of readability. If not mentioned otherwise, all translations are my own, with special thanks to Viktorija Romascenko.

5. See Aristotle *Rh.* 1.2.2: "Of the pisteis, some are atechnic ["nonartistic"], some entechnic ["embodied in art, artistic"]" (trans. George A. Kennedy, Aristotle 1991).

6. Research literature on evidence often refers to Booth; see, e.g., Campe 1997, 219.

7. According to the *Grand Robert de la Langue Française* (2001, ed. Alain Rey, 2nd ed. Paris: Dictionnaires le Robert, 317), the Anglicism "interview" (in the *Journal illustré* even spelled "interwiew") was first mentioned in France by the Goncourt brothers in their *Journal des Goncourt. Mémoires de la vie littéraire* (2nd series. 5th vol. 1872–1877. Paris: Bibliothèque-Charpentier, 1891). The French equivalent was "entrevue," but the term was not widely used.

8. Even Reynes (1981, 156) has pointed to the authenticity of the interview by accentuating Chevreul's manner of speaking: "Chevreul answers in a tongue that is totally soaked in the perfume of the eighteenth century, but with a youthfulness in humor that astonishes."

9. Bigg (2007, 170–71) also outlines the commercial character of these remarks.

10. See also, almost in similar words, Paul Nadar in a letter to the French Photographic Society from January 7, 1887 (quoted in Auer 1999, 31–32).

11. A part of Nadar's autobiography has been translated by Thomas Repensek as "My Life as a Photographer," see Nadar (1978).

12. See, for example, an amateur short film called *First Photo Interview—1886* on YouTube, https://www.youtube.com/watch?v=erT2W5sxaFY, accessed February 15, 2018.

13. See the GIF on Wordpress, https://victorstavaroiu.files.wordpress.com/2012/07/first_interview_002.gif, accessed October 11, 2021.

14. Nadar wrote in his drafts: "While paying tribute to the great savant, I turned a bit to caricature, to *satire* in the spirit of the amusing journals of my time; I couldn't forget that I once edited the *Journal pour rire*. By the way, Chevreul contributed to it with his sense of irony," quoted in Reynes (1981), 157.

15. In this section, Chevreul refers to his own belief, but one could also read the line as a reference to the photo series on the last page, as if to say, "now look at the following pictures!"

16. A central feature of liveness according to television philosopher Stanley Cavell (1982, 89), is namely the "monitoring mode," where the composition of the "text" is motivated, "by requirements of opportunity and anticipation—as if the meaning is dictated by the event itself."

17. *Le Petit Journal* is considered to be a symbol for the change and the acceleration of journalism. It preferred simpler forms of presentation and more illustrations and had a wider audience and more success than the *Journal illustré* (see Gervais 2009, 20).

18. "L'art de vivre cent ans" remained an avant-garde act. It was not until 1889 that another photo interview was published in the *Figaro*, again with Paul Nadar as the photographer (see Gervais 2009, 24).

## Works Cited

Aristotle. 1991. *On Rhetoric: A Theory of Civic Discourse*. Translated by George A. Kennedy. New York, Oxford: Oxford University Press.

Auer, Michèle. 1999. *Le premier interview photographique. Chevreul—Félix Nadar—Paul Nadar*. Neuchâtel, Paris: Photogaleries.

Bacot, Jean-Pierre. 2004. "Le moment 1864: la naissance du *Journal Illustré* ou la rencontre tardive de l'actualité, de la gravure et du peuple." In *Production(s) du populaire*, edited by Jacques Migozzi and Philippe Le Guern, 51–61. Limoges: Presses Universitaires Limoges.

Barthes, Roland. [1968] 1986. "The Reality Effect." In *The Rustle of Language*, translated by Richard Howard, 141–48. New York: Hill and Wang.

Baudry, Jean-Louis. 1986. "The Apparatus: Metapsychological Approaches to the Impression of Reality in Cinema." In *Narrative, Apparatus, Ideology: A Film Theory Reader*, edited by Philip Rosen, 299–318. New York: Columbia University Press.

Bigg, Charlotte. 2007. "The Scientist as Personality: Elaborating a Science of Intimacy in the Nadar/Chevreul Interview (1886)." In *Science Images and Popular Images of the Sciences*, edited by Bernd Hüppauf and Peter Weingart, 159–79. New York et al.: Routledge.

Blumenberg, Hans. 1981. *Wirklichkeiten, in denen wir leben*. Stuttgart: Reclam.

Booth, Wayne C. 1983. *The Rhetoric of Fiction*. 2nd ed. Chicago, London: University of Chicago Press.

Campe, Rüdiger. 1997. "Vor Augen stellen: Über den Rahmen rhetorischer Bildgebung." In *Poststrukturalismus: Herausforderung an die Literaturwissenschaft*, edited by Gerhard Neumann, 208–25. Stuttgart, Weimar: J.B. Metzler.

—. 2004. "Evidenz als Verfahren: Skizze eines kulturwissenschaftlichen Konzepts." In *Vorträge aus dem Warburg-Haus*, vol. 8, edited by Uwe Fleckner, Wolfgang Kemp, Gert Mattenklott, Monika Wagner and Martin Warnke, 105–33. Berlin: Akademie Verlag.

—. 2006. "Epoche der Evidenz: Knoten in einem terminologischen Netzwerk zwischen Descartes und Kant." In *Intellektuelle Anschauung: Figuration von Evidenz zwischen Kunst und Wissen*, edited by Sibylle Peters and Martin Jörg Schäfer, 25–43. Bielefeld: Transcript.

Cavell, Stanley. 1982. "The Fact of Television." *Daedalus* 111 (4), 75–96.

Cicero. 1951. *On the Nature of the Gods. Academics.* Translated by H. Rackham. Revised and reprinted ed. Cambridge, London: Harvard University Press.
—. 2001. *On the Ideal Orator.* Translated by James M. May and Jakob Wisse. New York and Oxford: Oxford University Press.
Crowley, David and Paul Jobling. 1996. *Graphic Design. Reproduction and Representation Since 1800.* Manchester et al.: Manchester University Press.
Cuntz, Michael, Barbara Nitsche, Isabell Otto and Marc Spaniol, eds. 2006. *Die Listen der Evidenz.* Cologne: DuMont.
Ellis, John. 2000. *Seeing Things. Television in the Age of Uncertainty.* London, New York: Tauris.
Friedman, James. 2002. "Attraction to Distraction: Live Television and the Public Sphere." In *Reality Squared: Televisual Discourse on the Real*, edited by James Friedman, 138–54. New Brunswick et al.: Rutgers University Press.
Gernsheim, Helmut and Alison Gernsheim. 1969. *The History of Photography from the Camera Obscura to the Beginning of the Modern Era.* Revised and enlarged edition. London: Thames and Hudson.
Gervais, Thierry. 2009. "L'interview photographique d'Eugène Chevreul: une entreprise journalistique avant-gardiste." In *Photo de presse. Usages et pratiques*, edited by Gianni Haver, 11–24. Lausanne: Editions Antipodes.
Goffman, Erving. 1969. *Strategic Interaction.* Philadelphia: University of Pennsylvania Press.
Gosling, Nigel. 1977. *Nadar: Photograph berühmter Zeitgenossen. 330 Bildnisse aus der Hauptstadt des 19. Jahrhunderts.* München: Schirmer/Mosel.
Grimm, Thomas. 1886. "L'art de vivre cent ans." *Le Petit Journal*, no. 8649, August, 1.
Hickethier, Knut. 1995. "Dispositiv Fernsehen. Skizze eines Modells." *montage/av* 4 (1), 63–83.
Holschbach, Susanne. 2006. *Vom Ausdruck zur Pose. Theatralität und Weiblichkeit in der Fotografie des 19. Jahrhunderts.* Berlin: Reimer.
Jäger, Ludwig. 2005. "Evidenzverfahren." *Transkriptionen* 5, 10–13.
Kemmann, Ansgar. 1996. "Evidentia, Evidenz." In *Historisches Wörterbuch der Rhetorik*, edited by Gert Ueding, vol. 3, 37–38. Tübingen: Niemeyer.
Lausberg, Heinrich 1960. *Handbuch der Literarischen Rhetorik.* München: Hueber.
Meyrowitz, Joshua. 1985. *No Sense of Place. The Impact of Electronic Media and Social Behavior.* New York, Oxford: Oxford University Press.
Müller, Jan-Dirk. 2007. "Evidentia und Medialität: Zur Ausdifferenzierung von Evidenz in der Frühen Neuzeit." In *Evidentia: Reichweiten visueller Wahrnehmung in der Frühen Neuzeit*, edited by Gabriele Wimböck, Karin Leonhard and Markus Friedrich, 59–81. Berlin: Hopf.
Nadar [Tournachon], Gaspard-Félix, and Paul Nadar [Tournachon]. 1886. "L'art de vivre cent ans. Trois entretiens avec Monsieur Chevreul photographiés à la veille de sa cent et unième année." *Le Journal illustré* 23 (36) (September) 281–88.

Nadar [Tournachon], Gaspard-Félix. [ca. 1900]. *Quand j'étais photographe*. Paris: Flammarion.
—. 1978. "My Life as a Photographer." Translated by Thomas Repensek. *October* 5, 6–28.
Nadar [Tournachon], Paul. 1892. "Progrès et application de la photographie." *Paris-Photograph. Revue mensuelle illustrée* 2 (7), July 30, 1892, 280–91.
Nichols, Bill. 2008. "Evidence, Rhetoric, and Documentary Film." In *Rethinking Documentary: New Perspectives and Practices*, edited by Thomas Austin and Wilma de Jong, 29–38. Maidenhead and New York: McGraw Hill/Open University Press.
Nohr, Rolf F., ed. 2004. *Evidenz ... Das sieht man doch!* Münster: Lit Verlag.
Prinet, Jean and Antoinette Dilasser. 1966. *Nadar*. Paris: Armand Colin.
Reynes, Geneviève. 1981. "Chevreul interviewé par Nadar, premier document audiovisuel (1886)." *Gazette des Beaux Arts* 98, 154–84.
Rosa, Hartmut. 2013. *Social Acceleration. A New Theory of Modernity*. New York: Columbia University Press.
Ruchatz, Jens. 2014. *Die Individualität der Celebrity. Eine Mediengeschichte des Interviews*. München: UVK.
Schudson, Michael. 1996. *The Power of News*. Cambridge, MA, and London: Harvard University Press.
Sennett, Richard. 1986. *Fall of Public Man*. London: Faber.
Tuchman, Gaye 1972. "Objectivity as Strategic Ritual: An Examination of Newsmen's Notions of Objectivity." *American Journal of Sociology* 77 (4), 660–79.
Tupicoff, Dennis. 2011. *La première interview*. Australian Broadcasting Corporation, Jungle Pictures Pty Ltd, Film Victoria, and Screen Australia. Recording available online at https://www.youtube.com/watch?v=Z6QNQrtOxpo, accessed February 15, 2018.
Walde, Alois. 1965. *Lateinisches Etymologisches Wörterbuch*. Vol. 1. Heidelberg: Carl Winter.
Zettl, Herbert. 1981. "Television Aesthetics." In *Understanding Television. Essays on Television as a Social and Cultural Force*, edited by Richard P. Adler, 115–41. New York: Praeger.

# 13 "The Best Battlefield Scene of All Time": The Feeling of History and the Problem of Realism in *Saving Private Ryan*

*Philipp Löffler*

## Introduction

In a number of ways, Steven Spielberg's movie *Saving Private Ryan* (1998) responds to and affirms what a number of critics have labeled the "return of history" after the alleged end of history in 1989.[1] By "the return of history," I mean specifically a particular strategy of evidence creation that relies on a somewhat old-fashioned idea of historical realism. This idea of realism has been central to a broad number of filmic, literary, and national-political moments of historical commemoration, especially in the US, that have occurred over the past twenty-five years in seeming contrast to the self-reflexive irony of postmodernist art and theory. What I want to argue in the present chapter is this: *Saving Private Ryan* may be read as a very concrete cinematographic statement about the necessity to embrace the past in order to define and understand the historical present, that is, the cultural logic of the post-Cold War world. At the same time, the movie can also be viewed in conjunction with several more theoretical transitions that occurred with the decline of postmodernist vocabularies in recent film and literature. *Saving Private Ryan*'s commitment to a novel form of historical realism as a means of evidence creation connects both readings and thus illustrates on a broader scale the analogy between the political end of the Cold War and the fading relevance of postmodernist theory paradigms.

What makes *Saving Private Ryan* so relevant and at the same time controversial is its denial of traditional historiographical strategies of sense making that value the objectivity of historical representation against the subjectivity of individual experience. Traditionally, the assumption of historians has been that there is a virtual objectivity-subjectivity divide in historical writing. Good and reliable inquiries into past worlds are inspired by the ambition to remain objective, accurate, and thus scientific. In turn, any hint of subjectivity, indicated by individual feeling, political bias, and overt selectivity, must be denounced as detrimental to the ideal of objectivity, limited, misleading, and tainted by ideological agendas. However implausible this distinction, the fantasy of the objective, which may or may not be attained, continues to inform our sense of what it means to make history available in the contemporary present.[2]

*Saving Private Ryan* breaks with this tradition by proposing a quite paradoxical argument about the nature of historical representation. The movie's implicit claim is this: to attain truth in the representation of history, one needs to start out from the most subjective viewpoint possible, that is, the subject position of the historian as involved observer. *Saving Private Ryan* celebrates the subject position of the observer as the precondition for reaching a higher notion of historical truth. As successful observers, we must be radically particularist. Only then will we be able to understand and pass on what "really happened." Or, quite boldly: we must be as American as possible to be as truthful as possible. The movie makes it quite clear that this is not at all a contradiction.

I develop my argument in three related parts. In the first part, I comment briefly on the return of realism from a historical point of view. I then propose a close reading of *Saving Private Ryan* to illustrate some of the more profound theoretical implications of this return of realism for the problem of historical evidence creation. This part will be centered around the following question: How can the subjectivity of an individual historical agent be turned into the precondition for generating the idea of a universal historical truth? In my conclusion, I offer a more general discussion of Spielberg's movie as a reflection of the political world that has emerged in the aftermath of the Cold War's end.

## The Return of Realism

It may seem counter-intuitive to declare a return of realism in recent historical writing and film because the idea of historical realism is itself relatively young. The term did not exist before the invention of modern historiography in the early nineteenth century. Until then, using *historical realism* as a conceptual or genre category would have seemed odd, since the majority of people did not think of history as anything else but reality—a past reality, to be sure.[3] To speak of historical realism would not have made much sense because the idea of history was believed to be largely synonymous with reality in any event: an assemblage of hard facts that one could record and archive in chronicles. This is not to argue that capturing this sense of reality was beyond methodological debate. In fact, the opposite is true, as the large number of treatises on the writing of history since the Early Modern period reveals—both in the British North American colonies and continental Europe. The point, however, is that the term *realism*, as opposed to *non-realistic* accounts of the past, did only gain significance in as much as it was theorized within a broader debate surrounding the relationship between fiction and history. That discourse, unlike its Early Modern precursors, did not begin to take on relevance until the later eighteenth century.

We must keep in mind, however, that the proponents of this theoretical debate have never represented a broad cultural consensus. Even today the awareness that writing history can be quite problematic is limited to communities of scholars in the humanities, but it has not been a general point of concern outside the bounds of the academy. This is all the more surprising since history pervades contemporary social life in a variety of formats: in history school books, when generations of pupils learn about the glory of the American revolution or the perils of National Socialism; in movie theatres, when the educated middle class reencounters the fate of slave life in movies like *Amistad* (1997), *Django Unchained* (2012), and *12 Years a Slave* (2013); in novellas and novels, such as Günter Grass's *Im Krebsgang* (2002), Toni Morrison's *Beloved* (1987), and Jonathan Littell's *The Kindly Ones* (2006), not all of which concerned with slavery, to be sure; and in museums and at monuments, where diverse groups of people acknowledge the fact that the past still matters for our present day lives.

Despite the fact, however, that engaging history seems to be such an integral part of contemporary social life, there are a number of theoretical questions about the uses of history that continue to complicate the commonsensical belief in realism as a pertinent historiographical standard. Can we ever know what history feels like? Is there any way for us today to recreate a sense of reality that was never ours? What are adequate representations of historical events? Can we ever reliably define adequacy in historical representation? Do we really have to think about why we believe that some accounts of past events are more likely to be truthful than others?

Especially since the period that Reinhart Koselleck aptly defined as the "Sattelzeit,"[4] the question whether and how history can be recorded in meaningful ways has been at the center of debates about the purposes, function, and adequacy of historical writing and, more recently, historical film within and without history departments. The invention of modern historiography at the beginning of the nineteenth century has turned the study of history itself into an institutionalized form of academic self-introspection. Starting around 1800, people began speculating about historical evidence creation instead of simply assuming that historical facts existed as parts of a given reality. This was the time when historians began to reflect upon their own discipline and its underlying methodologies in the pursuit of scientific objectivity, accuracy, and adequacy. In the twentieth century, particularly following the advent of deconstructionist literary and cultural criticism during the 1960s, the problem of evidence creation became associated more frequently with a skepticist stance that questioned the idea of historical representation as such. In fact, for a limited period of time, claiming that there is no way to distinguish between historical events themselves and their textual appropriation was more likely to find scholarly approval than insisting on seemingly old-fashioned notions of realism, neutrality, and objectivity (see, e.g., Foley 1986; Hutcheon 1988; White 1974).

With the decline of postmodernist theory paradigms, these skepticist interventions have lost much of their original appeal, and since the early 1990s, the idea of realism has enjoyed a powerful comeback both on the academic theory market and as the expression of a more general, non-academic desire to reencounter history "as it actually were," to use Leopold von Ranke's notorious definition.[5] Especially in the US, the idea of a new historical realism attained unprecedented relevance in the years immediately after the end of the Cold War. With the fall of the Berlin Wall and the demise of the Soviet Union, people began looking back on the bygone years of the Cold War, while trying to gauge the signatures of a still unknown future. Writing about history became the primary mode of defining the present. In addition, a number of fifty-year anniversaries played crucial roles in the collective historical imagination of many Americans: Pearl Harbor, D-Day, the end of World War 2, and the bombings of Hiroshima and Nagasaki to name just the most memorable ones. This sense of looking back was taken up in rhetorically powerful ways by major TV and Hollywood movie productions simultaneously. The Ken Burns Series started in 1994, CNN launched its History Channel in 1995, and then historical movies such as *Schindler's List*, *Pearl Harbor*, and *Saving Private Ryan* became box office best sellers. After decades of self-reflexively distanced irony that we still associate with the legacies of literary or cinematographic postmodernism, a new sense of sincere historical sentiment emerged in the wake of the Cold War ending. This return of history brought back the question of realism with a vengeance, and thus also the problem of evidence creation for all those aspiring to promote this novel sense of realism.

## Saving Private Ryan

Steven Spielberg's and Robert Rodat's award winning war movie *Saving Private Ryan* has been widely acclaimed for its historical realism, especially in its minute reconstruction of the American landing on Omaha Beach. The movie features a platoon of American soldiers under the command of Captain John Miller (Tom Hanks) on their way to Ramelle, Normandy, where the group must locate paratrooper James Francis Ryan to bring him back home safely to America. Ryan is the youngest of the four Ryan brothers and the only survivor of the war in Europe. All his three brothers died in combat. The group accomplishes the rescue mission successfully—Ryan is eventually shipped back to America—even though Miller, along with four others of his unit, dies, reminding Ryan at the end of the movie that he must "earn this, earn it."

*Saving Private Ryan*'s authentic appropriation of Word War 2 reality owes much to its semi-autonomous, twenty-three-minutes long opening sequence, which was voted "the best battlefield scene of all time" by *Empire* magazine. The success of the movie's opening arguably has to do with Spielberg's decision to minimize the viewers' distance to the events depicted. Instead of creating the illusion of an objective, neutral narrative standpoint, Spielberg tries to engage his audience psychologically and emotionally in a collective encounter (or re-encounter) with a set of events that have long been considered both as hardly representable but also crucial parts of the collective national memory of the US. Spielberg's movie thus invokes a sample of both ethical and epistemological concerns that have also come to dominate equally immediate and detailed representations of September 11: "What are the strategies of emplotment needed to present the events as part of a coherent historical narrative?" "What are the technical requirements necessary to create images that are reliable and persuasive?" "Are there appropriate and inappropriate means of representation?" "How is appropriateness defined?"

Like the Normandy military landing, the attacks of September 11 have been viewed by politicians and scholars alike as events that, on the one hand, evade conventional historiographical modes of representation and, on the other hand, require objectifiable forms of commemoration. This conundrum defines the opening of *Saving Private Ryan* in exemplary fashion.

"The Best Battlefield Scene of All Time" 261

Figure 1. *Saving Private Ryan*, D-Day scene. Copyright © 1998 Paramount Pictures/DreamWorks LLC/Amblin Entertainment.

Figure 2. *Saving Private Ryan*, D-Day scene. Copyright © 1998 Paramount Pictures/DreamWorks LLC/Amblin Entertainment.

Figure 3. *Saving Private Ryan*, D-Day scene. Copyright © 1998 Paramount Pictures/DreamWorks LLC/Amblin Entertainment.

Figure 4. *Saving Private Ryan*, D-Day scene. Copyright © 1998 Paramount Pictures/DreamWorks LLC/Amblin Entertainment.

Only loosely connected with the over-all narrative of the movie, the scene presents viewers with an intense and extremely detailed reconstruction of the American military arrival in France on June 6, 1944. Featuring Miller and his soldiers, the Omaha Beach landing sequence makes the viewer part of the brutality and contingent violence of battlefield reality. The opening of *Private Ryan* alternates between wide angle shots of the beachhead, thus providing a general panorama of suffering and death, and close-ups and medium close-ups that personalize the savagery of combat, as if forcing the viewer to acknowledge that war is—after all—a very real, physical, and merciless business. Rhetorically speaking, the scene's underlying idea for evidence creation not only relies on an *ad-hominem* address of the viewer. The strategy, rather, is to drag the viewer into the very scene itself. Hence, we are forced to watch soldiers losing their limbs and crying for their mothers; we see body parts exploding and fractured skulls with protruding brains. The physical reality of combat action is backed additionally by the conscious use of sounds—screams, sudden explosions, or machine gun fire—that underline the unpredictability of action and thus enhance the atmosphere of suspense and terror.

While Spielberg's objective-historical rendering of war depends much on advanced filmmaking technologies, the images he creates and uses "rely for their inspiration on those old, grainy combat photos and newsreels that have been the iconic symbol of the D-Day invasion since the end of the war" (Auster 2002, 102). The photographs of Robert Capa in particular serve as the underlying aesthetic script for the movie's pursuit of historical accuracy. Following this ideal, the sections that feature battlefield action depend much on intuitive, at times free-handed camera movements and contain scenes that are shot through blood and water spotted lenses to authenticate the images and actions as historically reliable. Hence, the movie's narrative perspective and its individual stylistic features all point to a deliberate strategy to make the viewer part of what happened and thus construct the illusion of authenticity; rather than distanced neutrality, the movie's goal is to achieve physical and emotional involvement on the part of its audience. On a more particular rhetorical level, this strategy reveals the movie's commitment to classical *ad-hominem* strategies of persuasion, especially if one looks at the uses of emotions, the idea of lived, physical experience, and the primacy of the wounded body.

In another, frequently quoted scene, the physicality of lived historical experience is brought to extremes, when Private Mellish (Adam Goldberg), after desperately defending himself, is eventually stabbed by his German opponent. The scene consists of a series of medium close-ups that feature Mellish's death as the big hunting knife is shown in painstaking detail intruding slowly into Mellish's upper body.

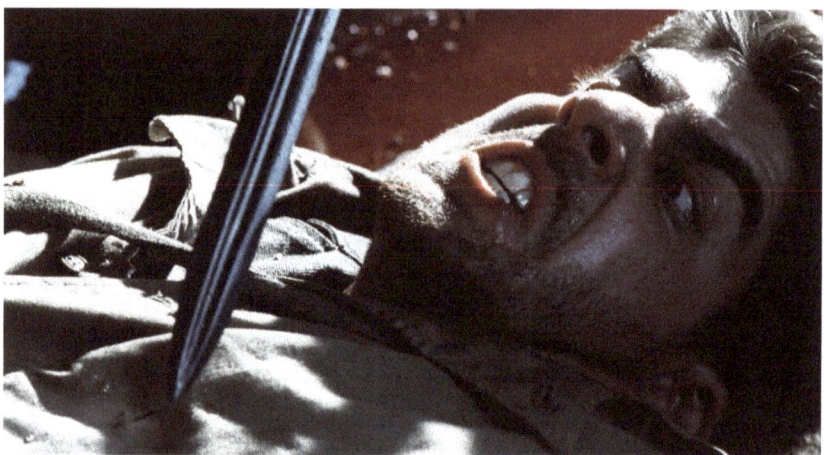

Figure 5. *Saving Private Ryan*, Private Mellish. Copyright © 1998 Paramount Pictures/DreamWorks LLC/Amblin Entertainment.

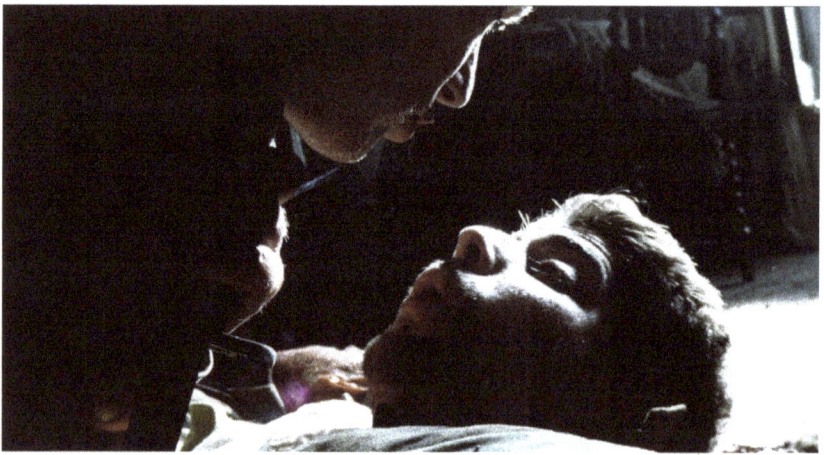

Figure 6. *Saving Private Ryan*, Private Mellish. Copyright © 1998 Paramount Pictures/DreamWorks LLC/Amblin Entertainment.

The scene's underlying assumption is that viewers automatically identify with Private Mellish as the good guy and viewers are also expected to identify with the moment of torture depicted, so much as if they were experiencing the fight and subsequent death struggle with their own bodies. They are not detached but in the middle of the depicted situation. Rather than learn about or study history, viewers feel and experience history in Spielberg's movie, as an anonymous *YouTube*-commenter reacts in response to the Mellish-scene: "This fight I like it the most in the movie, I feel it, even I feel the stab" (Ahmed 2011).

In that sense, the movie expands on a traditional *sub oculis* concept, in which the human body becomes central as evidence carrier. The physicality of lived historical experience is turned into the theoretical precondition for the movie's claim to realism. Feeling replaces knowledge, which is a conceptual shift that not only characterizes the above quoted scenes but also structures the movie as a whole. The primacy of the body connects the movie to a well-known rhetorical strategy in classical oratory, and on that basis, it also signals a turn away from conventional ideals of objectivity and neutrality that historians can resort to in order to define the success or failure of historical writing.

Understanding how the movie functions technically and rhetorically, however, does not necessarily uncover its broader theoretical and political frameworks. What does it really mean when we personalize historical reality, and how can we capture this sense of subjectivity in more theoretical terms?

*Saving Private Ryan*'s message is of course not that World War 2 history should be perceived as a purely subjective and thus random assemblage of veteran memories. By contrast, the movie posits the reality of war as a universal frame of historical events that we cannot and should not question, because these events entail the truth about World War 2 history, as it were. The movie is explicitly universalistic in its claims of objectivity because it insists on the truth-value of its images. Yet, at the same time, the viewer is constantly reminded that war—though masses of people were involved—is eventually a very personal, intimately emotional, and psychological event. What the movie quite emphatically conveys is that the reality of war depends on the bravery of individual men like Captain Miller, and that it is through the viewer's subjective efforts to recreate or live through these lives again that the reality of the past is restored as historical truth. On the one hand, the movie invokes the universalist notion of truth as context-transcendent point of reference, as something that must be true for everyone regardless of how they feel or think about it. On the other hand, however, *Saving Private Ryan* promotes its truth claims constantly by insinuating that the actual experience of war depends on the particularist dimension of subjective experiences—those of the soldiers who have witnessed the events as they happened, and those of the viewers as they learn to identify themselves with the fate of the soldiers around Captain Miller. *Saving Private Ryan* is a movie about the general history of World War 2, but it is also a movie about the American landing on Omaha Beach; the movie depicts in great detail and seemingly objectively the realities of the battlefields in Northwestern France, but it presents these images by asserting the experience of American soldiers as the carriers of historical truth.

Spielberg's movie is as much about American identity as it is about the reality of World War 2, eventually suggesting that the depiction of the Normandy landing and the subsequent rescue mission of James Ryan is so convincing because it is so American. This is no surprise. Hayden White and other theoreticians of history have shown that the production and dissemination of historical narratives in various generic formats—textual as well as filmic—derive their claims for objectivity and truth as much from the events themselves as from the patterns of storytelling available to the historian. As White explains, once historical data material is encapsulated within a familiar plot structure, the "original strangeness, mystery, or exoticism of the events is dispelled, and they take on a familiar aspect, not in their details, but in their function as elements of a familiar kind of configuration" (White 1974, 284). What enables the reader or viewer to understand is not only the amount of information they have about a particular set of events but also their familiarity with a specific "cultural endowment" (White 1974, 283) that produces a recognizable number of possible plot structures. Understood from that perspective, the movie's claim for authenticity, and thus also for truthfulness, is conditioned by the specificity of culture, that is, by the specificity of the collective American subject position. Viewers are rewarded with the truth of history, as it were, but only if they believe in the idea of America.

Spielberg's obvious nationalism has provoked a fair number of critics to dismiss *Saving Private Ryan* as just another predictable Hollywood production designed to support the hegemonic structures and imperialist US ideologies. Marilyn Young (2003, 255), for instance, has claimed that *Saving Private Ryan* served as an "all-purpose propaganda instrument" because the movie aspires to achieve the most realistic setting, while nonetheless "screening out everything save the immediate context in which [soldiers] fight."

Unlike movies such as Oliver Stone's *Platoon* (1986) or Stanly Kubrick's *Full Metal Jacket* (1987), *Saving Private Ryan* presents the mission to find Ryan as inherently meaningful, as something good and worth risking one's life for. The realist surface of the movie, then, functions as a necessary veil of objectivity that covers a more fundamental ideological agenda. And yet, however plausible such a political critique may seem, distinguishing between the ideal of realism, on the one hand, and the ideological uses of realism, on the other, is in itself essentially impossible. The dismissal of Spielberg's movie on grounds of its ideological entanglements requires an impossible subject position, independent of both the ideological thrust of the movie and the truth of history the movie seemingly denies. The movie insists on this predicament in complex fashion, eventually suggesting that there is no way to logically think of any more truthful, more objective, or more authentic alternatives to its very own account of the events.

At first glance, this claim seems counter-intuitive because it thwarts any form of external skepticism. In its modes of evidence creation, the movie relies on the centrality of the American subject position, that is, the centrality of an assumed collective American identity, and since it is impossible to assess identities as either true or false, it becomes equally impossible to question the truth claims they carry as biased or ideology-driven. How, then, can we make sense of this apparent paradox that *Saving Private Ryan* champions the subjectivity of a uniquely American war experience, while all the while suggesting that this is the truth?

To solve this puzzle, we must abandon the idea that there is an unbridgeable gulf between a universal truth, as it were, and the particular and merely subjective dimension of individual or collective experiences. It is logically impossible to disentangle the one from the other. Both poles are reciprocally related; we cannot have them both separately, even though much theoretical work on the representation of history has relied centrally on such moments of separation. Early postmodernist literary and cultural theory, for example, was centrally concerned with the idea that meaning in history is produced rather than found and that accordingly the goal was to disentangle the individuality of the historian from universalizing conceptions of truth, objectivity, or verisimilitude. This idea is fleshed out prominently in poststructuralist redefinitions of the author function and the celebration of the "open text," that is, the belief in the impossibility of finite textual meaning (see, e.g., Barthes 1977; Hejinian 2000; Eco 1989, 1–24). Meaning in history is defined in these accounts not based on verifiable historical facts but as the result of distinct emplotment strategies through which historical facts can be incorporated into specific political or ideological narratives (see, e.g., White 1973, 1–43; Parrish 2008; LaCapra 1983, 13–72). Powerful as they may seem, such theories must assume a logical split between the real in history and its mere ideological appropriation. In *Saving Private Ryan*, we find an intriguing inversion of this assumption. Here, the subjectivity of the viewer is not positioned against the universality of historical truth; the subjectivity of the viewer is instead turned into the very precondition for thinking about historical truth. In that respect, we must think of Spielberg's movie not only as a quite intricate attempt to redefine the idea of historical evidence creation and corresponding truth claims; *Saving Private Ryan* must also be viewed as a quite articulate filmic statement against the poststructuralist critique of representation and the proclamation of the death of the subject.[6]

Featuring James Ryan as an old man on a military cemetery in France, the movie's framing narrative illustrates this theoretical idea from the beginning on:

Figure 7. *Saving Private Ryan*, cemetery scene. Copyright © 1998 Paramount Pictures/DreamWorks LLC/Amblin Entertainment.

Overwhelmed by a flashback of memories, Ryan collapses in front of Miller's gravestone. The scene then blends smoothly into the world of the past and the embedded main story of the movie begins with a close-up on Captain Miller seconds before he and his platoon are released into the terror of war. The subject position of Ryan and his personal memories thus featured provide the beginning for a cinematographic account of World War 2 that aspires to be objective and representative of a general historical truth.

In this scene, Ryan is used as the narrative focalizer as he walks through a seemingly infinite number of gravestones. The infinity of suffering is then juxtaposed with Ryan's particular emotional outburst that is triggered by his very own limited memories and the story he shares with Captain Miller and his platoon. This aspect is further underlined as the scene ends with a sequence of close-ups of Ryan's face, so as if to suggest that viewers are literally entering the mind of Ryan. Hence, the American experience of war—expressed in Ryan's trauma—is used to make a more general statement about the value of history, a statement, however, that ultimately transcends the very subjective position it requires to be meaningful and reliable.

Against such a reading, viewers may obviously object that this old man is traumatized and thus also deluded and that it does not make much sense to instrumentalize the character of a deluded old man to propose a quite serious reading of World War 2. But again, what is the standpoint that would allow for denouncing the truth of Ryan's memories? What is the basis upon which such a moment of critique becomes meaningful? The only reason for denouncing James Ryan, the old man, and thus eventually the whole movie would be a standpoint that is politically opposed to *Saving Private Ryan*'s nationalism. Viewers may be reluctant to embrace the movie's broader political message. They may point out that the French or British are underrepresented throughout or complain about the fact that the Germans are portrayed as an almost anonymous mass of blood thirsty savages, while the Americans are used as personified emblems of humanism and camaraderie. All these points can be plausibly defended, but their plausibility has nothing to do with a more refined theoretical perspective on the problem of historical realism. The subjectivity of Ryan is not in itself political. And exactly in this sense, the movie opts for a separation rather than a conflation of theory and politics. The movie's commitment to the individual subject is distinct from its political instrumentalization, even if we are inclined to argue the other way around.

*Saving Private Ryan* is rich in scenes like the opening sequence in which the idea of historical truth, on the one hand, is juxtaposed with the collective subject position of America, on the other. The very title of the movie reveals an implicit narrative strategy that hinges primarily on the individual American soldier, rather than the idea of historical reality as such. Spielberg's piece is so compelling because it advertises the significance of American identity as something natural and politically necessary. The reason why Miller's platoon is sent out to find Ryan is not strategic, but patriotic. The decision is made to safeguard the integrity of American family ideals, and only as a contingent outcome of that to help to liberate France from the Germans. The commanders in chief send out Miller and his troop of soldiers as they receive the news that Mrs. Ryan had already lost three of her other sons, and so they conclude that it would be just inhumane, that is un-American, not to seize every opportunity to find James Ryan. Miller's men are courageous and fearful, prudent and, at times, helplessly irrational, and these human qualities make them typical of the great majority of soldiers who had fought in World War 2, regardless of citizenship or cultural identity.

Yet at the same time, citizenship and the idea of American culture is really all that matters in *Saving Private Ryan*. From a broad military perspective, locating Private Ryan is an insignificant action. But as we know, the movie is not meant to be a general statement about the suitability of specific military operations. The idea behind finding Private Ryan, and thus behind the movie in general, is the idea of America, and the movie suggests that this idea is something very special.

Miller's unit, therefore, is not just a group of randomly assembled soldiers. Spielberg presents these men as role models for a pluralist society, ethnically, socially, and religiously diverse, "a walking-talking example of the melting pot" (Auster 2002, 102). When the soldiers and commanders in the movie ponder the business of war from a more philosophical perspective, then they naturally seem to be able to quote Emerson or Lincoln without stuttering or hesitation. Significantly, Army Chief of Staff General Marshall (Herve Presnell) makes his decision to search for and bring home Private Ryan in a rush of nationalistic sentiment and not on grounds of military necessity. Weighing up the pros and cons of the operation, he eventually draws on the humanism of President Lincoln, as he recites emphatically one of his Civil War letters to Mrs. Lydia Bigsby, in which Lincoln consoles Bigsby on the combat death of her five sons. Hence, "invoking Lincoln's words takes the film out of the realm of mere realism and bathes it in the more luminous power of a sublime nationalism" (Auster 2002, 101). Thus, the movie eventually celebrates the collective subject position of the American nation, while it seems to give up on the notion of objectivity or truthfulness it initially promotes.

Again, it is of course possible to dismiss the movie because it seems to be endorsing questionable political agendas—many critics have in fact done this. What critics cannot do, however, is support their political aversions by arguing that the movie's theoretical premises are equally questionable. This would be to miss the movie's theoretical point: historical memory, rather than truth, is not tied to any particular political or ideological program. *Saving Private Ryan* is so remarkable in its strategies of historical representation because it proposes the reconfiguration of an originally epistemological question—"How can we know reality?"—as an issue of personal memory, albeit without questioning the status of the individual subject as the carrier of this experience. Truth claims can be argued, they can be defended, critiqued, or subverted, but memory—individual or collective—evades the conceptual frameworks of traditional epistemological inquiries. It simply does not make any sense to proclaim that memories are either correct or false. The movie uses its claims for authenticity as a strategy to tell us that feeling *means* knowing, that individual experience *verifies* truth claims, and, eventually, that we need to maintain the particularity of the individual self to safeguard the universality of historical truth.

## Conclusion

This shift from truth to memory and its corresponding commitment to a subject-based epistemology must be contextualized within a broader cultural transition that many prominent critics have identified as the demise of the postmodern. Minimally defined, the postmodernist world is premised on the possibility of either defending or subverting truth claims about the reality of the world and its representation. This is a classical deconstructionist gesture. To be able to subvert a dominant form of representation, one needs to believe in the superiority of one's own standpoint. Otherwise, the whole point of questioning some other person's position would be obsolete. The implicit assumption here is that of a difference in opinion. Opinions work independently of the people supporting them. They are detached from the subject position of a speaker or observer and derive their authority from their assumed proximity to ideals such as truth, reality, or knowledge. Yet, this logic seems to have lost much of its relevance in a world predominantly shaped by individual subject positions. There is no logically deducible foundation from which to ponder whether being American is any more truthful than being Japanese, or, say, Lithuanian. Insisting on a difference in opinion (which can be either true or false) does not work in contexts that are primarily shaped by the difference of cultures—be they defined nationally, ethnically, or religiously.[7]

In exactly this sense, I would suggest reading Spielberg's movie as part of a growing body of works in which subjectivity figures as the very precondition for evidence creation and not as a disclaimer against historical truth. This notion of truth as memory surfaces prominently in what we now categorize as 9/11 literature ("The Return of the Real") or contemporary ethnic historical fiction (e.g., post-slavery narratives), in which crucial periods in global or American history are reconstructed through the subjective experience of individual historical agents rather than on the basis of objective historical knowledge. These works—just like *Saving Private Ryan*—make the provocative claim that representations of history are not true *despite* the fact that they are subjective; they are only true *because* they are so subjective. To be sure, this may appear as a merely theoretical argument about a resurgent neo-realist discourse and its evolution since the 1990s. Yet, at the same time, it is hard to disregard the affinities between this neo-realist revival and the broader cultural and political transitions that occurred simultaneously in the aftermath of the Cold War. This is not to suggest that there is a direct causality between the aesthetics of movies like *Saving Private Ryan* and the emergence of the post-Cold War world. But there is a conceptual family resemblance between the idea of a world stripped of ideological antagonism and the claim promoted in and by Spielberg's movie that we need to replace truth with memory. What links the movie to its broader historical surroundings is a shift from the universal to the particular; in other words, on a mainly theoretical level, *Saving Private Ryan* reproduces the conceptual logic of Samuel Huntington's notion of culture, Jürgen Habermas' vision of a post-national constellation, and Francis Fukuyama's idea of a post-ideological world after the "end of history" (see Fukuyama 1992; Habermas 1998; Huntington 1996, 19–29;).

Returning to the title of the present paper helps to illustrate this claim: the opening scene of *Saving Private Ryan* may in fact legitimately be called the best battlefield scene of all time because it urges viewers to reconsider the theoretical problem of historical evidence creation on the one hand, and its potential political or ideological appropriations on the other. As counterintuitive as this may sound, the movie proposes the disarticulation of theory from politics—and not vice versa. *Saving Private Ryan* exposes the problem of realism in as much as it points out that the realist paradigm—understood as a particular theoretical challenge—does not itself require any political commitment. In that sense, it may indeed be symptomatic of the general climate of change and the shuffling around of traditional left-right distinctions that so drastically characterized the 1990s and the post-Cold War world. In a world bereft of ideological antagonisms, the realism of Spielberg's movie announces the beginning of an era where truth claims have become equivalent to subject positions. The trick of the movie is that it reproduces the value of cultural difference and hybridity—key terms in the post-national theory arsenal—on the level of epistemology as a pluralist memory discourse.

One thing is clear: Spielberg himself may have never been conscious of this theoretical dimension of his movie. The fact, however, that *Saving Private Ryan* has attained canonicity in contemporary cultural studies departments in Germany and the US proves how timely the discussions it triggered in fact are. The great and yet often unacknowledged strength of the movie is that it broaches questions about the conditions under which it makes sense to stake claims to realist modes of representation. *Saving Private Ryan* evades the confines of its rather limited thematic scope as a World War 2-movie by additionally emphasizing its political and theoretical situatedness in the contemporary historical present. The question of realism is the key tool to highlight this very connection.

## Notes

1. The end-of-history debate started again in 1989, when Francis Fukuyama proposed in *The National Interest* to view the demise of the Cold War world as the final step towards the end of history in the Hegelian sense of the term. Fukuyama offered a more comprehensive account of his idea in a monograph of the same title in 1992. "At the end of history," Fukuyama claims, "there are no serious ideological competitors left to liberal democracy" (Fukuyama 1992, 211). Fukuyama, however, is also cautious to maintain that while the political relevance of ideological antagonism has clearly diminished since the end of the Cold War, the post-Cold War world is not necessarily freed from potential sites of conflict. Yet, these sites of conflicts, now cultural conflicts, do not invalidate the view that the "liberal idea" has turned out to be victorious. They ultimately attest to the historical triumph of liberal democracy, spotlighting prominently how the universal frameworks of the liberal idea allow for a multiplicity of competing (but equal) identities in politics and culture. To illustrate his point Fukuyama (1992, 45–46) remarks that the "end of the Cold War in Europe was followed immediately by a challenge to the West from Iraq, in which Islam was arguably a factor". A comprehensive overview of the Fukuyama controversy is presented in Loptson (2005). See also Michaels (1996). The return of history after the alleged "end of history" is discussed with great clarity in Cohen (2009).

2. For an impressive summary of this genealogy and its re-appropriation in postmodernist literary and cultural theory see Scholz-Williams (1989).

3. The disciplinary evolution of history and historiography is discussed in great detail in Koselleck et al. (1975).

4. The term *Sattelzeit* refers to the period that saw the emergence of what we nowadays refer to as modernity in the late eighteenth and early nineteenth century. The technological and political progress associated with the years following the French revolution went hand in hand with a growing awareness of one's own historicity (see Koselleck 2014, 131–51).

5. The original quote by Leopold von Ranke can be found in Ranke (1824, 6). The neo-realist debate in literary studies is captured comprehensively in Versluys (1992). A more recent account of the neo-realism question in contemporary philosophy can be found in Gabriel (2013).

6. The theoretical implications of the alleged death of the subject are outlined in detail, for example, in Foucault (1972).

7. As Walter Benn Michaels (2004, 10) claims, the "difference between what you want and what I want is just a difference between you and me;

the difference between what you see and what I see is just the difference between where you're standing and where I'm standing—literally, a difference in subject position."

## Works Cited

Amed. [A comment on the video] "Saving Private Ryan—Shh . . ." *YouTube*, 2011. http://www.youtube.com/watch?v=g1I4P3umnzk. Accessed November 15, 2017.

Auster, Albert. 2002. "Saving Private Ryan and American Triumphalism." *Journal of Popular Film and Television* 30 (2): 98–104.

Barthes, Roland. 1977. "The Death of the Author." In *Image, Music, Text*, edited by Stephen Heath, 142–49. London: Fontana.

Cohen, Samuel. 2009. *After the End of History*. Iowa City: University of Iowa Press.

Eco, Umberto. 1989. *The Open Work*. Translated by Anna Cancogni. London: Hutchinson Radius.

Foley, Barbara. 1986. *Telling the Truth: The Theory and Practice of Documentary Fiction*. Ithaca, NY: Cornell University Press.

Foucault, Michel. 1972. *The Archeology of Knowledge and the Discourse on Language*. First edition. New York: Pantheon Books.

Fukuyama, Francis. 1992. *The End of History and the Last Man*. New York: Free Press.

Gabriel, Markus. 2013. *Warum es die Welt nicht gibt*. Berlin: Ullstein.

Habermas, Jürgen. 1998. *Die postnationale Konstellation: Politische Essays*. Frankfurt a.M.: Suhrkamp.

Hejinian, Lyn. 2000. "The Rejection of Closure." In *The Language of Inquiry*, 40–59. Berkley: University of California Press.

Huntington, Samuel. 1996. *The Clash of Civilizations and the Remaking World Order*. New York: Council on Foreign Relations.

Hutcheon, Linda. 1988. *A Poetics of Postmodernism: History, Theory, Fiction*. London, New York: Routledge.

Koselleck, Reinhart, Christian Meier, Odilo Engels, and Horst Günther. 1975. "Geschichte." In *Geschichtliche Grundbegriffe: Historisches Lexikon zur politisch-sozialen Sprache in Deutschland*, edited by Otto Brunner, Werner Conze, and Reinhart Koselleck. Vol. 2: E–G, 593–717. Stuttgart: Klett.

Koselleck, Reinhart. 2014. *Vom Sinn und Unsinn der Geschichte: Aufsätze und Vorträge aus vier Jahrzehnten*. Berlin: Suhrkamp.

LaCapra, Dominick. 1983. *Rethinking Intellectual History: Texts, Contexts, Language*. Ithaca, NY: Cornell University Press.

Loptson, Peter. 2005. "The End-of-History Idea Revisited." *CLIO* 35 (1): 51–73.

Michaels, Walter B. 1996. "Posthistoricism." *Transition* 70 (2): 4–19.

—. 2004. *The Shape of the Signifie: 1967 to the End of History*. Princeton, NJ: Princeton University Press.

Parrish, Timothy. 2008. *Postmodern History and American Fiction. From the Civil War to the Apocalypse*. First edition. Amherst, MA: University of Massachusetts Press.

Ranke, Leopold von. 1824. *Geschichten der romanischen und germanischen Völker von 1494–1535*. Berlin, Leipzig: Reimer.

Scholz-Williams, Gerhild. 1989. "Geschichte und die literarische Dimension. Narrativik und Historiographie in der Anglo-Amerikanischen Forschung der letzten Jahrzehnte: Ein Bericht." *Deutsche Vierteljahrsschrift für Literaturwissenschaft und Geistesgeschichte* 63 (2): 315–92.

Versluys, Kristiaan, ed. 1992. *Neo-Realism in Contemporary American Fiction*. Amsterdam: Rodopi.

White, Hayden. 1973. *Metahistory. The Historical Imagination in 19th-Century Europe*. Baltimore: John Hopkins University Press.

—. 1974. "The Historical Text as Literary Artifact." *CLIO* 3 (3): 277–303.

Young, Marilyn. 2003. "In the Combat Zone." *Radical History Review* 85 (4): 253–64.

# 14 An Analysis and Criticism of Chaïm Perelman's Approach to Evidence and Argument as Developed in *The New Rhetoric*

*John W. Ray*

This chapter examines the concept of the *universal audience* and the distinct method it provides for viewing what constitutes sound argumentation and convincing evidence. Included in this discussion is a consideration of the nature of the universal audience, how the universal audience functions as a criterion for judging sound argumentation and the importance of the universal audience for Perelman's theory of rhetoric. I also examine the philosophical antecedents of the universal audience in the works of Jean-Jacques Rousseau, Denis Diderot, and Immanuel Kant. My conclusion is that the universal audience does not provide a usable test of evidentiary adequacy.

## Evidence and Argument

Evidence is commonly defined as any data, facts or expert opinion statements that can prove or disprove a contention, assertion, thesis or proposition. Evidence can help to form a conclusion or belief. Evidence is commonly seen as the starting point of argumentation, for arguments are grounded in and proceed from evidence.

Evidence comes from the Latin and French words meaning obvious or evident. But, the question must be asked: obvious or evident to whom?

By its very nature, the concept of evidence presupposes that evidence must be viewed within a rhetorical context with particular attention paid to the concept of *audience*. By asking the question evidence or evident for whom, one is assuming that the evidence is "publicly" presented and judged by others, that is, an audience. After all, for Aristotle, a major audience function is to give a judgment as to the worthiness of the arguments that are addressed to it. Arguments are publicly presented and publicly judged. As Aristotle contended, we do not argue about that which is certain but about the probable. It is the audience that determines and constitutes rhetorical truth. I would argue that evidence, apart from the public context, is meaningless. Evidence, which exists in the particular, is only important when it is united to the universal.

## Perelman's Theory of Evidence and Argument as Rhetorical Constructs

Chaïm Perelman's theory of rhetoric and argumentation helps to answer the question: Evident to whom? As we shall see, Perelman's answer would be: evident to the universal audience.

Before we get to the universal audience, we need to summarize Perelman's theory of evidence and argument. For Perelman, agreement is the starting point of argument. Agreement of whom? Perelman answers: agreement of an audience is required. "We will constantly need a notion correlative to agreement, that of the audience. A fact is important in argument because it is considered as forming the object of universal agreement: it must be accepted by everyone" (Perelman 1963, 169). As Perelman (1963, 155) states argumentation cannot take place without an audience: "the development of all argumentation is a function of the audience to which it is addressed and to which the speaker is obliged to adapt himself." For Perelman (1963, 169), the notion of audience is correlative to that of agreement.

> The part played by the audience in rhetoric is crucially important, because all argumentation, in aiming to persuade, must be adapted to the audience, and hence based on beliefs accepted by the audience with such conviction that the rest of the discourse can be securely based upon it. (Perelman 1979, 15)

For Perelman, the quality of the audience determines the quality of the arguments addressed to it. Perelman reaches this conclusion because "argument is, in its entirety, relative to the audience to be influenced" (Perelman and Olbrechts-Tyteca 1969, 19).

Perelman sought rules and rational bases for practical activity and for argumentation. Since, according to Perelman, empiricism cannot provide a satisfactory basis for morals, he saw his task as similar to Kant's—to provide a non-empirical ground upon which to base and justify morals.

Agreement with the universal audience, which is really a form of self-evident agreement, is the major test of evidence, more powerful than conformity to any argumentative rules.

> The characteristic of rational argumentation is the aim to universality—an aim whose realization is never insured. It is useless to try to define rational argumentation the way we define a demonstrative technique, namely, by its conformity to certain prescribed rules. (Perelman 1967, 83)

That which is self-evident to the universal audience is true. That which contradicts the universal audience, or is not the product of the universal audience, is false:

> But my conception of reason differs from the classical conception. I do not see it as a faculty in contrast to other faculties in man. I conceive of it as a privileged audience, the universal audience. The appeal to reason is but an attempt to convince the members of this audience . . . by addressing them. To achieve his end, the philosopher must use a rational argumentation conforming to Kant's categorical imperative. His postulate and his reasoning must be valid for the whole of the human community. (Perelman 1967, 82)

The appeal to reason is the appeal to the universal audience. The goal of argumentation is to develop arguments that the universal audience finds convincing. The crucial importance of the universal audience, in Perelman's (1970, 30) terms, is that it provides a "norm for objective argumentation." For Perelman (1970, 31), the highest point of argumentation "is reached when there is agreement of the universal audience."

Perelman's *New Rhetoric* is a rhetoric of argumentation and a fundamental component of that rhetoric is the concept of audience. Perelman said: "All argumentation aims at gaining the adherence of minds, and, by this very fact, assumes the existence of an intellectual contact" (Perelman and Olbrechts-Tyteca 1969, 14). The best arguments are those that are directed to the universal audience. According to Perelman, the highest point in the argumentative process "is reached when there is agreement of the universal audience" (Perelman and Olbrechts-Tyteca 1969, 31). The universal audience is the ideal audience and is addressed when an appeal to reason is made. The universal audience has no ontological status except as a mental concept or construct of the speaker. Therefore, all evidence becomes a form of self-evidence. Facts and evidence have no real existence apart from an audience.

Perelman (1963, 188) notes: "When does a judgment express a fact? As long, we have seen, as it is believed to be valid for a universal audience . . . ." The universal audience provides universal agreement by which facts are established. "Facts and truths can be characterized as objects that are already agreed to by the universal audience, and, hence, there is no need to increase the intensity of adherence to them" (Perelman 1979, 15).

## The Criteria of the Universal Audience

The universal audience provides the criteria for judging the quality of arguments and for judging the quality of the evidence used in support of an argument. For Perelman, the fundamental starting point of argument is agreement. Perelman notes that "from start to finish, analysis of argumentation is concerned with what is supposed to be accepted by the hearers" (Perelman and Olbrechts-Tyteca 1969, 65). A fact or evidence in general is valid only if it is subject to the universal agreement of the universal audience. When the universal audience questions a fact, it is no longer a fact. Presumption is also grounded in universal agreement. In short, the agreement of the universal audience is a necessary condition for the starting place of argument, evidence. "Everything in argumentation that is deemed to relate to the real is characterized by a claim to validity vis-à-vis the universal audience" (Perelman and Olbrechts-Tyteca 1969, 66).

In an ontological sense, a fact is a fact and evidence is evidence only when sanctioned by the universal audience.

> Argumentation addressed to a universal audience must convince the reader that the reasons adduced are of a compelling character, that they are self-evident, and possess an absolute and timeless validity, independent of local or historical contingencies. (Perelman and Olbrechts-Tyteca 1969, 32)

According to Perelman, the universal audience is a means of bridging the bifurcation between evidence and thesis, data and claim, and fact and inference. The universal audience unites the subjective and objective poles of evidentiary based argumentation.

Of course, if arguments seek to convince the universal audience, how do we know that the universal audience has been convinced? How do we know that the universal audience assents? Are there certain rules to follow in determining what the universal audience accepts? How are we to recognize those arguments that are sanctioned by the universal audience? Are we reduced to saying that the universal audience is convinced if the universal audience follows the rules of logic and argumentation? (Remember Perelman eschews rule following as a guide to adequate argumentation. Perelman wants to get beyond logical consistency as a test of a good argument. Yet this is how you determine the assent of the universal audience.)

Echoing Kant, Perelman contends that arguments sanctioned by the universal audience must be "valid for the reason of every man" and "necessarily valid for everyone" (Perelman and Olbrechts-Tyteca 1969, 32), and that the criterion of Kant's categorical imperative—rational universality—is the criterion of the universal audience. Facts, presumptions, values are only valid if sanctioned by the universal audience.

The universal audience is an enterprise of trying to make the subjective universal. The universal audience expresses Perelman's desire to make the particular general and the general particular. For Perelman, argumentation and logic becomes a branch of ontology.

## Rousseau's and Diderot's General Will

Perelman's concept of the universal audience is very close to Rousseau's and Diderot's concept of the *general will*. Before comparing the universal audience to the general will, it is necessary to define what Rousseau and Diderot meant by the general will.

It is the social contract that creates a state that has a general will. The general will is to be distinguished from particular/individual wills and even the will of all in that the general will is general and universal, both in terms of its essence and the object toward which it is directed which is the general good. In fact, when the general will gets directed toward some particular object, it loses its moral force. For Rousseau and Diderot, the general will cannot be represented. Although the general will is found by counting votes, the greater the unanimity of a decision the more likely the general will is being followed (cf. Rousseau 1950, 106).

The general will is the universal and necessary will of the members of the state and is "universal justice emanating from reason alone" (Rousseau 1950, 54). The general will is a pure act of the understanding that functions as a rational standard against which the actions of people are judged (cf. Diderot 1967, 173–75). As such it is never wrong.

## Similarity of the Universal Audience to the General Will

In the same way that Rousseau and Diderot distinguish the general will from the particular will, Perelman distinguishes the universal audience from the particular audience. The universal audience provides the rational norm against which the value of the arguments of a discourse can be judged. Arguments sanctioned by the universal audience ought to be convincing to all rational people. Arguments which are persuasive for the particular audience make no universal claims, whereas the universal audience only accepts universal claims. As the imagined will of all reasonable people, both the general will and universal audience are a universal standard of judgment. Like the general will, the universal audience, as a universal standard of judgment, loses its force when it is brought to bear on particular questions in concrete, practical situations.

In short, just as the general will is a rational and infallible standard against which a person's moral actions are judged, so also the universal audience is an infallible rational standard in terms of which of a speaker's arguments are developed and against which the arguments of a speaker are judged.

## Kant's Ethical Theory

Kant, like Perelman, seeks to establish his moral theory not on empirical ground, which can yield no universal and necessary standards of conduct, but upon *a priori* reason. What Kant seeks to provide is a metaphysic of morals, a metaphysic that will provide a standard for moral action.

The standard for judging the ethical worth of a moral principle or standard of action is whether or not the maxim, a subjective principle of individual volition, can be willed without contradiction as a universal law for all. For example, we could not will lying as a universal maxim for all without contradiction.

For Kant, what must be sought is an absolute grounding for the will which has absolute worth and is an end in itself (cf. Kant 1949, 5–6, 18–21, 44–45, 58, 63–64, 71).

## The Categorical Imperative and the Universal Audience

As does Kant, Perelman argues that no universal standard, against which the validity of the arguments of a discourse could be appropriately judged, can be produced from empirical existence. Also like Kant, Perelman places little hope in a rationalist metaphysic as the producer of ultimate, acceptable standards of judgment. Using an approach equivalent to Kant's, Perelman attempts to solve the dilemma by introducing a standard that claims no ontological existence and is purely hypothetical but which can, nevertheless, as a purely mental concept, serve as an absolute standard not dependent upon empirical experience. For Kant, this standard is the categorical imperative; for Perelman, it is the universal audience.

Like Kant's categorical imperative, the universal audience is the product of reason—reason not determined by empirical experience, for empirical experience is always particular and can not yield universal standards. To establish the standard of the categorical imperative is to will without contradiction that a maxim should be a universal law for all people. Perelman (1968b, 22), too, speaks of universality and non-contradiction as the standards by which to judge what is sanctioned by the universal audience.

## Criticisms of the General Will, Categorical Imperative, and Universal Audience

The general will, the categorical imperative, and the universal audience are all attempts to provide a universal standard for correct or ethical action whether in the field of argumentation, ethics, or politics. An examination of the universal audience shows that it shares in the same difficulties as does the general will and the categorical imperative.

1. Criticisms that can be leveled against the concepts and constructs of the general will, the categorical imperative, and the universal audience. All three attempt to produce a transcendental grounding for, respectively, political, ethical, and rhetorical theory.
2. All three are excessively formal and abstract.
3. All three fail to provide an answer as to the question of who is to interpret the general will, categorical imperative, or universal audience. For example, the rhetor has no way of knowing if his/her personal concept of the universal audience is correct.
4. All three sometimes fall into the trap of arguing that what exists embodies the universal audience. For example, the zeitgeist of the times—the status quo. (We would do well to remember Nietzsche's admonition that all things are subject to interpretation, whichever interpretation prevails at a given time is a function of power not truth.)
5. Perelman sometimes argues that the content of the universal audience is empirical—historically based and contingent, sometimes timeless.
6. If, on the one hand, judgments of the universal audience are supposed to have some timeless and absolute validity, and if each individual, in isolation (as Perelman says), forms a construct of the universal audience, are we to have as many universal audiences as

we have speakers? Were this the case, we would face the anarchic situation of each individual's universal audience being as good as anyone else's universal audience, since no *a priori* standard is given that would enable us to choose between them. If this were the case, the universal audience would be a needless concept because it would not represent any advance over the old notion that each orator has a concept of the audience addressed.

7. How are we to characterize the relationship between these different, individually based conceptions of the universal audience? Would we need a third universal audience to express the relationship between the first two, and so on to infinity?

8. If, on the other hand, we are to take Perelman seriously when he says that the content of the universal audience varies with each historical epoch and place, then he is in fact reduced to saying that whatever each particular epoch and place sanctions is right—a position that Perelman explicitly wants to reject. However, if each historical epoch does give content to the universal audience, the inventional job of the orator would be simply that of discovering the prevailing moods of the time—a view of the inventional process that Perelman also wants to reject. Were the content of the universal audience variable with time and place, it would have to be history—in the sense of a particular culture's or country's acts, values, ideas, and events—which dictates the content of the universal audience. If this were the case, Perelman (1968a, 169) would have to argue explicitly that history is rational, because the appeal to the universal audience is the "appeal to reason." This would be, as Hegel would say, subjectivism run rampant.

9. To be consistent, Perelman would have to argue further that the message of history is self-evidently discoverable by reason, for, if it is not, there is no way of knowing whether the interpretation of the historical epoch by the orator is correct. Nowhere does Perelman argue that history is rational or that the message of history is self-evident. What we really end up with, because Perelman provides no synthetic *a priori* method of determining the content of the universal audience, is the existing facts, truths, and presumptions of a society confirming and constituting the universal audience.

10. All three are tautologies. For example, Perelman's universal audience is what is rational for all people, but it also should be the standard for determining what is rational for all people. This is a tautology. The general will and the categorical imperative are what are rational/ethical for all people but should also be the standard

for determining what is rational/ethical for all people. Again, they are both tautologies.
11. Is universal audience to be determined, like Kant's categorical imperative, according to rules of logical non-contradiction? If following the rules of logical non-contradiction, would it not be possible to will radical evil without contradiction?
12. All three provide a poor standard of argumentation that cannot be applied to specific situations, which is what Perelman says of the universal audience.

## Conclusion

In the past there have been many attempts to provide a universal and rational foundation for argumentation and rhetoric. Plato spoke of a rhetoric capable of persuading the gods as a noble rhetoric, unlike what the sophists were doing. Rawls in *A Theory of Justice* constructs a hypothetical audience capable of producing genuine principles of justice. Habermas, who espouses a consensus theory of truth, postulates an "ideal speech situation" as producing an audience whose criteria for fact, truth, and argumentation incorporates a rational, universal standard of universal agreement much like Perelman's universal audience. Fisher speaks of the equivalent of the universal audience in developing his narrative paradigm. All these attempts flounder on the rock of excessive abstraction and formality and represent an age-old search for certainty where it cannot be found.

If we accept the universal audience as a necessary and sufficient standard for judging argumentative adequacy, are we not ignoring Aristotle's warning not to look for certainty where it cannot be found? After all, as Aristotle ([1954, trans. Roberts], *Rh.* 1.2) said, "about things that could not have been, and cannot now or in the future be, other than they are, nobody who takes them to be of this nature wastes his time in deliberation."

The search for an absolute standard by means of which an argument can be judged would, if successful, lead to dogmatism. ("A dog barks when his master is attacked. I would be a coward if I saw that God's truth is attacked and yet would remain silent." John Calvin) After all, if there is one Truth and someone does not agree with that Truth, it could be because they are ignorant, or it could be because of a perverse will. If it is because they are ignorant, try to instruct them. If instruction does not work, force may be used to convert or to punish for failure to accept the truth.

For example, in mathematics, a wrong answer has no intrinsic value. It is wrong. If an answer does not conform to the universal standard of what, for that particular problem, constitutes a correct answer, we afford it no worth or probative value. A math student who consistently clings to a wrong answer, even after he/she is instructed as to how to derive the correct answer, is the victim of some perverse will or social pathology. The answer to a mathematical problem does not depend on a popular vote of those in the class. The correct answer to a math problem just is.

Using the universal audience as the standard of argumentation seeks to impose certainty and exactness where it does not belong. The universal audience presents a self-certifying truth. The universal audience offers an *a priori* standard to which all practical argumentation must conform. The universal audience conflates knowledge and true belief. The universal audience would make all deliberative questions, because deliberation presumes contingency, into judicial questions. The universal audience conflates ethics and epistemology. The universal audience could actually elevate my true belief to the level of Truth without foundation.

Perhaps the universal audience could be used as a device of rhetorical criticism. What is the universal audience of the particular speaker or piece of rhetoric? How would you characterize the rhetor's universal audience? What is the universal audience behind a rhetor's narration? What is the universal audience that is informing the rhetor's particular argument?

Where we run into significant problems is when we use the universal audience as it was primarily intended, that is, as a standard for judging the quality of arguments and argumentation. The search for the repose of certainty is going to fail.

## Works Cited

Aristotle. 1954. *Rhetoric*. Translated by W. Rhys Roberts. New York: The Modern Library.

Diderot, Denis. 1967. "Natural Rights." In *The Encyclopedia: Selections*, edited and translated by Stephen J. Gendzier, 173–75. New York: J. and J. Harper Editions.

Kant, Immanuel. 1949. *Fundamental Principles of the Metaphysic of Morals*. Translated by Thomas K. Abbott. Indianapolis: The Bobbs-Merrill Company.

Perelman, Chaïm. 1963. *The Idea of Justice and the Problem of Argument*. Translated by John Petrie. London: Routledge and Kegan Paul.

—. 1967. *Justice*. New York: Random House.

—. 1968a. "Reply to Mr. Zaner." *Philosophy and Rhetoric* 1 (3): 168–70.

—. 1968b. "Rhetoric and Philosophy." *Philosophy and Rhetoric* 1 (1): 15–24.

—. 1970. "The New Rhetoric: A Theory of Practical Reasoning." In *The Great Ideas Today*, translated by E. Griffin-Collart and O. Bird, edited by Robert M. Hutchins and Mortimer J. Adler, 273–312. New York: Encyclopedia Britannica.

—. 1979. *The New Rhetoric and the Humanities: Essays on Rhetoric and Its Applications*. Dordrecht: D. Reidel Publishing Company.

Perelman, Chaïm, and L. Olbrechts-Tyteca. 1969. *The New Rhetoric: A Treatise on Argumentation*. Translated by John Wilkinson and Purcell Weaver. Notre Dame: University of Notre Dame Press.

Rousseau, Jean-Jacques. 1950. *The Social Contract and Discourses*. Translated by George D. H. Cole. New York: E.P. Dutton and Company.

# 15 Carl Friedrich von Weizsäcker's Rhetorics of Evidence Construction

*Klaus Hentschel*

Carl Friedrich von Weizsäcker was not only an exceptional physicist, philosopher, and peace researcher, but also a skilled and articulate speaker and a highly successful author. Dozens of his books were published in tens of thousands of copies despite their highly nontrivial content. This wide impact—according to one of the claims made in this paper—was due to his sophisticated style and his often subcutaneous, clever rhetoric. The analysis here is based on hand-picked samples from a variety of primary texts (talks, scientific and popular papers, books, and verses). Weizsäcker easily found ways to make his theses sound "evident"—convincing, at least for the duration of a given speech—albeit doubts might arise on second thoughts. Strangely enough, this interesting stylistic and rhetorical facet of his oeuvre has not been analyzed in detail before, despite its crucial importance for his multifarious audiences of physicists, philosophers, social scientists, and the general public at large. This chapter strives to make this analysis of Weizsäcker's highly innovative style and rhetoric accessible to an international readership.

## Initial Thesis and Basic Idea

The physicist, philosopher, and peace scholar Carl Friedrich von Weizsäcker (1912–2007) was influential well beyond his own fields of expertise. His speeches, essays, and books affected the general public of his day. My initial thesis is that this was due to his broad multidisciplinary thinking and his masterful command of the language. The arguments and rhetoric of his oral and written presentations were carefully chiseled. He did not leave things to chance. His texts were thoroughly planned, from the general run of the argument down to the detailed wording, and each was carefully adjusted to the target audience. That is how he could reach and captivate such a broad public. This tactic also provoked opposition, however. It fed the minority complexes of his lesser contenders; others suspected so much solicitous rhetoric as disingenuous. Whoever has once debated with von Weizsäcker knows how difficult it was to stand firm against him and how easy it was to become "entangled" in his verbal argument. Von Weizsäcker raised claim to intellectual and moral leadership, but some would criticize that he was a "charmer." How easily he could put forward evidence for his hypotheses, which would hold at least for the duration of his disputation! The longer one considered such contentions, however, the more doubts would creep in. What exactly had been proven? A seeming proof would tend to fade into contention, suggestion, if not mere subtle insinuation. Thus, it is surprising that hitherto—as far as I can see—the rhetorical style of Carl Friedrich von Weizsäcker has not been examined more closely. This essay intends to address (but, clearly, not yet to close) this gap in the research, while, at the same time, making it accessible to an international audience by means of faithful English translations of the primary texts analyzed.

My guild of historians of science unfortunately tends to be averse to analyses of rhetorical style. Thus, von Weizsäcker's speeches and writings have yet to be thoroughly analyzed from the rhetorical point of view. Some monographs and collections of essays on rhetoric in the natural sciences do exist (see, e.g., Gross 1990 and 2006, Myers 1990, Moss 1993, Fahnestock 1999, Ceccarelli 2001). They examine, among other things, the copious rhetorics in the writings of Galileo, Einstein, or Schrödinger. Overall, though, the bias still dominates to limit any historical analysis of scientific works authored by scientists to their content and historical contexts. By contrast, it is a matter of course that all texts penned by literary writers be subjected to the full arsenal of linguistic and rhetorical probings. The scientists themselves practically never mention this level, incidentally. We can even quote von Weizsäcker on this, at the beginning of his speech on language in a series of talks before the Bavarian Academy of Sciences in 1959. He alludes to his own abstention from broaching the topic in a playfully altered verse of Goethe:[1]

| | |
|---|---|
| Mein Freund, Du hast den Braten gerochen | My friend, you've smelt the beef |
| Ich habe nie über die Sprache gesprochen. | 'Bout speech ne'er did I speak. |
| (Weizsäcker 1971, 106; reprint in Weizsäcker 1981b, 39–41) | |

Having (almost) never *spoken* about speech, even about his own, does not mean that von Weizsäcker never *thought* about it. Quite the contrary. This modification of Goethe's verse demonstrates how masterfully he could make use of the full linguistic repertory to express his thoughts. This verse—even more so Goethe's original, where the subject is thought, not speech—hints at the philosophical problem of disturbing any thinking about the process of thinking by means of thought.[2] Similarly, von Weizsäcker does not necessarily always consciously reflect on his use of language.[3] Even if much in his writings took shape quasi-automatically by virtue of his confident style and great linguistic proficiency, it is still legitimate—if not essential—to take a look at these texts specifically from this perspective of stylistic rhetoric.

Let me eliminate one possible misunderstanding at the outset. This approach to von Weizsäcker from the perspective of language and rhetoric (rather than by subject matter) is not an attempt at presenting scientific content by way of stylistic analysis. This is unfortunately occasionally done when rhetorical analyses of scientific texts claim to expose such texts as "mere rhetoric" to characterize science as a social construct or as sheer power play by other means. Far be it from me to reduce science to rhetoric alone. My entire output in the history of science to date is sufficient proof of that. However, I would not deny interdependencies between form and content of a text, and I do detect rhetorical facets in many texts written by scientists. Wherever such an interdependence occurs multiply—for instance, as a recurrent stylistic device—this finding becomes historically interesting. It could open new avenues to a person no longer living among us.

The great numbers of preserved sources on von Weizsäcker, in the form of texts, images and acoustical recordings, beckon. As we shall soon see, this approach does yield some fruit. We shall start by investigating conspicuous general traits of von Weizsäcker's style, taking into account conscious as well as unconscious ones along with aspects of speech and argumentation. Only in rare cases will sources such as private letters allow proof that certain features were chosen explicitly with rhetorics in mind (see below for an example from the correspondence with the scholar Staiger). Intercomparison of von Weizsäcker's multifarious texts also helps further in this regard. Other publications have treated in greater depth further correlations pertaining to his public persona, or "habitus," and the mentality of associated groups.[4]

Why is this approach particularly suitable for Carl Friedrich von Weizsäcker? Among the twentieth-century scientists I have looked at, few can boast such thoroughly planned and polished writings. This applies to his major lengthy textbooks, with print runs of up to 100,000 copies and translations in many of the world languages, just as much as to his shorter articles, his sermons, verses, or speeches as well as to his correspondence not actually intended for publication. However, an ample and interesting selection of his letters was published during his lifetime, in 2002. All these various types of writings were stylistically "composed," some of them extremely finely, by an author with a quite indisputable feel for verbal expression and a rich inventory of stylistic tools. As we shall likewise soon demonstrate, they were in many cases consciously and carefully employed to cater to concrete groups.[5] To that extent, von Weizsäcker's texts are unusually promising for an analysis of rhetorical style, and I am surprised how little this has been noticed and investigated up to now.

The arguments presented in favor of this approach thus far could perhaps be described as "sufficient." Now, however, I would also like to plead for their "necessity." Only thus are we going to be able to understand this scholar's great impact among professional as well as nonscientific circles. It is most intimately connected with this verbal elegance. Without his perfected language, von Weizsäcker could not have fulfilled his "civic role" as a "'nuclear weapons philosopher' and a sought-after society and peace analyst"[6] in the heavily mined no man's land between science, philosophy, and politics. The adherents of this "universal man of our day" would say that, thanks to his clear exposition purposefully free of foreign words, his writings were accessible to people of all age groups and walks of life.[7] His critics would protest that this catchy, seemingly simple verbal form caused particularly many people to "fall into the trap" of this "enlightened mystic," chameleon or, at very least, grand simplifier.[8] The journalist Johannes Gross complained in the *Frankfurter Allgemeine Zeitung* of October 9, 1981, about the "distinguished pompous prose of great facility" that was "as deep as it was hollow"[9] and even mocked von Weizsäcker's demeanor as it was being "marketed" in countless photographs in the press:

> The deeply set eye of a Pietist, the turned-down corners of the mouth, the entire self-staging, demands respect—a grand actor, a model to emulate. Certainly, also an important physicist . . . but hardly a knower and foreseer of the future.[10]

The nuclear physicist Lise Meitner occasionally could not refrain from criticizing "so much mysticism in-between many a very lucid formulation" either, and never was entirely of one mind with her former Berlin colleague.[11]

## Peculiarities of Carl Friedrich von Weizsäcker's Diction and Rhetoric

Let us start by assembling some stylistic and linguistic characteristics that crop up as one reads through von Weizsäcker's addresses—and that are confirmed elsewhere in tape recordings and television clips (see, e.g., Weizsäcker 1992b, a talk in Bamberg that was later also released as a DVD by a local radio-station) of his addresses:

- a very lucid, transparent structure for any given text by him
- an explicit exposition of its architectonics (occasionally, even a justification for it)
- repeated orientation in this structure within the flow of the argument (by such statements as "What have we already shown? What are we setting aside? What remains to be done?")
- conspicuously short, pithy sentences
- a quasi-melodic phraseology and feel for language
- many (rhetorical) questions and turning points in the narrative
- subtle paradoxes as hitches
- the rhetorical juxtaposition of opposite extremes
- followed by "saving" ways out
- well-chosen analogies and metaphors
- construed (Platonic) dialogues, anecdotes and allegories
- equally well construed thought experiments, etc.

It was by no means conventional to lay out the architectonics of an address the way Weizsäcker does in his texts. They are in the form of very detailed tables of contents incorporating not only chapter headings but also many subsections and sometimes especially inserted passages. Orientational paragraphs at the beginning explain the planned course, and other suitably placed ones demarcate the points reached and lay out the further course. Frequent rhetorical questions or temporary interruptions in the flow of the argument at turning points strengthen the reader's impression of being led by an author superior to him in both knowledge and skill.

Von Weizsäcker's extraordinary sense for quasi-melodic phraseology is particularly obvious in his verses and spoonerisms, for instance, the ones he composed during his internment under British control in Farm Hall in 1945 (cf. Hoffmann 1993). He was well-known for peppering a conversation with them at appropriate points, for the general amusement of his friends. Weizsäcker's relatives and acquaintances report that in a playful mood he was able to produce such verses spontaneously.[12] Here is one of his notorious limericks:[13]

| | |
|---|---|
| Es waren zehn Forscher in Farm Hall | There were once ten scientists at Farm Hall |
| Die galten als fürchterlich harmvoll, | They counted as terribly harmful, |
| Beim jüngsten Gericht | On Judgment Day |
| Erschienen sie nicht, | They stayed away, |
| Denn sie saßen noch immer in Farm Hall. | 'Cause they were still stuck at Farm Hall. |

Notice his playful fabrication of the word "harmvoll" (in German more properly "schädlich") to make it rhyme. At the same time, it forms a chiasmus because the capital letters of "Farm Hall" follow in reverse order ("harmful"). "Gericht" and "nicht" ("Day" and "away") rhyme imperfectly and the reiteration of "Farm Hall" right at the end is an epiphora to round off the whole thing.

Another limerick von Weizsäcker repeatedly used was passed on to me by members of his family;[14] it is about the philosophy of science:

| | |
|---|---|
| Es füllte der Geist einst das Segel | Spirit once filled up the mainsail |
| der Deutschen von Kant bis zu Hegel | of Germans from Kant to Hegel |
| und noch bis zu Nietzsche, | and still up to Nietzsche, |
| doch jetzt herrscht das Gequietsche | yet now there's but screechen', |
| der Sucht nach Methode und Regeln. | besotted by method and labels. |

EXAMPLES

We begin our examples of Carl Friedrich von Weizsäcker's style with the most elementary observation: astonishingly succinct, pithy sentence structure for German prose. It is quite refreshing and sets him apart as an author; it constitutes the first character trait of our focus. Here is an excerpt from the beginning of one of his most widely read works, *Garten des Menschlichen* (first published in 1977):

> The garden of human affairs. What is the topic here? Humanity, hence about the human being, hence about ourselves. But we humans are perpetually talking about ourselves. So let's not talk about ourselves now. Let's not express our wishes in the self-confident manner of that daily and political routine, or pass judgment on ourselves and our fellow human beings: We are suspicious of this self-confidence. We seek detachment from ourselves. We seek detachment for the sake of truth.[15]

If we count the subordinate clauses separated by commas as separate units, we obtain for this passage an average of some 5.8 words/unit—ultra-short for typical academic prose. This short excerpt is structured further by means of an anaphora in the third sentence (the two-fold "hence," in the mode of a logical deduction), followed by a six-fold anaphora, introduced each time by the first-person plural "we" or "us" ("wir" or "uns"), followed by a verb. This stylistic device of purposefully setting clauses in parallel appears in poetic passages of the Old Testament, as well as in sermons or mathematical proofs. Von Weizsäcker employs it also in entirely different contexts. For example, this anaphora in his letter to Emil Staiger on the occasion of his seventieth birthday in February 1978:

> A person is very dear to you, you feel elementarily at ease in his company, you've learned very much from him, think much of his judgment, exchange fragments of a Goethe verse reconstructed from memory across the dinner table and find it finer and almost more serious than earnest occupation with the so-called problems of the world;—and then, on the occasion of some date in the calendar, you're supposed to put all of this in a well-phrased speech; then you're at a loss for words. Then you resort to the familiar literary figure about why one cannot write; and that's how this address comes about.[16]

The longer subordinate clause about the joint effort to reconstruct a poem from memory, the sole passage in this excerpt in which the staccato of short parallel-structured clauses is dropped, gains emphasis by virtue of its placement in such a field of succinctness. The consciously construed contrast lends it additional weight. Furthermore, von Weizsäcker admits here outright that he does specifically employ rhetorical figures of speech, such as here the topos of writing about something ineffable. Thus, the conceivable argument is discounted that such characteristics in his style involved an unconscious choice of expressive forms.

Another excerpt out of this same letter to a good friend of his, a scholar of German literature, shows that this author also knows how to implement the melodic line of longer sentences for his own purposes:

> I believe I can fully fathom your way of perceiving things by my own and yet did have the feeling I could perhaps even offer you some assistance if in conversation with you I expressed what I do perceive differently in such a way that it harmonized with your way of perceiving things.[17]

A wonderful example of playful inversion construes a surprising paradox, as a catch or hitch to make its point. It comes from von Weizsäcker's foreword to his technical publication on the effects of nuclear explosions:

> Sometimes the statement hits me:
> Either the technological era will eliminate war,
> or war will eliminate the technological era.[18]

The way the idea is relegated to the final two clauses of the statement, with its rigid either–or structure, transforms it almost into proper verse. The built-in paradox that wars generally don't eliminate eras but rather, at best, trigger them (at least, according to common usage), only strikes one upon reconsidering the message. Thus, the intended point is underscored that sets apart this era of the present day—with all its risks of nuclear war—from all preceding periods. Nevertheless, the epistemological status of the above statement remains unclear: Is he just toying with a thought that "sometimes hits" him? Or is this a serious assertion?—Is it, even, a proof with a rigorous dichotomic decision on a case for which there are no alternatives?

Occasionally, von Weizsäcker developed such paradoxes further into an inner contradiction, an aporia. The following passage from his draft of the Göttingen Manifesto of 1957 (see Lorentz 2011, 125–27, 187, 263–65) is one instance. The West German government headed by Adenauer and Strauß wanted to arm the military with nuclear weapons (some of the co-signers of the manifesto against this policy considered this excerpt excessive and insisted on having it struck from the final text):

> These [atomic] bombs fulfill their purpose only if they are never dropped. If, however, everyone knows that they are never going to be dropped, they don't fulfill their purpose either.[19]

Should it necessarily follow from this aporia that we must forego nuclear armament? Was this a key proof or just a witty remark?

Another formula attributable to von Weizsäcker is more condensed still: the "transformation of erstwhile foreign policy into world domestic policy."[20] This ingenious insight turns the vocabulary upside-down. What had hitherto—throughout centuries of strategic policy-making—appeared to be foreign policy, is henceforth restyled by a philosophical historian into domestic policy of the world. Something that had hitherto been external is internalized. Even the seemingly completely spontaneous remark: "The nuclear shield has holes,"[21] during an interview in June 1972 is at once amusing and highly consternating, because, taken literally, this "dead" metaphor (a "nuclear shield") suddenly regains new vitality. Yet, are these anything more than aptly fitting metaphors?

In some instances, von Weizsäcker would expand uncomfortable alternatives into an aporia to develop his own point, such as in a letter to one of his students:

> If a scientist has become 50 years of age and still understands his students, then he doesn't have any good students. When you become 50 in a couple of years time, you are therefore going to have to choose which unpleasant realization you would prefer to make: that you still understand your students or that you do not understand them.[22]

The first alternative would mean that Meyer-Abich did not have any good students of his own, the second would mean that they had outgrown him intellectually: neither of these two alternatives is particularly "pleasant." The actual positive connotation of the ability to understand is inverted in the assessment to become an indicator of a negative connotation. Obversely, not being able to understand anymore, actually a deeply unsettling circumstance, turns into the reassuring guarantee of the quality of a student. Nonetheless: What follows from this beyond a smile from the person being addressed, in acknowledgment of the success of a profound quip?

Rhetorically posed oppositions dominate countless other passages of von Weizsäcker's oeuvre. Here is just one example, also taken from his foreword to *Kernexplosionen*:

> The inclination to inform oneself is strangely weak for many people of our time. The reasons apparently come from opposite directions. Nuclear war is not going to take place, says the optimist. So why should I trouble myself about it? If a nuclear war does take place, then everything is done for, says the pessimist. Why should I study ahead of time how we are going to perish?[23]

This rhetorical juxtaposition of contrasting positions is followed without fail by a "saving" way out. It can only be found if the extreme positions are abandoned, which both don't lead in the desired direction:

> In truth, optimism and pessimism mean two varieties of the same fault. . . . Nuclear war is not impossible precisely because optimists and pessimists together create a state of mental repression and lethargy in which people do not do the reasonable thing that they could very well do.[24]

At this point, in support of this middle course, von Weizsäcker presents an allegory that gives the whole matter an almost existential turn:

> Let me retell an old story a little differently. Three frogs fell into a barrel of milk: one optimist, one pessimist, and one rationalist.
> The optimist said: "What a pretty pond!" He dropped down into the milk, it clogged up his gullet and lungs and he drowned.
> The pessimist said: "I'm going to drown, and nothing can save me!" He also drowned.
> The rationalist realized that the pessimist was right and saw no way out either, but he didn't give up. He tredded for hours on end, until he felt a soft but solid mass under his feet. He had churned the milk into butter. It gave him a foothold. He hopped out of the barrel and was saved.[25]

The allegorical form disguises the fact that there is no strictly logical basis for choosing the third course and that other courses could also exist that are not addressed at all. Is rationality really the sole alternative to optimism and pessimism? Von Weizsäcker's prose assigns to these highly construed alternatives and solutions the status of absolute inevitability. I see this as his typical rhetoric in action. It circumvents constraints and smoothes over gaps in the argument. In these types of passages there is a "misleading" element for the inattentive reader, who will perhaps much later be astonished at how convinced he had been to accept everything without realizing it and not to immediately object.

Another stylistic device that Carl Friedrich von Weizsäcker liked to use, and effectively so, was the analogy or comparison. A short but sweet example is his comparison of mathematics to poetry—two not exactly closely related fields. They are linked together by a sophisticated remote analogy,[26] in which the "higher precision of expression" in von Weizsäcker's train of thought turns out to be the *tertium comparationis*:

> The difficulty among philosophers is that they often cite our assertions, formulated in 'prose,' without understanding the associated 'poetry,' namely, the mathematics. Other definitions from what we meant then sneak in unnoticed.
> (This comparison between mathematics and poetry appeals to me because I have the feeling that both excel in higher precision of expression above everyday prose. Philosophy attains the same precision only in a few places, where for that very reason it becomes entirely incomprehensible to the so-called normal person.)[27]

By the way, this passage also illustrates how perceptive von Weizsäcker was to shifts in meaning and equivocations becoming the source of incomprehension. For the sake of lucidity, he was even willing to pay the high price of inserting "linguistic clarifications" or definitions of unavoidable technical terminology (cf. Köhler 1992, 75–77, 214–15). He consistently avoided jargon. The opposition between the "normal" person and an enlightened élite, which appears right at the end of the quote, is characteristic. Von Weizsäcker obviously counted himself among the latter. He was fully aware of the irresolvable tension between what is of general interest and the esoteric subtleties of many of the points he addressed:

> I naturally am somehow moved and honored at the great numbers in which you have appeared; and have . . . the problem . . . that I must presume that if I recount what I would actually have had to present to my colleagues in physics, there are very many here who would then not find it exactly what they would consider as particularly comprehensible.[28]

Carl Friedrich von Weizsäcker was keenly interested in elevated intellectual exchanges—not just with people whose views he shared. He certainly also liked to confront advocates of a contrary opinion. He enjoyed a good debate. His response to what he would have asked Plato if he had ever had the chance to meet him is interesting. It emphasizes in particular the open-endedness of such a conversation:

> If I should ever meet Plato in Hades, I would approach him with a gesture of cheerful respect and relatively soon offer to tell him a little about Heisenberg's physics. That would undoubtedly interest him, since he had written *Timaeous*. . . . That is how I would initiate a conversation with him at his prompting. I do not know where the conversation would ultimately lead us.[29]

One of his coworkers at the Starnberg Institute, Tilman Spengler, put it this way: Carl Friedrich von Weizsäcker "wasn't a know-all, but he did relish having gotten another thinker into a form of temporary uncertainty"[30]—hence, he was a kind of twentieth-century Socrates. Just as in a "political game of chess," with the two opponents assuming opposing positions and engaging their black or white figures against each other, in abidance by the complex rules of the game, he enjoyed the exchange only if his opponent acted according to the rules and argued on the same plane. In a letter to his fellow physicist Edward Teller, who was politically extremely conservative and upheld quite opposite views (e.g., on the issue of nuclear deterrence), Weizsäcker admonished him to keep to the rules:

> It is evident that we are not going to agree. But that's not even necessary. You have your Hungarian views about Mongols and Russians far too long for me to be able to dissuade you of them. I know these views too long for you to have a chance to convince me of them. One can nevertheless always orientate oneself better from more conversations in the arena of history of philosophy.[31]

The sense and purpose of this debate was not perhaps to persuade the opponent and draw him into his own camp but to improve his own survey by the exchange of arguments and facts. This could only work if his counterpart presented real arguments without stooping to mere emotional outbreaks.[32]

> But if you want my statements not to be such that they work contrary to your intentions . . . , you must put forward arguments that convince me and that I might possibly also be able to use. . . . I'm traveling to see you to learn of arguments: I have known your sentiments for a long time. Perhaps you can consider which arguments you consider expressible.[33]

This matches an observation by the biographer of the Weizsäcker family, Martin Wein:

> In fact, in his personal dealings, Weizsäcker shrank away from opening up completely to others; camaraderie was totally alien to him. Just as in Heisenberg's case, to him friendships were important primarily as opportunities for intellectual exchange.[34]

Notwithstanding the curiosity and distinguished amiability that the baron extended even to persons entirely unknown to him (for instance, to me when we first met at the Heisenberg conference at Leipzig in 1991), every one of his counterparts in conversation had to reckon with his penetrating, testing glances and a perceptible *reservatio mentalis* that he himself expressed very well in the following passage:

> In forming my opinion, I must everywhere rely not only on my assessment of the subject matter, but also essentially on my judgment of people. About each of my counterparts in conversation I have to form an opinion on his level of knowledgeability, his particular interests, his passions and degree of his intelligence, his self-criticism and his sincerity.[35]

## On Carl Friedrich von Weizsäcker's Career and *Habitus*

Having diplomats among his immediate family members certainly had a major influence on Carl Friedrich von Weizsäcker's style of thinking and general deportment.[36] He was the eldest son of the naval officer and diplomat Ernst von Weizsäcker, who was highly placed in the Foreign Ministry (*Staatssekretär* 1938–43) during the Weimar Republic and the Nazi period, and was sent as ambassador to Basel and Copenhagen, where Carl Friedrich attended school.[37] This offspring from the upper bourgeoisie, consequently, was raised from the cradle, so to speak, to think carefully before speaking or acting.[38] It was good preparation for his later role as advisor to Chancellors Willy Brandt and Helmut Schmidt. The following points are part of this mental diplomatic baggage that the son of a baron carried around with himself and colored his habitus throughout his life:

- "understanding" and "sympathetic grasping" of even contradictory positions (in close resonance with Bohr's principle of complementarity)
- no commitment to any one of these stances
- careful, unambiguous formulation of one's own standpoint
- at the same time, a lasting reserve and aloofness toward everyone
- no unrestrained revelation of one's own position
- mastery of odds by scaling the step toward the next "higher plane," that is, elitism (not presumptuously or conceitedly, but as a "specially elect,"[39] natural endowment)
- connecting remote chains of reasoning
- intellectual brilliance and rapid grasp of obstacles, core problems and suitable strategies to solve them

What emerges out of these points leads almost as a matter of course to the roles of spokesman and mediator. It fell upon him time and again, for instance, during his internment at Farm Hall after the war (see, e.g., Frank 1993 and Hoffmann 1993), as well as in drawing up the Manifesto of the "Göttingen 18" in 1957 (see Lorentz 2011, 125–27, 187, 263–65). This disposition explains why he did not give up his hopes of assuming a leadership and advisory role "near the levers of power" even during the Nazi era. This almost self-evident expectation of his conforms with von Weizsäcker's orientation in line with Plato's ideal of the impartial philosopher, standing above ordinary things, as the ruler's councilor. When prospects of building an atomic bomb began to appear realistic, von Weizsäcker was interested in it as a weapon "that no one can prevent from being traded" and that could serve as his key to the centers of power, to the uppermost leadership at Hitler's side.

He believed that his own expertise could steer Hitler—which was, of course, a fatal mistake, as Weizsäcker himself later admitted.[40]

In von Weizsäcker's view, scientists, and especially physicists, had a different status *per se* from other people. He justified this conviction as follows:

> I don't want to underscore particularly the position of scientists above other people; I would think that we are about as good or evil as other people. But simply the fact that we saw these consequences somewhat earlier than other people—because we could, of course, foresee them before they occurred—made us perhaps feel the shock about the forces being released there somewhat earlier than others. . . . nevertheless I would definitely like to say that on average especially the important scientists thought about the consequences of their actions and the moral responsibility attached to them much more and are much more deeply worried about it than the majority of people.[41]

The elite among atomic and nuclear physicists had a very prominent status in this view of von Weizsäcker's, to which he could entirely justifiably count himself, as a longtime coworker of Werner Heisenberg and member of the nuclear research group Uranverein, even if they, for their part, did not always perceive him as such.

> We atomic physicists in all the nations on Earth were the first to realize already in 1939 . . . that henceforth nuclear weapons would become possible. Many of us realized then already that given the existing structures of humanity . . . the building of such weapons could not be prevented practically. This necessarily drove our thoughts in the direction of seeing that in the long run the sole solution is to overcome the institution of war. This was my opinion already in 1939, and it still is my opinion today.[42]

The repeated use of the pronouns "we," "us," and "our" in the foregoing quotation is conspicuous. Contrary to reality, it implies the existence of a coherent group of physicists united by a common agenda and the same attitude. In truth, a tooth-and-nail battle was going on between the various groups of physicists in Germany, in the bitter struggle over scarce resources.[43]

What Carl Friedrich von Weizsäcker is doing here is *boundary work* in Thomas Gieryn's (1983) meaning: constructing a purportedly coherent social group and patching up cracks and zones of conflict with empty "us against them" phrases. He situates himself at the head of this movement—true to his leadership claim (see above). "This was my opinion already in 1939" (not putting in words but insinuating: as one of the first). At Farm Hall he was the first to recognize the far-reaching political implications of the dropping of the atomic bombs above Hiroshima and Nagasaki, as the preserved transcripts of conversations held at the time show. Over there, at Farm Hall in 1945–46, he became a kind of mediator between the camps of opportunistic pragmatists (among others, Gerlach and Harteck), the more-or-less sworn Nazi party-liners (Diebner and Bagge), and the fundamental researchers who considered themselves apolitical (Hahn, Heisenberg, and von Laue). Carl Friedrich von Weizsäcker's careful weighing of the arguments yielded that apologetic compromise currently under so much discussion, alleging that atomic-bomb development in Germany had been purposefully held back. On that formulation, the bickering Farm Hall internees could agree (see the translated transcripts of secretly recorded conversations at Farm Hall published in Frank 1993, and Hoffmann 1993).

Situations did, of course, exist in which even von Weizsäcker's great diplomatic facility hit its limit, for instance, during his period at the University of Hamburg during the late 1960s. Michael Drieschner reminisced:

> I still remember very well the "tribunal" session of rebellious students that intended to pass public judgment specifically on Weizsäcker's conduct and had invited him to attend. He actually did appear at the meeting and defended himself with very adept diplomacy against the student tribunalists, who were no match for him on that score.... But one did notice the immense effort this diplomacy cost him, confronted by the totally antidiplomatic, emphatically coarse behavior of the rest of the participants in the debate, which in view of his own manners and custom was visibly repulsive and exhausting for him.[44]

He found similar debates with his younger team members at the Starnberg Institute during the 1970s no easier to handle: sociologists, philosophers, and physicists wanting to test out new ideas of the 1968 movement.

> Weizsäcker was mostly the more diplomatically adroit debater but it was obviously straining and most distasteful to him. He certainly could understand the criticism expressed by those leftist students [and coworkers] against the real circumstances; the style was just so very contrary to his nature and he was at least as skeptical of the hoped-for solution to the problems proposed by the leftists as of those by their conservative opponents.[45]

One common characteristic in these and many other quoted passages and recollections is his tendency to rise above worldly strife, his attempt to transcend the quarrel between contending parties and seek an élitist metaposition beyond the zones of conflict. Whenever he was personally attacked by any individual combatant, his response was harsh and coldly repellent. This letter to a young woman protester in the campaign against nuclear energy in 1988 is one example:

> My first reaction is that, as I see it, demonizing the opponent never contributes toward a solution to the problems. I fear that although your letter shows that you really are concerned, precisely because of the indignation it conveys, it can be of very little use toward solving the problems.[46]

I find it remarkable that so many people sought to argue with von Weizsäcker, even when—as in this instance—true agreement was difficult and unlikely from the outset. Perhaps such discussions had some kind of psycho-therapeutic or cathartic effect. His role was then often that of a priest or sage,[47] whose advice, goodwill, and patience one could count on,[48] even if he was of a totally different opinion.

My impression is that Carl Friedrich von Weizsäcker's practical acknowledgment of a polyphony of opinions succeeded in the area of theology and religion. He carried on fruitful dialogues with members of diverse faiths, ranging from Christianity to Islam, Hinduism and Buddhism. He vigorously rejected exclusive claims to truth and wisdom by any given sect.

> [A]t fifteen years of age [came] the loss of my childhood faith, from the outset recognized as irrevocable, that is, henceforth I could only really accept whatever falls within the scope of a multiplicity of religions and unreligious views that I could confirm by my own experience or at least could regard as credible. . . . however, the exclusivity presented in the Christian Trinity doctrine is something that I basically cannot follow.[49]

By this inclination to escape clashing opposites by fleeing onto a metalevel, von Weizsäcker occasionally ran the risk of letting his own stance become unrecognizably blurred. The following excerpt is one instance. This essay, dated 1981, posed the rhetorical question: "Are we approaching a world culture of asceticism?"

> The bounds of reason in technocracy lie in that the rationality of the ends does not equal the rationality of the means serving them. The bounds of reason in protest lie in that protest just stays bound to the object of protest.[50]

This—in my view hardly convincing—rhetorical contrast made between technocracy and protest is directly succeeded by another subtitle, followed by the constraint:

> This essay was not written in order to propose models for solving our problems in economic policy, but in order to consider an attitude for the assessment of such models.[51]

We cannot fault von Weizsäcker for not having a finished model at the ready to solve every pressing problem. On the contrary, his frank confession not to be able to offer such solutions rather works in his favor. What is strange is his counterproposal: not "an attitude for the assessment of such models," but, more cautiously still, merely one "to consider."

At the end of the day, the irreconcilable opposition between technocracy and protest (as if there were no other intermediary forms) is swapped for an, at best, vaguely discernible way out of "democratic asceticism"—in other words, robbing Peter to pay Paul. This suits the essay's flowery conclusion, something between priestly good words and an oracular horoscope:

> The energy for such solutions only presupposes that one think of them and that one want them. One cannot want anything sensible, though, without self-restraint.[52]

How true! How almost tautologically true! Yet, how noncommittal, at the same time. This structurally defined weakness of von Weizsäcker's texts is possibly related to what his biographer Dieter Hattrup has called the "enigma of this person's present nonpresence, worthy of a sphinx."[53] Benno Parthier, then president of the German Academy of Sciences, put it in the form of a question in the preface to the volume reproducing all of Carl Friedrich von Weizsäcker's Leopoldina talks given in its annual meetings between 1965 and 1993: "How many enthusiastic listeners of your chiseled speeches will admit that enthusiasm is only of limited use in approaching the unattainable?"[54]

Despite great public success as an author and a good reception by the press, despite high print-runs for his books and much acclaim, Carl Friedrich von Weizsäcker's impact had little lasting effect specifically in professional publications—neither in physics nor in philosophy.[55] Hattrup relates this paradox to his typical role as a kind of "sage," who is pleasant to listen to without necessarily having to believe him or follow his advice:

> We want to listen to you but we don't want to do what you say. Listening to you in the "role of the venerable sage" has to suffice as action.[56]

It is difficult to identify the reason behind this noticeable lack of a dedicated popular following developing out of his broad readership. Presenting a finished philosophical system was not von Weizsäcker's ultimate aim.[57]

It was rather to demonstrate the "movement of thinking"; the process of seeking and testing, not the final result. His choice of the cyclical "round tour"[58] as his favorite thought motif agrees with this, which he explained in *Zeit und Wissen*:

> The round tour was, from the outset, not just meant as a literary tool but as a philosophical, methodological principle, as an alternative to the assumption of any 'hierarchical' philosophy that hopes to set out from a single unshakable foundation, whether it be experience or the certainty of the consciousness.[59]

Such a circuit was an evidence-generating tool for von Weizsäcker. On various occasions he even explicitly asserted that some insights, and in particular a correct overview, could only be gained by such a mental round tour, whereas other methods only offered distorted partial views:

> According to this interpretation of physics, a picture of that which we call reality can only be drawn, if at all, in a round tour.[60]

To illustrate by another example just how central and important this figure of the circular train of thought was to von Weizsäcker, let us take a look at his round tour from nature to mankind to science and back:

> With regard to science, the round tour has the precondition: Nature is older than man; man is older than science. Setting out from natural history, we shall attempt to understand man; from the history of mankind, the way in which he understands nature. One must walk around the circuit many times. Precisely for that reason is it possible to step into it anywhere along the way around.[61]

Experiencing such "thinking in motion" is impressive but does not convey any stable final results that can be remembered or concretely implemented. The still youthful Carl Friedrich already apologized to the auditors of his course in summer 1948 that he cannot "offer secure results" but can "only invite you to enter with me upon a particular movement of thought," in search of truths, and in this struggle broach much, yet without thinking it through to the end. He was able to offer "not more than a hint on many points."[62] The "unity of physics" and the "unity of nature," which are concepts he placed on the title pages of two of his works (Weizsäcker 1967; 1981b) and never stopped reaffirming, remained unattained. Weizsäcker perceived, for instance, the "collected papers" in *Einheit der Natur* "as members of one unit," but this unfortunate formulation already shows that this form remained an "externally confused way." He had to admit: "I have not managed, however, to present the ideas on the unity of nature in a systematic form."⁶³ Instead of concentrating on gathering the "harvest" of a rich life, the elderly Weizsäcker just continued to offer further "round tours" through the *Garten des Menschlichen*, picking up the odd fruit along the way, more like a connoisseur passing through the "garden" from one corner to another, than like a purposeful gatherer.⁶⁴

## Conclusion

A variety of examples taken from Carl Friedrich von Weizsäcker's available texts indicate that a seamless transition exists between stylistic findings on his language, style, and rhetoric, and the argumentative structure of his texts with the appropriate habitus. His texts aim at finding a grand synthesis. They adopt a distinguished ethos. They polysemously address various target audiences. They make refined use of metaphor and analogy. These components make them resemble texts written by other scientists that effectively reached an interdisciplinary public.⁶⁵ Von Weizsäcker's firm grip on his audience or reader is signaled by his numerous excursive references to the outline of the given text, by rhetorically posed questions, by explicit pointers to crossroads and alternatives calling for decisions. One characteristic figure of his is the "round tour" (*Kreisgang*), occasionally also referred to as a "circuit" (*Umlauf*): a number of points are mentally walked through, often many times over, in a kind of spiral motion, with somewhat more lucidity gained by each circuit through the examined terrain, even if it seems as if one has come full circle, arriving back at the same starting point. All the afore-mentioned rhetorical and linguistic turns of phrase were means to construct evidence to impress the audience and smooth over gaps in the argument.

Weizsäcker used his superior knowledge and linguistic and rhetorical skill to full effect and throughout implicitly developed his claim to leadership of his trusting audience. This habitus conforms with his aristocratic upbringing and natural air of authority, with which he was able to charm millions of people over the course of his life. This deportment should not be taken for arrogance or emotional indifference—on the contrary, he genuinely and deeply wanted to understand others. He never passed up on a debate held on a higher intellectual plane, employing his characteristic means of careful argument and finished form. He even seemed to enjoy such an altercation in his own particular way, like playing a challenging game. For all his delight in the heat of a debate well fought, which radiates from his correspondence with Edward Teller, for example, one does nevertheless notice that he stubbornly insisted on his own positions against critics or opponents and seems to have viewed such exchanges with the seriousness of a chess match.⁶⁶ His perceptible ambition to maintain his advantage and preserve his leadership role closely resembles his mentor Werner Heisenberg. On difficult points, where arguments alone could bring one no further, Carl Friedrich von Weizsäcker tended to toy with contrasts, reworking or transcending them.⁶⁷ References to Bohrian complementarity or to an ecumenical diversity of conceivable standpoints served him as a springboard onto the metalevel, his favorite retreat when he was tired of arguing or was still perhaps a little unsure of his own position. He was a master constructor of rhetorical evidence,⁶⁸ a sure navigator through the shoals of his challenging topics.⁶⁹

## Notes

1. Goethe's original verse is: "Mein Kerl, ich hab es klug gemacht / ich habe nie über das Denken gedacht." ("My fellow, I used my wits, / 'Bout thought ne'er did I think."); here and in the following, any translations not specifically referenced from existing translations are my own. To improve readability, most of the original German quotes are given within the endnotes. A nearly complete bibliography of von Weizsäcker's writings is available online at: http://www.cfvw.org/stiftung/images/stories/downloads/Z_2.1_Bibliographie_INT_Weizsaecker.pdf

2. An analogously constructed paradox that you cannot think about your own thinking without disturbing the latter forms the basis of a text by the Danish thinker Poul Martin Møller, *En dansk Students Eventyr*, that had once inspired von Weizsäcker's mentor Niels Bohr to come up with his physical principle of complementarity. It touches on an important point also in von Weizsäcker's philosophy and is a good example of "polysemous textual construction" in the meaning of Leah Ceccarelli (2001, 5, 163–64). Those familiar with Bohr's philosophy will infer different meanings as compared to other readers, who are perhaps rather amused by the paradoxical tautology.

3. Bohr tended to say to Aage Petersen: "vir hänger i sproget" ("We're snared in language.") See von Weizsäcker's comments printed in Köhler (1992, 152).

4. See Hentschel (2007) on the mentality of German-speaking physicists after 1945. That study incorporates some sources by and on von Weizsäcker, but looks for common traits among numerous physicists of the period rather than sketching individual portraits; see also Hentschel and Hoffmann (2014) on von Weizsäcker's habitus in connection with his rhetorics.

5. See, for example, von Weizsäcker in the foreword to *Deutlichkeit* (Weizsäcker 1981a, 7): "as the audiences differ, and consequently the diction in which I attempted to address each is also different." ("da die Adressatenkreise verschieden sind und folglich auch die jeweilige Diktion verschieden ist, in der ich versucht habe, sie anzureden.") On this aspect see also the obituary on von Weizsäcker by the politician Erhard Eppler (2007) of the Social Democratic

Party. Cathryn Carson (2003) has demonstrated such fine-tuning in von Weizsäcker's postwar lectures held within the context of the *Studium generale* at Göttingen University. They catered to an audience with little prior education owing to the war but avid to catch up.

6. "zivilgesellschaftliche Rolle" als "'Atomwaffenphilosoph' und gern gefragter Gesellschafts- und Friedensanalytiker." Quotes from Zacher (2008, 24), resp. Lorenz (2011, 98, 352–53).

7. Between 1946 and the 1990s, von Weizsäcker's speeches were downright euphorically received in Germany; see Hattrup (2004, 9) or Köhler (1992, 8). For an example within the scientific community, see Lise Meitner's report about an address delivered in the Harnack Haus in a letter to Max von Laue, dated 22 Nov. 1942, in Lemmerich (1998, 235–37): "The auditors were, without exception, greatly impressed." (Underscoring in the original.) "Universalgelehrten unserer Zeit" is a quote out of the obituary by Zacher (2008, 23).

8. Translations of quotes ("aufgeklärter Mystiker" / "auf den Leim gingen") of a colleague friend of mine who would rather not be named.

9. ". . . tiefe wie hohle distinguierte Imponierprosa von großer Fertigkeit."

10. "Das tiefliegende Pietistenauge, der herabgezogene Mundwinkel, die ganze Selbstinszenierung nötigt Respect ab – ein großer Darsteller, ein Vor-Bild. Gewiß auch ein bedeutender Physiker . . . ein Zukunftskenner und -seher . . . aber kaum."

11. "so viel Mystik zwischen manchen sehr klaren Formulierungen," in her letters to Max von Laue dated 25 Jul. and 9 Jan. 1944, published in Lemmerich (1998, 385, 341). When von Weizsäcker delivered a talk at the Deutsches Elektron Synchrotron (DESY) on 22 Nov. 1984, which I also attended, similar skepticism prevailed among the high-energy physicists present as well as among other scientific specialists.

12. See, for example, Spengler (2007, no. 8): "eine angenehm befremdliche Liebe zu Kalauern" ("a pleasantly uncanny love of puns").

13. This limerick is also cited, for example, in Schirach 2012, and in the review of this book in *Frankfurter Allgemeine Zeitung*, 3. Jan. 2013 („An der Bombe vorbei"), as well as online at http://newfilmkritik.de/archiv/2013-02/beim-jungsten-gericht-erschienen-sie-nicht. Accessed November 22, 2017.

14. My cordial thanks to Elisabeth, Christian, and Heinreich von Weizsäcker, who attended the conference at Halle and made helpful comments at some of the presentations.

15. "Der Garten des Menschlichen. Wovon soll die Rede sein? Vom Menschlichen, also vom Menschen, also von uns selbst. Aber wir Men-

schen reden unablässig über uns selbst. So wollen wir jetzt nicht über uns reden. Wir wollen nicht in der selbstsicheren Weise des Alltags und der Politik unsere Wünsche äußern, unsere Urteile abgeben über uns und die Mitmenschen. Wir sind mißtrauisch gegen diese Selbstsicherheiten. Wir suchen Distanz zu uns selbst. Wir suchen die Distanz um der Wahrheit willen." (Weizsäcker [1977] 1980, 11).

16. "Man hat einen Menschen sehr gerne, fühlt sich in seiner Gegenwart elementar wohl, hat viel von ihm gelernt, gibt viel auf sein Urteil, tauscht mit ihm quer über den Abendessenstisch Bruchstücke eines aus der Erinnerung zu rekonstruierenden Goethegedichtchens aus und findet das schöner und beinahe ernsthafter als die seriöse Beschäftigung mit den sogenannten Problemen der Welt—und dann soll man das anläßlich eines Kalenderdatums in eine wohlgesetzte Rede bringen, dann verschlägt es einem die Sprache. Dann wählt man die bekannte literarische Figur des Schreibens darüber, warum man nicht schreiben kann, und so kommt diese Äußerung zustande." Quoted from Hora (2002, 120).

17. "Ich glaube alle Gründe Ihrer Wahrnehmungsweise in mir nachvollziehen zu können und hatte doch das Gefühl, ich könnte Ihnen vielleicht sogar noch etwas Hilfe leisten, wenn ich das, was ich anders wahrnehme, im Gespräch mit Ihnen so ausdrückte, daß es mit Ihrer Wahrnehmungsweise harmonisiert." Von Weizsäcker to the expert on German literature Emil Staiger, February 3, 1978, quoted from Hora (2002, 120). The fact that the addressee was a man of letters may well have only encouraged further this particular attention to style.

18. "Manchmal drängt sich mir der Satz auf: Entweder wird das technische Zeitalter den Krieg abschaffen, oder der Krieg wird das technische Zeitalter abschaffen" (Weizsäcker 1961, 12).

19. "Diese [Atom-]Bomben erfüllen ihren Zweck nur, wenn sie nie fallen. Wenn aber jedermann weiß, daß sie nie fallen, dann erfüllen sie ihren Zweck auch nicht." Quoted from Lorenz (2011, 276).

20. "Verwandlung der bisherigen Außenpolitik in Weltinnenpolitik." On the history of this term, which in von Weizsäcker's case can be traced back to his award of the Peace Prize conferred by the German Book Trade in 1963, see Hattrup (2004, 197-98) and Ulrich Bartosch's contribution to Hentschel and Hoffmann (2014).

21. "Der Atomschirm hat Löcher," interview of von Weizsäcker in June 1972 (subsequently published in Weizsäcker 1972).

22. "Wenn ein Wissenschaftler 50 Jahre alt geworden ist, und er versteht seine Schüler noch immer, dann hat er keine guten Schüler. Wenn Sie in ein paar Jahren 50 werden, werden Sie sich also entscheiden müssen, welche unangenehme Feststellung Sie lieber treffen: daß Sie Ihre Schüler

noch verstehen oder daß Sie sie nicht verstehen." Von Weizsäcker to Klaus Michael Meyer-Abich, 17 May 1983, quoted from Hora (2002, 170). It remains open whether von Weizsäcker still understood his own student Meyer-Abich at that time.

23. "Die Neigung, sich zu informieren, ist bei vielen Menschen unserer Zeit merkwürdig gering. Die Gründe dazu kommen aus scheinbar entgegengesetzter Richtung. Der Atomkrieg findet nicht statt, sagt der Optimist; warum soll ich mir also über ihn Sorgen machen? Wenn der Atomkrieg stattfindet, ist alles aus, sagt der Pessimist; warum soll ich vorher studieren, wie wir zugrunde gehen werden?" (Weizsäcker 1961, 7)

24. "In Wahrheit bedeuten Optimismus und Pessimismus zwei Spielarten desselben Fehlers. . . . Der Atomkrieg ist genau deshalb nicht unmöglich, weil Optimisten und Pessimisten gemeinsam einem Zustand seelischer Verdrängung und Lethargie schaffen, in dem die Menschen das Vernünftige nicht tun, das sie sehr wohl tun könnten" (Weizsäcker 1961, 7).

25. "Es sei erlaubt, eine alte Geschichte ein wenig umzudichten. Drei Frösche fielen in ein Milchfaß: ein Optimist, ein Pessimist und ein Vernünftiger. | Der Optimist sagte: 'Welch hübscher Teich!' Er geriet unter die Milch, sie verklebte den Schlund und Lunge und er ertrank. | Der Pessimist sagte: 'Ich werde ertrinken und nichts kann mich retten!' Auch er ertrank. | Der Vernünftige sah, daß der Pessimist recht hatte, und wußte auch keinen Ausweg, aber er gab nicht auf. Er strampelte stundenlang, bis er unter seinen Füßen eine weiche, aber feste Masse fühlte. Er hatte aus der Milch Butter gemacht. Sie bot ihm Widerhalt. Er sprang aus dem Faß und war gerettet." (Weizsäcker 1961, 7). One section in *Die Einheit der Natur* (Weizsäcker 1981b, sec. I.6.2), carries the heading: "Eine Anekdote als Blickfang" ("An anecdote as an eye-catcher.")

26. On analogies and the distinction between close and remote analogies (Nah- und Fernanalogien), see Hentschel (2008).

27. "Die Schwierigkeit bei den Philosophen ist, daß sie sich oft auf unsere in 'Prosa' formulierten Behauptungen berufen, ohne die 'Poesie' dazu, nämlich die Mathematik zu verstehen. Dabei schleichen sich dann unmerklich andere Wortbedeutungen ein, als wir sie gemeint haben. | (Der Vergleich der Mathematik mit der Poesie gefällt mir deshalb, weil ich das Gefühl habe, daß beide durch die höhere Präzision des Ausdrucks von der alltäglichen Prosa ausgezeichnet sind. Dieselbe Präzision erreicht meinem Gefühl nach die Philosophie nur an wenigen Stellen, an denen sie ebendeshalb dem sogenannten normalen Menschen völlig unverständlich wird.)" Von Weizsäcker to Erwin Schrödinger, 20 May 1952, quote from Hora (2002, 9). On analogies as stylistic tools of rhetoric in science, see Gross (1990, 21–32) and Myers (1990).

28. "[I]ch bin natürlich irgendwie gerührt und geehrt über die große Anzahl, in der Sie erschienen sind, und habe . . . das Problem, . . . daß ich vermuten muß, daß, wenn ich dasjenige erzähle, was ich den Fachkollegen in der Physik eigentlich vorzutragen gehabt hätte, ganz viele da sind, die das dann nicht genau als das finden, was sie eigentlich besonders verständlich finden." The opening line of von Weizsäcker's public lecture before the Leopoldina on 22 March 1977; quoted from the transcript of the tape recording in Köhler (1992, 107).

29. "Ich würde, wenn ich Platon in Hades treffen sollte, mit einer Geste heiterer Verehrung ihm gegenüber treten und ihm relativ bald anbieten, ich könnte ihm etwas von Heisenberg's Physik erzählen. Das würde ihn, da er doch den *Timaios* geschrieben hat, ohne Zweifel interessieren. . . . So würde ich in das Gespräch mit ihm eintreten, das er mir anbieten würde. Ich weiss nicht, wohin das Gespräch uns schließlich führen würde." Quoted from Weizsäcker's conversation with Erwin Koller (1987, 36).

30. ". . . kein Rechthaber, doch es behagte ihm schon, einen anderen Denker in eine Form der vorläufigen Ungewißheit versetzt zu haben." Spengler (2007) in his obituary on his former colleague, subordinate point 3 (his example was Martin Heidegger).

31. "[E]s ist evident, daß wir uns nicht einigen werden. Das ist aber auch gar nicht nötig. Du hast Deine ungarischen Ansichten über Mongolen und Russen schon zu lange, als daß ich Dich davon abbringen könnte. Ich kenne diese Ansichten schon zu lange, als daß Du jetzt eine Chance hättest, mich noch davon zu überzeugen. Man kann sich aber trotzdem im geschichtsphilosophischen Feld durch weitere Gespräche immer besser orientieren." Von Weizsäcker to Edward Teller, 30 April 1976, published in full in Hora (2002, 112). This anthology of correspondence is—very fittingly, I think—entitled: "Dear Friends—Dear Foes!" ("Liebe Freunde – Liebe Gegner!")

32. See furthermore Edward Teller's interesting article on "understanding" ("Das Verstehen") in Meyer-Abich (1982, 55–64), where the personality differences between him and von Weizsäcker come out very clearly: Teller, on the side of thorough knowledge, somewhat fearful of making a mistake; von Weizsäcker, striving for "breadth and tolerance," albeit—Teller does not say this explicitly but does clearly imply it—thereby remaining less precise, less pointed and far less sure of himself.

33. "Wenn Du aber willst, daß meine Äußerungen nicht so sind, daß Sie Deinen Absichten . . . entgegenwirken, so mußt Du Argumente vorbringen, die mich überzeugen und die ich womöglich auch verwenden kann. . . . Ich reise zu Dir, um Argumente zu lernen: Deine Stimmung kenne ich seit langem. Vielleicht kannst Du Dir überlegen, welche Argu-

mente Du für aussprechbar hältst." Von Weizsäcker to Edward Teller, 30 April 1976, quoted from Hora (2002, 112); see also Spengler (2007, no. 3).

34. "Tatsächlich scheute Weizsäcker im persönlichen Umgang davor zurück, sich anderen ganz zu öffnen, und Kumpanei war ihm völlig fremd. Freundschaften hatten für ihn, wie im Fall Heisenberg, vor allem als Möglichkeiten des geistigen Austauschs Bedeutung" (Wein 1988, 424). This also agrees with Wolfgang Pauli's complaint subsequent to the conferral of von Weizsäcker's postdoctoral degree (*Habilitation*) in Leipzig in 1936, about his "moral superiority respecting his own faults, that [were] legitimized neither by his age nor by his achievements to date" ("moralische Erhabenheit gegenüber eigenen Fehlern, die weder durch sein Alter noch durch seine bisherigen Leistungen gerechtfertigt").

35. "Ich bin überall bei meiner Meinungsbildung nicht nur auf mein Urteil über Sachen, sondern auch wesentlich auf mein Urteil über Menschen angewiesen. Ich muß mir bei jedem meiner Gesprächspartner selbst eine Meinung darüber bilden, welches sein Kenntnisstand, sein Particularinteresse, seine Leidenschaft, und der Grad seiner Intelligenz, seiner Selbstkritik und seiner Redlichkeit ist." Von Weizsäcker (1981a, 36) on 'nuclear energy' in *Deutlichkeit*.

36. See in this regard Michael Drieschner's (1996, 173–74) contribution to *Wissenschaft & Öffentlichkeit*: "Weizsäcker had worded this manifesto [the Göttingen Manifesto of 18 atomic and nuclear physicists in 1957] with great care, following the diplomatic tradition in which he had grown up."

37. Ernst von Weizsäcker was ambassador of the Third Reich in the Vatican from 1943 and was condemned to incarceration as a war criminal in 1945 in by an Allied tribunal court; see, for example, Wein (1988) as well as the helpful references in Ernst von Weizsäcker's German Wikipedia entry.

38. In his response to essays in Ackermann (1989, 96), von Weizsäcker described going on walks with his father, during which "he just spoke to me about politics and political history because he was a diplomat and a politically interested man. It was the air that the family breathed, so to speak." ("mit mir eben von Politik und politischer Geschichte redete, weil er ein Diplomat war und ein politisch interessierter Mann war. Das war sozusagen die Lebensluft der Familie.") Cf. Lise Meitner's remark about him in a letter to Max von Laue, 24 Dec. 1944; published in Lemmerich (1998, 427): "He unfortunately takes after his father in not always drawing the consequences out of his thinking, who is, you know, let's say, so overly much of a diplomat." ("Daß er im Handeln nicht immer die Konsequenzen

aus seinem Denken zieht, das hat er leider von seinem Vater, der ja, nun, sagen wir, ein gar zu großer Diplomat ist.")

39. Philipp Sonntag aptly described his rare élitist sense of awareness as a kind of self-imposed "duty to high quality in making assertions and acting." See Sonntag (2012) and Hentschel and Hoffmann (2014, 271–73).

40. Cf. von Weizsäcker's *Spiegel* interview, published on 22 Apr. 1991: "I was crazy!" ("Ich war verrückt!") For further details on the background on this see, e.g., Hattrop (2004, 170–71).

41. "Ich möchte nicht etwa den Stand der Wissenschaftler besonders über andere Menschen hervorheben, ich würde denken, daß wir etwa so gut oder schlecht sind wie andere Leute auch. Aber einfach die Tatsache, daß wir etwas früher als die anderen Menschen diese Folgen gesehen haben, weil wir sie ja schon voraussehen konnten, ehe sie eintraten, hat gemacht, daß wir vielleicht etwas früher als die anderen den Schreck darüber erlebt haben, welche Mächte da entfesselt werden. . . . so entschieden möchte ich doch sagen, daß im Durchschnitt gerade die bedeutenden Wissenschaftler über die Folgen ihres Handelns und die damit verbundene moralische Verantwortung viel mehr nachgedacht haben und viel tiefer beunruhigt sind als die Mehrzahl der Menschen." Von Weizsäcker to Heinrich Barth, 26 July 1956, published in Hora (2002, 46–48, quote on 47).

42. "Wir Atomphysiker in allen Nationen der Erde waren die ersten, die schon 1939 . . . realisierten, daß nunmehr nukleare Waffen möglich werden würden. Mehrere von uns haben schon damals eingesehen, daß bei der bestehenden Struktur der Menschheit . . . der Bau solcher Waffen praktisch nicht würde verhindert werden können. Dies drängte unsere Gedanken notwendigerweise in die Richtung, auf die Dauer die Überwindung der Institution des Krieges als die einzige Lösung zu sehen. Dieser Meinung war ich schon 1939, und ich habe sie auch heute noch." Von Weizsäcker to Ernst Honecker, July 17, 1987, published in Hora (2002, 221).

43. On the polycracy in physics in Germany during the Nazi period, see, e.g., Hentschel (1996) and the primary and secondary sources cited there.

44. "Ich erinnere mich noch sehr gut an die Sitzung des 'Tribunals' von aufmüpfigen Studenten, das öffentlich speziell über Weizsäckers Verhalten zu Gericht sitzen wollte und ihn dazu eingeladen hatte. Er erschien tatsächlich zu der Sitzung und schlug sich diplomatisch sehr geschickt gegen die studentischen Tribunalisten, die ihm in diesem Punkt nicht gewachsen waren . . . . Aber man merkte ihm die ungeheure Anstrengung an, die ihn diese Diplomatie kostete, angesichts des ganz und gar antidiplomatischen, betont ruppigen Benehmens der übrigen Diskussionsteilnehmer, das ihm

angesichts seiner eigenen Umgangsformen und Gewohnheiten sichtlich zuwider und strapaziös war." According to Michael Drieschner (1996, 178).

45. "Weizsäcker war meistens der diplomatisch Geschicktere, aber sichtlich angestrengt und angewidert. Dabei war ihm die Kritik, die die linken Studenten [und Mitarbeiter] an den bestehenden Verhältnissen äußerten, durchaus einleichtend; nur war ihm der Stil natürlich sehr konträr, und gegen die von den Linken erhoffte und propagierte Lösung der Probleme war er mindestens so skeptisch wie gegen die der konservativen Gegner." From a recollection by Michael Drieschner (1996, 179), one of his former coworkers.

46. "Meine Reaktion ist zuerst, daß meines Erachtens die Verteufelung des Gegners niemals dazu beiträgt, die Probleme zu lösen. Ich fürchte, daß Ihr Brief genau wegen der Empörung, die aus ihm spricht, zwar zeigt, daß Sie wirklich beunruhigt sind, aber sehr wenig dazu nützen kann, die Probleme zu lösen." Von Weizsäcker to G. Clemens-Höck, March 1, 1988, printed in Hora (2002, 226–228).

47. Alternatively as a "spiritual father-figure of the Federal Republic of Germany" ("geistiger Vaterfigur des bundesrepublikanischen Deutschland"), as he was repeatedly characterized—especially by the press. In the 1980s von Weizsäcker described himself as a "peddler priest in matters of peace" ("Wanderpriester in Sachen Frieden").

48. Thus also the "emotional sum-up" ("emotionale Fazit") of the sympathetic eye-witness report by Philipp Sonntag (2012). The observations by the biographer Dieter Hattrup also fit here. He described von Weizsäcker's ability "to wait with his own view until he had heard the other view" ("mit der eigenen Ansicht zu warten, bis er die andere Ansicht vernommen hat") and his endeavor to incorporate those other voices into his own texts: Hattrup (2004, 69). Cf. Hattrup (2004), the section "Wer spricht hier?"

49. "[I]m Alter von fünfzehn Jahren [kam] der totale und von vornherein als unwiderruflich erkannte Verlust des Kinderglaubens, d.h. von nun an konnte [ich] nur das im Bereich der Vielheit der Religionen und der nichtreligiösen Anschauungen wirklich akzeptieren, was ich aus meiner Erfahrung bestätigte oder zumindest als glaubwürdig ansehen konnte. . . . hingegen die Ausschließlichkeit, die in der christlichen Trinitätslehre vorgetragen wird, ist etwas, was ich im Grund nicht nachvollziehen kann." Von Weizsäcker to Helmut Schnelle, May 28, 1990, published in Hora (2002, 270–72, quote on 271). His conversation with Erwin Koller (1987, 60–63) reveals more about his religious attitude; see Hattrup (2004, part IV).

50. "Die Grenze der Vernünftigkeit der Technokratie liegt darin, daß die Rationalität der Zwecke der Rationalität der ihnen dienenden Mittel nicht gleichkommt. Die Grenze der Vernünftigkeit des Protests liegt dar-

in, daß Protest eben an das gebunden bleibt, wogegen er protestiert." Von Weizsäcker: "Gehen wir einer asketischen Weltkultur entgegen?" in *Deutlichkeit* (Weizsäcker 1981a, 56–86, quote on 79).

51. "Dieser Aufsatz ist nicht geschrieben, um Lösungsmodelle für unsere wirtschaftspolitischen Probleme vorzuschlagen, sondern um eine Haltung zur Beurteilung solcher Lösungsmodelle zu erwägen" (Weizsäcker 1981a, preface).

52. "Die Kraft zu solchen Lösungen setzt nur voraus, daß man sie denkt, und daß man sie will. Wollen aber kann man nichts Sinnvolles ohne Selbstbeherrschung" (Weizsäcker 1981a, 86).

53. "Rätsel einer präsenten Nichtpräsenz dieses Menschen, einer Sphinx würdig" (Hattrup 2004, 9).

54. "Wie viele der begeisterten Zuhörer Ihrer druckreifen Reden werden zugeben, daß Begeisterung nur bedingt zur Annäherung an das Unerreichbare taugt?" (Benno Parthier in his preface to Köhler 1992, 8).

55. Von Weizsäcker liked to set himself apart from professional philosophers, because his period as an active full-time professor of philosophy had just been limited, 1957–69. E.g., in *Die Einheit der Natur* (v. Weizsäcker 1981b, 26): "Having had this as my professional duty for over a decade is the gift that came with the transition from the field of physics into the field of philosophy. My fellow philosophers will recognize, and perhaps excuse me for having remained a dilettant, i.e., an enthusiast." ("Mehr als ein Jahrzehnt dies zur Berufspflicht gehabt zu haben, ist das Geschenk, das mir der Übergang aus dem Fach der Physik ins Fach der Philosophie gebracht hat. Daß ich in diesem Fach ein Dilettant, d.h. ein Liebhaber, geblieben bin, werden die philosophischen Kollegen erkennen und vielleicht entschuldigen.")

56. "Wir wollen Dich hören, aber wir wollen nicht tun, was Du sagst. Dich in der 'Rolle des verehrten Weisen' anzuhören muß als Tun genügen" (Hattrup 2004, 9) —von Weizsäcker is quoting his own letter to Richard von Weizsäcker, November 18, 1982 (Hora 2002, 163).

57. This is supported, e.g., by the following assertion (from Ackermann 1989, 98): "that I personally actually never did claim, basically perhaps also never had the aim of positing anything like a philosophical system." ("daß ich für mich als Person niemals eigentlich in Anspruch genommen habe, im Grunde vielleicht auch nie das Ziel gehabt habe, so etwas wie ein philosophisches System aufzustellen.")

57. The term *Kreisgang* for this thought motif occurs seventy-eight times in the CD-ROM edition of von Weizsäcker's collected works, edited by Michael Drieschner (2011). To these are added synonyms and related

ideas, such as circular path, roundabout walks, two half-way routes, many passes through, etc.

59. "Der Kreisgang war von vorneherein nicht nur als ein literarisches Hilfsmittel gemeint, sondern als ein philosophisches methodisches Prinzip, als Alternative zu jedem Ansatz einer 'hierarchistischen' Philosophie, die von einem einzigen unerschütterlichen Fundament auszugehen hofft, sei es nun Erfahrung oder Selbstgewißheit des Bewußtseins" (Weizsäcker 1992a, 594).

60. "Nach dieser Auffassung der Physik kann ein Bild dessen, was wir die Wirklichkeit nennen, wenn überhaupt, dann nur in einem Kreisgang gezeichnet werden" (Weizsäcker 1977/80, 194).

61. "Im Blick auf die Naturwissenschaft hat der Kreisgang die Voraussetzung: Die Natur ist älter als der Mensch; der Mensch ist älter als die Naturwissenschaft. Von der Geschichte der Natur her werden wir versuchen, den Menschen zu verstehen, von der Geschichte des Menschen her die Weise, wie er die Natur versteht. Man muß den Kreis mehrmals durchlaufen. Eben darum kann man an irgendeiner Stelle in ihn einsteigen" (Weizsäcker 1992a). Other examples include his analysis of Descartes, where he treats twelve characteristic points in two "walks around," the first walk through is a neutral review, the second one takes on a critical note. See Weizsäcker (1971, 11).

62. "nicht gesicherte Resultate bieten, sondern Sie nur auffordern . . . mit mir in eine bestimmte Bewegung des Denkens einzutreten," "in vielen Punkten nicht mehr als eine Andeutung" (Weizsäcker [1948] 2004, introduction, 4 and preface, 1).

63. "gesammelten Aufsätze als Glieder einer Einheit," "äußerlich zerstreute Weise," "Es ist mir jedoch nicht gelungen, den Gedanken der Einheit der Natur in systematischer Form vorzutragen" (Weizsäcker 1981b, preface, 9 and unpaginated introduction, 11).

64. On the contrast between purposeful "harvesting" and a noncommittal "round tour with a stop at this or that particular plant or at outlooks into the garden or beyond the garden," see M. Drieschner (1992).

65. On this species of "texts that seek to catalyze community," see esp. Ceccarelli (2001, chapters 1 and 8), which was developed out of an analysis of Theodosius Dobzhansky's *Genetics and the Origin of Species* (1937) and Erwin Schrödinger's *What Is Life?* (1944, esp. 158), on the trademark of such texts being a "synthesis rather than original research." On von Weizsäcker's quest for a grand sythesis rather than producing individual contributions to academic research, see, e.g., the obituaries by Hampe (2007), Lindinger (2007), Spengler (2007) as well as in Ackermann (1989).

66. See Köhler (1992, 76) for a direct provocation by von Weizsäcker of the mathematician van der Waarden: "I additionally say that now, to vex him enough to contradict." ("außerdem sage ich das jetzt, um [ihn] hinreichend zu reizen, damit er widerspricht.")

67. See, e.g., Lorenz (2011, 280) on the position von Weizsäcker aspired to as a "neutral, ideologically incorruptible, and, as a consequence, credible far-sighted thinker . . . In his numerous publications there is a notable effort, by rigorous factuality," not to be relegated to either of the belligerent parties, to be nonpartisan instead ("neutraler, ideologisch unbestechlicher, infolgedessen glaubwürdiger Vordenker ... Seinen zahlreichen Publikationen ist in Bestreben anzumerken, durch eine strenge, vermittels der Einnahme von verschiedenen Perspektiven suggerierte Sachlichkeit . . .")

68. In this sense, see, for example, E. Buchwald in the Laudatio on the occasion of von Weizsäcker's election into the Leopoldina 1959: Von Weizsäcker "expressed the inexhaustible wealth of his thoughts with polished clarity not only in these writings, even more so in his addresses, where is expressed in addition to his plentiful ideas, his model gift of speaking and the harmony of his whole personality." ("hat den unerschöpflichen Reichtum seiner Gedanken nicht nur in diesen Schriften mit vollendeter Klarheit zum Ausdruck gebracht, mehr noch in seinen Vorträgen, wo neben der Gedankenfülle seine vorbildliche Redegabe wie die Harmonie seiner ganzen Persönlichkeit zum Ausdruck kommt.")

69. This chapter was translated from German by Ann M. Hentschel.

## Works Cited

Ackermann, Peter, ed. 1989. *Erfahrung des Denkens—Wahrnehmung des Ganzen. Carl Friedrich von Weizsäcker als Physiker und Philosoph*. Berlin: Akademie-Verlag.

Carson, Cathryn. 2003. "Bildung als Konsumgut. Physik in der westdeutschen Nachkriegsliteratur." In *Physik im Nachkriegsdeutschland*, edited by Dieter Hoffmann, 73–85. Frankfurt: Verlag Harri Deutsch.

Ceccarelli, Leah. 2001. *Shaping Science with Rhetoric. The Cases of Dobzhansky, Schrödinger and Wilson*. Chicago: University of Chicago Press.

Dobzhansky, Theodosius. 1937. *Genetics and the Origin of Species*. New York: Columbia University Press.

Drieschner, Michael. 1992. "Im Garten der Philosophie." *Die Zeit*, no. 50 (December): 14.

—. 1996. "Die Verantwortung der Wissenschaft." In *Wissenschaft und Öffentlichkeit*, edited by Tanja Fischer and Rudolf Seising, 173–93. Frankfurt am Main: Lang.

—, ed. 2011. *Carl Friedrich von Weizsäcker im Kontext. Gesammelte Werke auf CD-ROM.* Berlin: Info-Software Karsten Worm.

Eppler, Erhard. 2007. "Leise reden im Tumult." *Die Zeit*, no. 19 (May): 12.

Fahnestock, Jeanne. 1999. *Rhetorical Figures in Science.* Oxford: Oxford University Press.

Frank, Charles, ed. 1993. *Operation Epsilon. The Farm Hall Transcripts.* Bristol: Institute of Physics Publ.

Gieryn, Thomas F. 1983. "Boundary-Work and the Demarcation of Science from Non-Science: Strains and interests in professional ideologies of scientists." *American Sociological Review* 6 (48): 781–95.

Gross, Alan G. 1990. *The Rhetoric of Science.* Cambridge, MA: Harvard University Press.

—. 2006. *Starring the Text: The Place of Rhetoric in Science Studies.* Carbondale, Illinois: Southern Illinois University Press.

Gross, Johannes. 1981. *Frankfurter Allgemeine Zeitung* of October 9, 1981.

Hampe, Michael. 2007. "Teilung des Atoms, Einheit der Natur." *Neue Zürcher Zeitung*, no. 99 (April): 23.

Hattrup, Dieter. 2004. *Carl Friedrich von Weizsäcker. Physiker und Philosoph.* Darmstadt: Primus.

Hentschel, Klaus, ed. 1996. *Physics and National Socialism. An Anthology of Primary Sources.* Basel: Springer.

—. 2007. *The Mental Aftermath: The Mentality of German Physicists 1945–1949.* Oxford: Oxford University Press.

Hentschel, Klaus, ed. 2008. *Analogien in Naturwissenschaften, Medizin und Technik*, Stuttgart: Wiss. Verlagsges. (= Acta Historica Leopoldina, 56).

Hentschel, Klaus, and Dieter Hoffmann, eds. 2014. *Carl Friedrich von Weizsäcker—Physik, Philosophie und Friedensforschung.* Stuttgart: Wissenschaftliche Verlagsgesellschaft [Acta Historica Leopoldina 63].

Hoffmann, Dieter. 1993. *Operation Epsilon. Die Farm-Hall Protokolle oder die Angst der Alliierten vor der deutschen Atombombe.* Reinbek: Rowohlt.

Hora, Eginhard, ed. 2002. *Carl Friedrich von Weizsäcker: Lieber Freund! Lieber Gegner! Briefe aus fünf Jahrzehnten.* Munich: Hanser.

Köhler, Werner, ed. 1992. *Carl Friedrich von Weizsäckers Reden in der Leopoldina.* No. 282 of Nova Acta Leopoldina, new series vol. 68. Halle: Deutsche Akademie der Naturforscher Leopoldina.

Koller, Erwin. 1987. *Carl Friedrich von Weizsäcker—Die Unschuld der Physiker? Ein Gespräch.* Zürich: Pendo.

Lemmerich, Jost. 1998. *Lise Meitner—Max von Laue. Briefwechsel 1938–1948.* Vol. 22 of Berliner Beiträge zur Geschichte der Naturwissenschaften und der Technik. Berlin: ERS-Verlag.

Lindinger, Manfred. 2007. "Synthesen eines Jahrhundertmannes." *Frankfurt Allgemeine Zeitung*, no. 100 (April): 35.

Lorenz, Robert. 2011. *Protest der Physiker. Die "Göttinger Erklärung" von 1957.* Bielefeld: Transkript.

Meyer-Abich, Klaus M. ed. 1982. *Physik, Philosophie und Politik. Für Carl Friedrich von Weizsäcker zum 70. Geburtstag*. Munich: Hanser.
Moss, Jean D. 1993. *Novelties in the Heavens. Rhetoric and Science in the Copernican Controversy*. Chicago: University of Chicago Press.
Myers, Greg. 1990. *Writing Biology. Texts in the Social Construction of Scientific Knowledge*. Madison, Wisc.: University of Wisconsin Press.
Podak, Klaus. 2007. "Ein aufgeklärter Mystiker." *Süddeutsche Zeitung*, April 30. Accessed November 10, 2017. http://www.sueddeutsche.de/wissen/carl-friedrich-von-weizsaecker-ein-aufgeklaerter-mystiker-1.833741.
Schirach, Richard von. 2012. *Die Nacht der Physiker. Heisenberg, Hahn, Weizsäcker und die deutsche Bombe*. Berlin: Berenberg Verlag.
Schrödinger, Erwin. 1994. *What Is Life? The Physical Aspect of the Living Cell. Based on lectures delivered under the auspices of the Dublin Institute for Advanced Study at Trinity College in February 1943*. Cambridge: Cambridge University Press.
Sonntag, Philipp. 2012. *Ja, aber was ist die eigentliche Frage?* Unpublished manuscript.
Spengler, Tilman. 2007. "Ein Denker universaler Zusammenhänge." *Tagesspiegel*, April 30, 2007. Accessed November 10, 2017. http://www.tagesspiegel.de/weltspiegel/gesundheit/ein-denker-universaler-zusammenhaenge/840826.html.
Wein, Martin. 1988. *Die Weizsäckers. Geschichte einer deutschen Familie*. Stuttgart: DVA.
Weizsäcker, Carl Friedrich von. 1946. *Die Geschichte der Natur, 12 Vorlesungen*. Göttingen: Vandenhoeck & Ruprecht.
—. 1958. *Mit der Bombe leben*. Hamburg. Offprint of 4 articles in *Die Zeit*.
—. 1961. Preface to *Kernexplosionen und ihre Wirkungen*. Frankfurt am Main: Fischer.
—. 1967. "Die Einheit der Physik." *Physikalische Blätter* 23 (1): 4–14.
—. 1971. Voraussetzungen des naturwissenschaftlichen Denkens. Munich: Hanser.
—. 1972. "Der Atomschirm hat Löcher." In *Interviews*, edited by Adelbert Reif, 169–77. Hamburg: Hoffmann und Campe 1972.
—. (1977) 1980. *Der Garten des Menschlichen*. Munich: Hanser.
—. 1981a. *Deutlichkeit. Beiträge zu politischen und religiösen Gegenwartsfragen*. Munich: DTV.
—. 1981b. *Die Einheit der Natur. Studien*. Munich: Hanser.
—. 1991. "Ich gebe zu, ich war verrückt." *Der Spiegel*, April 22: 227–30.
—. 1992a. *Zeit und Wissen*. Munich: Hanser.
—. 1992b. *Die Philosophie eines Physikers*. [Talk in Bamberg, June 22, DVD], Quartino SWR.
—. (1948) 2004. *Der begriffliche Aufbau der theoretischen Physik: Vorlesung gehalten in Göttingen im Sommer 1948* [Göttingen lectures, summer term 1948], edited by Holger Lyre. Stuttgart: Hirzel.
Zacher, Hans F. 2008. "Nachrufe—Carl Friedrich von Weizsäcker." In *Jahresbericht der Max-Planck-Gesellschaft* 2007, supplement, 23–26. Munich: Max-Planck-Gesellschaft zur Förderung der Wissenschaften.

# 16 Timeless Demonstration: Abraham Lincoln's Cooper Union Address and Cicero's *Officia Oratoris*: To Teach, to Delight, and to Move

*William M. Purcell*

## Introduction

The Address at Cooper Union is one of Abraham Lincoln's best known, most appreciated, but least studied speeches. Indeed, as Michael C. Leff and Gerald P. Mohrmann noted in 1974, this speech—which has been called a model of "'logical analysis and construction'"[1]—has "failed to generate a critical response in kind." Previous scholarship, they wrote, has been focused on the background of the speech and various trivia such as "the price of tickets or the fit of Lincoln's new shoes." Those analyses, they argued, did not enhance our appreciation of the "speech as a speech" (Leff and Mohrmann 1974a, 346).

Scholars of rhetoric, of course, know Leff and Mohrmann's classic pieces from 1974, "Lincoln at Cooper Union: A Rhetorical Analysis of the Text" and "Lincoln at Cooper Union: A Rationale for Neo-Classical Criticism."[2] The first piece provides an example of how an analysis based on classical concepts can "illuminate" a speech. The second provides a cogent argument for the use of classical concepts in performing criticism. Neither, however, seems to have spurred much scholarship on the Cooper Union Address or neo-classical criticism. Harold Holzer returned to the Cooper Union Address in a fairly recent work, *Lincoln at Cooper Union: The Speech that Made Lincoln President* (2004), and concurred with the position that the address had been understudied and underappreciated. While Holzer's work provides a fine contextual and historical overview for the address, he also considers the fit of Lincoln's shoes and suit, as well as the price of tickets. Leff, Mohrmann, and Holzer do provide some fine textual analysis, particularly for the section where Lincoln systematically develops a refutation to the assertion that the founding fathers had not intended that slavery ever be regulated. There is more to be learned, however, from the perspective of "neo-classical criticism." As Holzer (2004, 3) argues so forcefully, the Cooper Union Address, and its subsequent publication and wide distribution, lifted Lincoln from the status of "prairie stump speaker" to that of an orator whose abilities surpassed those of his Republican rival, William Seward, and his eventual Democratic opponent, Stephen Douglas. This chapter returns to neo-classical criticism, particularly Cicero's "duties of the orator," as a means of appreciating this landmark speech in its entirety.

## Neo-Classical Approaches to Speech Analysis

Leff and Mohrmann used their neo-classical approach as a jumping off point for genre criticism, quite properly identifying the address as a campaign speech:

> [T]his type does not fall within the tripartite Aristotelian division [forensic, epideictic, and deliberative]. The anomaly becomes evident when we consider the campaign speech in relation to audience and purpose, the basic components of Aristotelian distinction. One who listens to a campaign speech is a judge of a future event, and he is urged to do something (i.e., vote for a particular candidate). This corresponds to the function of audience in deliberative oratory. The object of judgment, however, is not a policy, as it is in deliberative speaking, but a person, as it is in epideictic. Ends are also blurred; the deliberative orator examines the "expediency or the harmfulness of a proposed course of action"; and the epideictic orator must "praise or attack a man" in order to prove "him worthy of honour or the reverse."[3] Now, the end of campaign oratory is to make the candidate appear worthy and honorable. (Leff and Mohrmann 1974b, 464)

Clearly, the Cooper Union Address is of a different type than the three delineated in Aristotle's *Rhetoric*. Aristotle's, however, is not the only rhetoric in the classical corpus. Just as the limitations of neo-Aristotelianism led to a wide variety of critical methods (including Leff and Mohrmann's neo-classical approach), so too do they lead us to consider other neo-classical approaches. One such approach comes from the later, mature works of

Cicero, but first let us consider the ideas of a man who may be considered the earliest rhetorician of them all, Gorgias of Leontini (ca. 480–380 BCE).

Gorgias espoused a kind of "proto" rhetoric that drew from what he regarded as the magical, incantational power of poetry and its power to act on the soul. Gorgias produced an "elaborate, artificial, jingling style" (De Romilly 1975, 19) of speech by means of what have been called the Gorgianic Figures: homoeoteleuton (adjacent clauses with similar endings), isocolon (clauses with near equal number of syllables), antithesis (opposed ideas in adjacent clauses), and parison (parallel construction). The orator may use the figures in a way that uses the poetic qualities of language to impart "the action of speech on the soul" (De Romilly 1975, 14). Jacqueline De Romilly wrote:

> Gorgias' magic rests on the notion that all truth is out of reach. Sacred magic was mysterious; Gorgias' magic is technical. He wants to emulate the power of the magician by a scientific analysis of language and of its influence. He is the theoretician of the magic spell of words. (De Romilly 1975, 16)

It is this magical, stylistic quality that is an important aspect of Cicero's duties of the orator and, ultimately, the Cooper Union Address.

Cicero first mentions the concept of an ideal orator in *De oratore*. There, the concept is developed by means of a dialogue staged between distinguished orators of Cicero's youth. Later, in *Orator*, he outlines the obligations incumbent upon this ideal orator:

> The man of eloquence whom we seek . . . will be one who is able to speak in court or in deliberative bodies so as to prove, to please, and to sway or persuade. To prove is the first necessity, to please is charm, to sway is victory. (Cicero [1921, trans. Hubbell] *Orat.* 69)[4]

The means to each of these "officia oratoris," or duties of the orator, are the three levels of rhetorical style: plain, middle, and grand. The speaker using the plain style will avoid rhythm and other embellishments. He will use arguments, make refutations, resolve problems, answer questions, offer interpretations, and engage in demonstrations. It should be "sprinkled with salt of pleasantry," utilizing both humor and wit (Cic. *Orat.* 75–90.). The speaker using the middle style will speak with a "minimum of vigor and a maximum of charm." All types of rhetorical devices are acceptable in this style. This type of "speaker will . . . develop his arguments with breadth and erudition and use commonplaces without undue emphasis" (Cic. *Orat.* 91–96). The grand style (97–99) is "magnificent, opulent, stately, and ornate," featuring exhortations and upbraidings and stirring the emotions. No speaker can maintain the grand style for long. It must be moderated by the plain and middle styles:

> But this orator of ours whom we consider chief, grand, impetuous and fiery, if he has natural ability for this alone, or trains himself solely in this, or devotes his energies to this only, and does not temper his abundance with the other two styles, he is much to be despised. For the plain orator is esteemed wise because he speaks clearly and adroitly; the one who employs the middle style is charming; but the copious speaker, if he has nothing else, seems to be scarcely sane. (Cic. *Orat.* 99).

The duties of the orator were also utilized by St. Augustine, particularly as a means of developing sermons. Ĉelica Milovanović-Barham (1993) looked at Augustine's reemployment of the duties and their use in the writings of Augustine, Gregory of Nazianus, and Cyprian—and noted that while Cicero employed the rhetorical figures more explicitly in his rhetorical composition, focusing on ways to present content, the latter rhetoricians followed the influence of the Second Sophistic in stylistically crafting their works with emphasis on periodic sentence structure.

Milovanović-Barham found the plain style is also marked by syllogisms, epicheiremes, logical definition, divisions and partitions, use of concluding quotations, medium sized cola, gentle and swaying variation, and use of the longest quotation at the beginning of the passage. The middle style was ornamented and restrained in emotion. It featured parallel sound and structure and broad, drawn out sentences. It was catalog like, poetic, long winded, and often featured a period at the beginning. The grand style utilized a heightened tone; used supplication, invective and reprimand, direct address, rhetorical questions, varied sentence structure, avoidance of parallel sound, short and long cola, alternation between short and long questions, and iambic rhythm (Milovanović-Barham 1993, 3–22).

The Ciceronian approach to reaching the different levels of style emphasized the rhetorical figures used in changing the meaning of words: metonymy, catachresis, metaphor, and allegory, for example (Cic. *Orat.* 92–95). In contrast, the Augustinian approach paid more attention to the figures comma, clause, period, and climax (see Augustine [1958, trans. Robertson] *De doct. Chr.* 4.7.11). Both views help our understanding, though Lincoln may be closer to the Augustinian, and by extension, Gorgian styles. The duties of the orator, then, provide us with particular rhetorical figures and strategies by which to read and appreciate a speech.

## Abraham Lincoln's Cooper Union Address: An Analysis

Indeed, when applied to the Cooper Union Address, the concepts of the duties and styles allow a much fuller appreciation of Lincoln's rhetorical artistry.

First, we might consider the audience for Lincoln's speech. Certainly, there is the immediate audience attending the lecture at Cooper Union. They are opinion leaders whose impressions will go far in establishing Lincoln's credibility as a candidate. Then, as Leff and Mohrmann (1974a, esp. 353–57) note, there is the absent audience of Southerners with whom he might reason, or at least consider. But Lincoln speaks also here to future voters and, indeed, to posterity. He addresses pivotal issues in the development of the country as it teeters toward crisis. Why is the nation on the brink of civil war? Why is it necessary to halt the idea of popular sovereignty right then and now? Lincoln provides the evidence, but he must also make the appeal to evidence popular and rouse his audience to action. Candidate Lincoln is running against not only his fellow Republicans, but more particularly against the presumptive Democratic opponent, Stephen A. Douglas, also his opponent in the senate race in Illinois in 1858.

Lincoln's opening section is a clear example of plain style. He motivates the section with a quotation from a recent speech by Douglas. Douglas had advocated his position of "popular sovereignty," that the citizens of new territories and states in the United States should have the right to determine whether or not slavery should be legal in those territories. Douglas maintained that the founding fathers had supported his contention stating: "'Our fathers, when they framed the government under which we live, understood this question just as well, and even better than we do now'" (Lincoln 1953, 522). Lincoln takes the statement as a point of departure for an analysis of original intent. He takes Douglas' statement and divides it into six particular questions that must be answered in order to determine the founders' intentions:

> What was the understanding those fathers had of the question mentioned?
> What is the frame of the government under which we live?
> Who were the fathers that framed that constitution?
> What is the question, which according to the text, those fathers understood "just as well, and even better than we do now?"
> Does the proper division of local from federal authority, or anything in the constitution, forbid *our Federal Government* to control as to slavery in *our Federal Territories*?

> Let us inquire now whether the "thirty-nine," or any of them, ever acted upon this question; and if they did, how they acted upon it—how they expressed that better understanding? (Lincoln 1953, 522–23)

Lincoln then turns Douglas' question back on him, defining "our fathers" as the thirty-nine original signers of the Constitution and the Constitution as the "frame of the government under which we live" (Lincoln 1953, 523–35). Though clearly mocking Douglas by repeating some variation of the quote over thirty-five times, Lincoln speaks primarily to the issue here. The question, of course, is whether the founding fathers felt it proper for the federal government to regulate slavery in federal territories. Lincoln builds a careful case, block by block, answering each of the questions with precise definitions and explicit marshaling of evidence. Lincoln reviews systematically the seven instances in which slavery in federal territories had been regulated by the federal government: Northwest Ordinance (1784), Ordinance of 87 (1787), Constitution (1787), Bill of Rights (1789,) Mississippi Territory (1798), Louisiana Purchase (1804), and the Missouri Compromise (1819/20), and demonstrates that twenty-three of the thirty-nine "fathers" had served on bodies that enacted the statutes and twenty-one of those twenty-three had affirmed or not objected to the federal government's right to regulate slavery. Only two were on the record as having opposed the position. The presentation is catalog like, repetitive and rendered in a syllogistic form that specifically shows how the various fathers had affirmed the regulation of slavery:

| | |
|---|---|
| Major premise: | Act provided for the regulation of slavery in Federal Territories. |
| Minor premise: | Founding fathers voted for/affirmed that act. |
| Conclusion: | These founding fathers understood that the Constitution allowed for the regulation of slavery in the territories. |

The pattern is repeated some seven times and is folded into an overall syllogism (actually, an epicheireme, because each premise is supported with evidence) that affirms that a majority of the founding fathers understood that the Constitution allowed for the regulation of slavery in Federal Territories. Lincoln repeatedly utters the same phrases: "the fathers," "thirty-nine," "who framed the government under which we now live," and "understood as well, and even better than we do now." The repetition builds in such a fashion that the audience anticipates, enthymematically, the conclusion and renders absurd Douglas' contention that regulation was not allowed. In addition to the cataloging, ratiocination, syllogisms, epicheiremes, and repetition, Lincoln varies the length of his clauses throughout. There is little parallelism nor periodic structure.

In the second section of the speech, Lincoln shifts into the middle style to delight his Republican audience, and the tone is hardly conciliatory: "And now," he begins, "if they would listen—as I suppose they will not—I would address a few words to the Southern people." The Southerners, he says, are calling Republicans names: "reptiles," "outlaws," and "Black Republicans" (Lincoln 1953, 535–36). He asks them to discuss and reason through the issue. He proceeds via ratiocination, asking and answering some four questions regarding sectionalism. The substance of the section is not as remarkable as is its presentation: nearly four hundred words in short, choppy clauses that build to artful periods via antitheses, homoeoteleuta, isocola, parallelisms, and climaxes.

I have rendered the paragraph below by sentences and clauses, with a syllable count at the end of each line. It begins with a series of homoeoteleuta and fairly regular clause length, and then moves to a series of climaxes that lead to an antithesis at the mid-point. A second series of climaxes leads to points where the audience responded with applause.[5]

> You say that we are sectional. (8)
>   We deny it. (4)
> That makes an issue; (5)
>   and the burden of proof is upon you. [loud applause] (10)
> You produce your proof; (5)
>   and what is it? (4)
> Why, (1)
>   that our party has no existence in your section— (13)
>     gets no votes in your section. (7)
> The fact is substantially true; (9)
>   but does it prove the issue? (7)
> If it does, (3)
>   then in case we should, (5)
>     without change of principle, (7)
>       begin to get votes in your section, (10)
>         we should therefore cease to be sectional. [great merriment] (10)
> You cannot escape this conclusion; (10)
>   and yet are you willing to abide by it? (11)
> If you are, (3)
>   you will probably soon find that we have ceased to be sectional, (16)

for we shall get votes in your section this very year. [loud cheers] (14)
You will then begin to discover, (9)
  as the truth plainly is, (6)
    that your proof does not touch the issue. (9)
The fact that we get no votes in your section, [Here begins a climax leading to the passage rendered in italics. The two passages in italics are antitheses.] (11)
  is a fact of your making, (7)
    and not of ours. (4)
And if there be fault in that fact, (8)
  that fault is primarily yours, (8)
    and remains until you show that *we repel you by some wrong principle or practice.* (21)
If *we do not repel you by any wrong principle or practice* (17)
  the fault is ours; [another climax begins] (4)
    but this brings you to where you ought to have started— (12)
      to a discussion of the right or wrong of our principle. [loud applause] (15)
If our principle, [climax begins] (5)
  put in practice, (4)
    would wrong your section for the benefit of ours, (12)
      or for any other object, (8)
        then our principle, (5)
          and we with it, (4)
            are sectional, (4)
              and are justly opposed and denounced as such. (12)
Meet us, [climax begins] (2)
  then, (1)
    on the question of whether our principle, (11)
      put in practice, (4)
        would wrong your section; (5)
          and so meet it as if it were possible that something may be said on our side. [applause] (20)
Do you accept the challenge? (7)
No! (1)
Then you really believe that the principle which "our fathers who framed the government under which we live" thought so clearly right as to adopt it, [climax begins] (36)
  and indorse it again and again, (9)
    upon their official oaths, (8)

> is in fact so clearly wrong as to demand your condemnation without a moment's consideration. [applause] (26)
> (Lincoln 1953, 536)

This is middle style at its very best. Lincoln leads his audience artfully to climax after climax (and ovation after ovation) via the Gorgianic Figures, using words as a magic spell.

Lincoln (1953, 536–37) goes on to identify the charge of sectionalism as stemming from Washington's warning against such in his Farewell Address. Lincoln rebuts the charge by noting that Washington, eight years before, had signed an act prohibiting slavery in the Northwest Territory. Would Washington, he asks, have "cast the blame of sectionalism upon us?" He begins his analysis with a series of antitheses: conservative/revolutionary, old and tried/new and untried, divided on new plans and policies/unanimous in rejecting the old plan of the fathers. Lincoln changes the opposed pairs with an artful dissociation, pointing out that the so-called revolutionary policy is old while the so called conservative one is quite new:

> We stick to, contend for, the identical old policy on the point of controversy which was adopted by "our fathers who framed the government under which we live;" while you with one accord reject, and scout, and spit upon that old policy, and insist upon substituting something new. (Lincoln 1953, 537)

He goes on to address the issue of the deregulation of slave trade with more parallelisms, antitheses, and balanced clauses. He begins with a series of parallel clauses, of equal syllable count, punctuated by the references to the popular sovereignty, and leading to the negation of these ideas with the reference back to "the fathers." There is a regularity of syllable count in the third to fifth "some" clauses, separated by several clauses, but then matched in the final clause referring to the fathers. Each of the positions is totally devastated by the final antithesis, which shows the logical inconsistency of the overall position:

> *Some* of you are for reviving the slave trade; (11)
>    *some* for a Congressional Slave-Code for the Territories; (16)
>      *some* for Congress forbidding the Territories to prohibit Slavery with their limits; (23)
>          *some* for maintaining Slavery within the Territories through the judiciary; (22)
>            and *some* for the great principle that if one man would enslave another, [great laughter] (18)

>             no third man should object, (6)
>                 fantastically called "Popular Sovereignty;" [renewed
>                 laughter and applause] (14)
>                     but never a man among you is in favor of federal
>                     prohibition of slavery in federal territories, (31)
>                         according to the practice of "our fathers who framed
>                         the government under which we live." (23)
> Consider, (3)
>     then, (1)
>         whether your claim of conservatism for yourselves, [Antithesis] (13)
>         and your charge of destructiveness against us, (11)
>         are based on the most clear and stable foundations. (12)
>                                                 (Lincoln 1953, 537–38)

Lincoln denies boldly the charge that Republicans made slavery a bigger issue than ever before. He points out that the issue is prominent because Southerners and Democrats had "discarded the old policy of the fathers". Their resistance to the old policy raised the issue's importance. Embedded within the rebuke is his ridicule of Stephen Douglas and the way he uttered "great principle" (Lincoln 1953, 538).

Lincoln then moves to the issue of John Brown's raid on Harper's Ferry. Brown, he asserts, was not a Republican, and no Republican had been shown to be a part of Brown's movement. Further, he argues, Republicans have not promoted slave insurrections. Indeed, the largest slave insurrection occurred in 1832, long before the formation of the Republican Party. Moreover, he argues, Brown's raid was not a slave insurrection. Rather, it was an attempt by white men to rouse the slaves to action. He questions whether all the talk of John Brown and the like is just another attempt to break up the Republican Party. He says, "There is a judgment and a feeling against slavery in this nation, which cast at least a million and a half of votes" (Lincoln 1953, 541–42). They can destroy a political party, but not the sentiment behind it. The consequences would be disastrous:

> You can scarcely scatter and disperse an army which has been formed into order in the face of your heaviest fire; but if you could, how much would you gain by forcing the sentiment which created it out of the peaceful channel of the ballot-box, into some other channel? What would that other channel probably be? Would the number of John Brown's be lessened or enlarged by the operation? But you will break up the Union rather than submit to a denial of your Constitutional rights. (Lincoln 1953, 542)

Finally, Lincoln comes to the Dred Scott decision and must do a bit of a balancing act. The Supreme Court had presumably decided the issue, but Lincoln, in a time before the judicial review function of the court had been established firmly (Dred Scott was only the second instance), does not let it go. He notes how the decision had been justified by the Fifth and Tenth Amendment and was the basis for Senator Douglas' position. He is powerful in his opposition to such interpretation. Earlier, in the first section of the speech, he had noted that the framers of the Constitution allowed for regulation of slavery in its subsequent legislation, asking a series of rhetorical questions:

> Is it not a little presumptuous in any one at this day to affirm that the two things which that Congress deliberately framed, and carried to maturity at the same time, are absolutely inconsistent with each other? And does not such affirmation become impudently absurd when coupled with the other affirmation from the same mouth, that those who did the two things, alleged to be inconsistent, understood whether they really were inconsistent better than we—better than he who affirms that they are inconsistent? (Lincoln 1953, 534)

Reviewing that thinking here, Lincoln argues strongly that a right "plainly written in the constitution" is being denied. Indeed, Lincoln (1953, 543) says, "we . . . deny that such a right has any existence in the constitution, even by implication." The Dred Scott decision, he states, allows slaveholders to take slaves into federal territories and retain them as property. The decision was made by a slim majority (actually, 7–2), with widespread disagreement as to the reasons for affirming it. Lincoln (1953, 544) says it was made on a mistaken assumption of fact: "'that the right of property in a slave is distinctly and expressively affirmed in the constitution.'" No such right, he observes, is expressed. The judge made a mistake. He is sure that the judges will rescind their mistaken opinion in time (This was only the second time in history that the court had engaged in judicial review to nullify a law). He then moves back to the familiar line about "our fathers, who framed . . ." in a long period that now includes the notion of mistaken fact. The first part of the paragraph, which refers to "the fathers," is rendered in clauses of nearly equal length. The second part follows with clauses of varied length, which accentuate the inconsistency of the rationales used to support the Dred Scott decision. The third and final clauses are balanced, reinforcing the position of the "fathers" and the mistake of the court:

> And then it is to be remembered that "our fathers, (14)
> who framed the Government under which we live"— (12)
> decided the same Constitutional question in our favor, (16)
> long ago— (3)
> decided it without division among themselves, (13)
> when making the decision; (7)
> without division among themselves about the meaning of it
> after it was made, (21)
> and, (1)
> so far as any evidence is left, (10)
> without basing it on any mistaken statement of fact.
> (16)
> (Lincoln 1953, 546)

It is perhaps the weakest point of his address, but he sells it with a solid foundation created earlier in the speech. Could there be any question at this point as to whether Lincoln had a superior legal mind to those of the divided justices on the court?

The section addressed to the Southerners (Lincoln 1953, 535–47) is not conciliatory at all. Rather, it is an up front, in your face, ridicule of the Southern position. It is, in essence, a knock-down, drag out, stump speech, aimed not so much to a Southern audience but at them. Popular sovereignty is deemed "fantastic." Lincoln mimics Douglas' speaking style in calling popular sovereignty the "gur-reat pur-rinciple." He speaks of purported Republican connections to John Brown and slave rebellions and mocks the Southern support of the Dred Scott decision while at the same time saying that the election of a Republican President is not grounds for destroying the union. With this he asks the final question of the Southerners:

> Under all these circumstances, do you really feel yourselves justified to break up this Government unless such a court decision as yours is, shall be at once submitted to as a conclusive and final rule of political action? But you will not abide the election of a Republican president! In that supposed event, you say, you will destroy the Union; and then, you say, the great crime of having destroyed it will be upon us! That is cool. A highwayman holds a pistol to my ear, and mutters through his teeth, "Stand and deliver, or I shall kill you, and then you will be a murderer!" (Lincoln 1953, 546–47)

Lincoln's style is fairly regular, and he uses common examples, particularly the one of the highwayman, to make his point. It is the type of oratory aimed at belittling opposing positions in a way that arouses a sympathetic crowd.

At this point, Lincoln shifts into his final appeal and into the grand style. As Leff and Mohrmann (1974a, 356) noted, "antithetical elements appear in the penultimate paragraph, but the opposed clauses are subordinated within the long periodic flow of the final sentence, a flow that builds emotionally to a union with [George] Washington's words and deeds." Lincoln's conclusion begins with five, long periodic sentences rendered in undulating clauses and ends with two successively shorter sentences. The first sentence features seven unequal clauses and is followed by a relatively short sentence comprised of three nearly equal clauses. The third sentence is set up with a long clause and then accentuated with four consecutive antitheses rendered in clauses of near equal length. The next seven clauses are of irregular length and marked by three more antitheses that place Republicans on the side of Washington. The final two sentences are resolute exhortations to have faith in their convictions and to do their duty:

> Wrong as we think slavery is, (8)
>   we can yet afford to let it alone where it is, (13)
>     because that much is due to the necessity arising from its actual presence in the nation; (26)
>       but can we, (3)
>         while our votes will prevent it, (7)
>           allow it to spread into the National Territories, (15)
>             and to overrun us here in these Free States?
>               [Applause, laughter, and comments] (10)
> If our sense of duty forbids this, (9)
>   then let us stand by our duty, (8)
>     fearlessly and effectively. (8)
> Let us be diverted by none of those sophistical contrivances wherewith we are so industriously plied and belabored— (34)
>   contrivances such as groping some middle ground between the *right* and the *wrong*, (19)
>     vain as the search for a man who should be neither a *living* nor a *dead* man— (19)
>       such as a policy of *"don't care"* on a question about which all true men *do care*— (21)
>         such as Union appeals beseeching true *Union men* to yield to *Disunionists*, (23)
>           reversing the divine rule, (7)
>             and calling, (3)
>               not the *sinners*, (4)
>                 but the *righteous* to repentance—

>                [prolonged cheers and laughter] (9)
>            such as invocations to Washington, (10)
>                imploring men to *unsay* what Washington *said*,
>                (12)
>                    and to *undo* what Washington *did*. (9)
> Neither let us be slandered from our duty by false accusations against us, (21)
>     nor frightened from it by menaces of destruction to the Government nor
>     of dungeons to ourselves. [applause] (27)
>        LET US HAVE FAITH THAT RIGHT MAKES MIGHT, (8)
>        AND IN THAT FAITH, (4)
>          LET US, (2)
>            TO THE END, (3)
>              DARE TO DO OUR DUTY AS WE UNDERSTAND IT.
>              [three rousing cheers, standing ovation] (12)
>                                            (Lincoln 1953, 550)

## Conclusion

As my analysis has shown, Lincoln's Cooper Union Address was presented via the three Ciceronian duties: to teach, delight, and move, and in the attendant styles: plain, middle, and grand. Lincoln started his speech by slowly and carefully taking his audience through the legal precedents—strikingly applying many signatures of the plain level of style in the process: He cataloged the issue; asked and answered questions, used repetition; and carefully demonstrated his points with syllogisms, epicheiremes, and enthymemes. In general, he used relatively short sentences with simple construction, all of which facilitated a better understanding of the issues at stake—and actively allowed for the audience to follow his points. Having established his factual case, Lincoln then used the middle style to address the imagined Southern audience. There, he employed the Gorgianic Figures to delight his audience with colorful and humorous allusions in language encoded in the textural devices of style. He shifted from the persona of the lawyer into that of the stump speaker. Finally, to arouse his immediate audience of Republicans and to speak to the nation and to posterity, he adopted the persona of the statesman as he moved into the grand style, presenting his final exhortation in a jagged, moving series of periodic clauses and sentences. Taken as a whole, the Cooper Union address is an exemplar of speech which fulfills the *officia oratoris* at their fullest.

There can be little doubt that there is substance in Lincoln's argument, but his use of the various styles goes beyond argument and the marshaling of evidence to marshal the aural texture of language to reinforce and, indeed, carry his points. As St. Augustine (1958, *De doct. Chr.* 4.5.7) wrote, "some do these things dully, unevenly, and coldly, while others do them acutely, ornately, and vehemently . . . ." The devices of style are the difference between the former and the latter.

The question of whether Lincoln had read Cicero, or his speeches, is difficult to answer. He had very little formal education, and the various surveys of what Lincoln had read indicate little direct contact, if any, with the works of Cicero (cf. Bray 2007). That said, his experience as a courtroom lawyer no doubt exposed him to others educated in the Ciceronian tradition. Nan Johnson (1991, 255) indicates that Cicero was the second most cited rhetorician in North American textbooks between 1800 and 1850. Still, Lincoln no doubt had an innate facility with words and language just as Gorgias did. We do know that what little formal education Lincoln had featured oral recitation, and that Lincoln was an oral reader. Mildred Freburg Berry (1943, 834) quoted Lincoln's law partner, William Herndon, "'Singularly enough Lincoln never read any other way but aloud,'" a habit that annoyed Herndon, "almost beyond the point of endurance."

A speech is not merely a written text. It is a record of words that were uttered out loud. A written text is merely a representation of those words. Many speech texts are vessels for words, but lifeless outside the voices uttering them. Other speeches are infused with the personality and life of the orator who composed and delivered them. Style infuses an argument with life. The duties of the orator and the rhetorical styles are the means by which that life and personality are imparted. The people who wrote the ancient treatises on rhetoric were active participants in an oral culture that valued the nuances of the spoken word. Our contemporary culture, strongly based on the written text, is hard pressed to appreciate the tension between text and speech. The classical canon of rhetorical theory gives us a critical apparatus with which to appreciate the oral magic locked into a speech text. A rhetoric of evidence must consider the nuances of oral rhetoric to be complete. Attention to the oral/aural dimension of language brings speech and speaker together in appreciation of the timeless demonstration wrought by the spoken word.

## Notes

1. Leff and Mohrmann (1974a, 346) cite this quote from Smith (1962, 272).

2. These two essays were originally written as one. Because of its length, the *Quarterly Journal of Speech* published it as two pieces. Names of the authors were reversed from the first essay to the second to ensure equal au-

thorial credit. In this chapter, to avoid potential confusion, the two pieces are not differentiated by author order, but as Leff and Mohrmann (1974a) and Leff and Mohrmann (1974b).

3. The passages Leff and Mohrmann quote here are taken from: Aristotle *Rh.* I.3, 1358b. For the English translation, see Aristotle 2010.

4. The English translation by H. M. Hubbell indicated here (Cicero 1921) is also used in the following quotations from Cicero's *Orator*.

5. Harold Holzer (2004) has reviewed accounts of the speech which record instances of audience response and inserted the responses in the Appendix to his book. I have inserted the responses in this and subsequent passages.

## Works Cited

Aristotle. 2010. *Rhetoric*. Edited by William D. Ross. Translated by William Rhys Roberts. New York: Cosimo Classics.

Augustine. 1958. *On Christian Doctrine*. Translated by D. W. Robertson, Jr. New York: MacMillan.

Berry, Mildred Freburg. 1943. "Abraham Lincoln: His Development in the Skills of the Platform." In *History and Criticism of American Public Address*, edited by W. Norwood Brigance. Vol. 2, 825–58. New York: McGraw-Hill.

Bray, Robert. 2007. "What Abraham Lincoln Read—An Evaluative and Annotated List." *Journal of the Abraham Lincoln Association* 28: 28–81.

Cicero. 1921. "Orator." In *Cicero, Brutus, Orator*. Translated by H. M. Hubbell. Cambridge: Harvard University Press.

De Romilly, Jacqueline. 1975. *Magic and Rhetoric in Ancient Greece*. Cambridge: Harvard University Press.

Holzer, Harold. 2004. *Lincoln at Cooper Union: The Speech that Made Lincoln President*. New York: Simon and Schuster.

Johnson, Nan. 1991. *Nineteenth-Century Rhetoric in North America*. Carbondale: Southern Illinois University Press.

Leff, Michael C., and Gerald P. Mohrmann. 1974a. "Lincoln at Cooper Union: A Rhetorical Analysis of the Text." *Quarterly Journal of Speech* 60:346–58.

Leff, Michael C. and Gerald P. Mohrmann. 1974b. "Lincoln at Cooper Union: A Rationale for Neo Classical Criticism." *Quarterly Journal of Speech* 60:459–67.

Lincoln, Abraham. 1953. "Address at Cooper Institute, New York City." In *The Collected Works of Abraham Lincoln*, vol. 3, edited by Roy P. Basler, 522–50. New Brunswick: Rutgers University Press.

Milovanović-Barham, Ĉelica. 1993. "Three Levels of Style in Augustine of Hippo and Gregory of Nazianus." *Rhetorica* 11:1–25.

Smith, Franklin R. 1962. "A Night at Cooper Union." *Central States Speech Journal* 13 (5): 270–75.

# Contributing Authors

**Kirsten Brukamp**, MD, MS, MA, is a Professor of Health Sciences at the Protestant University in Ludwigsburg (Germany). She obtained academic degrees in medicine, philosophy, and cognitive science. Her research areas of interest include evidence and efficacy in health care, neuromedicine, theory of neuroscience, and ethics of medicine and health care.

**C. Giovanni Galizia** is Professor for Zoology and Neuroscience at the University of Konstanz (Germany) and Director of the Zukunftskolleg at the same institution. He studied Biology at the FU Berlin and attained a PhD in Zoology in Cambridge (UK). After research times in Tübingen and Berlin, he was Associate Professor at the University of California, Riverside (USA). His current research focuses on understanding the mechanisms of insect olfaction

**Jeffery Gentry** is Professor of Communication and formerly Dean of the College of Fine Arts at Eastern New Mexico University, Portales (NM, USA). He conducts research on rhetoric and political communication and has produced six public-affairs specials for television.

**Robert Hariman** is Professor in the Department of Communication Studies at Northwestern University in Evanston, Illinois (USA). Together with John Louis Lucaites, he has co-authored *No Caption Needed: Iconic Photographs, Liberal Democracy, and Public Culture* (2007) and *The Public Image: Photography and Civic Spectatorship* (2016) and developed the blog nocaptionneeded.com.

**Klaus Hentschel** is Professor for the History of Science and Technology at the University of Stuttgart (Germany). He held fellowships at the TU Berlin and at the MIT in Cambridge, MA (USA), and was Ernst-Cassirer-Visiting-Professor at the University of Hamburg. He works *inter alia* on the interplay of instruments, experiments and theory formation, research technologies, and on the development of scientific concepts and of visual cultures in science and technology.

**Colleen E. Kelley** is Associate Professor Emerita of Rhetoric and Communication at Penn State-Erie, The Behrend College in Pennsylvania (USA). Educated at the University of Oregon, her research addresses the interface between strategic communication and science as well as political culture. She is the author of *The Rhetoric of Hillary Rodham Clinton, Post-9/11 American Presidential Rhetoric, A Rhetoric of Divisive Partisanship* and *Democratic Disunity: Rhetorical Tribalism in 2020*.

**Joachim Knape** is Senior Professor of Rhetoric at the Rhetoric Department of Tübingen University (Germany). His research interests comprise the theory and history of rhetoric, rhetorical semiotics, media rhetoric, textual rhetoric, rhetoric of images, poetics, and aesthetics as well as renaissance studies and German language and literature.

**Hubert Knoblauch** is Professor for Theories of Modern Societies at the Institute of Sociology at Berlin Technical University (Germany). His main areas of research center around theories of modern society and the sociology of knowledge.

**Eric Lettkemann** is a postdoctoral researcher at the Institute of Sociology at Berlin Technical University. His main research interests are in the field of science and technology studies. He is currently researching the effects of locative media on encounters in public places.

**Philipp Löffler** teaches American literature at the University of Heidelberg and at the Heidelberg Center for American Studies (HCA). He is the author of *Pluralist Desires: Contemporary Historical Fiction and the End of the Cold War* (2015). He has edited a number of books, most recently *The Handbook of American Romanticism* (2021) and *How to Read the Literary Market* (2021). His next monograph will be a cultural history of US literary professionalism in the nineteenth century.

**John Louis Lucaites** is Provost Professor Emeritus in the Department of English, Indiana University in Bloomington, Indiana (USA). Together with Robert Hariman, he has co-authored *No Caption Needed: Iconic Photographs, Liberal Democracy, and Public Culture* (2007) and *The Public Image: Photography and Civic Spectatorship* (2016) and developed the blog nocaptionneeded.com.

**Michael Pelzer** leads the project area "Knowledge Design" at the Research Center for Science Communication at Tübingen University (Germany). His research focuses on visual rhetoric, theories of evidence, and the communicative construction of collective memories. He develops and leads workshops to foster competence in the field of visual science communication.

**William M. Purcell** is Professor of Communication and Chair of Communication and Journalism at Seattle Pacific University (WA, USA). He teaches courses in Rhetorical Theory, Argumentation, Public Speaking, and Interpersonal Communication—and is author of *Ars poetriae: Rhetorical and Grammatical Invention at the Margin of Literacy* (1996) and *The Rhetorical Short Story* (2009).

**John Ray** is Professor of Public Policy and Communications in the Liberal Studies Department at Montana Tech of the University of Montana in Butte, Montana (USA). He holds a PhD in Political Science and a graduate degree in Communication Arts from the University of Wisconsin-Madison. His research interests comprise rhetorical theory, history of public address, environmental politics, and political theory.

**Jenny Rock** holds a BA in human ecology and a PhD in the biological sciences, with many years of experience as a research scientist. She has held Senior Lecturer and Adjunct Professor positions both teaching and researching in science and society interaction at University of Otago in Dunedin (New Zealand), College of the Atlantic (Maine, USA), and the University of the Westfjords (Isafjordur, Iceland). She researches on participatory practice, the aesthetics of science, creative science communication, and socio-environmental issues of climate change.

**David M. Schultz** is Professor of Synoptic Meteorology within the Centre for Atmospheric Science, Department of Earth and Environmental Sciences, University of Manchester (UK). He is the winner of several university teaching awards, Chief Editor of *Monthly Weather Review* (2008–2022), and author of *Eloquent Science: A Practical Guide to Becoming a Better Writer, Speaker and Atmospheric Scientist*.

**Julia Siebert** worked at the German Centre for Integrative Biodiversity Research (iDiv) Halle-Jena-Leipzig in Germany where she completed a PhD in global change ecology. She also coordinated an integrative postdoc project assessing the transformative potential of citizen science in high school education. Besides, Julia Siebert has a background in rhetoric and philosophy and is experienced in science communication and the facilitation of stakeholder dialogues. She now works at the Ministry of the Environment, Climate Protection and the Energy Sector Baden Württemberg, Germany.

**Thomas Susanka** leads the project "Science Notes" at the Department of Rhetoric at Tübingen University (Germany). Central areas of his research are visual communication, design and science communication. In his PhD thesis, he examined *The Rhetoric of Photography—James Nachtwey's War Photography* (in German).

**Anne Ulrich** is tenured Lecturer at the Institute for Media Studies of Tübingen University (Germany). Her research interests center around media philosophy, visual rhetoric and digital culture. Her current project examines the spectral metaphor in media theory and notions of spectrality in contemporary media culture. She is the co-author of *Trump and Television*, *Media Rhetoric of Television*, and *Contested Credibility: Visual Strategies of Television Journalism in the 2003 Iraq War* (all in German).

**René Wilke** is a postdoctoral researcher at the Institute of Sociology at the Berlin Technical University. His main interests are in the field of sociology of knowledge and the sociology of communication as well as in videography and qualitative research data management. He is currently working on a research data infrastructure for audio-visual research data.

# About the Editors

**Olaf Kramer** is Professor of Rhetoric and Knowledge Communication at the Rhetoric Department of Tübingen University (Germany), where he also heads the associated Research Center for Science Communication. His main areas of research comprise literary aesthetics around 1800, communicative competence and continuing education, political communication, and strategic positioning, as well as fiction and virtual reality.

**Michael Pelzer** leads the project area "Knowledge Design" at the Research Center for Science Communication at Tübingen University (Germany). His research focuses on visual rhetoric, theories of evidence, and the communicative construction of collective memories. He develops and leads workshops to foster competence in the field of visual science communication.

# Index

**addressee**, xx, xxviii, 9, 30, 36–37, 40, 49–51, 55, 58, 79–82, 90, 93, 95–96, 110, 131, 144, 146, 157, 208, 210, 211–214, 216, 220–222, 224, 227, 229, 234, 238, 241, 245, 247, 249, 262–267, 279, 291, 296, 305, 308, 333

**adequacy**, xvii, xx– xxi, xxviii, 55, 70, 79, 125, 213–214, 225, 258–259, 276, 280, 284

**aesthetics**, xviii, 4–5, 22–23, 47, 49, 51–53, 64, 67, 72, 142, 148, 155–156, 161, 164, 210, 216, 219–220, 222, 228, 245, 263, 271

animation, xx

**appeal**, xvi, xviii–xix, 45, 48–49, 53–55, 57–58, 176, 213, 259, 278, 283, 323, 331

aptum → adequacy

**argumentation**, xxviii-xxix, 9, 14–22, 31, 35, 48, 52, 54–57, 63–67, 117–118, 122–123, 127–134, 142, 144, 161–165, 170–173, 182, 193, 195, 197–198, 216–229, 240, 271–272, 276–285, 288–293, 298, 305, 332–333

**Aristotle**, xi, xv–xviii, xx, xxx, 4, 5, 8, 12–13, 16–17, 19, 21, 23–25, 30–31, 36, 48, 52, 58, 147–148, 162–165, 179, 181, 186–187, 218, 230, 240, 252–253, 277, 284–285, 320, 334

**art**, xi, xxix, 22–23, 32, 64, 75, 117, 163, 186, 190, 209–217, 219, 221, 227–229, 233–237, 241–246, 248–254, 256

**authenticity**, xxviii, 33, 47, 221, 246, 252, 260, 263, 266–267, 270

**authority**, 12–13, 19, 30, 120, 144, 147, 193–194, 238, 271, 305, 323

Bacon, Francis, 24, 57–58

**Barthes, Roland**, 4, 23–25, 228, 230, 239, 253, 267, 274

**Blumenberg, Hans**, 6–8, 13, 18, 25, 251, 253

**Booth, Wayne C.**, 51, 59, 240, 252–253

**Brecht, Bertolt**, 9, 11, 14, 18–25

**Burke, Kenneth**, 21, 25, 146, 158

**certainty**, xxiv, 16, 30, 35, 37–38, 40, 103, 177, 195–196, 284–285, 304

**Chevreul, Michel-Eugène**, xxviii, 233–234, 236, 238–239, 242–243, 245–255

**Cicero, Marcus Tullius**, xv–xvii, xix–xx, xxix, xxxi, 5, 20, 23, 25, 30, 35–36, 48, 59, 147, 158, 234, 251, 254, 319–322, 332–334

**clarity**, xi, xvi–xvii, xx–xxii, 35–36, 40–42, 48, 54–55, 75, 80, 110, 123, 152–153, 156, 179, 181, 220, 223, 234, 257, 323

**color**, xiii, xxv–xxvi, 36, 40, 68, 69, 70, 76, 79, 80, 82, 85, 86, 87, 89, 90–97, 120, 137, 213, 299, 332

**communicator**, xiii, xvi, xix–xx, xxii, xxiv, xxix, 3, 5, 9, 19, 23, 36, 55–56, 58, 283, 320–322, 333

**context**, xx–xxi, xxvi, 5–7, 14–17, 48, 56–58, 90, 94, 102, 110–111, 116–119, 123–128, 133–136, 144–145, 160, 177, 197, 200, 228, 234, 240, 243, 249, 265–277, 283–284

**criticism**, xiii, xxv, xxvii, 14, 29, 32–33, 38, 40, 42, 65, 69, 70, 74, 79, 94, 143, 154, 160–163, 176, 186, 194, 202, 213–217, 220,

228–229, 241, 259, 285, 298, 301, 315, 319–320, 333

**culture**, xi, xiv, xxiii, xxvii, xxix, 4, 8, 31–34, 65, 87, 116, 120–121, 134, 179–180, 191–192, 196, 199, 210, 212–215, 217–218, 228, 251, 256, 258–259, 266–267, 269, 271–273, 283, 302, 333

**Darwin, Charles**, Darwinian, xii, 166, 169, 196, 198

**data**, xxi, xxiii, xxvi, xxviii, 31, 41, 63, 67, 70–71, 73, 76, 79–80, 85–87, 88, 90–95, 98, 106, 113, 122, 130, 132, 135, 136, 146, 156, 161, 186, 193, 198, 266, 276, 279

**deixis**, xix–xx, xxix, xxx, 9, 15, 21, 51, 65, 85, 89, 90, 94, 103, 220, 223, 238, 240, 242–243, 249, 250

Descartes, Réné, xx, 253, 315

**details** → evidence: descriptive evidence / enárgeia

**Diderot, Denis**, xxix, 276, 280, 285

**digitalization**, xii, xiii, 33, 79, 119, 121, 201, 210, 217

**discourse**, xiii, xviii, xxvii, 5, 7–8, 32, 34, 52, 122, 128, 157, 162–165, 176, 178, 190, 192–197, 199–201, 209, 210, 212, 214–216, 228–229, 240–241, 258, 271–272, 277, 281

**discussion**, xii, xv–xvi, xviii, xxv–xxix, 11, 13, 52, 146, 193, 200–201, 216–217, 243, 249, 257, 276, 301, 321, 326

**education**, xxiii, xxix, 3, 53, 65, 102, 111, 136, 178, 194, 215, 226, 307, 333

**emotion**, 24, 45, 52, 54, 71–72, 144, 163, 186, 208, 216–217, 263, 265, 268, 298, 305, 313, 322

**empiricism**, xii, xxvi, 13, 20, 75, 115, 117–118, 122, 135, 141, 192, 198, 209, 228, 277–278, 281–282

**ethics**, xii, xiii, xxvi, 12, 17–18, 34–35, 42, 80–81, 96, 142–143, 147, 154, 190, 199, 208, 213, 216, 222, 257, 260, 281–285, 296, 302

**ethos**, 52, 144, 163, 176, 186, 199, 305

**evidence**:

    **descriptive evidence / enárgeia**, xiv–xx, xxiii–xxiv, 8, 20–21, 30, 35–39, 42, 48–52, 54–58, 69, 91, 93, 103, 121, 134, 136, 141, 150–151, 155, 161, 170, 172, 191, 215, 222–224, 234, 238–239, 263, 265, 273, 287;

    **dynamic evidence / enárgeia**, xi–xii, xiv–xx, xxii–xxv, xxix, 9, 21, 36–42, 48–51, 55, 58, 79, 89–92, 94, 96, 101, 135, 169, 182, 234, 238–239, 243, 245, 251, 304, 305;

    **epistemic evidence**, xiv–xv, xx–xxix, 3–9, 12–22, 30–42, 51–54, 67–76, 115–136, 141–145, 161–164, 172–180, 186, 190–201, 207–219, 224–229, 239–242, 248–249, 256–260, 265–272, 276–285, 288–305

    **evidentia**, xi, xv–xvii, xix, xxii, xxiv, xxvii–xxviii, xxx, 8–9, 20, 30–42, 48, 51–58, 75, 80, 141, 156, 179, 208, 217, 219, 227, 234, 238–240, 250, 273, 276, 279, 316;

    **forensic evidence**, xi, xiv, xxi, 5, 19, 20, 31, 115, 135, 164, 197, 202, 204, 217, 219, 222, 229, 281–282, 311, 320–321, 329, 330, 333;

    **narrative evidence**, xxii, xxvi–xxvii, 18–21, 45–47, 50–58, 141–157, 163–166, 169, 172–173, 176–178, 185, 191–193, 196–198, 225–226, 240, 258–263, 266, 268–269, 271, 284–285, 291, 296, 306;

    **self-evidence**, xx, xxiii, 8, 18, 30, 35–42, 51, 161, 208, 278–279, 283, 299;

**verbal evidence**, xi–xii, xiv–xviii, xxii–xxiv, 17–23, 36–39, 45–58, 71–76, 110, 117, 129–130, 133–135, 141–150, 153–157, 161–165, 193, 222, 234–235, 238–240, 246, 287–298, 304–306, 321–333;

**visual evidence**, xiii–xvii, xix–xx, xxii–xxiii, xxv–xxxi, 19–21, 29, 31–42, 46, 49, 63–76, 80–95, 103, 112, 120, 123–125, 128, 131–137, 146, 149, 151, 155, 167, 207–229, 232, 233–253, 304

**Fallada, Hans**, xxiv, 45–59, 164

**film**, xiv, xix–xx, xxviii, 29, 38, 66, 89, 112, 209, 245, 252, 256–274

**Fisher, Walter**, 52, 59, 160–166, 178, 188, 284

**Foss, Sonja K.**, 37, 39, 42, 75, 77

**Galileo, Galilei**, xii, 9–21, 24, 28, 288

**Gorgias, of Leontini**, 321, 333

**Grice, Paul**, 55, 59, 146, 158

**Habermas, Jürgen**, 134–135, 138, 204, 272, 274, 284

Hegel, Georg Wilhelm Friedrich, xxix, 283, 292

**Heidegger, Martin**, 5, 7, 24–25, 310

**history**, xxviii, 17–21, 45–46, 52, 210–211, 222, 228, 233–234, 242, 249–250, 256–260, 263–273, 288–289, 294, 298, 304, 308, 311, 319, 329

**Husserl, Edmund**, 5, 8, 23, 25, 115, 117, 138

**identification**, 143–147, 199

**imagination**, xvi–xviii, xxii, xxv, xxviii, 20, 36, 48–51, 55–58, 76, 172, 180–181, 209–215, 219–221, 224–229, 234, 245, 259

**Jäger, Ludwig**, xxii, xxx, xxxi, xxxii, 8, 23, 26, 240, 254

**journalism**, xxviii, 216, 220–221, 233, 238–241, 246–247, 250, 253

**Kant, Immanuel**, xxii, xxix, 16, 26, 253, 276, 278–285, 292

**Kennedy, John F.**, xviii–xxiv, 3–4, 8

**knowledge**, xi–xiii, xxii, xxvi–xxvii, xxix, 3, 7, 9, 12, 35, 54, 65–70, 99–100, 115–122, 124, 128–136, 141–142, 145, 147, 161, 178, 190–195, 197, 200–201, 207–208, 216–218, 221, 227, 265, 271, 285, 291, 305, 310; *see also* evidence: epistemic evidence

**Kuhn, Thomas S.**, xiii, xxxi, 14, 18, 119, 142–145, 150, 153–154, 193

**Lincoln, Abraham**, xxix, 270, 319–334

**logos**, 23, 52, 144, 163–164, 186, 199

**Luhmann, Niklas**, 15–16

**McLuhan, Marshall**, xii, xxxi

**media**, xi–xii, xiv, xviii, xix, xxii, xxvii–xxviii, 29, 51, 58, 66, 80, 96, 118, 164–165, 173, 176, 178, 180–182, 185, 197, 201, 207–212, 215–216, 219, 221, 227–229, 233–234, 240–241, 247, 250, 262–263, 322

**metaphor**, 41, 145, 199, 295, 305, 322

**Mitchell, William J. T.**, xiii, xxxi, 33, 43, 65, 75, 78, 228, 231

**Nadar, Gaspard-Félix**, xxviii, 233–255

**narration** → evidence: narrative evidence

**objectivity**, xii–xiii, xxvii, 4–7, 16, 19–20, 30–34, 50–51, 55, 71, 74–76, 79, 119–120, 145–146, 161–163, 190–194, 198, 207–210, 217– 220, 227, 241–242, 248, 256–272, 277–279, 282–285, 302, 333

**pathos**, 24, 52, 144, 163, 186, 216, 322

**Perelman, Chaim**, xxviii, 193, 203, 276–286

**persuasion**, xii, xvi, xviii, xxi, xxii, xxiv, xxvii, xxix–xxx, 4, 16, 29, 35–36, 40, 42, 48, 52–55, 63, 65, 117, 142, 144–148, 156–157, 160–164, 173–176, 181, 192–194, 198–199, 229, 234, 240, 260, 263, 266–281, 287, 298, 302, 321

**philosophy**, xiv, xxv, xxviii–xxix, 5, 7–8, 36, 63–65, 70–74, 135, 142, 164, 210, 218, 235, 238, 248, 270, 273, 276, 289–294, 298, 303–306, 314

**photography**, xiv, xx, xxvii–xxviii, 32–34, 38, 64–69, 80, 90, 207–229, 232–236, 238, 239, 241–253

**Plato**, 4, 7, 21, 30, 229, 284, 291, 297, 299

**plausibility**, xiii, xxiv, 3, 9, 14–17, 102, 115, 167, 169, 176, 193, 234, 248, 266, 269

**poetry** → evidence: verbal evidence

**politics**, xxviii, 4–5, 9, 22, 30, 54–55, 115, 143, 147, 161, 179, 192–193, 196, 198–199, 201–203, 210, 213, 216–227, 256–257, 265–267, 269–273, 282, 290, 292, 297, 300, 311, 328, 330

**presentation**, xi, xix–xx, xxvi, xxx, 38, 55, 106, 117–118, 121–122, 130–139, 146, 197, 207, 210, 236, 241, 244, 247, 253, 324–325

**proof**, xi, xiv, xxi, xxiii, 13, 19, 21, 30–34, 42, 63, 67, 69, 74, 135, 144, 163, 174, 176, 192, 228, 240–242, 251–252, 288–289, 294, 325–326

**psychology**, 63–64, 67, 70–73, 93, 122, 136, 142, 147, 265

**Quintilian, Marcus Fabius**, xvi–xviii, xx, xxii, xxx, xxxii, 9, 18–21, 24, 27, 30–31, 35–36, 44, 48, 60, 147, 159

**realism**, xxviii, 51, 209–210, 212, 214–215, 219, 228–229, 256–260, 265–266, 269–273

**responsibility**, xii–xiii, 128, 143, 157, 196, 300

**rhetoric**, xi–xiv, xvi, xx–xxix, 3–9, 14–23, 29–39, 42, 48–65, 70, 74–75, 99, 115–118, 124–125, 134–135, 141–147, 156–157, 160–165, 176–182, 190–194, 197–201, 234, 238–242, 247–251, 276–278, 284–285, 288–289, 305–306, 319–323, 333

**rhetoric of science**, xiii, 143, 160, 161, 200

**Rousseau, Jean-Jacques**, xxix, 276, 280, 286

**science communication**, xi–xii, xiv, xxi–xxvii, xxx, 3, 5, 14, 17, 20, 30, 39, 54, 63–76, 79, 85, 87, 89, 93, 96, 98, 107, 115–122, 128, 135, 136, 141–145, 148–157, 160–164, 169, 178–181, 186, 190–204, 212, 241, 248, 288–292, 304, 309

**Searle, John R.**, 5, 76, 78

**semiotics**, 4, 29–32, 36, 214, 228, 238, 240

**simulation**, 4–6, 13, 21–22, 24, 46–47, 50–51, 54, 57–58, 95, 121, 229

**showing** → deixis

**society**, xi–xiv, xxiii, xxvii–xxviii,

xxx, 3, 6, 14–16, 54, 65–66, 74–75, 94–95, 116, 119, 141–144, 147–148, 156–157, 162, 178–179, 191–195, 199–201, 208–209, 213, 215, 221, 223, 226, 270, 278, 283, 290, 307, 315

**storytelling** → evidence: narrative evidence

**strategy**, xii–xiii, xviii, xxi–xxiv, xxviii, 9, 14, 16, 47, 51–54, 65, 123, 143–145, 195, 196, 200, 224, 246, 249, 256, 260, 263, 265, 267–270, 299, 322

**style**, xvi, xxii, xxv, xxix, 48–51, 54, 145–146, 163, 176, 181, 195, 197, 208, 218, 263, 287–293, 296, 299, 301, 305, 308–309, 321–323, 325, 327, 330–333; *see also* evidence: verbal evidence

**subjectivity**, xxviii, 32, 51, 70–71, 74, 76, 116, 120, 147, 175, 177, 179, 186, 216, 256–257, 265, 267–271, 279–281

**truth**, xiii, xxii, xxviii, 4–5, 7, 16, 19–20, 30–31, 40, 75, 115, 120, 143, 177, 190–193, 200, 209–210, 217–218, 224, 227, 257, 265–272, 277, 279, 282–285, 292, 295, 300, 302, 304, 321, 326

**uncertainty**, xiii, 99, 101–102, 105–112, 193, 297

**visuality** → evidence: visual evidence

**vividness**, xi–xvii, xxi–xxii, xxiv–xxv, xxviii–xxx, 8–9, 18, 20–21, 30, 35–42, 48–58, 68, 71, 80, 87, 123, 131, 135, 141, 147, 182, 192–196, 199, 233–234, 238–245, 247, 251–252, 257, 272–273, 304

**vivification** → evidence: dynamic evidence / *enérgeia*

**Weizsäcker**, Carl Friedrich von, xxix, 287–318

www.ingramcontent.com/pod-product-compliance
Lightning Source LLC
Chambersburg PA
CBHW041624020526
44116CB00047B/2967